Minooka Comm. H.S. South
Channahon, IL 604

Praise for Jill Lepore's

THE MANSION OF HAPPINESS

"[Lepore] manages to spin a larger narrative that both fascinates and informs, showing that our taken-for-granted ideas about every stage of life are culturally specific, very much a product of our times."

—*The Washington Post*

"Lepore has mastered the neat trick of writing imaginatively and often humorously for a general audience without checking her scholarly swing . . . she gets you thinking like she does, and you can ask no more from a historian."

—*The Daily Beast*

"One of the pleasures of Lepore's work is the way she uses a single, deftly chosen artifact to crack open a much wider cultural vista. . . . If the bonds between the disparate subjects and motifs in *The Mansion of Happiness* sometimes seem to be sustained by Lepore's own personal version of extraordinary measures, there are plenty that hold firm. They can't be disputed or endorsed like traditional theories, but they can dazzle and illuminate and inspire. And that's just what they do."

—*Salon*

"Lepore has a brilliant way of selecting just the right historical detail to illuminate a larger point. . . . The most valuable lesson here is that of impermanence. Everything changes. And although, as Lepore writes, 'it's best to have a plan,' as her multifaceted, sometimes dizzying joyride of a book reveals, the next roll of dice could, in fact, change everything."

—*The Boston Globe*

"This fascinating book explores a few centuries' worth of ideas about life and death—you know, just a light beach read. But for all its analysis of Darwin and Aristotle, *The Mansion of Happiness* is a lot of fun. . . . [Lepore] is always engaging, even surprising." —*Entertainment Weekly*

"A series of engaging and wonderfully perceptive essays on how individuals caught in time made sense of life and death. Jill Lepore is one of America's most accomplished and imaginative historians."

—Linda Colley, author of *The Ordeal of Elizabeth Marsh*

Minooka Comm. H.S. South Library
Channahon, IL 60410

"A stunning meditation on three questions that have dominated serious reflection about human nature and cultures for centuries: How does life begin? What does it mean? What happens when we die? . . . Lepore's refreshing and often humorous insights breathe fresh air into these everlasting matters."
—*BookPage*

"A breezy, informative, wide-ranging book . . . singular, always stimulating."
—*The American Scholar*

"Lepore's prose is thoroughly engaging and witty. . . . Covers enough of mankind's earnest curiosity about life and death to both entertain and provoke thought."
—*Booklist*

"Lepore chooses quirky, though always revealing, lenses through which to examine the changing definitions of conception, infancy, childhood, puberty, marriage, middle age, parenthood, old age, death, and immortality. . . . Through sheer force of charisma, Lepore keeps her readers on track: this book, with all its detours and winding turns, is a journey worth taking."
—*Library Journal*

"Engaging. . . . Lepore writes about our striving to understand our existence. *The Mansion of Happiness* is an important addition to the effort."
—*San Francisco Chronicle*

"This is why Jill Lepore is becoming my favorite historian: wise, witty, wide in scope and deep in spirit."
—James Gleick, author of *The Information*

"Equip a profound scholar with H. L. Mencken's instinct for running down charlatans and chuckleheads, and you get this book. It will amuse and embarrass those of us ever befuddled by the rogues in her gallery."
—Garry Wills, author of *Lincoln at Gettysburg*

"Written with sardonic wit and penetrating intelligence, *The Mansion of Happiness* is a fascinating and startlingly original guide to the ways in which the human life cycle has been imagined, manipulated, managed, marketed, and debased in modern times."
—Stephen Greenblatt, author of *The Swerve: How The World Became Modern*

JILL LEPORE

THE MANSION OF HAPPINESS

Jill Lepore is the David Woods Kemper '41 Professor of American History at Harvard University and a staff writer at *The New Yorker*. Her books include *The Story of America*; *The Whites of Their Eyes*; *New York Burning*, a finalist for the Pulitzer Prize; and *The Name of War*, winner of the Bancroft Prize. She lives in Cambridge, Massachusetts.

Minooka Comm. H.S. South Library
Channahon, IL 60410

Minooka Comm. H.S. South Library
Channahon, IL 60410

ALSO BY JILL LEPORE

· NONFICTION ·

*The Whites of Their Eyes: The Tea Party's Revolution
and the Battle over American History*

*New York Burning: Liberty, Slavery, and Conspiracy
in Eighteenth-Century Manhattan*

*A Is for American: Letters and Other Characters
in the Newly United States*

*The Name of War: King Philip's War
and the Origins of American Identity*

· FICTION ·

*Blindspot: By a Gentleman in Exile
and a Lady in Disguise* (with Jane Kamensky)

THE MANSION OF HAPPINESS

Minooka Comm. H.S. South Library
Channahon, IL 60410

THE MANSION OF
HAPPINESS

A History of Life and Death

JILL LEPORE

VINTAGE BOOKS
A DIVISION OF RANDOM HOUSE, INC.
NEW YORK

Minooka Comm. H.S. South Library
Channahon, IL 60410

FIRST VINTAGE BOOKS EDITION, MARCH 2013

Copyright © 2012 by Jill Lepore

All rights reserved. Published in the United States by Vintage Books, a division of
Random House, Inc., New York, and in Canada by Random House of Canada Limited,
Toronto. Originally published in hardcover in the United States by Alfred A. Knopf,
a division of Random House, Inc., New York, in 2012.

Vintage and colophon are registered trademarks of Random House, Inc.

Portions of this book originally appeared in *The New Yorker.*

Frontispiece: *The Life and Age of Man* (c. 1840). Courtesy of the Library of Congress,
Prints and Photographs Division.

The Library of Congress has cataloged the Knopf edition as follows:
Lepore, Jill.
The mansion of happiness : a history of life and death / Jill Lepore.—1st ed.
p. cm.
Includes bibliographical references and index.
1. United States—Social life and customs. 2. United States—Social conditions. 3. United
States—Intellectual life. 4. Politics and culture—United States—History. 5. Popular
culture—United States—History. 6. Life—Social aspects—United States—History.
7. Life (Biology)—Social aspects—United States—History. 8. Life cycle, Human—Social
aspects—United States—History. 9. Death—Social aspects—United
States—History. 10. Happiness—Social aspects—United States—History.
I. New Yorker. II. Title.
E169.1.l5295 2012
973—dc23
2011050566

Vintage ISBN: 978-0-307-47645-6

Author photograph © Rose Lincoln
Book design by Maggie Hinders

www.vintagebooks.com

Printed in the United States of America
10 9 8 7 6 5 4 3 2 1

To John Demos

Minooka Comm. H.S. South Library
Channahon, IL 60410

At this amusement each will find

A moral fit t'improve the mind.

—THE MANSION OF HAPPINESS

Minooka Comm. H.S. South Library
Channahon, IL 60410

Minooka Comm. H.S. South Library
Channahon, IL 60410

Contents

Preface xi

INTRODUCTION The Mansion of Happiness xv

1. Hatched   5

2. Baby Food   23

3. The Children's Room   38

4. All About Erections   61

5. Mr. Marriage   81

6. Happiness Minutes   97

7. Confessions of an Amateur Mother   111

8. Happy Old Age   137

9. The Gate of Heaven   152

10. Resurrection   169

LAST WORDS 189

A Chronology 193

Notes 199

Index 267

Minooka Comm. H.S. South Library
Channahon, IL 60410

Preface

This book is a history of ideas about life and death from before the cradle to beyond the grave. It starts with a seventeenth-century Englishman named William Harvey, who had the idea that life begins with an egg, and it ends with an American named Robert Ettinger, who, in the 1970s, began freezing the dead. If Victor Frankenstein were in this book, he'd fit right in, halfway between the egg man and the iceman. But Frankenstein's not here. In a history of life and death—which, really, could include just about anything—you have to leave rather a lot out.

To write history is to make an argument by telling a story. This is, above all, a book of stories. Each story here stands alone, but each makes an argument about the past, and, taken together, they offer an interpretation of the present. The tales I have to tell range over centuries and circle around a bit, but pause, for a goodish while, in the seventeenth and the late nineteenth and early twentieth centuries and, again, at the 1960s and '70s, because my argument is that the age of discovery, Darwin, and the space age turned ideas about life on earth topsy-turvy. New worlds were found; old paradises were lost. Many of these ideas were ideas about America.

Life used to be a circle: ashes to ashes, dust to dust. Fortune used to be a wheel that turned, and turned again. Aristotle wrote about three ages of man: youth, the prime of life, and old age. Morning, noon, and night. Medieval writers wrote about three, too, or maybe four, like the seasons, from the spring of childhood to the winter of old age, or seven, like the planets. Whatever the number, the metaphor was always drawn from the natural world, and went round and round. Then life lengthened, and the stages of life multiplied. In 1800, the fertility rate in the United States was over seven births per woman, the average age of the population was sixteen, and life expectancy was under forty. By 2010, the fertility rate had fallen to barely two, the average age of the population had risen to thirty-seven, and the average American could expect to live to nearly eighty. This demographic transition has been going on the world over. Life is no longer a circle.

When life lengthened, all those circles became lines: fortune, a number in a ledger; life, an evolution and, above all, a progression. In the latter part of the twentieth century, talk of progress was replaced by talk of innovation, but, really, it was the same hobbyhorse. Meanwhile, the contemplation of matters of life and death moved from the humanities to the sciences, from the library to the laboratory.

A line, unlike a circle, has an end. Or does it? Linear, scientific narratives of progress promise a different sort of eternity—humanity, undying—right up to the vague and halfhearted notion that one day, when the earth dies, humans will simply move to outer space, as if in the heavens, if not in heaven, will be found, at long last, life everlasting. When thinking about life and death moved from the library to the laboratory, the light of history dimmed. The future trumped the past. Youth vanquished age, and death grew unthinkable. The more secular ideas about immortality have become, the less well anyone, including and maybe especially doctors and scientists, has accepted dying, or even growing old. Freezing the dead, like living forever in another galaxy, is cockamamie, but it's not so far from anti-aging cream as you might suppose.

A word about this book's tone: questions about how life begins, what it means, and what happens when you're dead are so big that when people presume to answer them, or even to ask them, they can get awfully grandiose. "The only source of the true ridiculous," Henry Fielding once observed, "is affectation." Fielding, I like to think, would have found it difficult to read *The Day of a Godly Man's Death Better Than the Day of His Birth*, a frightfully bombastic sermon preached by Thomas Foxcroft in Boston on a bitterly cold February day in 1722, without wondering how far into the sermon Foxcroft had gotten before his parishioners slumped in their pews and nodded off. Sometimes, I wonder about that kind of thing, too.

This, also, must be said: matters of life and death have to do with faith and knowledge and hope and despair. They are not, inherently, political, though they are quite commonly turned to political ends. Generally, the trouble begins when people who think they've found the answers start bullying other people into agreeing with them. Wars have been fought over far less. In the last few decades, charged and painful debates about what have been termed "culture of life" issues, including abortion, end-of-life medical care, stem cell research, and the right to die, have become battles in what has been called a war for the soul of America. These debates, which are usually understood as having to do with science and religion, have also to do with history. When people do battle over matters of life and death, they often believe, passionately and even devoutly, that their own ideas, and no one else's, are eternal. But even antique ideas have histories—sacred in one era, profane in another—and some seemingly timeless truths, like "the sanctity of life" or "death with dignity," turn out to be of fairly recent vintage. Those histories are worth excavating. Still, the past, while always edifying, is rarely dispositive: people believe and hold dear what they believe and hold dear for more reasons than what happened long ago. This book is a history; it's not a catechism.

The chapters of this book follow the stages of life, or what used to be called the ages of man: they start with life before birth and end with life after death. In between lie chapters on infant care, childhood, growing up, marrying, working, having children, growing old, and dying. But first comes an introduction, about the idea that life is a game, which is where this book gets its title: the Mansion of Happiness used to be the most popular board game around. A book, like life, is a voyage; this one begins with the unborn and ends with the undead. The game board is your map.

Introduction

THE MANSION OF HAPPINESS

In 1860, the year Abraham Lincoln was elected president, a lanky, long-nosed, twenty-three-year-old Yankee named Milton Bradley invented his first board game, played on a red-and-ivory checkerboard of sixty-four squares. He called it the Checkered Game of Life. Play starts at the board's lower left corner, on an ivory square labeled Infancy—illustrated by a tiny, black-inked lithograph of a wicker cradle—and ends, usually but not always, at Happy Old Age, at the upper right, although landing on Suicide, inadvertently, helplessly, miserably, and with a noose around your neck, is more common than you might think, and means, inconveniently, that you're dead.

"The game represents, as indicated by the name, the checkered journey of life," Bradley explained. There are good patches and bad, in roughly equal number. On the one hand: Honesty, Bravery, Success. On the other: Poverty, Idleness, Disgrace. The wise player will strive "to gain on his journey that which shall make him the most prosperous, and to shun that which will retard him in his progress." But even when you're heading for Happiness, you can end up at Ruin, passed out, drunk and drooling, on the floor of a seedy-looking tavern where Death darkens the door disguised as a debt collector straight out of *Bleak House:* the bulky black overcoat, the strangely sinister stovepipe hat.[1]

The history of games of life contains within it a history of ideas about life itself. The Checkered Game of Life made Milton Bradley a brand name. His company, founded in 1860, survived his death in 1911, the Depression,

and two world wars. In 1960, to celebrate its centennial, the Milton Bradley Company released a commemorative Game of Life. It bears almost no
resemblance to its checkered nineteenth-century namesake. Instead, Milton Bradley's antebellum game about vice, virtue, and the pursuit of happiness was reinvented as a lesson in consumer conformity, a two-dimensional
Levittown, complete with paychecks and retirement homes and medical
bills. In Life, players fill teensy plastic station wagons with even teensier pink
and blue plastic Mommies and Daddies, spin the Wheel of Fate, and ride
along the Highway of Life, earning money, buying furniture, having pink
and blue plastic babies, and retiring, if they're lucky, at Millionaire Acres.
Along the way, there are good patches: "Adopt a Girl and Boy! Collect Pres-
ents!" And bad: "Jury Duty! Lose Turn." Whoever earns the most money
wins. (The game's motto: "That's *Life*!") Inside the game box are piles and
piles of paper: fake automobile insurance, phony stock certificates, pretend
promissory notes, and play money, $7.5 million of it, including a heap of
mint-green fifty-thousand-dollar bills, each featuring a portrait of Bradley,
near the end of his days: bearded, aged, antique.[2]

As the years passed, Life came to look more and more like that portrait
of old man Bradley. Only a handful of games have had as long a shelf life.
After all, not for long did anyone play Park and Shop, another game sold
by the Milton Bradley Company in 1960, whose object was "to outsmart
the other players by parking your car in a strategic place, completing your
shopping quickly, and being the first to return home."[3] In the 1990s, Hasbro, which bought the Milton Bradley Company in 1984, revised Life to
market it to the baby boomer parents who had grown up with it: the station wagons swelled into minivans and it became possible, a few miles
down life's highway, to have a midlife crisis. The update was a disappointment. And so, in 2006, in an attempt to Botox the shiny, puffy nowness of
youth into a gray-whiskered game, Hasbro decided to start again, to design
a new game of life, by asking, What would Life be like if it were invented
today? That's a question about the present. If you turn it around, though,
you can make it into a question about the past: Why did Milton Bradley
invent the Checkered Game, the way he did, when he did? How, in short,
did Life begin?

A great many questions about life and death have no answers, including,
notably, these three: How does life begin? What does it mean? What hap-

pens when you're dead? These questions are ancient; they riddle myths and legends; they lie at the heart of every religion; they animate a great deal of scientific research. No one has ever answered them and no one ever will, but everyone tries; trying is the human condition. All anyone can do is ask. That's why any history of ideas about life and death has to be, like this book, a history of curiosity.

"How did the *game* of life begin?," though, isn't an existential question; it's a historical one, and you can find answers to historical questions in libraries, museums, and archives, like the U.S. Patent Office. "I, MILTON BRADLEY, . . . have invented a new Social Game," Bradley wrote on his patent application. "In addition to the amusement and excitement of the game, it is intended to forcibly impress upon the minds of youth the great moral principles of virtue and vice."[4] It was a new game, but the genealogy of the Checkered Game of Life stretches back centuries and across oceans. Bradley's invention is descended from a family of ancient Southeast Asian games—members of a genus called "square board race games"—whose common ancestor is probably over a thousand years old. Nepal has the "game of karma"; Tibet has the "game of liberation." In India, Jñána Chaupár, the game of knowledge, is played much like the Checkered Game of Life: land on a virtue and you get to climb a ladder toward the god Vishnu; land on a vice and you're swallowed by a snake. Life has its ups and it has its downs. Then you die, the snake spits you out, and you start again.

In the nineteenth century, games from the farthest reaches of the British Empire and beyond found their way into middle-class Victorian parlors. A Persian game of life was collected, probably about 1810, by a British major general serving in northern India. The American firm of Selchow & Righter packaged pachisi as the Game of India at least as early as 1867. The New York–based McLoughlin Brothers sold the ancient Japanese game of Go as Go-Bang in 1887. Beginning in 1892, Jñána Chaupár was available in Britain as Snakes and Ladders; in the United States it was sold, entirely unhinged from its Indian origins, and decidedly karma-free, as Chutes and Ladders.[5]

Unfortunately, although Milton Bradley kept a diary all his life, he never put his papers in an archive, and most of them have been lost, which, notwithstanding his patent application, makes it something of a challenge to know exactly how a young New Englander came, on the eve of the Civil War, to adapt an ancient Southeast Asian game to a red-and-ivory checkerboard featuring an American vision of the good life.[6] He certainly never traveled to India. Still, he didn't have to look half a world away to find what he was after.

That life's a game that can be played well or badly is a very old idea, in the West no less than in the East. The people in Thomas More's 1516 *Utopia* play a game of life, "not much unlike the chesse," in which "vices fyghte wyth vertues, as it were in battell." (The origins of chess are murky. It is thought to have been invented either in India before A.D. 600 or in China about A.D. 800.)[7] How to win and what the rules are—whether you're playing against yourself or against God or Satan—are matters of much speculation. In 1640, the English poet George Herbert put it this way:

> *Man's life's a game at tables and he may*
> *Mend his bad fortune, by his wiser play;*
> *Death plays against us, each disease and sore*
> *Are blotts.*[8]

In Man versus Death, being clever helps, but the best you can hope for is to prolong the game. Death always wins. Death is a bastard. Death cheats.

Milton Bradley took a different view. In the Checkered Game of Life, you can win and you can lose and you can even be ruined, but there's no square called Death. Unless you land on Suicide, you can't actually die. Also, you have some control over your fate. "The journey of life is governed by a combination of chance and judgment," he explained.[9] There's what you roll, and there's where you choose to go. The Checkered Game of Life is a game of destiny checked by strategy. This really was new, because Milton Bradley came from a family ruled for generations by nothing so much as an angry God.

The Bradleys arrived in New England in 1635, when Daniel Bradley, an apothecary's son, settled in Salem, in Massachusetts Bay, just five years after the Puritans founded their city on a hill. Their sufferings were biblical. Daniel Bradley was killed by Indians in 1689; six years later, his fifteen-year-old son, Isaac, was taken captive. In 1697, another son, his wife, and two of their children died in an attack on the town of Haverhill, during which Hannah Bradley, the wife of still another of Daniel's sons, was captured, whereupon her husband, Joseph, trudged after her, through waist-high snows, with his dog and a purse of coin. He meant to ransom her.

To be rescued from captivity was to be redeemed. It took Joseph Bradley two years, but he finally redeemed his wife and brought her home. Then, in the winter of 1704, Indians returned to Haverhill and broke into the Bradleys' house all over again. This time, Hannah, who was eight months pregnant, fought back. "Perceiving the Misery that was attending her, and having boiling Soap on the Fire," she "scalded one of them to Death," as the minister of Boston's North Church, Cotton Mather, described it in an account of her trials and tribulations. She hid her sister and one of her children in the back of the house; eventually, she surrendered. She was then forced to walk, for weeks, over hundreds of miles, northward; she lived on nuts, bark, and wild onions. Once, she was allowed a piece of moose hide. She prayed "that the Lord would put an end unto her weary Life!" Six weeks into her captivity, she gave birth, "with none but the Snow under her, and the Heaven over her." When the baby cried, the Indians "threw hot Embers in its Mouth," which rendered its "Mouth so sore, that it could not Suck . . . So that it Starv'd and Dy'd." She endured by faith alone. "She had her Mind often Irradiated with Strong Perswasions and Assurances, that she should yet *See the Goodness of God,* in this Land of the Living." At last, "her tender and Loving Husband . . . found her out, and fetch'd her home, a Second time." And what, upon her redemption, did she pray? "*O magnifie the LORD with me, and let us Exalt his Name together.*" The next time an Indian came to her door, she shot him. She lived to be ninety.[10]

In 1707, when Mather wrote about Bradley's captivity and redemption, he used her story as an allegory for the Puritans' errand into the wilderness, quoting Virgil: "*Ab una Disce omnes.*" From one, learn all. That same year, he delivered a sermon called "The Spirit of Life Entering into the Spiritually Dead," preaching from the gospel of Luke: "He was Dead, and is Alive again." Resurrection is redemption from the captivity of death, but Mather spoke, too, about another kind: redemption from the captivity of sin. Sinners are dead souls, dry bones, but they can be quickened, made alive. There wasn't much you could do to be saved; the Lord would decide, on the Day of Judgment. You can hearken: "O ye Dry Bones, Hear the word of the Lord." And you can pray: "*Lord, I am Dead! I am Dead! Oh! Let me ly no longer among the Dead.*"[11]

Hannah Bradley's life was in God's hands; her captivity was a blessing, her redemption a lesson. She was far from helpless, but she was pursuing neither happiness nor even happy old age. Hers was a story not of success or failure but of fate: God had chosen to visit her with affliction, and there was nothing she could do but praise him, remembering Psalms 119:50: "This is my comfort in my affliction: for thy word hath quickened me." Hannah Bradley didn't think of life as a game. There was no game; there was only God, his word, and the quick and the dead.

The first game called Life, in English, wasn't Milton Bradley's. It was the New Game of Human Life, a board game engraved and inked in 1790 by John Wallis, a London printer and mapmaker. Card and table games were fashionable in eighteenth-century London, which is where Hoyle's books of rules were first published. Board games look like maps, and they were made by mapmakers. The first board game sold to children, Journey Through Europe, or the Play of Geography, was printed in London in 1759. The first jigsaw puzzle, Europe Divided into Its Kingdoms, also a map, was sold seven years later. Wallis's New Game of Human Life is a map, too: its life is a journey along a twisty path from birth to death, with eighty-four stops on the road, one for each year.[12]

The notion of life as a voyage goes way back. Plato, in *The Republic,* wrote about old men as "travelers who have gone a journey."[13] Francis Bacon, in his *History of Life and Death,* described life as a "pilgrimage through the wilderness of this world." (It might be a long trip, Bacon warned, so be careful not to wear your shoes out: you might need them in the afterlife.)[14] In Wallis's game, life is a voyage to salvation, just as it is in John Bunyan's *Pilgrim's Progress,* first printed in 1678.[15] (Either salvation or that other place: "I saw that there was a way to hell," Bunyan wrote, "even from the gates of heaven.") Your progress is speeded up by virtue and slowed down by vice. Each stop is a "character." You begin at the Infant. Whoever dies first wins. Your reward is to become, at eighty-four, the Immortal Man. There are setbacks at every turn, Jñána Chaupár all over again. Land on the Married Man, at the square marked 34 (the thirty-fourth year of your life), and you get to advance to the Good Father, at 56; but land on the Duelist, at 22, and you'll be sent back to age 3, for acting like a child. There is some slight sense of improvement—the acquisition of wisdom, maybe—not unlike that captured in a proverb Benjamin Franklin once printed in *Poor Richard's Almanack:* "At 20 years of age the Will reigns; at 30 the Wit; at 40 the Judgment."[16] The Benevolent Man, age 52, has much to recommend him. Still, there are rogues and knaves all over the board, from the Thoughtless Boy, a ten-year-old, to the Troublesome Companion, at eighty-one. Every age has its folly.

The New Game of Human Life borrowed its board and rules from the Royal Game of Goose, invented in Florence in the sixteenth century, and one of a class called "spiral race games." The oldest spiral race game may be the Hyena Game, played for centuries by Arabs in Sudan, in a groove traced in the sand with a stick. It involves a race between pebbles representing the players' mothers, who leave their village and head to a well at the spiral's center, where they must wash their clothes and return home before a hyena catches them. (A similar game, from ancient Egypt, is known as Hounds and Jackal.)[17] Wallis adapted the spiral race game to the idea that life is a voyage in which travelers are buffeted between vice and virtue. It was this allegory that gave the New Game of Human Life its "UTILITY and MORAL TENDENCY." Parents were instructed to play with their children and "request their attention to a few moral and judicious observations explanatory of each Character as they proceed & contrast the happiness of a Virtuous & well-spent life with the fatal consequences arriving from Vicious & Immoral pursuits." The game is a creed: life is a voyage that begins at birth and ends at death, God is at the helm, fate is cruel, and your reward lies beyond the grave. Nevertheless, to Puritans, who considered gambling the work of the devil, playing a game of life was, itself, an immoral pursuit. As the English poet Nathaniel Cotton put it, in 1794:

> That life's a game, divines confess;
> This says at cards, and that at chess;
> But if our views be center'd here,
> 'Tis all a losing game, I fear.[18]

The New Game of Human Life showed up in the United States not long after George Washington was inaugurated, and it was still being played as late as the 1870s; although, by then, an essayist who wrote about it made it sound quaint, an antique game played "on a queer old parchment."[19] The fearsome hand of providence made the New Game of Human Life, by latter-day board game standards, unbearably dull. There's no strategy, just dutiful to-ing and fro-ing, in abject obedience to the roll of the die and the rules of the game. Even worse, there's a dispiriting absence of adversaries; you're racing against other players, but you're not competing with them, not the way you are in, say, Monopoly, when you get to charge them exorbitant rents. And, as for parents offering up "a few moral and judicious observations" at each square, I have tried this—giving my best impression of an eighteenth-century father—and all I can say is: no dice. When my six-year-old landed on the Docile Boy, I asked him, "Do you know what 'docile' means?"

"No."

"It means you should do what I say, you little blister."

"Oh yeah?" He narrowed his eyes. "Your roll."

Two more games of life, the Mansion of Bliss and the Mansion of Happiness, were both produced in England beginning around 1800.[20] They look a lot like the New Game of Human Life: spiral race games adapted to the pilgrimage of life. Both represent immortality, life's final destination, as a heavenly mansion; this was then a popular Christian conceit, taken from John 14:2: "In my Father's house are many mansions." "O Lord! deliver us from sin," prayed one American evangelical in 1814, "and when we shall have finished our earthly course, admit us to the mansion of bliss and happiness."[21] Or, as the rules to the Mansion of Bliss had it:

> *Who enter the mansion of bliss,*
> *Will have cause to rejoice at his claim;*
> *So well has he travell'd thro' life,*
> *He has happily ended the game.*[22]

In the United States, the Mansion of Bliss never really made a mark, maybe because the phrase "the mansion of bliss" was also used by Americans to refer to an especially alluring woman's breasts.[23] But the Mansion of Happiness, the most popular board game in Britain, had an extraordinarily successful American career. It was sold in the United States at least as early as 1806. In 1843, an American edition, based on revisions to the English game made by Anne Wales Abbott, the editor of a Boston-based juvenile magazine called the *Child's Friend,* was offered by W. and S. B. Ives, a printing company in Salem. In ten months, Ives sold nearly four thousand of what went on to become the century's most enduring game. It became a staple of Victorian parlors; it made its way west on the Overland Trail.[24]

The Mansion of Happiness is abundantly pious. Its rules begin:

> *At this amusement each will find*
> *A moral fit t'improve the mind;*
> *It gives to those their proper due,*
> *Who various paths of vice pursue,*
> *And shows (while vice destruction brings)*
> *That good from every virtue springs.*
> *Be virtuous then and forward press,*
> *To gain the seat of happiness.*

You can hear, in these lines, echoes of the earliest Puritan primers: "In Adam's fall, we sinned all." And the last couplet alludes, quite particularly, to the beginning of John Milton's *Paradise Lost* (1667), in which Man waits for the son of God to "Restore us, and regain the blissful seat."[25]

No game is more didactic: "At this amusement each will find / A moral fit t'improve the mind." Whether it's amusing is difficult to say. The Mansion of Happiness is hard to finish, mostly because the wages of sin are so harsh—"Whoever becomes a SABBATH BREAKER must be taken to the WHIPPING POST and whipt" (a retreat of six squares)—that you're forever going backward and losing turns. However popular the Mansion of Happiness was with the parents who purchased it, the game boards that survive in archives are in such suspiciously good condition that at least one historian has wondered whether children—who must, invariably, have been given the game as a gift—could ever bear to play it. Its rules read like a sermon: "Whoever possesses AUDACITY, CRUELTY, IMMOD-ESTY, or INGRATITUDE, must return to his former situation till his turn comes to spin again, and not even *think* of Happiness, much less partake of it."[26]

Milton Bradley was born in Vienna, Maine, in 1836, two centuries after Daniel Bradley crossed the Atlantic, by which time the Bradleys had not yet begun to think of happiness, much less partake of it. He was the great-great-grandson of Jonathan Bradley, one of the many members of the Bradley family killed by Indians. He was his parents' only son. He was named after the Puritan author of *Paradise Lost*. As a boy, he read *Pilgrim's Progress*. When he was ten, his family moved to Lowell, Massachusetts, so that his father, Lewis, an insolvent, itinerant craftsman, could work in the textile mills.[27]

The nineteenth century was an age of machines: the steam engine, the cotton gin, the power loom. Inventors abounded; the patent office could barely keep up. "Men of progress" they were called, and "conquerors of nature." Their machines were better than poetry. The genius of Eli Whitney was said to rival that of Shakespeare. The head of the U.S. Patent Office declared the steamship "a mightier epic" than the *Iliad,* and any fool could see that James Watt had a thing or two over Cicero. Machines were thought to be the engines of progress, the "index of the degree in which the benefits of civilization are anywhere enjoyed," as James Mill, John Stuart Mill's father, put it, in his six-volume *History of British India.* (Having never been to India proved no obstacle to Mills's claiming that Indians were stalled on the march to progress, as measured by their "great want of ingenuity and completeness in instruments and machinery.")[28]

But the age of machines had its critics. Thomas Carlyle considered faith in machines a kind of spiritual bondage, something akin to a religious fallacy but worse, and every bit as much a delusion as seventeenth-century New Englanders' belief in witchcraft. Faith in progress is faith in the future, but if we think that machines liberate us from the past, Carlyle argued, we are wrong; it is we who are their prisoners. "Practically considered," he wrote, "our creed is Fatalism; and, free in hand and foot, we are shackled in heart and soul with far straighter than feudal chains." We may be blind to those shackles, blinded by a fog as thick as London's, as he put it, but we are just as surely "fettered by chains of our own forging."[29]

What Carlyle was describing, and what the Bradleys, like everyone else, were caught up in, was a quite extraordinary transition, a shift in where people were seeking answers to questions about the meaning of life: from the ancients to the moderns, from the pulpit to the patent office, from books to machines, from the arts to the sciences. Not just the source but the nature of authority changed. Answers you used to find in the past you were now expected to find in the future. And you were supposed to find them yourself.

The secularization of progress and the rise of individualism had a great deal to do with another transformation: the shape of a life was changing. Life used to begin where it ended; it ended where it began. A lot of other things used to be circular, too. Everything went round and round: day and night, the seasons, the crops in the field, fate. In an unraveling that had begun even before Daniel Bradley sailed to Salem, all those circles were turning into lines. The sun still set at the end of every day, but now you could turn on the lights and day would never end. The very idea of history came to a kind of close. The world of tomorrow was infinitely more interesting than the world of yesterday. Novelty replaced redemption.[30]

While his father worked in the mills, Milton Bradley attended Lowell's grammar and high schools. Then he went to the Lawrence Scientific School at Harvard, where he likely studied with Jacob Bigelow, Harvard's Rumford Professor of Physical and Mathematical Science. In a widely read treatise called *Elements of Technology,* Bigelow used the word "technology" to describe "the application of the sciences to the useful arts."[31] (Before that, technology was something you made by hand. Bigelow's usage soon found a place in the name of a new school: the Massachusetts Institute of Technology.) Technology, Bigelow said, was "promoting the progress and happiness of our race."[32] That's neither what Bunyan meant by progress nor Milton by bliss. No machine can take you into the mansion of happiness or even to the gate of heaven.

Lewis Bradley did not find happiness shackled to a new and improved loom. He left Lowell for Hartford, in search of better work, which meant that his son had to drop out of school. Here, though, was yet another novelty: the Bradleys could travel from Lowell to Hartford by train. At the time, the locomotive was the symbol of progress, pictured, in prints and paintings, chugging across the continent, conquering nature, unstoppable. You could measure it: each mile of railroad track was another mile of progress. In the 1840s, train tracks reached across Massachusetts, much to the distress of Henry David Thoreau, who had built on the banks of a pond in Concord a very different mansion of happiness: a cabin in the woods. While the train to Fitchburg rode by, its whistle screeching, its smokestack puffing, Thoreau wrote that all those machines were merely "improved means to an unimproved end": "We boast that we belong to the nineteenth century and are making the most rapid strides of any nation," but that, he believed, was humbug. "We do not ride on the railroad; it rides upon us."

Thoreau planted a hill of beans and spent his time hoeing, reading, writing, picking huckleberries, and listening to bullfrogs trumping, hawks screaming, and whip-poor-wills singing vespers.[33] "Mr. Thoreau is thus at war with the political economy of the age," one reviewer of *Walden* complained in 1854. But Thoreau wasn't so much battling progress as dodging it. He had the idea "not to live in this restless, nervous, bustling, trivial Nineteenth Century, but stand or sit thoughtfully while it goes by." No one can manage that. Ralph Waldo Emerson drafted a letter, never sent: "My dear Henry, A frog was made to live in a swamp, but a man was not made to live in a swamp. Yours ever, R."[34]

Milton Bradley, no frog he, did not sit out the restless, nervous, bustling, trivial nineteenth century. He kept striving. He left Hartford. By 1856, he had made his way to Springfield, Massachusetts, where, two years later, he opened his own business: "MILTON BRADLEY Mechanical Draftsman & Patent Solicitor." In an age of machines, he would write not poems or prayers but patents. The next year, when Sa'id Pasha, the Ottoman viceroy of Egypt, hired a Springfield firm to build a $300,000 railroad train on which he might travel the newly laid tracks between Cairo and Alexandria, it was Milton Bradley who designed and supervised the construction of a rosewood-and-mahogany observation car, from sketches supplied by an Egyptian artist.[35]

In 1860, Bradley started a lithography business and brought out an immensely popular election-year lithograph of a clean-shaven Abraham Lincoln. But then, just when it seemed the young striver had finally crawled his way to Success, he nearly sank into Ruin: Lincoln grew a beard, making Bradley's inventory worthless. One evening, a friend came over to cheer him up, bringing with him a board game; from descriptions, it sounds as though this must have been the Mansion of Bliss or a near knockoff. Bradley loved it. He decided to invent his own game, with materials he had near to hand: a chessboard and wooden men.[36]

He always claimed to have invented the Checkered Game of Life from scratch, but that's not strictly true. Most of its ideas were, by then, hackneyed. "Life is a kind of chess," Benjamin Franklin once wrote. By playing chess, you could learn foresight, circumspection, caution, and perseverance.[37] An 1834 engraving called *The Chess Players; Or, The Game of Life*, by the German artist Moritz Retzsch, depicted life as a game of chess between Man and Satan, held in the nave of a Gothic cathedral. Americans reenacted Retzsch's engraving in *tableaux vivants*. It inspired short stories, novels, and plays. In 1848, one abolitionist complained about compromises with slaveholding states by arguing, "The North is as unequally matched with the South in this Game of Life as the youth in Retzsch's chess-players, with his Satanic adversary."[38]

In Bradley's game, you don't play against the devil; you play against other men. And you don't play for your soul; you play for success. Bradley found more in Franklin than in Retzsch. Born in Boston in 1706 into a family much like Hannah Bradley's, Franklin grew up listening to Cotton Mather's sermons. But the story of his life, as he told it, wasn't the story of dry bones quickening; it was the story of a voyage "from the Poverty and Obscurity in which I was born and bred, to a state of Affluence and some degree of Reputation in the World." It was the story of "the way to wealth."[39]

This, then, was the genius of Milton Bradley's invention: he took a game imported from India and made it into the story of America. He turned a game of knowledge into the path to prosperity. He wrote a set of rules and lithographed a board. After he had manufactured enough boxes to make a sales trip, he took a train to New York, walked into a stationery store, and said to the manager, "How do you do, sir. I am Milton Bradley of the Milton Bradley Company of Springfield. I have come to New York with some samples of a new and most amazing game, sir. A highly moral game, may I say, that encourages children to lead exemplary lives and entertains both old and young with the spirit of friendly competition. May I demonstrate how it is played?" He sold out his stock, went back to Springfield, and, with a pocketful of cash, got engaged. He was married later that year. He was twenty-four.[40]

The Checkered Game of Life is deceptively simple. Twirl the teetotum, a numbered, six-sided top, and move your wooden man around the board, collecting points by landing on any of the eight point-value squares. Whoever earns 100 points first wins. Some squares help you along, little lithographed hands pointing the way, as when Perseverance leads you to Success, worth 5 points. (Very Franklinian, that.) Spinning a 2 from the red square between Ruin and Fat Office forces you to land on Suicide, where, ignominiously, you die, but almost any spin from nearly every other square involves a decision, a choice among as many as eight possible moves. Unlike The New Game of Human Life or the Mansion of Happiness, the Checkered Game of Life requires you to make decisions, lots of them. Nothing is in God's hands. It's best to have a plan.

Most players, I find, try to go to School, and then to College (worth 5 points), heading slowly toward the top of the board and Happy Old Age, worth a whopping 50 points. But your chances of going to School are not good: from your starting position, at Infancy, you have to spin either a 3 or a 6. You're quite likely to end up at Poverty instead. Despair not. "It will be seen that poverty lies near the cradle," Bradley wrote in the rules of the game, explaining why he had placed Poverty just two squares from Infancy. But because "in starting life, it is not necessarily a fact that poverty will be a disadvantage, so in the game it causes the player no loss." Even if you skip School altogether, you may be rewarded by landing on Honesty, and sent from there directly to Happiness.

It's possible to win the Checkered Game of Life without ever reaching Happy Old Age—after all, people do die young—but it's not easy. And, as Bradley warned, "Happy Old Age is surrounded by many difficulties": land on Idleness, and you'll be sent to Disgrace, at the very bottom of the board, which means that you have to climb back up all over again. Ignore Bradley's warning at your peril. Here's another word of advice: don't enter Politics, if you can possibly avoid it. You'll go to Congress and earn 5 points, but you'll be carried away from Happy Old Age and you'll woefully increase your chances of landing on Crime and ending up in Prison, where you lose a turn, "for any person who is sent to prison is interrupted in his pursuit of happiness."

When Bradley brought out his Checkered Game of Life, in 1860, parents, apparently, greeted it as merely "a new form of the game dear to children as The Mansion of Happiness."[41] In his patent application, Bradley himself insisted that his game was "intended to forcibly impress upon the minds of youth the great moral principles of virtue and vice."[42] But the Checkered Game of Life is vastly darker and more ruthless than its predecessors. In the Mansion of Happiness, landing on Truth—which you can't avoid, if a spin of the teetotum sends you there—advances you six squares; in the Checkered Game of Life, Truth exists, and you can choose to seek it out, but it has no value whatsoever. (Thoreau would not have approved: "Rather than love, than money, than fame, give me truth.")[43] Bradley's game rewards only those virtues that lead to Wealth and Success, like Industry and Perseverance. It has no use for Patience or Charity, which aren't even on the board. By 1866, the game even promoted betting on the stock market, on a square called Speculation.[44] In sixty-four squares, Bradley's game both celebrated and made possible his own rags-to-riches rise. The Checkered Game of Life isn't a race to heaven; it's a series of calculations about the best route to collect the most points, fastest. Accumulate or fail.

Bradley accumulated. He sold forty thousand copies of his game in its first year, and made his fortune when he decided to sell Games for Soldiers, a portable box of games (the Checkered Game of Life, backgammon, checkers, and chess), just as the Civil War broke out. The Checkered Game of Life found a place in the knapsack of nearly every Union soldier. Poverty . . . Industry . . . Perseverance . . . Success.

Not long afterward, Mark Twain wrote a piece for the *New York Tribune* called "The Revised Catechism":

What is the chief end of man?
A. To get rich.

In what way?
A. Dishonestly if we can, honestly if we must.

Who is God, the only one and True?
A. Money is God. . . .

Do we progress?
A. You bet your life.[45]

And that, in nineteenth-century America, was how you played the checkered game.

"You could never in a million years sell it today," Mel Taft told me. Taft used to be vice president of research and development at the Milton Bradley Company. In 1959, when Taft and his colleagues were preparing for the company's centennial, they—wisely—never considered reviving Bradley's original game. It was quaint; it was old-fashioned; good grief, it even had a square for Intemperance. They decided, instead, to hire a California company that had started the hula hoop craze to develop a new game of life. When Taft first saw what they'd come up with, he knew it was a doozy: "It looked like a million bucks."

What it doesn't look like is the Checkered Game of Life, but, curiously, it does rather resemble the Mansion of Happiness, just with lots of pieces of plastic attached to it.[46] The 1960 Game of Life is a spiral race, its serpentine path representing the voyage of life, from high school graduation to retirement. (In Life, you never die; you just quit working.) Some squares offer rewards: "Contest Winner! Collect $5,000." Others mete out penalties:

"Buy Furniture. Pay $2,000." But neither is morally freighted; instead of a battle between virtue and vice, it's an accounting of income and expenses. The game's most important squares are those that announce, in red letters, "Pay Day!" What you earn depends on a choice you make on your very first move: Will you go to college or take a job? The Checkered Game brought together choice and chance, but Life has only one real fork in the road: work or study. If you start work, you can collect paychecks right away; if you go to college, you have to take out loans and pay them back, but you earn more when you eventually do start getting paychecks. After that there are occasional financial decisions to be made—do you want to buy life insurance? would you like to invest in the stock market?—but these, and the piles of paper and the cars full of babies, serve mainly as a distraction from the play's passivity. Like the Mansion of Happiness, Life is a journey along a fixed path, where only one thing matters. At Life's "Day of Reckoning," you count your cash, not your good deeds. Like all earlier spiral race games of life, Life is about fate—not whether you're fated to become an Immortal Man, but whether you're fated to retire to Millionaire Acres. By 1960, the mansion of happiness was a five-thousand-square-foot house in a swank retirement community.

The 1960 Game of Life was a smash. Children liked it because it's like playing dress-up; you get to pretend to be a grown-up. One speaks, of course, only for oneself, but this game is just for kids—unless you're eight, it's a drag. And, as the years passed, it drew criticism: it is, after all, relentlessly amoral and shamelessly cash-conscious. In the Wall Street 1990s, a team of designers charged with updating it gave up; whenever they tried to make the game less about having the most money, it made no sense. All they could come up with was to add "life tiles," which allowed players to do good deeds. But the only way to be rewarded for your virtue was in the game's sole currency: cash. Save an endangered species: collect $200,000. Solution to pollution: $250,000.[47]

In 2007, just before a global financial meltdown involving securities fraud, subprime mortgages, and bad debt, Hasbro introduced a wholly reimagined game: the Game of Life: Twists and Turns. In this version, life is . . . aimless. There's a place to begin, but it's called Start, not Infancy or High School Graduation. There's no place on the board called Happy Old Age and no Millionaire Acres, either. Plainly, the Gate to Heaven is out of the question. The game board is divided into four squares—Learn It, Live It,

Love It, and Earn It—through each of which a colored path snakes its way. (The game is a mishmash of a square board and a spiral one.) You decide how you want to spend your time: go to school, have kids, hang out, travel the world. Whatever. You begin using a tiny plastic skateboard as a game piece; if you want, you can convert it to a car. You can buy a house, from "Modest," for $200,000, to "Mansion," for $1,000,000. You pay 10 percent a year on your mortgage. The rules advise: "Because houses increase in value by 6% a year, higher-priced homes earn more over time than lower-priced homes. Just be sure to offset these earnings by any debt you carry." How players (ages nine and up) would do that is unclear. This game is paperless. Instead of cash, each player gets a Visa-brand credit card—made out in Milton Bradley's name—to swipe in the game's electronic Life Pod. Only the computer—a battery-powered mechanical deity—knows how much money you have.[48] Accused of wantonly advertising credit cards to kids through the Hasbro-Visa deal, a Visa spokesman insisted, "We are not marketing to kids. We are helping to educate kids. It's never too early."[49] Suffice it to say, Twists and Turns has a remarkably forgiving attitude toward the highly leveraged player. "If you're in debt in Monopoly," George Burtch, vice president of Hasbro's games division, told me, "you're watching. But in this game, you can be hugely in debt but you're still playing, and no one knows it!"[50] In the Mansion of Happiness, there's a square for that kind of thing. It's called the Road to Folly.

What is the meaning of life? In Twists and Turns, whoever ends up with the most "Life Points" wins, although, technically, the object of the game is to "experience all that LIFE has to offer!" With Milton Bradley's Visa card in hand, you can do whatever the hell you want. "A THOUSAND WAYS TO LIVE YOUR LIFE!" the game box screams. "YOU CHOOSE!" No one dies; no one grows old; no one even grows up. You can play for five minutes or five hours. Or you can just quit, which, all things considered, I recommend.

"Men have an indistinct notion that if they keep up this activity of joint stocks and spades long enough all will at length ride somewhere," Thoreau wrote.[51] But where? Twists and Turns failed, not because it was aimless, but because it wasn't aimless enough. By the time it came out, kids were busy leading virtual lives online, some of them in a place called *Second Life*, a simulated world where you could live your life all over again, or instead, forever.[52]

If the history of games of life tells a story, it's a story about a voyage to nowhere. God, machines, markets, science: each new faith, even faith in uncertainty, is its own creed. Each has its philosophers, each its hucksters, and between them lies a history of beliefs about the beginning, meaning, and end of life. Twists and Turns is the aimless, endless game of secular, liberal modernity. How does life begin? What does it mean? What happens when you're dead? Who knows. YOU CHOOSE!

History can't answer existential questions about life and death; it can only investigate and use evidence to tell stories that make arguments about the relationship between the living and the dead, like the story of Milton Bradley. After the Checkered Game of Life, Bradley lost interest in games.[53] In an age when success made the man—when to fail was to *be* a failure—he spurned his own achievement.[54] He reached Fat Office, and then he walked out. Beginning in the 1870s, he devoted his energies not to board games but to the nascent kindergarten movement, a plan to offer free education to four-, five-, and six-year-olds, and especially to the children of the poor.

Increased wealth brought increased want, as Henry George pointed out in *Progress and Poverty,* in 1879: "Discovery upon discovery, and invention after invention, have neither lessened the toil of those who most need respite, nor brought plenty to the poor." What could be done? The restless, nervous, steam-powered nineteenth century had this how-the-other-half-lives underside: social welfare efforts aimed to rescue the people who were being ridden over by the engine of progress. Enthralled by the idea that very young children could learn through art, a kind of learning that would set them up not only for future academic success but for happiness, too, Bradley started manufacturing crayons, colored paper, color wheels, flash cards, and watercolors, for classrooms. He invented the one-armed paper cutter. He set up a printing shop in Springfield in order to publish, in 1887, *The Paradise of Childhood,* a lavishly illustrated manual for kindergarten teachers, adapted from the writing of the movement's German founder, Friedrich Froebel. Soon he was printing a monthly journal, the *Kindergarten Review.*[55]

Then he entered his decrepitude and, next, his dotage. He began falling asleep at his desk. He started taking naps in his office; he ordered the presses in his factory stopped for half an hour after lunch every day, so as not to disturb his rest. He retired in 1907; he was seventy-one. In 1910, his colleagues toasted him and gave him the gift of a book of tribute essays titled *Milton Bradley: A Successful Man.* But, writing in the *Kindergarten Review,* Bradley reflected that, of all he had done, he was most proud of his educational inventions, which had earned him barely any money at all. "In using the word success, I do not wish to confine its meaning to that cheap interpretation which sees only the glitter of gold or the glamour of elusive fame. In my case, I cannot overestimate the feeling of satisfaction which has been with me all these years at the thought that I have done something, if only something prosaic in character, to place the kindergarten on its present solid foundation."[56] It was a lesson any clever child might have drawn from playing the Checkered Game of Life: Beware of Ambition. It sounds good, but if you land there, you are promptly sent to Fame, a square that not only has no value, in itself, but also puts you perilously close to Jail, Prison, and Suicide. Success isn't everything.

"The journey of life is governed by a combination of chance and judgment," Bradley had written, in his rules for the game, while still a young man. "In starting life, it is not necessarily a fact that poverty will be a disadvantage, so in the game it causes the player no loss." But the older he grew, the better Bradley came to see that he had been wrong. Some people are given better chances than others. There are such things as lousy starts, rotten luck, and bad cards. Maybe he even regretted that he had placed Poverty so close to Infancy and made the chances of getting to School no better than one in three. The kindergarten movement was about beating those odds. Maybe, as he neared the mansion of happiness, Milton Bradley saw in making crayons for kindergartners not only their second chance but his, too: redemption, at last.

THE MANSION OF
HAPPINESS

Be virtuous then and forward press,

To gain the seat of happiness.

—THE MANSION OF HAPPINESS

Minooka Comm. H.S. South Library
Channahon, IL 60410

[CHAPTER 1]

Hatched

On April 30, 1965, seven years after *Sputnik* orbited the earth and four years before *Apollo* landed on the moon, a pink fetus appeared on the cover of *Life* magazine. Curled up inside a diaphanous white membrane set against a black background flecked with what looked to be clusters of stars, a tiny human being floated in space, as if traveling the Milky Way in a ship the shape of an egg. "Living 18-week-old fetus shown inside its amniotic sac," read the text. "Unprecedented photographic feat in color." The magazine promised to reveal, for the first time, the "DRAMA OF LIFE BEFORE BIRTH."

Inside, a seven-page spread, complete with centerfold, documented "the stages in the growth of the human embryo." After photographs of sperm swimming in a blue ocean and of a "ripe egg" lying in wait, there followed highly magnified color close-ups, taken by the Swedish photographer Lennart Nilsson, of embryos at three and a half weeks, four, five, and more, all the way to a fetus of twenty-eight weeks. Said one gynecologist, "This is like the first look at the back side of the moon."[1]

Nilsson's photographs, which also appeared in *Paris Match* and London's *Sunday Times,* were published just after Easter. Eight million copies of the magazine sold in just four days. In September, a New York publisher released a book version with the nativity-themed title *A Child Is Born.* (It has since sold more copies than any other illustrated book in the history of publishing.) The following May, the American Society of Magazine Photographers named Nilsson Photographer of the Year. Before long, his photographs came to stand for humanity itself. In 1977, NASA launched Nilsson's portfolio into outer space, on board the *Voyager* probes, as evidence of life on earth.[2]

There was, nevertheless, something altogether untethered about those haunting and beautiful *Life* photographs: page after page of embryos and fetuses, with not a pregnant woman in sight, which made it look as if those embryos and fetuses were living all on their own. But, of course, embryos and fetuses do not live on their own. Nilsson's embryos and fetuses were dead: miscarriages, abortions, hysterectomies. Only a single photograph captured a living fetus: "the first portrait ever made of a living embryo inside its mother's womb." (The mother was not pictured.) The remaining photographs, including the eighteen-week-old fetus on the much-reproduced cover, had been—as the fine print explained—"surgically removed."[3]

The day *Life* published Nilsson's photographs, *Time* reproduced its cover to illustrate a story in its own pages, called "The Unborn Plaintiff," about the rights of fetuses in criminal court cases. ("A pregnant woman is knocked down by a car and injured. Can she recover damages? Certainly— if the driver was at fault. But what about the unborn child? If he is born with a defect caused by the accident, can he go to court and sue for an injury?")[4] Nilsson's photographs went on to galvanize opposition to abortion and to serve as the iconic symbol of what would come to be called the pro-life movement.[5] But, billed as portraits of life, Nilsson's photographs were, in fact, portraits of death. Weirder still is that they were portraits of humans who looked as if they had been incubated in eggshells, like chickens, and launched into outer space, like so many baby-sized intergalactic rockets.

How life begins is a mystery. The facts of life used to be called the secrets of generation because how life began was not just any mystery but *the* mystery, the great mystery of life. Everyone could see that conception required a man ejaculating into a woman's body; past that, what else was needed, and what followed, was anyone's guess. From antiquity to the Renaissance, most anatomists believed that people came not from eggs but from seeds (*semen* is Latin for "seed"). Beginning in the fifth century B.C., a Hippocratic tradition maintained that conception required two seeds, male and female. A century later, in *On the Generation of Animals,* Aristotle argued that only one seed was needed; human life began, he believed, when a man's seed mixed with a woman's menstrual blood, inside the uterus. In the second century A.D., Galen rejected Aristotle; he believed that the woman contributed a seed, too. This debate lasted for eighteen hundred years.

One-seeders and two-seeders agreed, more or less, on two points. First, conception happened when sex turned matter into life, by way of heat. The seed or seeds supplied the matter; orgasm supplied the heat. Because this happened inside a woman's body, her orgasm, as much as the man's, was often thought to be required for conception to occur (which is why, for a long time, in some places, a woman couldn't charge a man with rape if he had gotten her pregnant). Second, women and men had the same sexual organs, the only difference being that women's are on the inside. This requires a certain exercise of the imagination. Galen offered this instruction: "Turn outward the woman's, turn inward, so to speak, and fold double the man's, and you will find the same in both and every respect."[6]

Aside from stretching your imagination to its limits, was there another way to get at this problem? Aristotle, for one, thought about how life begins by investigating it: dissecting the fetuses of animals, including an "aborted embryo," probably human, and cracking open the eggs of chickens. "Which came first, the chicken or the egg?" is a question Aristotle actually asked. "A bird comes from an egg. There could not have been a first egg to give a beginning to birds," he insisted, "or there should have been a first bird which gave a beginning to eggs."[7]

Setting aside the philosophical conundrum, the fact that eggs come from birds and birds from eggs has been clear enough, for quite a long time. The ancestor of the chicken was domesticated, probably in India, five thousand years ago. Chickens were raised in ancient China, and sometime after hens were introduced to Egypt from Mesopotamia, in about 1400 B.C., chicken eggs were artificially incubated, in brick ovens, by the thousands.[8] Chicken eggs are big. Human eggs are teensy. Bird eggs vary in size, in proportion to the size of the bird—think of the difference between a sparrow egg and an ostrich egg—but the egg of an elephant is about the same size as the egg of a mouse. If you pour out a handful of sand on a table, spread it out, and look for the smallest grain—the speck just barely visible to the naked eye—that grain is about the size of the egg of a human, a horse, a whale, or a shrew.[9]

Chickens are obvious. People are not. People come from people, not from eggs; people are born, not hatched. You can crack open an egg and look inside; you can't crack open a person, although you can see a fetus by cutting open the uterus of a dead pregnant woman, which is what Leonardo da Vinci did, in the fifteenth century, producing a drawing whose wondrous detail wouldn't be matched for centuries but that calls to mind nothing so much as an egg, cracked open.

The first person to imagine that people come from eggs, and not from seeds, was the Englishman William Harvey, born in Kent in 1578. In 1600, when he was twenty-two, Harvey went to study at Padua with the Italian anatomist Hieronymus Fabricius. Fabricius, an Aristotelian, had just finished a book called *The Formed Fetus*. He had also dissected hens' eggs; his *Formation of the Egg and of the Chick* was published posthumously.[10] Harvey earned his MD in 1602, returned to England, and, two years later, married Elizabeth Browne, the daughter of the king's physician. That same year, the king, James, ordered a team of scholars to undertake an English translation of the Bible. In the King James Bible, published in 1611, the word "seed" appears more than two hundred times ("And I wil make thy seed to multiply as the starres of heaven," God tells Abraham); the word "egg" appears not once.

Harvey became a member of London's Royal College of Physicians and succeeded his father-in-law as James's physician. According to a friend of his, the gossip-mongering John Aubrey, Harvey was the first man in England "that was curious in anatomie." While Harvey attended the king at court, a fleet of English ships, led by the *Discovery*, sailed across the ocean to establish what would become England's first permanent colony in the New World. The settlers named it Jamestown. They starved, not because the land was barren, but because they were unable to govern themselves. "Had we beene in Paradice it selfe," John Smith complained, "it would not have beene much better." The colony's lieutenant governor, George Percy, described the settlers running around naked, "so Leane thatt they Looked lyke anatomies." Most of the colonists were men, which, as Smith saw it, was part of the problem. One of the women, Percy reported, met a bad end: "one of our Colline murdered his wyfe Ripped the Childe outt of her woambe and threwe it into the River and after Chopped the Mother in pieces and sallted her for his foode." (Added another settler: "Now whether shee was better roasted, boyled or carbonado'd, I know not, but of such a dish as powdered wife I never heard of.") Jamestown, Smith reported, was "a misery, a ruine, a death, a hell." Nevertheless, in 1620, Pilgrims hoisted the sails of the *Mayflower* and headed to a land Smith had named "New England."[11]

When James died, in 1625, his son Charles became king, and William Harvey became Charles's physician. He continued his study of anatomy, making discoveries by way of vivisection. In 1628, two years before John Winthrop and his band of Puritans settled Massachusetts Bay, and seven years before Milton Bradley's ancestors washed up in Salem, Harvey announced the discovery for which he is now best known: the circulation of the blood.[12] In this seafaring age, Harvey thought of himself as an explorer, inspired by "the Sedulity of Travellers" who had discovered lands unknown to the ancients, on the other side of the ocean. "To Us the whole Theatre of the World is now open," Harvey wrote. He, too, had explored a whole new world: the inside of the human body, which he navigated by way of the blood vessels. One poet compared Harvey to Francis Drake, calling him the "Fam'd Circulator of the Lesser World."[13] The body was his earth.

"In the beginning," Locke wrote, "all the world was America." In the age of discovery, theories about the origin of life were very often bound up with ideas about the New World. What William Harvey thought about men and beasts and kings and courts and worlds new and old, he put into his work. So, too, his thoughts about men and women.

Harvey, something of a misanthrope, kept a monkey. "He was wont to say that man was but a great mischievous baboon," Aubrey wrote. Harvey also liked to say "that we Europaeans knew not how to order or governe our woemen, and that the Turkes were the only people used them wisely." He thought a harem a good idea. He was not vaunted for his fidelity, Aubrey noted: "He kept a pretty young wench to wayte on him, which I guesse he made use of warmeth-sake as king David did." Married for over forty years, he never had any children. His wife kept a parrot. More than that, about their marriage, is not known.[14]

At the time, theories about what caused childlessness abounded. *The Birth of Mankind*, a midwifery manual first published in English in 1550, explained that the best way to discover the problem, in a barren couple, was to have husband and wife urinate onto seeds of wheat, barley, and beans, seven of each, and then plant the seeds in separate pots, filled with soil, and water them, every day, with urine. Whoever's seeds failed to sprout was thought to be the cause of the barrenness.[15] It's for this kind of thing that doctors used to be called piss prophets.

William Harvey was keenly interested in discovering the secrets of generation, but not by way of piss prophecy. He wanted to bring to this question deduction, reason, and experiment. He started by speculating.

"A *Man*, was first a *Boy*," he began. "Before he was a *Boy*, he was an *Infant*; and before an *Infant*, an *Embryo*." So far, so good. "Now we must search farther," he urged, venturing into the unknown. "What hee was in his Mothers Womb, before he was this *Embryo*, or *Foetus*; whether *three bubbles*? or some *rude* and *indigested lump*? or a *conception*, or *coagulation* of *mixed seed*? or whether any thing else?"

Following Aristotle and Fabricius, Harvey first sought the answer by cracking open hens' eggs, which were "cheap merchandize," and ready to hand.[16] He may have begun this work on first returning to England from Padua, even before he took up his study of the circulation of the blood. He regretted that he was unable to gather evidence about his own species, "for we are almost quite debarred of dissecting the humane *Uterus*." Even barnyard animals were hard to come by: "to make any inquiry concerning this matter, in *Horses, Oxen, Goats*, and other Cattel, cannot be without a great deal of paines and expense." Fortunately, King Charles liked to hunt. "Our late Sovereign King *Charls*, so soon as he became a Man, was wont for Recreation, and Health sake, to *hunt* almost every week, especially the *Buck* and *Doe*." From the king's gamekeeper, Harvey claimed his catch: does, in the rutting season. "I had a daily oportunity of dissecting them, and of making inspection and observation of all their *parts*." Evidence suggests that Harvey's very good friend Thomas Hobbes attended at least one of these dissections.[17] (In his will, Harvey left Hobbes ten pounds, "to buy something to keepe in remembrance of mee.") The king, too, found Harvey's work fascinating and "was himself much delighted in this kind of curiosity, being many times pleased to be an eye-witness, and to assert my new inventions." Even the queen took an interest. "I saw long since a foetus of the magnitude of a Pease-cod, cut out of the uterus of a Doe," Harvey wrote. "I shewed this pretty Spectacle and Rarity of Nature to our late King and Queen. It did swim, trim and perfect, in such a kinde of White most transparent, and crystaline moysture (as if it had been treasured up in some most clear glassie receptable) about the bigness of a Pigeons egge." Harvey had seen human fetuses, too, including one "wherein the *Embryo*, who was as long as the *naile* of the *little finger*, did appear like a small *frogge:* having a *broad body*, a *wide mouth*, and his *armes* and *leggs* newly shot forth, like the young *buds* of *flowers*." And there was more:

Another *humane Conception* I saw (which was about fifty dayes standing) wherein was an *egge*, as large as an *Hen-egg*, or *Turkey-egg*. The *foetus* was of the longitude of a *large Bean*, with a very great *head*, which was over-looked by the *Occiput*, as by a *crest*; the *Brain* it self was in substance like *Coagulated milk*; and instead of a *solid scull*, there was a kind of *Leather-membrane*, which was in some parts like a gristle, distributed from the *fore-head*, to the *Roots* of the *Nose*. The *Face* appeared like a *Dogs snout*. Without both *Ears*, and *Nose*. Yet was the *rough Artery*, which descends into the *Lungs*, and the first *rudiment* of the *Yard*, visible. The two *deaf-ears* of the *Heart*, appeared like two *black eyes*.[18]

Harvey's descriptions are marvelous. A fetus was like a frog, a flower bud, a turkey egg, a large bean, something like milk, covered with leather, with a snout like a dog's. Still, while the human fetuses, like the spectacle of deer embryos floating in egg-shaped sacs as clear as glass, were wonderful, what Harvey was really looking for was an egg.

The famed circulator of the lesser world considered it a fallacy to believe, as most anatomists did, that different sorts of animals derived from different things: birds from eggs; vermin from worms; men from seeds. No, he insisted, they all came from eggs, even if, in some creatures, those eggs are incubated inside and, in others, out. He knew that this claim ran "counter to the common received tenets." In fact, it bordered on anatomical heresy. "An egg," he believed, turning prevailing wisdom on its head, "is the Common Original of All Animals."[19]

He didn't expect everyone to agree with him. At the time, all sorts of people were challenging ancient knowledge of the natural world and challenging, too, the very nature of knowledge, and even its limits. What could be known was what could be investigated, demonstrated, and explained.[20] Harvey's theory of circulation (which, like his theory of generation, happens to have been right) did not gain easy or ready acceptance, partly because no one, not even Harvey, could explain what circulation was *for.* Harvey told Aubrey, "Twas beleeved by the vulgar that he was crack-brained."[21]

Anticipating that his idea about eggs would be still more controversial, he was reluctant to publish his study of generation. And he never got around to publishing another book, which was to be called *The Loves, Lusts, and Sexual Acts of Animals.*[22] Not until the end of 1648 was he persuaded to prepare his treatise for publication. He was, by then, an old man, in considerable pain, suffering from gout, and burdened with disappointment. His wife had died. England was at war with itself. In 1649, while Harvey worked on his manuscript, Charles was beheaded, leaving the future of the monarchy uncertain. For a time, Harvey was banished from London. In a portrait taken to serve as an illustration for his new book, Harvey, a dying royalist, looked so miserable that, in the end, the likeness was left out. Then Harvey, who "believed it lawful to put an end to his life when tired of it," tried to kill himself by taking an overdose of laudanum. He failed.[23]

Harvey's *De Generatione animalium* was published, in Latin, in 1651. It was to be his lasting legacy, his own act of generation. A dedicatory poem noted at once Harvey's intellectual fecundity, his childlessness—"Thy *Brain* hath *Issue,* though thy *Loins* have none"—and the parentless state of England: "Let fraile *Succession* be the Vulgar care; / Great *Generation's* selfe is now *thy Heire.*"[24]

This analogy—between a theory of generation and a hereditary monarchy—was not uncommon. The state has been thought of as a body for a long time; in English, the phrase "body politic" dates to the fifteenth century. Anatomy is a good place for the discussion—literally, the embodiment—of a political order.[25] Harvey's *Generatione* was published the same year as Hobbes's *Leviathan.* In *Leviathan,* Hobbes postulated the existence of a primordial state of nature—a place, very much like Jamestown, where life is poor, nasty, brutish, and short—against which the leviathan, artificial man, civil society, is formed. "Life is but a motion of Limbs," Hobbes wrote, "the beginning whereof is in some principal part within." The leviathan, the state, is "but an artificial man," healthy in times of peace, sickened by treason, and felled by civil war.[26] In *Generatione,* Harvey attempted to deduce a state of nature, within the womb, out of which man was formed. In a state of nature, man is an egg.

But Harvey had not found an egg. When he dissected does that had just mated, he never found anything in their uteruses. Not female seed, not male seed. Weeks later, he did find something; he found an embryo. But he thought he had found something else, and he called what he found, in Latin, an *ovum,* a word that, before then, had been used only to talk about birds' eggs.[27] (Aubrey: "He wrote very bad Latin.")[28] In 1653, Harvey's Latin treatise was translated into English, and that *ovum,* the origins of life, an anatomical Eden, became an "egg." But nothing inside the book made Harvey's point so well as its frontispiece, which pictured Zeus opening an egg, out of which hatched all manner of creatures: a grasshopper, a lizard, a bird, a snake, a deer, a butterfly, a spider, and a baby. "*Ex ovus omnia,*" read the motto: Everything from an egg.[29]

"We shall call these vesicles *ova,* on account of the exact similitude which they exhibit to the eggs contained in the ovaries of birds," the Dutch anatomist Regnier de Graaf wrote, in 1672, when he finally found the egg Harvey was looking for—or, at least, when he thought he had found it, although what he had actually found is what is now called the ovarian follicle.[30] With de Graaf, what used to be called "female testicles" were renamed "ovaries." Harvey appeared to be triumphing. But Harvey, who died of a stroke in 1657, was right to worry that people would think he was crack-brained.

"Man comes not from an egg," Antoni van Leeuwenhoek insisted in 1683, "but from an animalcule in the masculine seed."[31] He had seen it himself. The microscope was invented in Holland between 1591 and 1608, and the Dutch Leeuwenhoek was the finest microscope maker in the world. He was not trained as an anatomist, but what he saw with his lenses led him, in letters to London's Royal Society, to challenge the authority of "your Harvey and our de Graaf."[32] He reported on the eye of a bee and the nose of a louse. He made a particular subject of himself. He looked at "a hair taken from my eyelid"; he looked at his spit. "I have often viewed the *Sweat* of my face," he wrote.[33] And then he looked at semen (the product, he took pains to point out, not of masturbation but of intercourse) and reported that he'd found in it "animalcules," tiny animals.[34] They could swim; they had heads and tails; they were microscopic men.

After that, it took rather a long time for anatomists to work out what men and women contribute to generation. But from Harvey and Leeuwenhoek, for all their differences, emerged, eventually, a consensus: women aren't men turned inside out, as Galen had thought. Women don't have testicles, like men; they have ovaries, like hens. Women don't make seeds; they make eggs.[35] Hobbes had argued that in a state of nature, there are no natural rulers—not a king over his people, not man over woman. Men enter a political state when they consent to be governed. But women don't consent to a government of men; they aren't even part of it. Women, therefore, must be not lesser men, not lesser members of the body politic, but no members at all.[36] "In everything not connected with sex, woman is man," Rousseau wrote. "In everything connected with sex, woman and man are in every respect related but in every respect different."[37] But different, how? The poet who supplied the dedication to Harvey's *Generatione* put it best:

> . . . *both the* Hen *and* Housewife *are so matcht,*
> *That her Son* Born, *is only her Son Hatch;*
> *That when her* Teeming *hopes have prosp'rous bin,*
> *Yet to* Conceive, *is but to* Lay within.[38]

Women are a great deal like men, except when they're more like chickens.

"I shall begin at the beginning," says the director of the Hatchery, while giving a tour to a group of students, in the opening chapter of *Brave New World,* Aldous Huxley's 1931 novel. The idea that eggs can exist outside of women's bodies was a mainstay of twentieth-century science fiction. "*Begin at the beginning,*" Huxley's students dutifully write in their notebooks. The tour continues: "'These,' he waved his hand, 'are the incubators.' And opening an insulated door he showed them racks upon racks of numbered test-tubes. 'The week's supply of ova.'" In Huxley's dark and terrible world, yet another new world, there are no mothers and no fathers, no families at all. Humans are conceived in the laboratory, and fetuses grow in test tubes.[39]

Huxley's fiction was ahead of science, but not by all that much. Before human eggs could be incubated, they had to be found. Aristotle had studied chickens; Harvey, deer. After Harvey, there followed something of an egg hunt. In 1827, a German scholar named Karl von Baer finally found a mammalian egg, the ovum of a dog. "Led by curiosity," he wrote, "I opened one of the follicles and took up the minute object on the point of my knife, finding that I could see it very distinctly and that it was surrounded by mucus. When I placed it under the microscope I was utterly astonished, for I saw an ovule . . . so clearly that a blind man could hardly deny it."[40]

Meanwhile, Charles Darwin was undertaking his own investigation of genesis. *The Origin of Species* was published in 1859. *Water-Babies: A Fairy Tale for a Land Baby,* a children's book that doubled as a defense of Darwinism, was published four years later. The Huxley children, including Aldous and Julian, read it, not least because it featured a scene in which their grandfather T. H. Huxley, a supporter of Darwin's, inspects a baby in a bottle. "Dear Grandpater," Julian Huxley wrote to his grandfather when he was four, "have you seen a Water-baby? Did you put it in a bottle? Did it wonder if it could get out? Can I see it some day? Your loving JULIAN."[41]

In *The Eggs of Mammals,* in 1936, the Harvard-trained physiologist Gregory Pincus (who started out studying rats) offered a history of what happened next in the matter of hunting eggs: "Pfuger, 1863—cat; Schron, 1863—cat and rabbit; Koster, 1868—man; Slawinsky, 1873—man; Wagener, 1879—dog; Van Beneden, 1880—bat; Harz, 1883—mouse, guinea pig, cat; Lange, 1896—mouse; Coert, 1898—rabbit and cat; Amann, 1899—man; Palladino, 1894, 1898—man, bear, dog; Lane-Claypon, 1905, 1907—rabbit; Fellner, 1909—man."[42] The year 1909 is also when the word "ectogenesis" was coined.

By then, chicken and deer and dogs and cats and bats and rats were giving way to mice, largely through the pioneering research and promotional work of a single man, C. C. Little. Mice are small and cheap and quiet and easy to care for, and they reproduce very quickly; gestation takes only three weeks.[43] The first study of the egg of a mouse was published in 1883. A landmark account of conception, based on the study of mice, was published ten years later.[44] Little, born in 1888, began breeding mice as a student at Harvard, just after the rediscovery of the work of Gregor Mendel, who had deduced what became known as Mendel's laws of inheritance in the 1850s and '60s in an Augustinian monastery in Czechoslovakia.

At Harvard, Little worked under W. E. Castle at the dawn of the field called, beginning in 1906, "genetics"; it was Castle who popularized Mendel's long-forgotten work in the United States. Castle trained Pincus, as well.[45] J. A. Long and E. L. Mark, who also worked in Castle's lab and who, in 1911, published *The Maturation of the Egg of the Mouse,* bought their stock of mostly white and brown mice from dealers and fanciers.[46] Little wanted to breed his own mice, to save money and to standardize the stock, allowing for more controlled research. In 1920, he launched the Mouse Club of America; three years later, he started holding meetings in Maine. In 1929, the year after Mickey Mouse was first seen in theaters, Little founded the Jackson Laboratory, in Bar Harbor, and appeared on the cover of *Time.* (Because of Little's work, the mouse became the standard laboratory animal and Jackson Laboratory the leading supplier of mice for biomedical research, shipping, by the end of the twentieth century, more than two million mice annually. A mouse gene was the first gene ever cloned; the mouse genome was the first genome decoded.)[47]

Still, mice aren't men. There's a limit to arguing by homology. Until 1840, no one knew that human females ovulate monthly, the menstrual cycle remained a mystery, and the question of what determines the sex of a human embryo was uncertain. Anatomists in Germany began collecting the products of miscarriages and abortions in order to study ovarian, embryonic, and fetal development in humans. In 1890, an American named Franklin Paine Mall, who had studied in Germany, began teaching at a new university in Worcester, Massachusetts, from which he sent a circular letter to more than half the physicians in the United States:

My dear Doctor,

During the last few years the kindness of several physicians has enabled me to procure for study about a dozen human embryos less than six weeks old. As a specialist in embryology I ask if you can aid me in procuring more material. It is constantly coming into your hands and without your aid it is practically impossible to further the study of human embryology. . . . Any material which may come into your possession should not be injured by handling nor should it be washed with water. Carefully place it in a tumbler and as soon as possible preserve it in a bath of alcohol. . . . When a specimen is to be sent by express it should be placed in a bottle completely filled with alcohol, with a very loose plug of absorbent cotton both above and below it.

Thanking you in advance for any aid you may give me in procuring material, I am,

Very Truly Yours,
F. Mall.
Clark University, Worcester, Mass.[48]

Mall soon moved from Clark to Johns Hopkins, where he collected specimens from hospitals in Baltimore, a city filled with poor women and in which one out of every three children born out of wedlock died in infancy. He rarely kept records about the women from whose bodies his specimens came, but his scant notes include stories like this: a twenty-five-year-old woman, childless after four years of marriage, in whose uterus, examined after a hysterectomy, was found an embryo; a domestic servant who "fell into the hands of an abortionist"; a woman, one month pregnant, who committed suicide by swallowing lye. By 1917, Mall had gathered, into what had become the Carnegie Human Embryo Collection, more than two thousand embryos.[49]

Similar collections were made in Europe. All those embryos and fetuses stored in jars made an impression on J.B.S. Haldane, a Scottish biologist credited with uniting Mendelian genetics with Darwinian evolution and who happened to be a close friend of Aldous Huxley's. It was Haldane who gave Huxley the idea for the Hatchery. In 1923, Haldane delivered a lecture at Cambridge University, a meditation on "the influence of biology on history." He imagined a future in which a third of all children would be conceived and incubated in glass jars. Haldane's lecture, published as *Daedalus; Or, Science and the Future,* contains a fictional history—a very early science fiction fantasy, a founder of the genre—of the experimental work (including his own) that had led to ectogenesis:

It was in 1951 that Dupont and Schwarz produced the first ectogenetic child. As early as 1901 Heape had transferred embryo rabbits from one female to another, in 1925 Haldane had grown embryonic rats in serum for ten days, but had failed to carry the process to its conclusion, and it was not till 1940 that Clark succeeded with the pig, using Kehlmann's solution as a medium. Dupont and Schwarz obtained a fresh ovary from a woman who was the victim of an aeroplane accident, and kept it living in their medium for five years. They obtained several eggs from it and fertilized them successfully, but the problem of the nutrition and support of the embryo was more difficult. . . . France was the first country to adopt ectogenesis officially, and by 1968 was producing 60,000 children annually by this method. In most countries the opposition was far stronger, and was intensified by the Papal Bull "Nunquauam prius audito," and the similar fetwa of the Khalif, both of which appeared in 1960.[50]

What actually happened was different. In 1934, Gregory Pincus claimed to have fertilized a rabbit egg in vitro. "Rabbits Born in Glass: Haldane-Huxley Fantasy Made Real by Harvard Biologists," the *New York Times* reported. Three years later, Pincus was denied tenure at Harvard; his rabbit experiments had caused something of a scandal. In 1944, Pincus cofounded the Worcester Foundation for Experimental Biology, where, in the 1950s, he and his colleagues Min Chueh Chang and John Rock developed the oral contraceptive known as the Pill.[51] No ectogenetic child was produced in 1951. But in 1952 a young photographer named Lennart Nilsson did come across three jars containing human embryos, each only half an inch long, in an anatomy laboratory in the Karolinska Institute, in Stockholm.

Nilsson, born outside Stockholm in 1923, had always been interested in the mystery of life. "From the time he could toddle about Swedish countryside showed single-minded drive to explore secrets of nature," one *Life* press release put it. When he was five years old, he fell through the ice on a lake near his home and, when he was pulled out, reported calmly, "There were some very interesting things to see down there." When he was twelve, his father gave him a camera. By the time he was fifteen, he was selling his photographs to Swedish magazines. In that lab at the Karolinska, he took pictures of what was in those jars, and in 1953 he brought those pictures to New York, to show them to the editors at *Life*. Encouraged to pursue the work, Nilsson spent seven years in Swedish hospitals and gynecological clinics, taking pictures of dead embryos and fetuses, attempting to chronicle "the stages of human reproduction from fertilization to just before birth," a project that helped invent the idea of being unborn as a stage of human life, a stage that was never on any board game.[52]

Pincus's contraceptive pill was sold beginning in 1960; it went a long

Minooka Comm. H.S. South Library
Channahon, IL 60410

way toward separating sex from reproduction. But separating reproduction from women hadn't come nearly as far. Haldane had predicted that by 1968 sixty thousand children would be born ectogenetically in France alone. That prediction was wrong. Nevertheless, a great many people, including the millions of people who saw Stanley Kubrick's 1968 film, 2001, were thinking about ectogenesis.

Kubrick was born in New York in 1928. His father, a physician, gave him a camera, and Kubrick, as a very young man, became a photographer for Look magazine. He made a series of films in the 1950s and found box office success in 1960 with Spartacus, followed by Lolita (1962) and Dr. Strangelove (1964). Strangelove ends with a nuclear Armageddon: the extinction of all life on earth. The year Strangelove came out, Kubrick decided he wanted to make a science fiction film about outer space, where life might last forever, in another kind of mansion of happiness.

He enlisted the help of science fiction writer Arthur C. Clarke. The film, Clarke suggested, ought to be based on his 1948 story "The Sentinel," which is set in 1996, although Kubrick was, for a time, much more interested in a novel of Clarke's from 1953, called Childhood's End. Clarke liked to imagine men without women, worlds in which generation, if it takes place at all, is the work of men of science, or men of the future, or aliens who, however inhuman, are, somehow, male. He had the idea that he and Kubrick ought to write a novel together, then write a screenplay from the novel. They began collaborating on the novel, which was to be called Journey Beyond the Stars, in April 1964. Clarke was also working at the offices of Time-Life, finishing a book called Man and Space for Time-Life Books.[53]

Kubrick and Clarke consulted with NASA. They met with Marvin Minsky at MIT. They talked to Carl Sagan at Harvard's Smithsonian Astrophysical Observatory. They worked with IBM on HAL, the computer on board their fictional spaceship, Discovery. At the time, Kubrick was obsessed with sex, aging, death, and laboratory mice. He told Playboy, "I understand that at Yale they've been engaging in experiments in which the pleasure center of a mouse's brain has been localized and stimulated by electrodes; the result is that the mouse undergoes an eight-hour orgasm."[54] He met with Robert Ettinger, a physics teacher from Michigan who was interested in freezing the dead. He decided that the crew on board the Discovery would have to travel in cryogenic suspension.

In April 1965, when Nilsson's photographs of the "Drama of Life Before

Birth" were published in *Life*, Kubrick decided to call his film *2001: A Space Odyssey*. Two months later, an unmanned probe, *Mariner IV*, came within six thousand miles of Mars and sent twenty-two photographs of the planet back to earth. Kubrick contacted Lloyd's of London, "to price an insurance policy against Martians being discovered before the release of his film." In September, *A Child Is Born*, the book version of Nilsson's photographs, was published. On October 3, Kubrick decided how *2001* would end: its main character, David Bowman, a crew member on board the *Discovery*, would turn into an infant. Clarke wrote in his diary: "Stanley on phone, worried about ending . . . gave him my latest ideas, and one of them suddenly clicked—Bowman will regress to infancy, and we'll see him at the end as a baby in orbit." Shooting began in December. An unmanned Russian spacecraft landed on the moon in February 1966. On March 29, 1968, a special screening of *2001* was held for *Life*. The film was released in April and Clarke's novel in July. Within the year, Neil Armstrong and Edwin Aldrin walked on the moon.[55]

In *2001*, Kubrick and Clarke tell the story of human history; the film is *Pilgrim's Progress* as told by MIT and IBM, with extraterrestrials playing the part of God. It begins with the dawn of man. Apes on an African plain become men not by evolution but by way of aliens, who send to earth a stone slab, a rectangular monolith ("the New Rock," Clarke calls it in the novel), which makes possible conceptual leaps, including the use, by primates, of tools—the first machines. The discovery of a monolith on the moon in the year 1994 leads to another conceptual leap, interstellar travel, resulting in the voyage of the *Discovery* in 2001. Bowman serves as the ship's captain on a voyage intended to take a hibernating crew past Saturn. After HAL kills the crew, Bowman disconnects the computer and is left alone on the *Discovery*. Orbiting a satellite of Jupiter, he finds another monolith and rides in a space pod to get a closer look. He passes through some sort of star gate, which takes him on a journey past the stars and into a room in an eighteenth-century mansion—it has the look of Versailles—where he eats some blue goo, falls asleep, ages into a very old man, and regresses into a baby and then a fetus.[56]

As with the rest of the film, which contains very little dialogue, this regression is not explained, but in the novel, Clarke refers to the unborn Bowman as the Star-Child.[57] Both the novel and the film close with the Star-Child approaching a blue-green earth. "Down there on that crowded globe," Clarke writes, "history as men knew it would be drawing to a close."[58] The final scene of *2001* is that cover of *Life* magazine: a Lennart Nilsson–style shot of a fetus, cut out of a woman's body, floating through space, in an egg.

"Morally pretentious, intellectually obscure, and inordinately long," the American historian Arthur Schlesinger Jr. called *2001*, in a review in *Vogue*. Jay Cocks, a writer for *Time* who had been assigned a feature story about Kubrick, reported that at the appearance of the Star-Child at the first public screening of *2001*, one critic snorted and walked out. The reviews were, Cocks said, "almost uniformly devastating." *Time* canceled the feature.[59] Renata Adler and Pauline Kael, two influential reviewers who, to say the least, didn't often agree, despised it. They were both women. Adler, writing in the *New York Times*, found it extravagantly inane that *2001*, the story of human history, ends with man's "death and rebirth in what looked like an intergalactic embryo." Kael, writing for *Harper's*, called *2001* "monumentally unimaginative": "Kubrick's story line—accounting for evolution by extraterrestrial intelligence—is probably the most gloriously redundant plot of all time."[60] 'Twas believed by the critics that he was crack-brained.

Kubrick waved all this aside, dismissing his detractors as "dogmatically atheist and materialist and Earth-bound." And the reviews were far from uniformly devastating. *Life* celebrated the film's gadgetry and "hard science."[61] Audiences, meanwhile, adored it. It was a happening, good to watch while getting stoned, a different kind of voyage of life: *2001* was, as its ad campaign had it, "the ultimate trip."[62]

Kubrick's *2001* told the story of the origins of man—without women. Women, meanwhile, were campaigning for equal rights with men, for what they called "personhood." The National Organization for Women was founded in 1966, NARAL in 1969. In a speech in Chicago that year, Betty Friedan said, "There is no freedom, no equality, no full human dignity and personhood possible for women until we assert and demand the control over our own bodies." In 1972, the Equal Rights Amendment, written by Alice Paul and first introduced to Congress in 1923, passed and went to the states for ratification. Opponents of the ERA, led by Phyllis Schlafly, supported, instead, a "human life amendment," first proposed in 1973, eight days after the Supreme Court ruling in *Roe v. Wade*. The ERA was eventually defeated. The language of personhood was adopted by the pro-life movement. By the beginning of the twenty-first century, personhood amendments began appearing on state ballots. A 2011 Mississippi Person-hood Amendment read, "The term 'person' or 'persons' shall include every human being from the moment of fertilization." If a fertilized egg has con-stitutional rights, women cannot have equal rights with men. In American political history, this debate goes back only decades, but in the history of ideas, it goes back to a time before almost no one, least of all William Har-vey, could imagine the body politic as female.

"To Us the whole Theatre of the World is now open," Harvey had writ-ten, during the age of discovery. For Stanley Kubrick, it wasn't inner space but outer space that his *Discovery* explored, a whole new world. But, really, it was the same place, a world without women. In the space age, the secrets of generation were at last discovered, in a galaxy terribly far away.

CHAPTER 2

Baby Food

At the dawn of the twenty-first century, there were some new rules governing what used to be called "mother's milk," or "breast milk," including one about what to call it when it's no longer in a mother's breast. An explanation, nomenclatural: "expressed human milk" is milk that has been pressed, squeezed, or sucked out of a woman's breast by hand or by machine, but not by a baby, and stored in a bottle or a jar or, best for freezing, in a plastic bag secured with a twist tie. Matters, regulatory: Could a woman carry containers of her own milk on an airplane? Before 2008, not more than three ounces, because the U.S. government's Transportation Security Administration classed human milk with shampoo, toothpaste, and Gatorade until a Minneapolis woman heading home after a business trip was reduced to tears when a security guard at LaGuardia Airport poured a two-day supply of her milk into a garbage bin, leading protesting mothers to stage airport "nurse-ins"; Dr. Ruth Lawrence of the breast-feeding committee of the American Academy of Pediatrics to tell the press, "She needs every drop of that precious golden fluid for her baby"; and the TSA to reclassify human milk as "liquid medication."[1]

Could a woman sell her milk on eBay? It had been done and, so far, with no more consequence than the opprobrium of the blogosphere, at least until the Federal Drug Administration decided to tackle that one. Could women share their milk over Facebook? This, too, had been done (it was called "Eats on Feets," after Meals on Wheels), and, although the Canadian Paediatric Society deemed it inadvisable, what the Centers for Disease Control had to say about it remained to be seen.[2] That agency did, however, provide a fact sheet about "What to Do If an Infant or Child Is Mistakenly Fed Another Woman's Expressed Breast Milk," which could happen at day care centers where fridges were full of bags of milk, labeled in smudgeable ink. (The CDC solemnly advised that a switch "should be treated just as if an accidental exposure to other bodily fluids occurred.") During a nine-hour exam, could a woman take a break to express the milk uncomfortably filling her breasts? No, because the Americans with Disabilities Act did not consider lactation a disability.[3] Could a human milk bank pay a woman for her milk? (Milk banks supply pasteurized human milk to hospitals.) No, because making of human milk a cash cow violated the ethical standards of the Human Milk Banking Association of North America.[4] If a nursing woman drank to excess—alcohol flows from the bloodstream into the mammary glands—could she be charged with child abuse? Hadn't happened yet, but there had been talk. Meanwhile, women who were worried could test a drop with a product called Milkscreen; if the alcohol level was too high, the recommendation was: pump and dump.[5]

An observation, historical: all this seemed so new that people were making up the rules as they went along.[6] Before the 1990s, electric breast pumps, sophisticated pieces of medical equipment, were generally available only in hospitals, where they were used to express milk from women with inverted nipples or from mothers of premature or low-birth-weight infants too weak and tiny to suck and who needed to be fed milk through a tube snaked down the esophagus. But by the first decade of the twenty-first century, breasts pumps were so ubiquitous a personal accessory, they were more like cell phones than catheters.[7] During the 2008 presidential campaign, the Republican vice presidential nominee, Sarah Palin, told *People* magazine that she had often found herself having to "put down the Black-Berries and pick up the breast pump."[8] In 2010, staffers and newly elected politicians arriving in Washington and looking for a place to pump their milk availed themselves of six "lactation suites" known as "boob cubes."

The first was opened after then Speaker of the House Nancy Pelosi pushed for a pumping station in a room in the basement of the Capitol Building. It was equipped, the Associated Press reported, with "multiline phones, a TV often tuned to C-SPAN, and power outlets for laptops. Women who made calls from a phone in that room found that the caller ID read, 'INFANT LACTATION.' "[9] In 2011, First Lady Michelle Obama urged the IRS to give tax breaks for breast pumps.[10]

Ectogenesis was a still a science fiction fantasy, the stuff of Haldane and Huxley, but ectolactation was everywhere. There were as yet no Hatcheries, but there were boob cubes in the very halls of government. Strangest of all: not many people seemed to find this freakishly dystopian, merely troubling, or even objectionable.

A treatise, mercantile: Medela, a Swiss company founded in 1961, introduced its first non-hospital, electric-powered, vacuum-operated breast pump in the United States in 1991; five years later it launched the swank Pump In Style. Its sales soon quadrupled. The traffic in pumps was brisk, although accurate sales figures were hard to come by, not least because many people bought the top-of-the-line models secondhand. (Manufacturers pointed out that if you wouldn't buy a used toothbrush, you shouldn't buy a used breast pump; but a toothbrush didn't cost three hundred dollars, and most women figured that, so long as you sterilized the hell out of the thing, it wasn't unsanitary.) Then there was the swag. "Baby-friendly" maternity wards that had once sent new mothers home with free samples of infant formula began giving out manual pumps: plastic, one-breast-at-a-time gizmos that work like a cross between a straw and a bicycle pump. Walmart sold an Evenflo pump at a bargain. Avent made one "featuring new iQ Technology"; the pitch was that the pump's memory chip made it smart, but the name also played on well past dubious claims that human milk raises IQ scores.[11] Still swisher, state-of-the-art pumps whose motors, tubes, and freeze packs were wedged into bags disguised to look like black leather Fendi briefcases and Gucci backpacks were a must-have at baby showers; the Medela Pump In Style Metro Model—"the CEO of breast pumps"—was a particular rage; you could pick one up at any department store.

Medela also sold Pump & Save storage bags and breast shields (a shield is the hard plastic part of the contraption that fits over the breast; it looks like a horn of plenty). Plug Medela's no-hands model into your car's cigarette lighter: pump 'n' drive. Better yet, pump, drive, 'n' text: strenuous motherhood was de rigueur. Duck into the ladies' room at a conference of doctors, lawyers, or professors and, chances were, you'd find a flock of women with matching "briefcases" waiting—none too patiently and, trust me, more than a little sheepishly—for a turn with the electric outlet. Pumps came with plastic sleeves, like the sleeves in a man's wallet, into which a mother was supposed to slip a photograph of her baby because, Pavlovian, looking at the picture aids "letdown," the release of milk normally triggered by the presence of the baby, his touch, his cry. Staring at that picture when your baby was miles away: it could make you cry, too. Pumping is no fun—whether it is more boring or more lonesome I find hard to say—but it wasn't just common; it had become strangely trendy, too, so trendy that even women who were home with their babies all day long expressed their milk and fed it to their babies in a bottle. American women pumped milk like no other women in the world. Behind closed doors, the nation began to look like a giant human dairy farm.

Meanwhile, the evolving rules governing human milk, including a proposed Breastfeeding Promotion Act, made for nothing so much as a muddle. They indulged in a nomenclatural sleight of hand, eliding "breast-feeding" and "feeding human milk." They were purblind, unwilling to eye whether it's his mother or her milk that matters more to a baby. They suffered from a category error. Human milk is food. Is it an elixir, a commodity, a right? This question about life and death was, at heart, taxonomical. And, like most questions about life and death, it had been asked before.

Taxonomy follows anatomy: William Harvey sought the origins of life; the Swedish naturalist Carolus Linnaeus sorted the kinds of life. Linnaeus's parents had wanted him to follow in his father's footsteps and become a priest, but, from boyhood, he loved plants and their quirky names. In 1735, he was twenty-eight and just finishing his study of medicine when he published the first edition of his *Systema Naturae,* in which he proposed a system for classifying and naming all living things. At first, he placed humans in a category called Quadrupedia: four-footed beasts. This was heresy; in Genesis, men are not animals. (Linnaeus, a devout Lutheran, considered his work to be honoring God's creation, in that he was deducing, by observation, the divine order of nature.) But even those of Linneaus's critics who conceded the animality of man averred, none too gently, that people have two feet, not four. Ah, but hands are just feet that can grip, Linnaeus ventured. This proved unpersuasive. By 1758, in a process brilliantly reconstructed by the historian of science Londa Schiebinger, Linnaeus had abandoned Quadrupedia in favor of a word he'd made up: Mammalia, for animals with milk-producing nipples.

He derived this word from the Latin root *mamma,* meaning breast, teat, or udder. *Mamma* is closely related to the onomatopoeic "mama," mother, thought to come from the sound a baby makes while suckling. Mammals are mammals and humans are mammals because they make milk. As categories go, mammal is an improvement over quadruped, especially if you're thinking about what people have in common with whales. But, for a while at least, it was deemed scandalously erotic. (Linnaeus's classification of plants based on their reproductive organs, stamens and pistils, fell prey to a similar attack. "Loathsome harlotry," one botanist called it.) More importantly, the name falls something short of capacious: only female mammals lactate; males, in a strict sense, are not mammals. Plenty of other features distinguish mammals from Linnaeus's five other animal classes: birds, amphibians, fish, insects, and worms. (Tetracoilia, animals with a four-chambered heart, proposed by a contemporary of Linnaeus's, the Scottish surgeon John Hunter, was, quite possibly, a better idea.) And if it's the milk that matters most, why not gather the cetaceous with the human, male and female, under Lactentia: animals whose young suckle?

Linnaeus had his reasons; mostly, they were political. Naysayers might doubt that humans are essentially four-footed (whether on scriptural or arithmetic grounds), but no man born of woman, he figured, would dare deny that he was nourished by mother's milk. Then, too, while Linnaeus was revising his *Systema Naturae* from the fourteen-page pamphlet he published in 1735 to the two-thousand-page opus of 1758—and abandoning Quadrupedia in favor of Mammalia—his wife was, not irrelevantly, lactating. Between 1741 and 1757, she bore and nursed seven children (two of whom died young). The father of taxonomy was a father of five. He also taught medicine and treated patients—he specialized in syphilis—and lectured and campaigned against the widespread custom of wet-nursing.

The practice is ancient; contracts for wet nurses have been found on scrolls in Babylonia. (Poor women with milky breasts, hired to nurse their betters' infants, were known as wet nurses, as opposed to governesses, or "dry nurses.") Some women can't breast-feed, and wet nurses also save the lives of infants whose mothers die in childbirth. But in Linnaeus's time, extraordinary numbers of European mothers—as many as 90 percent of Frenchwomen—simply refused to breast-feed their babies and instead hired servants to do the work. In 1752, Linnaeus wrote a treatise entitled "Step Nurse," declaring wet-nursing a crime against nature. Even the fiercest beasts nurse their young, with utmost tenderness: surely women who resisted their mammalian destiny were to be ranked as lowlier, even, than the lowliest brute.[12]

Enlightenment doctors, philosophers, and legislators agreed: women should nurse their children. Rousseau prophesied in *Émile*, "When mothers design to nurse their own children, then morals will reform themselves." (Voltaire had a quibble or two about Rousseau's own morals: the author of *Émile* abandoned his five illegitimate children at birth, at a foundling hospital.) "There is no nurse like a mother," Benjamin Franklin wrote in 1785, after learning about an infant mortality rate of 85 percent at a foundling hospital in Paris that relied on wet nurses (the hospital where Rousseau's children all but certainly died); the discovery may explain why Franklin, in his autobiography, went to the trouble of remarking about his own mother, "She suckled all her ten children."[13] But Franklin's mother was hardly unusual; wet nurses were not nearly as common in colonial America as they were in eighteenth-century Europe. "*Suckle* your Infant your Self if you can," Cotton Mather commanded from his pulpit. Puritans found milk divine, even the good book gave suck. *Spiritual Milk for Boston Babes, Drawn Out of the Breasts of Both Testaments* was the title of a popular catechism.[14] By the end of the eighteenth century, breast-feeding had come to seem an act of citizenship. Mary Wollstonecraft, in her 1792 *Vindication of the Rights of Woman*, scoffed that a woman who "neither suckles nor educates her children, scarcely deserves the name of a wife, and has no right to that of a citizen." (More commonly, political theorists argued that what made women different from men meant that they could *not* be citizens.) The next year, the French National Convention ruled that women who employed wet nurses could not apply for state aid; not long after, Prussia made refusing to breast-feed a crime.[15]

There was also a soppy side to the age of reason. In 1793, Erasmus Darwin offered, in *Zoonomia; or, The Laws of Organic Life,* a good summary of the eighteenth century's passionate attitude toward the milky breast:

> When the babe, soon after it is born into this cold world, is applied to its mother's bosom; its sense of perceiving warmth is first agreeably affected; next its sense of smell is delighted with the odour of her milk; then its taste is gratified by the flavour of it; afterwards the appetites of hunger and thirst afford pleasure by the possession of their objects, and by the subsequent digestion of the aliment; and, lastly, the sense of touch is delighted by the softness and smoothness of the milky fountain, the source of such variety and happiness.[16]

If, on the one hand, there is nothing more animal about a woman than the milk in her breasts, there is, on the other hand, nothing more divine. Beliefs about mother's milk, like the secrets of generation, have often bordered on the mystical; what has changed over time is what kind of mystery people are talking about. A half century after Erasmus Darwin, across the Atlantic, this kind of thing turned into an even milkier cult of motherhood, abundantly illustrated in a craze for mammary photography; archives and museums all over the United States house daguerreotypes from the 1850s of babies suckling beneath the unbuttoned bodices of prim, sober American matrons, looking half Emily Dickinson, half da Vinci's *Madonna and Child.*[17]

Then, bizarrely and almost overnight, American women seemed to be running out of milk. "Every physician is becoming convinced that the number of mothers able to nurse their own children is decreasing," one doctor wrote. Another reported that there was "something wrong with the mammary glands of the mothers in this country."[18] That this happened in the latter half of the nineteenth century—just when the first artificial infant foods were becoming commercially available—is no mere coincidence. Cows were proclaimed the new "wet nurse to the human race." About the time Milton Bradley was hanging up a shingle in Springfield, setting himself up as a patent solicitor, the Texas beef industryman Gail Borden, who aspired to be "the World's Cook," applied for a patent for condensed cow's milk. Not long after, you could buy milk in a can.[19]

Most of what marketers said were the nutritive and curative properties of cow's milk—it soothes a burn; it helps you get to sleep; it makes your bones grow—were claims appropriated from conventional wisdom about human milk. Tragically, very many babies fed on modified cow's milk died, which is one reason why, in the United States, nineteenth- and early-twentieth-century physicians, far from pressing formula on their patients, urged them to breast-feed. Many women, however, simply refused, not unlike all those eighteenth-century Frenchwomen who hired wet nurses. Or, actually, what American women did was different: they insisted that they lacked for milk, mammals no more.

Evolution is the organic version of the mechanical idea of progress. It wasn't only machines that could get better and better, by invention; animals could improve, too, by evolution. In 1871, Charles Darwin published *The Descent of Man,* in which he speculated that the anomalous occurrence in humans of extra nipples represented a reversion to an earlier stage of evolution.[20] If our ancestors once suckled litters of four or six, and if—as was supposed—men had nipples because male mammals once produced milk, maybe women, too, were evolving out of the whole business. By 1904, one Chicago pediatrician could argue that "the nursing function is destined gradually to disappear." Gilded Age white American women considered themselves so refined, so civilized, so delicate. How could they suckle like bovines? (By the turn of the century, the cow's udder, or even her head, had replaced the female human breast as the icon of milk.) Behind this question lay another, darker and crueler: How could a white woman nurse a baby the way a black woman does? It was so . . . animal.

Linnaeus had claimed that African women make a prodigious amount of milk: "*Feminis sine pudoris; mammae lactantes prolixae*" (Women without shame; breasts lactate profusely).[21] In the United States, generations of black women, slave and free alike, not only nursed their own infants but also served as wet nurses to white babies. In the nineteenth century, racial theorists, who measured heads to classify the "races," measured milk for the same purpose: they ran microscopic tests of human milk and concluded that the whiter the mother, the less nutritious her milk. Hardly surprising, then, that well-heeled white women told their doctors they had insufficient milk. By the 1910s, a study of one thousand Boston women had reported that 90 percent of the poor mothers breast-fed but only 17 percent of the wealthy mothers. Doctors, pointing out that evolution doesn't happen so fast, tried to convince these Brahmins to breast-feed, but by then, it was too late.

The American "epidemic of lactation failure" depended, too, on the evolving design of baby bottles: so sleek, so clean, so scientific, so modern. The industrial-era rise of processed, bottled, canned, and packaged food was so precipitous that some historians refer to it as the Food Revolution. That age of machines that had locomotives chugging across the continent brought food from farms to factories, where it was canned and bottled and packaged. Cow's milk went from farms to factories, too. And, soon, you could pour that cow's milk that you could buy in a can into bottles that babies could suck. The first U.S. patent for a baby bottle was issued in 1841; the device, shaped like a breast, was to be worn over a mother's chest, as a prosthetic. But, year by year, bottles came to look less like breasts and more like silos. The familiar cylindrical bottle, called the "Stork Nurser," dates from the 1910s and is inextricably tied to the rise of the stork myth: babies come from storks; milk comes from the milkman. Perversely, Freud's insistence that infants experience suckling as sexual pleasure proved a boon to stork-style repression, too: mothers eager to keep infantile incestuous desire at arm's length propped their babies in high chairs and handed them bottles.[22] Arm's length, or further: patents for "bottle holders," taken out beginning in the 1890s, allowed for bottles to be propped on tables, hung from strings suspended from over cribs, and hooked to the tops of prams, not unlike the way water bottles are clasped to the sides of a hamster's cage.

Meanwhile, more and more women were giving birth in hospitals. This meant that, for the first time in human history, infants born prematurely or very small were given a chance of survival—if only there were enough milk and a way to get it out of a woman's breast and into the belly of a baby too tiny to suck.

In 1910, a Boston doctor, Fritz Talbot, spent three days searching for a wet nurse. He failed. Exasperated, he established a placement service, the Boston Wet Nurse Directory. Across town, Frances Parkman Denny, caring for a sick baby, asked a neighbor to hand-express her milk for him. When the infant improved after drinking just three ounces, Denny, a bacteriologist, became convinced of the "bactericidal power" of human milk. The year after Talbot started his Wet Nurse Directory, Denny opened the first human milk bank in the United States, collecting milk from donors using a breast pump whose design was inspired by bovine milking machines.[23]

The modern breast pump can be traced to two late-nineteenth-century developments: the birth of neonatology—the word "neonatal" was coined in the 1890s—and the industrialization of dairy farming. (Milking machines are cited in breast pump patents; at the level of basic engineering, Medela's Pump In Style wasn't very different from Dairymaster's Swiftflo.) Denny's plan worked better than Talbot's: families who needed and could afford human milk did not generally like having poor women living with them as in-house wet nurses; they preferred having their milk delivered in bottles. Talbot stopped placing wet nurses and instead distributed their milk; he renamed his agency the Directory of Mother's Milk.[24]

Once milk banks replaced wet nurses, human milk came to be treated, more and more, as a medicine, something to be prescribed and researched, tested and measured, in flasks and beakers.[25] Denny's bottled, epidemiological model prevailed. What happened next is a twice-told tale. Treating milk as a medicine promoted synthetic milk. Laboratory-made formulas improved; aggressive marketing of processed infant food—not just bottles of formula but jars of mush and all manner of needless pap—grew to something between badgering and downright coercion. The infant food industry grew. By the middle of the twentieth century, the majority of American women fed their babies formula. Babies sucked bottles, not breasts. But, all this while, Erasmus Darwin's rhapsodic view of the milky breast endured. "With his small head pillowed against your breast and your milk warming his insides, your baby knows a special closeness to you," advised The Womanly Art of Breastfeeding, first published by La Leche League in 1958. "He is gaining a firm foundation in an important area of life—he is learning about love."[26]

In the 1960s, nursing as a mammalian mommy-baby love-in began a comeback, at least among wealthier and whiter women. The history of food appears to follow this rule: when the rich eat white bread and buy formula, the poor eat brown bread and breast-feed; then they swap. Meanwhile, the more scientists studied milk, the less good formula looked. The same science that had brought formula brought a panic about formula. To encourage women to return to breast-feeding not long after they had been persuaded to abandon it (having been told by manufacturers that formula was more scientific), doctors had to talk about human milk as a medicine—a better medicine than formula.

This took some time to become a major public health issue. But in 1997, the American Academy of Pediatrics issued a policy statement on breast-feeding and the use of human milk, declaring human milk "species-specific" and recommending it as the exclusive food for the first six months of a baby's life, to be followed by a mixed diet of solid foods and human milk until at least the end of the first year. In that statement and in a subsequent revision, the AAP cited research linking breast-feeding with reduced incidence and severity of, among other things, bacterial meningitis, diarrhea, respiratory tract infection, ear infection, urinary tract infection, sudden infant death syndrome, diabetes mellitus, lymphoma, leukemia, Hodgkin's disease, obesity, and asthma. The benefits of breast-feeding, the report insisted, are unrivaled, and breast-feeding rates in the United States were abysmally low; the combination made for a public health emergency. In 1990, the Department of Health and Human Services announced a goal of increasing the proportion of mothers who breast-feed their babies "at initiation" (i.e., when they leave the hospital) from a 1998 baseline of 64 percent to a 2010 target of 75 percent; until the age of six months, from 29 percent to 50 percent; and at one year, from 16 percent to 25 percent.

Attempts to improve initiation rates met with spotty success. The Rush University Medical Center, in Chicago, which established a peer-counseling program called the Mother's Milk Club, achieved an initiation rate of 95 percent; nationally, the rate hovered around 70 percent. More difficult was raising the rates at six and twelve months. The CDC, which issued an annual Breastfeeding Report Card, reported that in 2010 the rate of exclusive breast-feeding at six months was only 13 percent (although the rate of *some* breast-feeding at six months had risen to 43 percent); only the initiation rate had been met.[27]

One reason so many women stopped breast-feeding after a matter of weeks was that, in the United States, more than half of the mothers of infants under six months old were leaving home to go to work—a change that began with industralization and the age of machines, which separated home from work. The 1993 Family and Medical Leave Act guaranteed only twelve weeks of (unpaid) maternity leave, and, in marked contrast to established practice in other industrial nations, neither the government nor the typical employer offered much more. The 2010 Health Care Act required employers to "provide reasonable break time for an employee to express breast milk for her nursing child for 1 year after the child's birth each time such employee has need to express the milk" and "a place, other than a bathroom, that is shielded from view and free from intrusion from co-workers and the public, which may be used by an employee to express breast milk"; but it was not clear how that would work out, as a matter of enforcement.[28] To follow doctor's orders, a woman who returned to work twelve weeks after childbirth had to find a way to feed her baby her own milk for another nine months. The nation suffered, in short, from a Human Milk Gap.

There were three ways to bridge the gap: longer maternity leaves, on-site infant child care, and pumps. Much effort was spent on the cheap way out: option 3. At the turn of the century, Medela distributed pumps in ninety countries, but its biggest market, by far, was the United States, where maternity leaves were so short, unpaid, and unsanctioned that many women, blue-, pink-, and white-collar alike, returned to work just weeks after giving birth. (Breasts supply milk in response to demand; if a woman is unable to put her baby to her breast regularly, she will stop producing milk. Expressing not only provides milk to be stored for times when she is away, it also makes it possible for a working woman to keep nursing her baby at night and on the weekends.) In 1998, Congress had authorized states to use food stamp funds granted to the USDA's Women, Infants, and Children nutrition program to buy breast pumps for eligible mothers.[29] Studies reported that breast-feeding rates rose with maternal age, education, and income. Medela offered a Corporate Lactation Program, which included free advice for employers seeking to reduce absenteeism and health insurance costs by establishing "Mother's Rooms." These would be equipped, ideally, with super-duper electric pumps because "breastpumps with double-pumping options save time and can even help increase a mother's milk supply." The loss of productivity, Medela promised, would be slight: "If each employee uses safe, effective, autocycling breastpumps, each visit to the Mother's Room should last no longer than 10 to 15 minutes."[30]

Even more intensive was the energy directed toward legislative reform. By 2008, forty-seven states had passed laws about breast-feeding. Most had to do with option 3. Must companies supply employees with refrigerators to store milk expressed during the workday, else it spoil? Twenty-one states, along with Puerto Rico and the District of Columbia, required employers to make a "reasonable effort" to accommodate nursing mothers and their bottled milk. These laws, however, were generally toothless: the National

Zoo's compliance consisted of putting a chair and a curtain in a ladies' room. (The posher the employer, the plusher the pump station. Baristas at Starbucks had to barricade themselves in loos intended for customers, while traders at Goldman Sachs could go online to reserve half-hour slots in designated lactation rooms.)[31] In 2007, Oregon became the first state to pass a law requiring companies with more than twenty-five employees to provide "non-bathroom" lactation rooms. (A national media campaign asked, reasonably enough, if you wouldn't make your kid a sandwich in a public restroom, why would you expect a woman to express her baby's milk in one?)[32] In California, the comedian Will Ferrell toted his wife's pump to the Golden Globe ceremony, though whether the Beverly Hilton has a dedicated, non-bathroom lactation room was a matter of hospitality and not of law. Did nursing in public violate state obscenity laws? In most places, no. In 2009, Virginia and Maryland joined twenty-three other states in exempting women who expose their breasts while suckling infants from indecency laws. Whether pumping in public is obscene had not yet been tested—and, honestly, who would want to?—but, what with all these lactation rooms, that seemed off the table.[33]

More rules were under consideration. Could a woman or her employer get a tax break for producing or storing milk, some kind of dairy subsidy? Maryland exempted breast pumps from its sales tax, but Congress was deadlocked over the Breastfeeding Promotion Act, introduced in 2007 and again in 2009. The goals of the bill were four: to add the word "lactation" to the Civil Rights Act of 1964; to define lactation as "the feeding of a child directly from the breast or the expressing of milk from the breast"; to provide a tax credit of up to $10,000 per year for companies that provide pumps to their employees; and to set and enforce performance standards and safety rules for pumps.[34] A better title for the proposed legislation might have been the Breast Pump Promotion Act. Some breast-feeding advocates argued that human milk fell under Article 25 of the U.N.'s 1948 Universal Declaration of Human Rights: "Everyone has the right to a standard of living adequate for the health and well-being of himself and of his family, including food, clothing, housing and medical care."[35] Expressing and drinking human milk, these people insisted, are human rights, but baby food had, by now, become a partisan trigger issue. In 2010, the IRS decided that flexible spending health care funds could not be used to buy breast pumps, the *Times* reporting that the health care consultant

Roy Ramthun (who worked at the Treasury Department) said tax officials were worried about allowing breaks for something that could be classified as food.[36] In 2011, Michelle Obama's support for breast pump tax breaks inspired Tea Party congresswoman and presidential aspirant Michele Bachmann to rejoin, "To think that government has to go out and buy my breast pump—You want to talk about nanny state, I think we just got a new definition."[37] When people talk about machines, everything seems new, even when it's old.

Breast pumps aren't sinister; they can be useful, even indispensable and, in some cases, lifesaving. But a thing doesn't have to be underhanded to feel cold-blooded. How different is a "boob cube" at the Capitol from a Hatchery? To be hooked up to a breast pump is to be chained to the age of the machine. Non-bathroom lactation rooms are so shockingly paltry a substitute for maternity leave, you might think that the Second Gilded Age's craze for pumps—especially the government's pressing them on poor women while giving tax breaks to big businesses—would have been met with skepticism by more people than Tea Partiers. Not so. The growth of the breast pump industry was not only not questioned by women's groups but had, in fact, been urged by them.[38] The National Organization for Women wanted more pumps at work; NOW president Kim Gandy complained, "Only one-third of mega-corporations provide a safe and private location for women to pump breastmilk for their babies."[39] What ever happened to asking for more than a closet?

The difference between employer-sponsored lactation programs and flesh-and-blood family life is stark. Breast-feeding involves cradling and cuddling your baby; pumping involves cupping plastic shields on your breasts and watching your nipples squirt milk down a tube. Rhode Island's Physicians' Committee for Breastfeeding gave an annual award for the most Breastfeeding-Friendly Workplace, a merit measured, in the main, by the comforts provided in pumping rooms; for instance, the Gold Medal winner's "soothing room" was equipped with "a sink, a lock on the door, and literature." It appeared no longer within the realm of the imaginable that, instead of running water and a stack of magazines, "breastfeeding-friendly" could mean making it possible for women and their babies to be together. Some lactation rooms even went so far as to make a point of banning actual infants and toddlers, lest mothers smuggle them in for a quick nip. At the University of Minnesota, staff members with keys could pump their milk at the "Expression Connection," but the sign on the door bore this warning: "This room is not intended for mothers who need a space to nurse their babies." When Playtex debuted a breast pump called the Embrace, no one bothered to scream, or even to murmur, that something you plug into a wall socket is a far cry from a whisper and a kiss.

Is milk medicine? Is suckling love? Of all questions about life and death, taxonomical questions are some of the trickiest. At the end of the twentieth century and the beginning of the twenty-first, breast pumps were handy; they were also a handy way to avoid a politically unpalatable topic about the artificiality of modern life: Is it the mother or her milk that matters more to her baby? Meanwhile, *mamma ex machina:* Medela offered a breakthrough model with "2-Phase Expression." Phase one "simulates the baby's initial rapid suckling to initiate faster milk flow"; phase two "simulates the baby's slower, deeper suckling for maximum milk flow in less time." These newest machines, the company promised, "work less like a pump and more like a baby."[40] More like a baby? Holy cow. We are become our own wet nurses.

Minooka Comm. H.S. South Library
Channahon, IL 60410

[CHAPTER 3]

The Children's Room

Anne Carroll Moore was born long ago but not so far away, in Limerick, Maine, in 1871. She had a horse named Pocahontas, a father who read to her from *Aesop's Fables*, and a grandmother with no small fondness for *Uncle Tom's Cabin*. Annie, whose taste ran to *Little Women*, was a reader and a runt. Her seven older brothers called her Shrimp. In 1895, when she was twenty-four, she moved to New York, where she more or less invented the children's library.[1]

At the time, you had to be fourteen, and a boy, to get into New York's Astor Library, which opened in 1854, the same year as the Boston Public Library, the country's first publicly funded city library, where you had to be sixteen. Even if you got inside, the librarians would shush you, carping all the while about how the "young fry" read nothing but "the trashy": Scott, Cooper, and Dickens. (One century's garbage being, as ever, another century's Great Books.) Samuel Tilden, who, before his death, in 1886, left his $2.4 million fortune to "establish and maintain a free library and reading room in the city of New York," nearly changed his mind when he found out that 90 percent of the books charged out of the BPL were fiction. Meanwhile, libraries were popping up in American cities and towns like crocuses at first melt. Between 1881 and 1917, Andrew Carnegie underwrote the construction of more than sixteen hundred public libraries in the United States, buildings from which children were routinely turned away on the grounds that they were noisy, messy, and careless but chiefly because they needed to be protected from books, especially novels, which would corrupt their morals. Something had to be done. In 1894, at the annual meeting of the American Library Association, established in 1876, the Milwaukee Public Library's Lutie Stearns read a "Report on the Reading of the Young." Stearns wondered, What if age limits were lifted? What if libraries were to set aside special books for children, shelved in separate rooms for children, "staffed by attendants *who liked children*"?[2]

In 1896, Moore, who didn't exactly like children but who did care about them—and who, in any case, needed a job—was given the task of running just such an experiment. The Children's Library of the Pratt Institute in Brooklyn was the first library in the country whose architectural plans included space for children, and this at a time when the Brooklyn schools' policy stated, "Children below the third grade do not read well enough to profit from the use of library books." Moore toured kindergartens—those rooms Milton Bradley was busy supplying with crayons and scissors and paper cutters—and made a list of what she needed for her room: tables and chairs sized for children, not grown-ups; plants, especially ones with flowers; artwork; and very, very good books.[3]

The year before Moore started at Pratt, the Astor and Lenox libraries and the Tilden Trust had joined forces to form the New York Public Library. Its cornerstone was laid, at Forty-second Street and Fifth Avenue, in 1902. Four years later, when the library's directors established the Department of Work with Children, they hired Moore to serve as its superintendent, a position in which she not only oversaw the children's programs at all of the branch libraries—including sixty-five paid for by a Carnegie bequest of $5.2 million—but also planned the Central Children's Room. After the New York Public Library opened its doors, in 1911, its Children's Room became a pint-sized paradise, with its pots of pansies and pussy willows and oak tables and candlelit corners and much-coveted window seats, so low to the floor that even the shortest legs didn't dangle.[4]

All this depended on the so-called discovery of childhood. Stages of life are artifacts, ideas with histories: the unborn, as a stage of life anyone could picture, dates only to the 1960s; adolescence is a useful contrivance; midlife is a moving target; senior citizens are an interest group; and tween-hood is just plain made up. There have always been children, of course, but in other times and places, people have thought about them differently. The idea that children are born innocent and need protection from the world of adults is a product of the Enlightenment. You can trace it, as a matter of child-rearing advice (in English, anyway), to John Locke's 1693 treatise *Some Thoughts Concerning Education*. Locke thought children needed to learn through play. "The chief Art," he argued, "is to make all that they have to do, Sport and Play, too." Even reading could be taught to children, he thought, without them ever "perceiving it to be anything but a Sport." Locke is why, beginning in 1744, the London printer John Newbery published books aimed to amuse and entertain children, including Mother Goose stories, Perrault's tales, *Aesop's Fables, The History of Little Goody Two-Shoes,* and a serial, the *Lilliputian Magazine.* When John Wallis printed the New Game of Human Life in 1790, he was following Locke's advice and Newbery's footsteps: teaching children about the journey of life by making it a game.[5]

A century later, when Anne Carroll Moore was a little Goody Two-Shoes herself, the amusing and precious and Lilliputian world of children had become a mainstay of Victorian middle-class culture: there were children's books, children's clothes, children's toys, and children's furniture. Annie Moore was sixteen, in 1887, when Milton Bradley published *The Paradise of Childhood.* In the age of progress, with all its machines, the world of adults was thought to be ruthless: cold, industrial, and grinding. Reformers wanted childhood, a world of little women and little men, to be a place apart, a paradise: the last mansion of happiness.

Most of what Moore did in the Children's Room at the New York Public Library had never been done before. She hired storytellers and, in her first year alone, organized two hundred story hours—and ten times as many two years later. She compiled a list of twenty-five hundred standard titles in children's literature. She fought for, and won, the right to grant borrowing privileges to children. (By 1913, children's books accounted for one-third of all the volumes borrowed from New York's public libraries.) She invited authors to come and talk about their work. Much against the prevailing sentiment of her day, she was convinced that her job was to give "to the child of foreign parentage a feeling of pride in the beautiful things of the country his parents have left in place of the sense of shame with which he too often regards it."[6] She celebrated the holidays of immigrants (reading Irish poetry aloud, for instance, on St. Patrick's Day) and stocked the shelves with books in French, German, Russian, and Swedish. In 1924, she hired the African-American writer Nella Larsen to head the Children's Room in Harlem, at the 135th Street branch (in her first year, Larsen bought over six hundred new books). In every one of the library's branches, Moore abolished age restrictions. Down came the SILENCE signs; up went framed prints of the work of children's book illustrators. "Do not expect or demand perfect quiet," she instructed her staff. "The education of children begins at the open shelves" was her watchword. In place of locked cabinets, she provided every library with a big black ledger; if you could sign your name in it, you could borrow a book. Moore considered signing the ledger something between an act of citizenship and a sacrament, to be undertaken only after reading a pledge, as solemn as an oath: "When I write my name in this book I promise to take good care of the books I use in the Library and at home, and to obey the rules of the Library." (Philip Roth once said that taking that pledge—at a public library in Newark in the 1940s—"had as much to do with civilizing me as any idea I was ever to come upon in the books themselves.") During both the First and the Second World Wars, soldiers on leave in the city climbed the steps, past Patience and Fortitude, the massive stone lions guarding the entrance, walked into the Children's Room, and asked to see the black books from years past.[7] They wanted to look up their names, to trace the record of a childhood lost, an inky, smudged, and quavering once-upon-a-time.

"Anne Carroll Moore is an occurrence," Carl Sandburg wrote admiringly.[8] In the first half of the twentieth century, no one wielded more power in the world of children's literature than Moore, a librarian in a city of publishers. The authors were more fretful, the editors smarter, the publishers cannier. But for gumption, for glove-fisted gumption, Moore smacked them all, right in the snoot. "Admit to no discouragement!" she liked to say. She never lacked for an opinion. "Dull in a new way," she labeled books she despised. When William R. Scott brought her copies of his press's new books, tricked out with pop-ups and bells and buttons, Moore snapped, "Truck! Mr. Scott. They are truck!" Her verdict, not any editor's, not any bookseller's, sealed a book's fate. She kept a rubber stamp at her desk and used it liberally while paging through publishers' catalogs: "Not recommended for purchase by expert."[9] The End.

The end of Moore's own influence came, years later, when she tried to block the publication of a book by E. B. White about a woman who gives birth to a mouse, a book that disturbed much that Anne Carroll Moore believed about life and death and everything she believed about childhood and adulthood. Watching Moore stand in the way of that book, White's editor, Ursula Nordstrom, remembered, was like watching a terrible accident: you tried not to look, but you couldn't help yourself. Or, no, Nordstrom thought, it was worse: it was like watching a horse fall down, its spindly legs crumpling beneath its great weight.[10]

E. B. White, born in Mount Vernon, New York, in 1899, was a generation Moore's junior. As a boy, he had a pet mouse; he thought he looked a little mousy himself. The common house mouse comes from Europe, and traveled the world during the age of discovery. Mice were bred in captivity as early as the seventeenth century. In the beginning of the nineteenth century, "fancy mice," bred in Japan, were brought to Britain. By the end of the nineteenth century, a trade in fancy mice was thriving in the United States and the United Kingdom. *Mus musculus* was bred to white; children took to keeping mice as pets. Anatomists began using them in laboratories, to uncover the secrets of generation and, especially, to study heredity, which is what C. C. Little was studying at Harvard when E. B. White was a boy.[11]

In 1909, when White was nine, he won a prize from *Woman's Home Companion,* for a poem about a mouse. He wanted to be a writer, and it always bugged him that there were books in his town library he wasn't allowed to look at.[12] The New York Public Library opened the year he turned twelve, the year he won a silver badge for "A Winter Walk," an essay published in the children's magazine *St. Nicholas,* which Anne Carroll Moore stocked on the shelves of her Children's Room.[13] In 1917, White went to Cornell, where he became the editor of his college paper, the *Cornell Daily Sun.* In 1918, Moore wrote her first book review, in the *Bookman.* That review marks the birth of serious criticism of children's literature. (The next year saw still more firsts: the first Children's Book Week, organized by Moore, and the appointment of Louise Seaman, soon-to-be Bechtel, to head the first children's department at a major publishing house, Macmillan.) Moore's column ran in *Bookman* until 1926, the year after Harold Ross, an upstart from Aspen, launched a magazine called the *New Yorker*.[14] Right away, Ross hired White as a writer and snapped up a crackerjack thirty-two-year-old freelancer named Katharine Angell as a reader of manuscripts. Not long after, Angell became the magazine's fiction editor.[15]

Along about this time, E. B. White fell asleep on a train and "dreamed of a small character who had the features of a mouse, was nicely dressed, courageous, and questing." White had eighteen nieces and nephews who were forever begging him to tell them a story, but he hated trying to make one up off the top of his head. He set to writing and stocked a desk drawer with tales about "his mouse-child . . . the only fictional figure ever to have honored and disturbed my sleep." (He was therefore not, he felt, at liberty "to change him into a grasshopper or a wallaby.") He named him Stuart.[16]

Anne Carroll Moore had an imaginary friend, too. "I have brought someone with me," she would say, singsongy, as she fished out of her handbag a wooden doll dressed as a Dutch boy. She named him Nicholas Knickerbocker. Moore also had letterhead engraved for her doll, and wrote and signed letters—to adults—as "Nicholas." ("I'm the sorriest little Dutch boy you ever knew over your accident," she once wrote to Louise Seaman Bechtel.) When Moore forgot Nicholas in a taxi, never to be found again, her colleagues, fair to say, did not grieve his loss.[17]

In 1924, Moore published her own children's book, *Nicholas: A Manhattan Christmas Story*. It begins with Nicholas's Christmas Eve arrival in a New York Public Library Children's Room filled with fairy creatures: "The Troll gave a leap from the Christmas Tree and landed right beside the Brownie in a corner of the window seat. Just then the Fifth Avenue window swung wide open and in walked a strange boy about eight inches high."[18] It has not aged well.

From 1924 to 1930, Anne Carroll Moore reviewed children's books for the *New York Herald Tribune;* beginning in 1936, her reviews also appeared in the *Horn Book*. She could be a tough critic, especially of books that violated her rules: "Books about girls should be as interesting as girls are" and "Avoid those histories that gain dramatic interest by appeal to prejudice. Especially true of American histories."[19] But merely in bothering to criticize children's books, Moore was ahead of everyone. Only in 1927 did the *Saturday Review* begin running a twice-monthly column called "The Children's Bookshop." The *New York Times Book Review* didn't regularly review children's books until 1930. It was a first, in 1928, when the *New Yorker's* Dorothy Parker, in her "Constant Reader" column, reviewed A. A. Milne's *The House at Pooh Corner.* (Moore called another Milne book "a nonsense story in the best tradition of the nursery.") Pooh's wasn't just a Good Hum and a Hopeful Hum. It was a hummy hum. "And it is that word 'hummy,' my darlings," Parker wrote, "that marks the first place in 'The House at Pooh Corner' at which Tonstant Weader fwowed up."[20]

In 1929, E. B. White married Katharine Angell. They soon had a son. In 1933, when the Whites' son, Joel, was three, Katharine, who also had two children from her first marriage, began writing the *New Yorker's* "Children's Shelf," an annual and sometimes semiannual roundup of children's books. Katharine White's taste in children's literature, if it fell short of Tonstant Weader's fwowing up, was more than spitting distance from Moore's indulgence in the adventures of Troll, Brownie, and Nicholas Knickerbocker. An A. A. Milne introduction to Jean de Brunhoff's *Travels of Babar,* White found "an unnecessary and misleading condescension, since de Brunhoff is witty without being Poohish, and Babar is an elephant who can stand on his own feet." White favored sturdy characters and spare prose. But there was something else at stake, too. White's "Children's Shelf," even in its title, called into question the very idea of a children's library. Maybe all they needed was a shelf?

Some of the very best prose and poetry, not to mention the best art, is to be found in books written for children—disciplined, inspired, even elevated by the constraints of the form. Katharine White loved very many books for children; above all, she admired the beauty and lyricism of picture books and readers for the under-twelve set. But about what was happening to children's literature, especially for older kids, she had her doubts:

> It has always seemed to us that boys and girls who are worth their salt begin at twelve or thirteen to read, with a brilliant indiscrimination, every book they can lay their hands on. In the welter, they manage to read some good ones. A girl of twelve may take up Jane Austen, a boy Dickens; and you wonder how writers of juveniles have the brass to compete in this field, blithely announcing their works as "suitable for the

child of twelve to fourteen." Their implication is that everything else is distinctly *un*suitable. Well, who knows? Suitability isn't so simple.[21]

And who decides what's suitable, anyway? Parents? Librarians? Editors? White had her own ideas about who should draw the line—if a line had to be drawn—between what was good for children and what was childish or just plain rotten. About Anne Carroll Moore she once fumed, "Critic, my eye!"[22]

Sometimes books labeled juvenile are, instead, antique. Children's literature, at least in the West, is utterly bound up in the medieval, as the literary scholar Seth Lerer has argued.[23] Lots of books for kids are about the Middle Ages (everything from *The Hobbit* to *Robin Hood* and *Redwall*); and the conventions of the genre (allegory, moral fable, romance, and heavy-handed symbolism) are also themselves distinctly premodern. It's not only that many books shelved as "children's literature"—the Grimms' fairy tales or *Gulliver's Travels* or *Huck Finn*—were born as biting political satire, for adults; it's also that books written for children in the centuries after the discovery of childhood tend to be distinctly, willfully, and often delightfully anti-modern. *The Phantom Tollbooth* has more in common with *Pilgrim's Progress* than it does with *On the Road*. Lurking in the stacks of every "children's library" are dozens of literary impostors: satires, from ages past, hiding their fangs; and shiny new books, dressed up in some very old clothes.

It would be convenient if Katharine White and Anne Carroll Moore stood on either side of a divide between anti-modernist and modernist writing. But their taste doesn't really sort out that way. A better way of thinking about it might be to say that Anne Carroll Moore did not like fangs. She loved what was precious, innocent, and sentimental. White found the same stuff mawkish, prudish, and daffy. "There are too many coy books full of talking animals, whimsical children, and condescending adults," White complained in the "Children's Shelf" in 1935. Katharine White also hated the word "juvenile," and sorely regretted, in the 1930s, that "it still adequately describes the calibre of the great majority of these books."[24] But what about her husband's teensy talking mouse-child? Whether he was juvenile remained to be seen because, for now, he was still stuck in that desk drawer.

·   ·   ·

While Katharine White stood her ground against Anne Carroll Moore, Harold Ross battled Henry Luce, who, with his Yale classmate Briton Hadden, had started *Time* magazine in 1923. The battle between White and Moore turns out to have a great deal in common with the battle between Ross and Luce: in a way, they were part of the same war, a war about babying readers.

Ross meant the *New Yorker* to be everything *Time* wasn't. ("But, Lester, is it *enough* just being against everything that 'Time' magazine is for?" read the caption beneath one *New Yorker* cartoon.)[25] *Time* sent out a flyer: "TIME has given such attention to the development of the best narrative English that hundreds of editors and journalists have declared it to be the greatest creative force in modern journalism."[26] The *New Yorker* published a parody: "Before a sentence may be used in THE NEW YORKER it must be cleaned and polished. The work of brightening these sentences is accomplished by a trained editorial staff of 5,000 men named Mr. March."[27]

Luce founded a business magazine in 1930. "Who reads *Fortune*?" Ross asked. "Dentists."[28] In 1936, Luce launched yet another magazine. "Life begins!" announced the first issue, alongside a photo of a doctor holding up a newborn baby. The week that issue hit newsstands, the *New Yorker* published a profile of Luce called "Time . . . Fortune . . . Life . . . Luce," a parody written by *New Yorker* editor Wolcott Gibbs in *Time*'s trademark style. "Backward ran sentences until reeled the mind," Gibbs wrote. "Where it will all ends, knows God." The next year, *Life* printed a photograph of Ross doodled on to make him look like Joseph Stalin. Ross toyed with starting a magazine called *Death*.[29]

In March 1937, the month after the publication of John Steinbeck's *Of Mice and Men*, Luce's staff ran a cover story about C. C. Little in *Time* and put an army of mice on the cover of *Life*, announcing, "Mice Replace Men on the Cancer Battlefield." The feature went a long way to achieving Little's goal of what he called "a New Deal for mice": he wanted the federal government to fund biomedical research and, especially, to pay for the use of mice in the fight against cancer. That goal was largely achieved, in June 1937, with the passage of the National Cancer Institute Act.[30]

Meanwhile, *Life* was struggling, $3 million in the red. "We have to get more and more remarkable pictures," Luce ordered.[31] The first week of April 1938, *Life*'s editors warned subscribers of a forthcoming story "without precedent among general magazines": "If your copy of LIFE is read by children, this letter will give you time in which to make up your mind whether they shall the see the story and under what conditions."[32] (Rejected was the idea of selling newsstand copies bound with a tape reading, "This issue of LIFE to be sold to adults only.") Apparently, very few subscribers received the warning before the magazine, since the letter was sent by third-class mail. *Life* also sent advance notices to nearly four thousand newspapermen; another four thousand to schoolteachers, mayors, and heads of women's clubs; two thousand letters to Protestant clergymen; and more than three thousand to doctors and hospitals.[33]

The offending issue contained a removable centerfold—the pages were supposed to arrive uncut—called "The Birth of a Baby." It consisted of thirty-five quite small black-and-white stills from a documentary film of the same title. For all the hoopla, the pictures were hardly prurient. The woman pictured was an actress named Eleanor King, and not pregnant.[34] The photographs contain no nudity (not even, really, the baby's). The caption for frame 25 reads: "Dr. Wilson supports the head as the body emerges and slowly turns, but lets the mother actually expel the baby." The baby emerges amid a sea of drapes.[35]

All the same, the stunt worked. Eleanor Roosevelt said she found that issue of *Life* "completely engrossing."[36] The film was shown in fifteen states. One reporter made the not unreasonable claim that "almost overnight, *The Birth of a Baby* became the most discussed picture since *The Birth of a Nation*."[37] *Life*'s "Birth of a Baby" issue was banned all over the country. By April 15, municipal officials in fifty cities in New York, New Jersey, Georgia, Louisiana, Pennsylvania, Arizona, Kansas, Illinois, Missouri, Ohio, Tennessee, Virginia, and every New England state had prevented its distribution, seizing copies from newsstands and threatening and arresting newsdealers. (*Life* paid all of the newsdealers' legal fees.) Pittsburgh safety director George E. A. Fairley ordered it off the city's newsstands, declaring, "The magazine outrages all common decency." When a Tucson police chief banned the sale of the magazine at newsstands, the *Arizona Daily Star* offered to sell it from its offices. In the Bronx, a Catholic district attorney named Samuel J. Foley called the photographs "lewd, lascivious, obscene" and "an outrageous affront."[38] Bronx police seized four thousand copies. After four Bronx newsdealers were arrested, Roy Larsen, *Life*'s publisher, went to Foley's office, sold a copy of the magazine to a policeman for a quarter, and was put in handcuffs. Larsen's trial began on April 19. Two days later, George Gallup issued the results of a nationwide poll. Asked, "In your opinion do these pictures violate the law against publication of material which is obscene, filthy or indecent?," 24 percent of respondents said yes; 76 percent, no. On April 26, a Bronx court ruled that the photographs were not indecent, and Larsen was released.[39]

This was just the kind of malarkey Harold Ross hated. The week after *Life* published "The Birth of a Baby," the *New Yorker* published a lampoon called "The Birth of an Adult," with text written by E. B. White accompanied by stills of a fictitious film—drawings by Rea Irvin, the artist who created Eustace Tilley—portraying "the waning phenomenon of adulthood." (Frame 1: "*The Birth of an Adult* is presented with no particular regard for good taste. The editors feel that adults are so rare, no question of taste is involved.") "The decrease in the number of mature persons in the world is a shocking indictment of our civilization," White wrote. That might have been satisfying but, in the meantime, seventeen million adults had seen that issue of *Life*. The *New Yorker* published a cartoon of two mailmen shouldering mail sacks stuffed with *Life;* one says, "If their circulation keeps going up, Joe, I swear I can't go on."[40]

At just that moment, E. B. White returned to his mouse. "I have written a fine parody of *Life*'s 'The Birth of a Baby,'" he wrote to James Thurber on April 16, 1938. "I also have a children's book about half done." He had finally opened his desk drawer. He wrote that letter from North Brooklin, Maine, where the Whites had moved. In Maine, White met C. C. Little. He got a dog from Little's laboratory in Bar Harbor ("he was usings dachshunds in his cancer-research experiments," White explained). White gave his mouse a last name. [41]

White next made a study of children's literature. In a November 1938 essay for *Harper's,* he complained that his house was chockablock with review copies of children's books, two hundred of them, sent to his wife by publishers; they were spilling out of the cupboards, stuck under sofa cushions, tumbling out of the wood box. About the only one he liked was Dr. Seuss's *The 500 Hats of Bartholomew Cubbins.* The rest were ruthlessly cloying, horribly written, and hopelessly naïve. ("One laughs in demoniac glee," White wrote, "but this laugh has a hollow sound.") What White found most depressing—and he was pretty discouraged in 1938, which he called "this year of infinite terror"—was the looming war that threatened to make the whole planet unsuitable for anyone, while, in the world of children's literature, "adults with blueprints of bombproof shelters sticking from their pants pockets solemnly caution their little ones against running downstairs with lollypops in their mouths."[42]

In his *Harper's* essay, White mused, as if he were merely mulling it over, that "it must be a lot of fun to write for children—reasonably easy work, perhaps even important work." After Theodor Geisel (Dr. Seuss) pointed White's essay out to Anne Carroll Moore, she wasted no time in sending White a letter. "I wish to goodness you would do a real children's book yourself," she wrote, from a return address of "Behind the Lions." "I feel sure you could, if you would, and I assure you the Library Lions would roar with all their might in its praise." White replied that he had, in fact, started writing a children's book but was finding it difficult. "I really only go at it when I am laid up in bed, sick, and lately I have been enjoying fine health. My fears about writing for children are great—one can so easily slip into a cheap sort of whimsy or cuteness. I don't trust myself in this treacherous field unless I am running a degree of fever."[43]

Moore pursued the correspondence. In early 1939, she pressed upon White no fewer than five letters. She sent him copies of her reviews. She gave him writing tips: "Let it *flow*, without criticizing it *too close* to its *creation*." She inquired after his family, asking, more than once, for his child's name. She was very, very keen to make the acquaintance of his wife: "I'd like to include *Mrs.* E.B. White in this letter for two reasons. The first that she is mother of the boy, or is it a girl? And second because she reviews children's books for the New Yorker or some other magazine." Most of all, she begged him to get back to his children's book. "Can't you achieve a *temperature*, without getting sick and finish it off?" She was attempting, as she often did, not only to cultivate this author but to claim him. "No one is more interested than I when your children's book is ready," Moore wrote on February 18. "Let me know if I can be of service at any stage."[44]

In April 1939, White sent an unfinished manuscript to his editor at Harper & Row, Eugene Saxton. "It would seem to be for children, but I'm not fussy who reads it," White offered, adding, "You will be shocked and grieved to discover that the principal character in the story has somewhat the attributes and appearance of a mouse." Saxton was far from grieved. He wanted *Stuart Little*, for a fall 1939 publication date. Anne Carroll Moore would have liked that, too; she was dying to take credit for the book. But that mouse would have to wait for a pack animal to budge. As White gently warned the pestering librarian, "I pull back like a mule at the slightest goading."[45]

Two books that *were* published in 1939, Gertrude Stein's children's book

The World Is Round and John Steinbeck's *Grapes of Wrath*, reveal a bit more about what was turning into a baby battle of the books. Of Stein's book, Anne Carroll Moore approved, with much enthusiasm. Katharine White found it numbingly insipid. (It begins, "Once upon a time the world was round and you could go on it around and around. Everywhere there was somewhere and everywhere there were men women children dogs cows wild pigs little rabbits cats lizards and animals. That is the way it was.") In her *New Yorker* column, White took aim at Moore: "A number of experts in children's literature have pronounced 'The World Is Round' a good book, but that does not surprise me, since, with a few exceptions, the critics of children's books are remarkably lenient souls. They seem to regard books for children with the same tolerant tenderness with which nearly any adult regards a child. Most of us assume there is something good in every child; the critics go on from this to assume there is something good in every book written for a child. It is not a sound theory."[46]

The Grapes of Wrath met with the disapproval not of Anne Carroll Moore but of Annie Dollard, the librarian of a private subscription library in Brooklin. "She was a tiny spinster with firm convictions about which books were fit to read," Katharine wrote. "The library had acquired 'The Grapes of Wrath,' but Annie took it off the shelf and placed it on her chair and sat on it. That solved that."[47] Of course, that didn't solve that, and Katharine White decided to do something about it. Those two hundred review copies her husband had been tripping over before Christmas? She hauled them to the Brooklin library.[48]

On November 26, 1939, the day after her "Children's Shelf" column was printed in the *New Yorker,* Katharine White wrote to "Miss Moore" for the first time, delicately hinting that the librarian ought to stop bothering her husband about *Stuart Little*—"I've decided that the less we say the sooner it will be done"—and steering the correspondence in another direction by seeking advice about how to apply for Carnegie funds for the Brooklin library. She also inquired, a little wickedly, after recommendations from the formidably humorless Moore for material for an anthology she and her husband were compiling, *A Subtreasury of American Humor.*[49]

Anne Carroll Moore did not write to E. B. White again until February 1941, alerting him, in confidence, of her plan to retire from the New York Public Library. "I am telling you because I would love to make one of my very final recommendations a large order for E. B. White's children's book," she wrote. White sent his congratulations, saying, "Mrs. White & I were interested to learn of your forthcoming retirement in the fall, & are impressed by your long and fruitful service to the children of the world. It is really one of the great and honorable careers—none finer." Of Moore's wanting to wheedle *Stuart Little* out of him as the capstone of her career, he did not utter a word. In her own letter, Katharine was sly. "Miss Moore," she began, "Children's literature cannot spare you."[50]

Katharine White had by now become something of a librarian herself. "Public libraries have more and more seemed to me a democratic necessity," she wrote in 1942, "so most of my war efforts so far, instead of going into civilian defense proper, have been devoted to keeping alive the little library in this town." Three years after she started her work, she reported to Moore that, what with all of her donations of the *New Yorker*'s review copies, her little library, now public and incorporated, and with vastly expanded hours, boasted "the best collection of children's books in the country." The only reason she was still continuing on the "Children's Shelf," she wrote, probably not entirely in jest, "is to have the books for the Brooklin Library."[51]

Her experience in Brooklin, however, only confirmed Katharine White's cynicism about children's literature. To her friend Louise Bechtel she wrote in 1941, "I think children's rooms must have greatly increased the children's reading and widened their horizons. Just to have the books assembled where they can be seen by the kids is all to the good. However, it occurs to me that there is a real danger in it and that is that these rooms isolate young readers and make it less easy for them to explore the books in the library proper." She laid much of the problem in the laps of librarians in big cities: "What public libraries need for kids, to my mind, are tough-minded, imaginative women, and men, too, as children's librarians . . . but I'm almost willing to bet that such librarians are easier to find in the small town library than in the big city library where the children's specialist holds sway."[52]

Katharine White believed, passionately, in public libraries, and in stocking them with books for children. What worried her were tiny spinsters sitting on books. Making a room for children is one thing. Guarding the door is entirely another. And then there's the matter of setting traps for mice.

The Subtreasury of American Humor was published in 1941. As for including humor from children's books: "We gave it up," the Whites confessed; they couldn't find any. Ross's battle with Luce raged on. E. B. White wrote a parody of a *Life* circulation announcement. Ross wanted to publish it in the *Times,* asking a colleague, "Too strong? But what the hell?" The plan was axed. An editor at *Fortune* alerted Ross to a *New Yorker* prank involving Luce's wife's underwear. "I don't know any more about it than you do," Ross wrote. "But I do know that there are a great many sallies of one kind or another between our two offices. It's morbid." By now, everybody was busy covering the war. "Honest to Christ," Ross wrote, "I'm more dilapidated at the moment than Yugoslavia."[53]

Meanwhile, Katharine White kept up her editorial work and her column, where she disagreed, as ever, with the librarian she only ever addressed as "Miss Moore." Moore adored Saint-Exupéry's 1943 *Little Prince;* White reported: "Every child I've ever pressed that one on was bored to death." In the winter of 1943–44, the Whites moved back to New York, to a top-floor apartment looking out on West Eleventh Street. Katharine began editing Nabokov. Her husband's nerves were shot. He felt like he had "mice in the subconscious": "The mouse of Thought infests my head, / He knows my cupboard and the crumb." Then, miraculously, over eight weeks in late 1944 and early 1945, he finally finished the book he had been writing all his life. Saxton, White's editor, had died in 1943. White sent the manuscript to Ursula Nordstrom, the director of Harper's Department of Books for Boys and Girls, who was known as the Maxwell Perkins of children's publishing; so great was her influence that she sometimes called herself Ursula Carroll Moore. (When the real Moore asked Nordstrom what could possibly qualify her to edit children's books, Nordstrom shot back, "Well, I am a former child, and I haven't forgotten a thing.")[54]

Anne Carroll Moore had been waiting for *Stuart Little* for seven years. During all this time, she had claimed E. B. White, the most celebrated American essayist of the century, as *her* writer. She may have been retired, but even in her retirement, her powers had scarcely dimmed. She still showed up for meetings at the New York Public Library; she even still *ran* those meetings, much to the dismay of her successor, Frances Clarke Sayers, who tried switching meeting places, to no avail. "No matter where you held them," Sayers remarked, "she was there." (In an oral history conducted at UCLA in the 1970s, Sayers admitted that she found it all but impossible to stand up to Moore, a pitiless tyrant who made her life "an absolute hell"; reduced Sayers's staff to tears by ripping up their lists of recommended books and substituting her own; and refused, utterly refused, to cede power: "She hung onto everything.")[55] Moore had come to think of recruiting E. B. White to the world of juvenilia as her final triumph—a victory over Tonstant Weader, a victory over Katharine White. *Stuart Little* was to be Anne Carroll Moore's lasting legacy to children's literature. In her mind, it was *her* book. There was nothing for it: Nordstrom sent her a set of galley proofs.

"I never was so disappointed in a book in my life," Moore announced.[56] She demanded that Nordstrom visit her at her rooms at the Grosvenor Hotel, where she warned her that the book "musn't be published."[57] She sent the Whites a fourteen-page letter, predicting that the book would fail and that it would prove an embarrassment and begging White to reconsider its publication. Exactly what the letter said is hard, now, to know. The Whites threw it away—"in disgust," Katharine reported. (Katharine White later insisted that Moore wrote not one letter but three: a relatively timid one to her husband and at least two more to her, each more vicious than the last.)[58] Even in what looks to be a redacted form—only six pages of a dubious copy in Moore's hand, rather than a typed carbon, survive—Moore's criticisms were severe: the story was "out of hand"; Stuart was always "staggering out of scale." Worse, White had blurred reality and fantasy—"the two worlds were all mixed up"—and children wouldn't be able to tell them apart. "She said something about its having been written by a sick mind," E. B. White remembered. About one thing, everyone agreed: Moore made a threat and meant to carry it out. "I fear *Stuart Little* will be very difficult to place in libraries and schools all over the country," she warned.[59]

"It is unnerving to be told you're bad for children," E. B. White allowed, "but I detected in Miss Moore's letter an assumption that there are rules governing the writing of juvenile literature—rules as inflexible as the rules for lawn tennis. And this I was not sure of." In the end, he shrugged it off. "Children can sail easily over the fence that separates reality from make-believe," he figured. "They go over it like little springboks. A fence that can throw a librarian is as nothing to a child."[60]

White did not write back. His wife did. "K refused to show me her reply," White told his brother, "but I suspect it set a new world's record for poisoned courtesy." It did and it didn't. "I agree with you that schools won't be likely to use 'Stuart Little,' " Katharine wrote to Miss Moore, "but, to be very frank, just as you have been, I can't imagine *libraries* not stocking it." And she couldn't help asking, "Didn't you think it even *funny*?"[61]

·   ·   ·

Stuart Little was published in October 1945. The book's pictures, by Garth Williams, share with its story a kind of quiet tenderness, hushed but somehow breezy, too. (Nordstrom and White had rejected seven other illustrators, whose mice looked too much like Mickey.) On the cover, little Stuart, in his shorts and shirtsleeves, paddling his canoe—a boat named *Summer Memories*—is at once so tiny and so grown-up that he might just as well have illustrated White's wistful 1941 essay "Once More to the Lake," about going camping with his son at a place in Maine where he once went with his father and in which White comes to realize that he isn't so sure, anymore, just who is who: "Everywhere we went I had trouble making out which was I, the one walking at my side, the one walking in my pants."[62]

On page 1, the most disappointing book Anne Carroll Moore ever read begins with these words:

> When Mrs. Frederick C. Little's second son was born, everybody noticed that he was not much bigger than a mouse. The truth of the matter was, the baby looked very much like a mouse in every way. He was only about two inches high; and he had a mouse's sharp nose, a mouse's tail, a mouse's whiskers, and the pleasant, shy manner of a mouse.[63]

Two days after *Stuart Little* was published, an unhappy Harold Ross stopped by White's office at the *New Yorker*. White recalled Ross's reaction:

> "Saw your book, White," he growled. "You made one serious mistake."
> "What was that?" I asked.
> "Why the mouse!" he shouted. "You said he was born. God damn it, White, you should have had him adopted."

Next, Edmund Wilson stopped White in the hall. "I read that book of yours," he began. "I found the first page quite amusing, about the mouse, you know. But I was disappointed that you didn't develop the theme more in the manner of Kafka." About all this—"the editor who could spot a dubious verb at forty paces, the critic who was saddened because my innocent tale of the quest for beauty failed to carry the overtones of monstrosity"—White tried to laugh.[64] But then Malcolm Cowley, reviewing the book in the *Times*, proved skeptical, too: "Mr. White has a tendency to write amusing scenes instead of telling a story. To say that 'Stuart Little' is one of the best children's books published this year is very modest praise for a writer of his talent."[65]

The real blow came when Frances Clarke Sayers, acting on Moore's orders, refused to buy *Stuart Little* for the library, sending a signal to children's librarians across the country: "Not recommended for purchase by expert."[66] In November, a syndicated *New York Post* columnist squibbed, "There will be a to-do about the New York Public Library's reluctance to accept 'Stuart Little.'"[67] For this unsavory gossip, White graciously apologized in a letter to Frances Sayers in November, assuring her that neither he nor Nordstrom had planted the notice to apply pressure, and that he much regretted the appearance of "dark and terrible goings on in the world of juvenile letters."[68]

One way to read *Stuart Little* is as an indictment of both the childishness of children's literature and the juvenilization of American culture. It might justifiably have been titled *The Birth of an Adult.* Whether Mrs. Frederick C. Little had given birth to a mouse or to a creature that just looked like a mouse was, especially in 1945, poignant social commentary. Just after the book came out, White wrote to Nordstrom asking her not to call Stuart a mouse in advertisements, noting, "He is a small guy who *looks* very much like a mouse, but he obviously is not a mouse." Later in the letter, though, White appears to suddenly realize that he himself had called Stuart a mouse on page 36: "I just found it. . . . Anyway, you see what I mean."[69] The one thing Stuart wasn't was a baby. Page 2: "Unlike most babies, Stuart could walk as soon as he was born." No bottles, no diapers, no nighttime feedings, no prams, no cribs ("Mr. Little made him a tiny bed out of four clothespins and a cigarette box"). No baby talk. No board books. From the first, Stuart dressed himself and was helpful around the house. His biggest problem was that he was too little to turn on the tap to brush his teeth. His parents' biggest problem was that "mice" were so badly treated in children's books. Tsk-tsk. Mr. Little "made Mrs. Little tear from the nursery songbook the page about the 'Three Blind Mice, See How They Run,'" something Mr. Little, Anne Carroll Moore–like, Annie Dollard–like, deemed too mousy for his second son. From books written for people bigger than him, Stuart needed to be protected.

"I don't want Stuart to get a lot of notions in his head," said Mr. Little. "I should feel badly to have my son grow up fearing that a farmer's wife was going to cut off his tail with a carving knife. It is such things that make children dream bad dreams when they go to bed at night."[70]

The Littles also questioned the suitability, the mouse-appropriateness, of "'Twas the Night Before Christmas," in which not a creature stirs, *not even a mouse*. "I think it might embarrass Stuart to hear mice mentioned in such a belittling manner," Mrs. Little told her husband. They settled, at last, on another kind of bowdlerizing:

> When Christmas came around Mrs. Little carefully rubbed out the word mouse from the poem and wrote in the word louse, and Stuart always thought that the poem went this way:

> > 'Twas the night before Christmas when all through the house
> > Not a creature was stirring, not even a louse.

Tearing the pages out of books and rubbing out words that might worry their little one—it was just what Katharine White had been complaining about ("Children can take subordinate clauses in their stride," she once insisted).[71] Her "Children's Shelf" column for 1946, a very thinly veiled repudiation of *Stuart Little*, offered a lament about writers who "are careful never to approach the child except in a childlike manner. Let us not overstimulate his mind, or scare him, or leave him in doubt, these authors and their books seem to be saying; let us *affirm*."[72]

Stuart Little leaves you in doubt, a good deal of doubt, really; it doesn't end so much as it's just, abruptly, over. In chapter 8, Stuart falls in love with a bird named Margalo, and when she flies away he goes on a quest. In the book's last chapter, he stops his coupe at a filling station and buys five drops of gas. In a ditch alongside the road, he meets a repairman, preparing to climb a telephone pole. "I wish you fair skies and a tight grip" is Stuart's fond wish. "I hope you find that bird," the repairman says. Then come the book's final, distressing lines:

> Stuart rose from the ditch, climbed into his car, and started up the road that led toward the north. The sun was just coming up over the hills on

his right. As he peered ahead into the great land that stretched before him, the way seemed long. But the sky was bright, and he somehow felt he was headed in the right direction.[73]

Stuart Little isn't Gregor Samsa. He's Don Quixote, turning into Holden Caulfield.

Anne Carroll Moore tried very hard to ensure that schools would ban *Stuart Little*. Some did. But some schoolteachers decided, instead, to teach the book. In February 1946, a fifth-grade teacher in Glencoe, Illinois, assigned her students the task of writing a different ending. Susan Alder managed, with felicitous economy, to get to a happy ending in just nine paragraphs:

> After talking to the repairman, Stuart took the road heading north. "Chug chug" went his car. "Five drops running out," thought Stuart. "I'll stop at that filling station just ahead." So he drove in.
>
> "What do you want?" said the man.
>
> "Five and one-half drops," said Stuart. "The last five drops I got didn't take me as far as I wanted to go." Just then Stuart saw a bird hop out of the filling station.
>
> "This is Margalo," said the man. "MARGALO!" yelled Stuart. "You must know each other," said the man.
>
> "I'll make you a deal," said Stuart. "I'll give you a whole ten dollars if you'll let me have your bird."
>
> "It's a deal," said the man.
>
> "Hop in, Margalo," said Stuart and away they went. They were married back in New York and raised a family of half mice and half birds.[74]

Susan Alder cleared that fence by a good three feet.

And the New York Public Library? Did the mouse scamper past the lions? In December, the library's director, Franklin Hopper, invited Louise Seaman Bechtel, the pioneering editor of children's books at Macmillan, to deliver an endowed lecture on book publishing. To her friend Katharine White, Bechtel pledged that if she couldn't prove to Frances Sayers that "S.L. is a *great* book," she would eat the Sunday paper. At the library, Bechtel discovered that although Sayers had bought a copy of *Stuart Little*, she kept it under her desk. Bechtel grabbed the book and took it to Hopper's office. She told him to read it. He did, and wrote to Bechtel the next day. He liked it very much. He was furious: "Have those who talk about its abnormalities no imagination?" Did Anne Carroll Moore think she could rule his library from the goddamn Grosvenor? Hopper ordered Sayers to take Stuart out of his hiding place. "He got into the shelves of the Library all right," E. B. White wrote, "but I think he had to gnaw his way in."[75]

For a while, many American libraries did ban *Stuart Little*. But the best librarians, like the best schoolteachers, have a genius all their own. In March 1946, the seventh graders at the Clifton School, in Cincinnati, Ohio, posted a letter:

> Dear Mr. White:
>
> We have just finished your book "Stuart Little." Our school
> librarian asked us to read it to help decide whether it would be a
> good book for the library. We think it would be.[76]

It's a quiet little letter. But that noise, the scritch-scratch of pen across paper, those thirty-eight seventh graders signing their names at the bottom of that letter? That's the sound of a horse falling down.

In January 1946, when Louise Bechtel delivered her lecture at the New York Public Library, Anne Carroll Moore was sitting in the front row, glaring. Undaunted, Bechtel made a point of plugging *Stuart Little,* saying, "I hope it gets all possible awards and medals." Moore made her disapproval known. "E.B.W. will be tickled to hear that A.C.M. sent me a blast," Bechtel wrote to Katharine afterward.[77] Very likely, he wasn't so tickled. He didn't much like the dark and terrible goings-on in the world of juvenile letters.

Moore, in her rage, fallen but still kicking, seems to have used her influence to shut *Stuart Little* out of the Newbery Medal, a prize named after the eighteenth-century printer of *Little Goody Two-Shoes* and awarded by a panel of librarians, including, that year, Frances Clarke Sayers. White's book was not even among the four runners-up. The day after the awards were announced, Bechtel was "still grinding my teeth in rage," she wrote to Katharine White, complaining about "these stupid *un-literary* women in charge" and suggesting that Nordstrom ought to have stamped on *Stuart Little*'s jacket, "The book all children of all ages love, that did *not* get the Newbery." ("Thank you for your gratifying grinding of teeth," Katharine wrote back.)[78]

Harper headed Moore's criticism off at the pass. "Some people—those who think they understand a thing if they can paste a neat label on it—will call 'Stuart Little' a juvenile," the press's publicity material read. "They will be right. They will also be wrong." In December 1946, while Katharine White was ushering J. D. Salinger's first *New Yorker* story to press (a story that turned into *The Catcher in the Rye*), Nordstrom told E. B. White that there were now a hundred thousand copies of *Stuart Little* in print. White invited his editor to a posh lunch to celebrate, saying, "You can eat 100,000 stalks of celery and I'll swallow 100,000 olives. It will be the E. B. White–Ursula Nordstrom Book and Olive Luncheon."[79] Not exactly happily ever after, but close.

Katharine White wrote her last "Children's Shelf" in 1948. Her own children were grown. The Brooklin library would survive without her review copies. But she was exasperated, too. "No one who has examined five hundred and more juveniles, as I have this year," a weary White wrote in 1948, "could say that the American child now occupies a submerged position in an adult world. There can surely be no childish taste, good, bad, or indifferent, that the eager publishers have not tried to satisfy."[80] In those years, you couldn't walk a block without bumping into a pram. Did American letters, too, have to make way for babies? The paradise of childhood had crowded out adulthood.

E. B. White published a second children's book, *Charlotte's Web*, in 1952. His wife said that he considered it "his only really completely satisfactory children's book," and it was adored, as far as I can tell, by everyone—everyone, that is, except Anne Carroll Moore, who complained that Fern's character was "undeveloped." Nordstrom, after hearing of Moore's reservations and reading a rave by Eudora Welty in the *Times,* gleefully wrote to White, "Eudora Welty said the book was perfect for anyone over eight or under eighty, and that leaves Miss Moore out as she is a girl of eighty-two."[81]

Anne Carroll Moore died in her rooms at the Grosvenor on January 20, 1961, the day John F. Kennedy was inaugurated.[82] "Much as she did for children's books and their illustrators at the start of her career," White wrote to Bechtel a few months later, "I can't help feeling her influence was baleful on the whole. Am I wrong?"[83]

Stuart Little has sold more than four million copies. In later editions, E. B. White made a tiny change. Mrs. Frederick C. Little's second son is no longer born. He arrives.

CHAPTER 4

All About Erections

I t was in the living room. My father was reading the newspaper. I was reading Sir Arthur Conan Doyle.

Sherlock Holmes sat up with a whistle. "By Jove, Peterson!" said he, "this is treasure trove indeed. I suppose you know what you have got?"

"A diamond, sir? A precious stone. It cuts into glass as though it were putty."

"It's more than a precious stone. It is *the* precious stone."

"Not the Countess of Morcar's blue carbuncle!" I ejaculated.

I looked up from my book. "Hey, Dad."

"Hmm?"

"What does 'ejaculate' mean?"

He put down the newspaper. He sighed.

I never did find out who stole the Countess's blue carbuncle.

At the start of the twenty-first century, kids with questions had another option: they could read a whole slew of books, with illustrations. "You already know a lot about your penis," Karen Gravelle remarked in *What's Going on Down There? Answers to Questions Boys Find Hard to Ask*. But she knew more.[1] In *Sex, Puberty, and All That Stuff: A Guide to Growing Up*, Jacqui Bailey offered this: "Whether her hymen is holey or whole, a girl is always a virgin if she has not had sexual intercourse."[2] Lynda Madaras's *On Your Mark, Get Set, Grow!* included a section called "All About Erections," although the Bette Davis joke was likely lost on her readers; they were supposed to be in fourth grade.[3]

"Pads are also called sanitary napkins," Robie Harris explained in *It's Perfectly Normal: A Book About Changing Bodies, Growing Up, Sex, and Sexual Health*, for ages ten and up, and then she had the good sense to add, "*Sanitary* means *clean*."[4] Harris's books, which include *It's So Amazing! A Book About Eggs, Sperm, Birth, Babies, and Families*, for ages seven and up, were genuinely sweet, in a genre where, for all its good intentions, there was a fairly despicable tendency to be edgy, brash, and cool, as if what kids put out must be what they want from grown-ups. She had a section called "What's Love?" and sensible, even existential answers ("Sometimes people just love each other"), along with a remarkably thoughtful discussion about love between men and men and between women and women. Harris's books also boasted by far the best illustrations, honest and tender drawings by Michael Emberly.[5] The worst? Robert Leighton's cartoons in Gravelle's books, which took their sensibility from *Mad* magazine—to wit, syphilis, gonorrhea, and chlamydia as bug-eyed, slimy monsters, and, for a mascot (most of these books have a mascot), a tiny, naked, bald homunculus who walks around with an erection. In an illustration for a discussion titled "How Much Does a Girl Bleed? Does She Have to Wear a Bandage?" that homunculus guy is taking a nap on a sanitary pad.[6]

Think of the genre as Kinsey for kids. The big hits in the 1970s were *Where Did I Come From? The Facts of Life Without Any Nonsense and with Illustrations* (1973) and *What's Happening to Me? The Answers to Some of the World's Most Embarrassing Questions* (1975), both written by Peter Mayle. If you put your mother and your father in a bathtub, Mayle suggested, you'd notice that they're different. "You've probably noticed that already," he granted, "but you notice it much more when you put them in the bath together." "Vagina" rhymes with "Carolina," Mayle explained, and an orgasm is like a sneeze.[7] Ah-choo?

While not the world's most embarrassing question, here's a good historical question: How did these books come to be? If the answers to life's secrets are to be found in books, why *these* books? Couldn't at least a few of life's secrets be discovered on a foggy day spent at the neighborhood branch of your local public library, even in the Children's Rooms started by Anne Carroll Moore, reading something else? What is love? Read a novel. Where did I come from? Philosophy, Religion. Dewey decimals 100–299. How are babies born? Librarians usually keep one or two well-illustrated anatomy textbooks near the reference desk. What does "ejaculate" mean? Dictionaries are *made* for this kind of thing. "E-jac-u-late, *v.* to eject semen." "Semen" gets you to "spermatozoa," which gets you to "ovum," and before you know it, you know it all. I once saw two cats go at it beneath a black-berry bush in a vacant lot after dark; later, one of those cats gave birth to a litter of kittens in our cellar and, although at first I thought they were three blind mice, that, *Webster's New Collegiate,* and *Gray's Anatomy* pretty well covered it, which was good, because the Holmes chat had left me wonder-ing, "Dr. Watson did *what?*"

Books about sex, usually offering advice about how to do it better, have been around for a long time. The most popular manual, even into the twentieth century, was *Aristotle's Master-piece; Or, The Secrets of Generation,* which was first published in English in 1684. It caused a stir in Northampton, Massachusetts, in 1744, when Jonathan Edwards discovered that a dozen young men in his congregation had "read Aristotle," a "nasty book, about womenkind."[8] It went through twenty-six American editions between 1766 and 1831 alone.[9] It wasn't exactly a masterpiece, and it certainly wasn't writ-ten by Aristotle. No one knows who wrote it; it's a hodgepodge. But it's got both handy anatomy lessons ("The Clytoris . . . is the Seat of Venereal Pleasure") and useful tips: "They that would be commended to their Wed-lock actions, and be happy in the fruit of their Labour, must observe to Copulate at distance of time not too often, nor yet too seldom."[10]

Aristotle's Master-piece, though, wasn't a kids' book; it was written and published before kids' books existed. Books explaining the facts of life to kids have been around only since the beginning of the twentieth century—the so-called golden age of children's literature—which is also when adolescence as a stage of life was invented. And, curiously, the books and the stage are tangled together, because adolescence, at least when it started, meant the time between when you learn about sex and when you do it.

Aristotle (the actual Aristotle) wrote about three ages of man: youth, the prime of life, and old age. In the seventeenth century, Boston's Puritan poet Anne Bradstreet followed medieval writers, by describing four:

> *Lo now! four other acts upon the stage,*
> *Childhood, and Youth, the Manly, and Old-age.*[11]

In early America, "youth" could mean anyone up to the age of thirty. Jonathan Edwards called the young men in his congregation who were reading *Aristotle's Master-piece* "boys"; their average age was twenty-four.[12]

The ages of man followed the order of the natural world—the days and the seasons. Morning, noon, night. Spring, summer, fall, winter. "One man in his time plays many parts, / His acts being seven ages." (There were seven planets.) Shakespeare's player goes straight from "the whining school-boy, with his satchel" to "the lover, / Sighing like a furnace." John Wallis's New Game of Human Life had seven ages, too. His character is a "boy" until twelve, when he turns into a "youth"; he's not a "man" until he's twenty-four.[13]

Rousseau talked about *l'adolescence* in *Émile* in 1762, which is one route by which the word, and the idea, entered the English vernacular.[14] He called adolescence a second birth. "We are born, so to speak, twice over; born into existence, and born into life." The time when a child "leaves childhood behind him," Rousseau warned, will be a time of peril: "he is a lion in a fever." If childhood is a paradise, the best plan, Rousseau thought, is to prolong it by staving off the onset of adulthood. This requires keeping the secrets of generation secret.

The problem is, the little pipsqueaks ask so many questions. " 'Where do little children come from?' This is an embarrassing question," Rousseau admitted, "which occurs very naturally to children, one which foolishly or wisely answered may decide their health and their morals for life." He recommended dodging it:

Should we enlighten children at an early period as to the objects of their curiosity, or is it better to put them off with decent shams? I think we need do neither. In the first place, this curiosity will not arise unless we give it a chance. We must therefore take care not to give it an opportunity. In the next place, questions one is not obliged to answer do not compel us to deceive those who ask them; it is better to bid the child hold his tongue than to tell him a lie. He will not be greatly surprised at this treatment if you have already accustomed him to it in matters of no importance. Lastly, if you decide to answer his questions, let it be with the greatest plainness, without mystery or confusion, without a smile. It is much less dangerous to satisfy a child's curiosity than to stimulate it.

That is, if you can't skirt these questions, better to be honest, early, before your child becomes a lion with a temperature of a hundred and three.[15]

The paradise of childhood was a product of the Enlightenment, but the storm of adolescence descended upon the United States with urbanization.[16] Children used to be able to see for themselves how animals mate, bear, and nurse their young. But when people left the farm and moved to the city to work in factories, the way Milton Bradley's father did, kids missed out on the chance to watch animals . . . sneezing.[17] And then, oddly enough, parents began solemnly informing their children that babies, swaddled in blankets, are dropped down the chimney by a tall bird with long legs and a heavy bill.

Storks, which are common in northern Europe, are known for taking particular care of their young. (Storks haven't always been associated with fertility; in fact, the reverse has just as often been the case. In eighteenth-century Philadelphia, syringes marketed as abortifacients were "ingenious things said to have been suggested by the stork." The stork feeds its young by inserting its bill down their throats, and a woman who thrust this syringe up her vagina and through her cervix could induce a miscarriage, or die trying.)[18] In the United States, the rise of the myth that babies come from storks dates to the publication in 1838 of "The Storks," a story by Hans Christian Andersen. In a nest on the roof of a house in a little village, a male stork guards a female and her hatchlings. Down below, a rascally boy sings:

> *Stork! stork! long-legged stork!*
> *Into thy nest I prithee walk;*
> *There sits thy mate,*
> *With her four children so great.*

> *The first we'll hang like a cat,*
> *The second we'll burn,*
> *The third on a spit we'll turn,*
> *The fourth drown dead as a rat!*

The baby storks tell their mother they would like to exact some vengeance on the boys below.

"Shall not we fly down, and peck out their eyes?" said the young ones.
"No, leave them alone!" said the mother.

Instead, she teaches them to fly.

"Now we will have our revenge!" said they.
"Very well!" said the mother; "I have been thinking what will be the best. I know where the pool is, in which all the little human children lie until the storks come and take them to their parents: the pretty little things sleep and dream so pleasantly as they will never dream again. All parents like to have a little child, and all children like to have a little brother or sister. We will fly to the pool and fetch one for each of the boys who has not sung that wicked song, nor made a jest of the storks; and the other naughty children shall have none."
"But he who first sung those naughty rhymes! that great ugly fellow! what shall we do to him?" cried the young storks.
"In the pool there lies a little child who has dreamed away his life; we will take it for him, and he will weep because he has only a little dead brother."[19]

And that is just what they do.

"The Storks" is as cruel as the darkest of the Grimms' tales, but it also explained, in one fell swoop, both birth and infant death. Andersen's fables were hugely popular in the United States.[20] Soon, the stork myth was everywhere: there were stork books, stork toys, stork baby bottles, and stork postcards. Nineteenth-century Americans, squeamish, but with eggs on their minds, grew all but obsessed with the idea that babies come not from women but from birds.

.   .   .

To all this, Sylvester Graham objected, strenuously. He was an anti-stork man. Graham was born in West Suffield, Connecticut, in 1794, the youngest of seventeen children. His grandfather, a Scottish emigrant, was a minister. His father, who died when Sylvester was a baby, had been a charismatic preacher during New England's Great Awakening, in the 1740s, when Jonathan Edwards was preaching—and banning *Aristotle's Master-piece*. After the death of her husband, Sylvester Graham's mother was deemed by the court to be "in a deranged state of mind" and unable to care for her children.[21] From the age of three, her youngest son was farmed out to neighbors and relatives; he never had much of a childhood. A wayward and melancholy youth, he once wrote an autobiographical poem about that uncomfortable, feverish age between childhood and manhood:

> *In gloom, in sadness, and in tears,*
> > *Through childhood's period then did'st languish;*
> *And up through manhood's early years,*
> > *Thy every pulse was beat in anguish.*[22]

In 1823, Graham began a course of study at Amherst. Then he had a breakdown. The next year, he married the daughter of a sea captain. And then he was born again. Like many young men of his day, Graham was swept away by what came to be known as the Second Great Awakening, a religious revival that aimed at a wholesale reformation in manners. Preachers shunned everything earthy, bawdy, and reckless in favor of everything refined, restrained, pious, and purposeful. In 1776, about one in six Americans belonged to a church; by 1850, that number had risen to one in three. In roughly the same period, the amount of alcohol Americans drank dropped from more than seven gallons per adult per year to less than two. Sobriety, orderliness, and punctuality: these were deemed essential traits for a people leaving farms and working, instead, in factories and in offices, striving to accumulate, achieve, invent, progress, and succeed.[23]

Although Graham was licensed to preach in 1826, he never established his own congregation, partly because he was plagued by ill health. He suffered from a series of vague ailments: dyspepsia, sciatica, rheumatism, and neuralgia. For a while, he made a living as a temperance reformer, warning of the dangers of drink. Then he began having visions of a coming apocalypse—an apocalypse of children. "Thousands and thousands of children are springing into existence, and rising up into civil and moral society, and becoming incorporated with the body politic of the nation, without receiving any regular moral culture of the heart," he preached in Philadelphia in 1829. A half-million children had already reached adulthood without having been given religious instruction, and some two and a half million children were in danger of following them into ruin. This river of children, he said, was more powerful than the Mississippi:

> The millions of children, which are now unseen and unfelt in our Country, with the thousands that are daily gushing into life,—if measures be not taken to qualify and direct their course, will inevitably, from their condition and circumstances, soon unite in one dark and mighty confluence of ignorance and immorality and crime, which will overflow the wholesome restraints of society, and sweep away the barriers of civil law, and sap the foundations of our Republican institutions.[24]

The more he considered the coming apocalypse, the more Graham came to believe that this wasn't so much a religious matter as a medical one. The problem at the heart of the body politic was a problem in the human body itself, and especially in the bodies of young men. They were overflowing; they were spurting: they were ejaculating.[25]

Graham didn't use the word "adolescence." He talked, instead, about "children" and, more often, about "youth." Still, the people he was worried about were between ten and twenty-four: growing up, but not yet married. He was more worried about boys than girls. He wasn't alone. In 1829, the Connecticut minister Joel Hawes remarked, in *Lectures to Young Men on the Formation of Character,* that on the voyage of life, the waters traveled between the ages of fourteen and twenty-one are the most perilous: "On this sea, my young friends, you are now embarking, with little knowledge of what is before you, and many of you, I fear, without line, or compass, or chart." Henry Ward Beecher warned, in his own *Lectures to Young Men,* that "a young man . . . feels in his bosom the various impulses, wild desires, restless cravings he can hardly tell for what." He is on a quest, "thirsting for happiness."[26]

All this worry about young men was by no means without cause. The period between childhood and adulthood was, at the time, getting longer.

Puberty was beginning earlier (at least as measured by the age of menarche, which was declining), and young people were starting work and marrying later. Girls remained dependent even after getting married, but prolonged dependence was a particular problem for boys, who were trying to grow into men in a nation that had revolted from its parent country and that prized no value more than independence. There were a great many young people around; the average age of the population was seventeen. And many of those young people were living near factories, as Dorus Clarke, a Springfield, Massachusetts, minister, remarked in his *Lectures to Young People in Manufacturing Villages* in 1836. Clarke preached that the first generation of Americans to come of age during the age of machines faced dangers unknown to any prior generation: "Never before was the world in such an excitable, impressible state."[27]

Graham started delivering his own *Lecture to Young Men* in the 1830s. He wanted to warn them about excitement by telling them about sex, not storks. In one thing, he sided with Rousseau: "Through a fear of contaminating the minds of youth, it has long been considered the wisest measure to keep them in ignorance." This would be fine, except that "the natural inquisitiveness of the young mind has been met by misrepresentation and falsehood, on the part of those who would preserve their purity." This, Graham believed, was a disaster, because young people are as curious as cats—theirs is a "restless and prying curiosity"—and they'll find out about sex, by hook or by crook, "So that while parents have been resting securely in the idea of the ignorance and purity of their children, these have been clandestinely drinking in the most corrupt and depraving knowledge from mercenary and polluted hands."[28]

People often called him "Dr. Graham," but Sylvester Graham was not a physician. Still, the confusion is a good illustration of the era's shifting source of authority for how to steer your course through the voyage of life: rules for conduct once laid down by clergymen were, more and more, made by doctors. Graham's lectures were based in morality—his was a theory, finally, about virtue and vice—but he called it something else. He called it "the science of human life."

Graham believed that the human body had two functions, nutrition and reproduction, connected by the same bundle of nerves. Stimulation of either system was debilitating. The nineteenth century's combination of excitements—the processed food of the factory and the frenzy of city life—was responsible not only for specific diseases, including devastating outbreaks of cholera, but also for a general American malaise, caused by overstimulation. All those hordes of unmarried young people living in cities were eating, instead of fresh farm foods, tinned meat and canned vegetables and bread made with processed flour. Worse, old enough to know about sex but not old enough to marry, they were masturbating. "Self-pollution," he said, "is actually a very great and rapidly increasing evil in our country."[29] Young Americans were spilling their precious bodily fluids; the nation was at risk.

This was, for Graham, a matter of national political urgency. The new republic—Young America it was called—was not only full of young people, it was a young country, and it was also the world's first modern democracy. It was precarious, an excitable experiment. Graham put it this way: "Whether a national Government can permanently and beneficially exist, whose ultimate power is in the hands of the people, and whose form of existence and mode of operation depend on the popular will, is yet a matter of experiment, with us; not only for ourselves, but for the whole human family; and it may be, for ages or forever!" No government in the history of the world, he argued, had so entirely depended on the virtue of its people. The United States was "the political POLE-STAR of the world; by which the political philanthropists of every nation, are endeavoring to govern their course."[30] The health of the nation's youth would determine the future of the republic. If the American body politic spent its time masturbating, what then?

Haranguers, of course, had damned masturbation before. In the 1790s, before Parson Weems wrote his *Life of Washington,* he sold *Onania,* a treatise against masturbation. (Weems, an itinerant bookseller, also pocketed tidy sums peddling *The Lover's Almanac* and, in 1799, a book dedicated to George Washington called *The Philanthropist; Or, A Good Twelve Cents Worth of Political Love Powder, for the Fair Daughters and Patriotic Sons of Virginia.*)[31] But Graham went much further than moralists who damned only masturbation—he also damned intercourse. For Graham, it wasn't solitude that was the problem; it was ejaculation. Before Graham, sex within marriage, at least, hadn't been bad; usually, it was considered good for you. *Aristotle's Master-piece* described intercourse as a release: "It eases and lightens the body, clears the mind, comforts the head and senses, and expels melancholy." The best sex was "furious": "The act of coition should be performed with the greatest ardor and intenseness of desire imaginable, or else they may as well let it alone."[32] The Garden of Eden, after all, was a "Place of Pleasure"; Adam and Eve were together, "compleating their mutual Happiness" in "the Paradise of Paradise itself."[33]

With all this, Graham could hardly have disagreed more strenuously. "Sexual excess within the pale of wedlock" was, he argued, a national crisis. If a man was exceptionally robust, and terribly lucky, he might indulge in it once a month without too much ill effect. Much more, and he would grow old before his time, and die an early and miserable death.[34] Graham did not consider marital sex a mansion of happiness. Ejaculation was an injury; even the most innocent sexual release was debilitating. "There is a common error of opinion among young men, which is, perhaps, not wholly confined to the young,—that health requires an emission of semen at stated periods, and that frequent nocturnal emissions in sleep are not incompatible with health. . . . All this is wrong,—entirely, dangerously wrong!"

Graham's lectures were wildly popular, and no wonder. He was a stagy talker, famous for shouting and sweating himself into a state of froth and fury. Nothing was so violent an overstimulation to the human body, he insisted, as sexual excitement. He compared arousal to a natural disaster: "the body of man has become a living volcano." During the climax of one of his lectures, when he described orgasm—"the convulsive paroxysms attending venereal indulgence"—he could barely contain himself: "The brain, stomach, heart, lungs, liver, skin, and the other organs, feel it sweeping over them with the tremendous violence of a tornado." All this, he said with a shudder, is "succeeded by great exhaustion, relaxation, lassitude, and even prostration."[35] And then, he nearly collapsed.

Gesundheit.

Curiously, what Graham described as the consequences of masturbation sound like nothing so much as the ravages of old age: "The sight becomes feeble, obscure, cloudy, confused, and often is entirely lost—and utter blindness fills the rest of life with darkness and unavailing regret." Masturbators were sure to suffer not only from loss of sight but also from diseases of the heart, lungs, kidneys, and liver, and, in the worst cases, memory loss, brain damage, and death.[36] "The skin loses its healthy, clear and fresh appearance, and assumes a sickly, pale, shriveled, turbid and cadaverous aspect;—becoming exceedingly susceptible to the injurious effects of cold, heat, moisture, and other disturbing causes."[37] (Graham also believed masturbation caused insanity. Under the influence of Graham's ideas, "masturbatory insanity" was a leading cause of admission to the State Lunatic Hospital, in Worcester, Massachusetts, second only to intemperance. And those suffering from masturbatory insanity had, of all inmates, the poorest chance of recovery.)[38]

What would happen to the United States if young Americans didn't stop masturbating? They, and the republic, would grow as feeble and decrepit as the Old World. Still, there was hope, boundless hope. If eating the wrong kind of food and having too much sex is what causes disease, then disease can be avoided. And if disease is what causes aging, then aging can be avoided, too. "If mankind always lived precisely as they ought to live," Graham explained, "they would—as a general rule—most certainly pass through the several stages of life, from infancy to extreme old age, without sickness and distress, enjoying, through their long protracted years, health, and serenity, and peace, and individual and social happiness, and gradually wear out their vital energies, and finally lie down and fall asleep in death, without an agony—without a pain." Illness and decline were unnatural. "Disease and suffering are, in no degree, the legitimate and necessary results of the operations of our bodily organs," Graham maintained, "and by no means necessarily incident to human life."

The science of human life promised to cure all disease and relieve all pain. The rules were simple. For the digestive system, Graham recommended abstinence from meat and processed food and prescribed cold plain foods, whole grains, and the digestive crackers that still bear his name. (John Harvey Kellogg, who read Graham as a boy, later founded the Battle Creek Sanitarium, in Michigan, where he prescribed enemas and cold—and eponymous—breakfast cereal, to stifle desire.)[39] For the reproductive system, Graham recommended sexual abstinence, or close to it. And then, decades would pass, but you wouldn't feel the years. You couldn't live forever, but you could live for a very long time, disease-free.

Grahamism marked a turning point between a religious conception of the good life and a medical one. With Graham, the wages of sin became the stages of life. "For the wages of sin is death; but the gift of God is eternal life through Jesus Christ our Lord" (Romans 6:23). Graham believed in Christ, death, and eternal life; he just didn't believe in sex, sickness, or aging. They weren't necessary. No, he said: "God made you to be happy."[40]

This led Graham to a rather uncomfortable position: to be saved, children had to be taught the facts of life. But to advocate this position was to court more controversy than he could bear.[41] "When I commenced my public career, as a Lecturer on the Science of Human Life, it did not, in any degree, enter into my plan, to treat on this delicate subject," he insisted. (He had also been attacked by mobs: once by a posse of commercial bakers, once by angry butchers, and once for delivering an arousing lecture about chastity to young women.)[42] But, at least as he told it, he had been persuaded of its necessity because so many very young men had approached him, complaining of all manner of illness and having not the least notion that their suffering was the consequence of masturbation. Something had to be done.[43]

Crowds thronged by the thousands to see him speak, thrillingly, about volcanoes and tornadoes. And they scooped up copies of his book, too. *A Lecture to Young Men, on Chastity, Intended Also for the Serious Consideration of Parents and Guardians* went through ten editions in fifteen years. He always insisted that it wasn't really appropriate for children: "It may, perhaps, be said, that this work is better calculated for adults than for young boys. This is true."[44]

He never discounted the idea of writing a book about the science of human life for young men and women, rather than for their parents. One day, he thought, it may "be found expedient and desirable that a work should be produced on the subject, more peculiarly adapted to young minds."[45] He never wrote it. Despite a strict adherence to his regimen, his health declined. He abandoned lecturing. He abandoned writing. He got sick, and then he got sicker. As he languished, at the end of his life, at his home in Northampton, Massachusetts, he tried eating meat, and even drinking alcohol.[46] Nothing helped. He died in 1851, at the age of fifty-seven. A postmortem was conducted, but no one was quite sure what had killed him. He seemed, simply, to have wasted away.[47] Before his final illness, he had been at work on a new book. It was to be called *The Philosophy of History.*[48]

"Perchance the mantle of Graham may fall upon the shoulders of some-one who, availing himself of all that Graham learned, and rejecting all his errors, shall carry on the work," observed one obituary writer.[49] The year Graham died, Granville Stanley Hall was seven years old and living on a farm in western Massachusetts, about twenty miles from Graham's house. Hall's father, a farmer, was also a temperance lecturer. He must have known Graham; he certainly knew of him. Young Stanley was said to have been "unusually inquisitive about the origin of babies." He asked a lot of ques-tions, including whether God had ever been a baby. He read everything he could get his hands on. Very likely, he read Graham's Lecture to Young Men. Told that masturbation causes leprosy, he tied himself up at night, with bandages.[50]

When Hall grew up, he went to study in Germany, where he learned all about kindergartens; he helped bring them to the United States. In the 1890s, he founded the child-study movement, which is what led to children's rooms at public libraries. He earned the first PhD in psychology awarded at an American university. Psychology was Hall's science of human life. He founded the American Journal of Psychology, and he founded and served as first president of the American Psychological Association. But what G. Stanley Hall is best remembered for is what Anne Carroll Moore cap-tured when she called him "the great explorer of adolescence."[51]

In Adolescence: Its Psychology and Its Relation to Physiology, Anthropol-ogy, Sociology, Sex, Crime, Religion and Education, an exhaustive, rambling, and at times downright bizarre two-volume study published in 1904 (and that sold more than twenty-five thousand copies), Hall finished what Gra-ham had begun, stirring in much of Darwin and a great deal of Freud, insisting that the time between childhood and adulthood is a stage of life all its own.[52] It happens, he explained, between the ages of fourteen and twenty-four. It is marked by Sturm und Drang, storm and stress. On the voyage of life, adolescence is when you have to steer your ship through a hurricane.

This stage of life was, to Hall, living in an age of psychological explana-tions, mostly in your head. "The dawn of adolescence is marked by a special consciousness of sex," he wrote. Its dusk is the act itself. Hall condemned masturbation, but, unlike Graham, he didn't condemn intercourse. Instead, in language no less fevered and millennialist than Graham's, he celebrated sex as the birth of the adult. The crisis of adolescence, Hall argued, is solved by the integration of religious fervor and sexual passion. That integration is accomplished by the realization—earned by experience—that sex is sacred. Here is Hall on intercourse:

> In the most unitary of all acts, which is the epitome and pleroma of life, we have the most intense of all affirmations of the will to live and realize that the only true God is love, and the center of life is worship. Every part of the mind and body participates in a true pangenesis. This sacrament is the annunciation hour, with hosannas which the whole world reflects. Communion is fusion and beatitude. It is the supreme hedonic narcosis, a holy intoxication, the chief ecstasy, because the most intense of experiences; it is the very heart of psychology, and because it is the supreme pleasure of life it is the eternal basis and guarantee of optimism. It is this experience more than any other that opens to man the ideal world. Now the race is incarnated in the individual and remembers its lost paradise.

It was a mansion of happiness, regained.[53]

Books like *Where Did I Come From?* came from G. Stanley Hall. It was Hall's work on adolescence that led, at the beginning of the twentieth century, to facts-of-life books for "teenagers" (the word, an Americanism, was coined not long after *Adolescence* was published).[54] Adolescent boys, Hall reported, spend nine-tenths of their time thinking about sex, and they don't know what to think.[55] He therefore argued for sex education; adolescents could enter that mansion of happiness only if they were taught about sex. They needed help: they needed something to read.[56]

Under Hall's influence, books explaining sex to kids, directly, and not through their parents, began to proliferate during Anne Carroll Moore's golden age of children's literature, which also happened to be a time when there was a lot of talk about sex. "Sex O'Clock in America" is what one pundit called it, in 1913.[57] At the same time, venereal disease had come to be seen as the cause of all manner of social problems, including a perceived crisis in the American family, marked by a falling marriage rate, a rising divorce rate, and a declining fertility rate, at least within the middle class. Teaching "sexual hygiene," celebrating chastity and marriage, was to be the solution.

Early-twentieth-century Progressives, who could make a science of lick-ing envelopes if they set their minds to it—which is why so many ideas about life and death hinge on this period—made a science of adolescence. Sex education in the public schools began in the 1910s; by 1922, the subject was taught in nearly half of all public schools in the United States.[58] The first sex books for kids were schoolbooks. About matters anatomical, they were candid. About the dangers of venereal disease, they were concerned. But as for that question Rousseau mentioned—"Where do little children come from?"—they were, as yet, coy.

"All live things start from eggs," wrote Winfield Scott Hall in 1912 in *Life's Beginnings: For Boys of Ten to Fourteen Years.* Hall, a professor of physiol-ogy at Northwestern University, and no relation to G. Stanley Hall, was, at the time, America's foremost sexologist.[59] The author of such classics as *From Youth into Manhood,* he wrote with a winning frankness ("Turn-ing our attention now to the testicles . . .") and had been particularly com-mended for his forgiving attitude toward the nocturnal emission ("It is a perfectly natural experience that results in no loss of vitality, only a slight depletion of material").[60] His books about what he called "the great truths of life" included a twenty-five-cent pamphlet titled *Instead of "Wild Oats"* and a collaboration with his wife, Jeannette Winter Hall, *Girlhood and Its Problems: The Sex Life of Woman,* although he was perhaps best known for a 320-page manual, *Sexual Knowledge: In Plain and Simple Language,* published by the International Bible House in 1913 and available, for two dollars, bound in morocco.[61]

In *Life's Beginnings,* a twenty-five-cent primer published by the YMCA, Winfield Scott Hall aimed to explain the birds and the bees by way of the barnyard, as if every boy were William Harvey: "All boys are interested in live things, therefore all boys are interested in eggs. The best place to see all kinds of eggs is out on a farm."[62] Let's go out to the country, he told his readers, city boys all. In the henhouse, a "motherly old biddy" sits on a nest of eggs. Where do those eggs come from? Let's follow the farmer's wife into the kitchen, where she's butchering chickens for Sunday dinner. "When the farmer's wife opens the bodies of these hens to remove their internal organs, she finds in each an ovary or egg-sack, with many eggs in differ-ent stages of development," Hall explains. "If the egg is to develop into a chicken it must be fertilized. Every day the rooster deposits the fertilizing fluid in the pouch or *cloaca* of the hen."[63] Next he takes his readers down to the pond, to watch the frogs spawn. By chapter 3, he's moved on to kittens and puppies, colts and calves. Do these animals come from eggs, too? "Yes, all these animals begin as tiny little eggs. But they are so delicate that, if they were deposited in any nest outside of the body, they would surely be destroyed, so nature has provided that in all these animals the delicate eggs should be held within a sort of nest in the mother's body. This nest is called the *womb*." And then, somewhat abruptly, our tour comes to a close:

> You return to the city after three months on the farm, to be introduced to a baby sister, who came into your home two weeks ago. When you come into the house and see your little sister you find that she is in the act of taking her dinner from her mother's breast, and after the first rush of joy at the sight of them both—joy and surprise nearly smothering you—it all comes over you that little baby sister has come in the same way the little baby colts and calves and kittens and lambs came. "Mother," you ask, "was my sister formed from an egg and did she grow within your body?" Your mother will of course answer "Yes," and you will go away and think it over.[64]

That, it hardly needs to be said, leaves rather a lot to the imagination.

E. B. White was thirteen years old when Winfield Scott Hall published *Life's Beginnings: For Boys of Ten to Fourteen Years.* In 1929, the year he married Katharine Angell, White, with his officemate, James Thurber, published his first book, *Is Sex Necessary?* (Their answer: not strictly, no, but it beats raising begonias.) *Is Sex Necessary?* is a lampoon of the sex books that White had grown up with. It features fake Freudian sexologists (viz., the undersized Dr. Samuel D. Schmalhausen) and a chapter, written by White, addressing the child's perennial question: "What shall I tell my parents about sex?" The answer: "Tell them the truth. If the subject is approached in a tactful way, it should be no more embarrassing to teach a parent about sex than to teach him about personal pronouns. And it should be less discouraging."[65]

White's first children's book, *Stuart Little*, could easily have been titled *Is Childbirth Necessary?* (Not strictly, no, but it beats banning books.) Plenty of grown-ups got the joke about how the tale of the mouse was, among other things, a sly commentary on Progressive-era sex education. The *Washington Post* even ran a review that took the form of a loving imitation of *Is Sex Necessary?* right down to the idiotic Freudian sexologists, in this case, Dr. Hans Von Hornswoggle, who asserts that *Stuart Little* must be a hoax: " 'Lacks verisimilitude from the very first line,' said Herr Von Hornswoggle. 'Man or mouse, homo sapiens or *Mus musculus*—no little rodent can sail a ship in Central Park lagoon while still teething. Much, much too Jung.' "[66] Kids, though, were too young to get that one.

"Have you ever thought about an egg, perhaps the one you know best, the chicken egg?" Books like *Window into an Egg: Seeing Life Begin,* which explained the story of life through pictures of a chicken egg with a piece of the shell missing, were still being published in 1969.[67] But that same year also saw the publication of *Everything You Always Wanted to Know About Sex (But Were Afraid to Ask),* which rather dramatically raised the stakes (and inspired a Woody Allen film). Sex left the farm.

The possibility that books explaining sex to kids could become far more explicit came into play after 1957, when, in *Roth v. United States,* the Supreme Court drew a distinction between sexual explicitness and obscenity, which meant that, if being explicit had a redeeming social value, you could be explicit.[68] By the 1960s, sex education had become a partisan battleground, especially after the founding of both the Sexuality Information and Education Council of the United States and a flock of local organizations, like the New York League for Sexual Freedom. Their reforms of the sex education curriculum in public schools—which consisted not only of greater explicitness but also of a rejection of the Progressives' chastity-and-marriage curriculum, the promotion of contraception, and the discussion of homosexuality—led to campaigns to regulate it by organizations including the John Birch Society, whose founder called sex education a "filthy communist plot."

Is the School House the Proper Place to Teach Raw Sex? was the title of a pamphlet published by the Christian Crusade in 1968.[69] In the 1970s, the battle over sex education got nastier, especially in the wake of *Roe v. Wade.*[70] Kids trying to figure out sex were caught in the middle. Then came AIDS. During all this time, a great deal remained as unspeakable as it had been in the days of Sylvester Graham's brimstone. In 1994, U.S. surgeon general

Joycelyn Elders was asked, at an AIDS forum, whether it might not be a good idea to discuss masturbation with children. "I think that it is something that's part of human sexuality and it's part of something that perhaps should be taught," Elders said. "But we've not even taught our children the very basics. And I feel that we have tried ignorance for a very long time and it's time we try education." Within hours, Elders was asked to resign.[71]

Teaching sex became a political minefield. And facts-of-life books changed. They no longer involved going to a farm or studying other animals; this is not zoology class. We are not dissecting frogs; we are thinking about ourselves. Late twentieth-century books were full of anatomical drawings of the insides of kids' bodies, with cross sections of gonads on every page. That's partly because, outside a laboratory or a surgery, some of those things had only recently been photographed, Lennart Nilsson–style. But it's also because of the culture's inward looking. Eggs and sperm aren't to be found out there in the barnyard or on some farmer's wife's kitchen table: they are inside of *you*.

By the beginning of the twenty-first century, nothing was left to the imagination anymore: "1 sperm + 1 egg = 1 baby," Robie Harris explained, in *It's NOT the Stork! A Book About Girls, Boys, Babies, Bodies, Families, and Friends* (2006). "When grownups want to make a baby," she went on, "most often a woman and a man have a special kind of loving called 'making love'—'having sex'—or 'sex.' This kind of loving happens when the woman and the man get so close to each other that the man's penis goes inside the woman's vagina."[72] *Life's Beginnings* was for boys ten to fourteen; *It's NOT the Stork* was for kids as young as four.

Over the course of a century, where babies come from had become baby stuff. Books for kids older than about seven or eight covered that subject, but they were far more concerned with the perils of puberty. Adolescence seemed to be starting earlier and earlier and, somehow, to be getting harder and harder. Since the beginning of the nineteenth century, every generation of Americans has found adolescence to be stormier than it had been, ever before. Meanwhile, the beginning of life, a mystery that evolved into a science, became yet another form of therapy, as if every kid needed Von Hornswoggle. The disorder it treated was growing up.

"It is much, *much* harder to be a teenage girl now than ever before," insisted the gynecologist Jennifer Ashton in 2009, in *The Body Scoop for Girls: A Straight-Talk Guide to a Healthy, Beautiful You.*[73] "Am I weird?"

you wonder. "*No!*" Lynda Madaras insisted, in *Ready, Set, Grow!* "You are not weird. You are 100% NORMAL! You're just starting puberty." Madaras's book included a chapter called "B.O. and Zits."[74] You're 100 percent normal, but you stink, and if you would only be more careful about your grooming, you could look so much better. "If puberty is something that just happens, why do you need to read about it?" Louise Spilsbury asked in *Me, Myself and I: All About Sex and Puberty,* in 2009. Her answer: "Finding out more about puberty will also help you deal with the practical side of it, from shaving to sanitary pads."[75] And, to be sure, there was in that era's crop of well-intentioned books an abundance of practical information. *The Care & Keeping of You: The Body Book for Girls,* published in 1998 by the makers of the American Girl dolls, had this to say about underarm hair: "Whether you want to remove it or leave it there is a very personal decision."[76] No subject was too small. How to shave your legs, how to shave your face ("take special care when shaving around pimples"), how to insert a tampon, how to ask someone on a date, what to say on a date, what not to say ("Never Tell Your Boyfriend You're on the Pill," advised Ashton), how to spy on your vagina with a hand mirror, how to brush your hair ("use a wide-tooth comb to detangle small sections"), even how to brush your teeth. If you find that your clothes are suddenly too small for you, one author patiently explained, that's because you're *growing,* dear.[77]

For adults, there were, at the turn of the twenty-first century, a new generation of books offering guidance on how to talk to kids about sex, including *Ten Talks Parents Must Have with Their Children About Sex and Character,* in which Pepper Schwartz and Dominic Cappello provided scripts, line-by-line instruction. "I'm reading this chapter about sex and character," you were supposed to begin, holding the book in your hands. "I need to talk to you for five or ten minutes."[78] Ten minutes? How much more can a kid take?

It was in the kitchen. I was reading the newspaper. A small, bookish boy sat by my side.

"Hey," he said.

"Hmm?"

"Do you need a conundrum for oral sex?"

I put down my newspaper. I sighed. And then, carrying on an ancient and honorable family tradition, I whiffed the bejeezus out of that one.

CHAPTER 5

Mr. Marriage

Dick Weymer, a forty-one-year-old engineer, was about to begin an affair. He was bored with his wife, Andrea. The Weymers had four children and had been married for twenty years. "He told me I was dull and stupid, uninteresting, that I did not inspire him," Andrea said. "Living with her," Dick said, "is like being aboard that ship that cruised forever between the ports of Tedium and Monotony." Can this marriage be saved? You bet. In 1953, the Weymers went to the American Institute of Family Relations in Los Angeles, the country's first, largest, and most successful marriage clinic, called, by reporters, "the Mayo Clinic of family problems." Urged by the clinic's staff to make herself more interesting, Andrea learned how to make better conversation, went on a diet, and lost eight pounds. The affair was averted, the marriage saved.[1]

The American Institute of Family Relations was founded by Paul Popenoe, the father of marriage counseling. Popenoe is best remembered for a column published in *Ladies' Home Journal:* "Can This Marriage Be Saved?"[2] For a quarter century, the stories in the magazine came from his clinic. He counseled more than a thousand couples a year.[3] At its height, Popenoe's empire included not only "Can This Marriage Be Saved?" but also stacks of marriage manuals; a syndicated newspaper column, "Modern Marriage"; a radio program, *Love and Marriage;* and a stint as a judge on a television show called *Divorce Hearing.* People called him "Mr. Marriage." They also called him "Dr. Popenoe," even though his only academic degree was an honorary one.[4]

Many modern ideas about marriage—and a great many ideas about American family life, including having, raising, and educating children—date to the Progressive era, when progress was no longer either John Bunyan's pilgrimage or a locomotive chugging across the continent. For Progressives, progress was science. And for Paul Popenoe, that science was eugenics.

The American Institute of Family Relations was funded by E. S. Gosney, the president of the Human Betterment Foundation, for which Popenoe served as secretary. Before he became "the man who saves marriages," Popenoe was a leader in the campaign to sterilize the insane and the weak of mind. He considered marriage counseling the flip side of compulsory vasectomy and tubal ligation: sterilize the unfit; urge the fit to marry. But what if the fit got divorced? "I began to realize that if we were to promote a sound population," he explained, "we would not only have to get the right kind of people married, but we would have to keep them married." He opened his marriage clinic in order "to bring all the resources of modern science to bear on the promotion of successful marriage and family life."[5] He didn't much mind if the marriages of people of inferior stock fell apart: "Divorcees," he wrote, "are on the whole biologically inferior to the happily married."[6] By saving the marriages of the biologically superior, though, Popenoe hoped to save the race.

The son of a California avocado farmer, Paul Popenoe was born in 1888. He went to Stanford, where he studied with the university's president, David Starr Jordan, a biologist who was much influenced by both Herbert Spencer and Charles Darwin. In 1906, the American Breeders' Association appointed Jordan to head a committee to "investigate and report on heredity in the human race" and to document "the value of superior blood and the menace to society of inferior blood."[7]

Darwin redefined what it meant to be human. Americans read his work avidly.[8] Animals had been bred for thousands of years. If people are animals, why not breed a better race? Maybe human suffering could be relieved, people hoped. Maybe disease and even poverty could be eradicated. That was one vision. Another was darker. If people are animals, and natural selection weeds out the unfit, others wondered, then why bother taking care of the weak? In the United States, what came to be called social Darwinism provided conservatives with an arsenal of arguments in favor of laissez-faire economic policies, against social welfare programs, and in support of Jim Crow. "The Negro," it was argued, was "nearer to the anthropoid or pre-human ancestry of men" than any other race, a living missing link; only slavery had prevented the extinction of the black American; if not for the peculiar institution, natural selection would have led to the death of the entire race.[9] New laws were put on the books, segregating the races. In 1891, Georgia was the first state to demand separate seating for whites and blacks in streetcars; five years later came *Plessy v. Ferguson*. By 1905, every southern state had a streetcar law, and more: in courthouses, separate Bibles; in bars, separate stools; in post offices, separate windows. In Birmingham, it was a crime for blacks and whites to play checkers together in a public park.[10]

The year the American Breeders' Association appointed Jordan to that committee, Robert Bennett Bean, a former student of Franklin P. Mall's, weighed and measured more than a hundred brains from Mall's anatomical laboratory and reported that parts of "the Negro brain" were smaller than those same parts of "the Caucasian brain." *American Medicine* published an editorial about Bean's research, noting, "Leaders in all political parties now acknowledge the error of human equality." It seemed but a short step to implementing policy. Perhaps, the editors suggested, the Fourteenth Amendment ought to be repealed, thereby removing "a menace to our prosperity—a large electorate without brains."

Bean's work did not go unchallenged. At Clark University, Mall had been a colleague of Franz Boas's. Boas, a German immigrant who was raised as an Orthodox Jew and had confronted anti-Semitism from childhood, railed against racial taxonomies, finding them to rest on nothing more than "the shackles of dogma."[11] Mall was inclined to agree with him (the two men had been colleagues at Clark). He repeated Bean's study, conducting his study blind, and found no difference in brain size.[12] "To those who stoutly maintain a material inferiority of the Negro race and who would dampen your ardor by their claims," Boas told a graduating class at Atlanta University in 1906, "you may confidently reply that the burden of proof rests on them, that the past history of your race does not sustain that statement." W.E.B. DuBois was in the audience that day. "I came then and afterwards," DuBois wrote, "to realize how the silence and neglect of science can let truth utterly disappear."[13]

In 1908, when nine-year-old E. B. White was publishing his first poem, about a mouse, and C. C. Little was embarking on the study of heredity in *Mus musculus,* Paul Popenoe left Stanford to master the subject of heredity by studying breeds of date palms. The next year, California passed a forced sterilization law. (Two-thirds of American states eventually did the same.)[14] In 1913, Jordan appointed Popenoe editor of the *Journal of Heredity;* C. C. Little contributed to an early volume.[15] The first National Conference on Race Betterment was held, in Battle Creek, Michigan, in 1914. (The Race Betterment Foundation was established by an early Grahamist, John Harvey Kellogg, and was endowed with proceeds from the sale of Kellogg's cereals.)[16]

The growing eugenics movement only really made national news in 1915, when Americans learned about the case of Baby Bollinger, born in a Chicago hospital on November 12. The baby, never named, was severely deformed, missing an ear and its neck, and with a blocked bowel and a malformed skull. Harry J. Haiselden, the surgeon called to the case, told the baby's parents that surgery could repair the bowel obstruction and save the baby's life, but he recommended against it. Baby Bollinger died five days later. Haiselden then cowrote and starred in a feature film about the case called *The Black Stork.*[17]

The Black Stork tells the story of the barely fictionalized Bollingers, here a man named Claude who marries a girl named Anne, after having been warned by a doctor, played by Haiselden, that he suffers from a heritable disease. The disease is traced to a grandfather who fathered a child with "a slave—a vile filthy creature who was suffering from a loathsome disease." (A "black stork" might bring a dead baby, but the phrase was also used at the time to refer to a stork delivering a black baby to a white mother. "The Wrong Address" is the caption on a postcard from 1905; it pictures a white stork carrying in its beak a sleeping black baby. From a window, an alarmed white mother throws a shoe at the bird, urging both bird and baby away.)[18] Before the film was released to theaters, that scene was reshot and the slave was replaced by a servant girl. The title was changed, too. By 1919, Haiselden's film was being screened as *Are You Fit to Marry?*[19]

Eugenics found its strongest foothold in California. Charting the progress of the state's sterilization project, Popenoe traveled from one asylum to the next, counting and inspecting the feeble, the insane, and the criminal. Under the auspices of human betterment, more than twenty thousand men and women were sterilized in California, more than in all the other states put together; over half the sterilizations in the United States were conducted there.[20] Popenoe's vision, though, was far grander; he estimated that about ten million Americans should be sterilized. At the time, that would have meant about a tenth of the population.[21]

But which tenth? Knowing whom to sterilize, like knowing who was fit to marry, came to depend on the idea that intelligence is a thing, a quantity, something that you're born with, something that can be measured. In 1906, Lewis M. Terman, a student of G. Stanley Hall's, had written a dissertation titled "Genius and Stupidity." For his subjects, boys aged ten to thirteen, Terman selected "the brightest or most stupid that could be found within easy distance of Clark University, in the city of Worcester." After subjecting them to a battery of tests, which reinforced his view that the seven bright boys were bright and that the seven stupid boys were stupid, he concluded that what lay between them was inherited and unchangeable.[22]

Terman then joined David Starr Jordan's faculty at Stanford, where he refined a test designed by the French psychologist Alfred Binet in 1905. Binet's test was meant to identify children who needed help learning. Terman standardized the scale, with a mean of 100, and developed what he called an "intelligence quotient," or IQ, the ratio of mental to physical age. For his test, which he named the Stanford-Binet, Terman took some of his questions from the Frenchman: "My neighbor has been having queer visitors. First a doctor came to his house, then a lawyer, then a minister. What do you think happened there?" But where Binet accepted "a death" as the only correct answer, Terman allowed "a marriage": the lawyer came to make the arrangements, and the minister to officiate. And the doctor came to see if the betrothed were fit to marry.[23]

In 1916, Terman published *The Measurement of Intelligence*. With Terman's work, the measurement of intelligence moved from anatomy to psychology, from weighing brains to administering tests. He recommended that all schoolchildren be subjected to the Stanford-Binet test, so that "real defectives" could be identified, not so much (as Binet had believed) because they needed dedicated instruction, but because "all feeble-minded are at least potential criminals."[24] His conclusions constituted an argument against not only equality but also philanthropy: "when charity organizations help the feeble-minded to float along in the social and industrial world, and to produce and rear children after their kind, a doubtful service is rendered."[25]

Like Bean's measurement of brains, Terman's measurement of intelligence did not go unchallenged. In the pages of the *New Republic,* Walter Lippmann attacked Terman's work as "quackery in a field where quacks breed like rabbits." Lippmann argued that Terman, "muddle-headed and prejudiced," had supplied no evidence that intelligence is either fixed or heritable. Terman had promoted a staggeringly dangerous idea, Lippmann said, an idea of whose danger he seemed utterly unaware. "I hate the impudence of a claim that in fifty minutes you can judge and classify a human being's predestined fitness in life," Lippmann wrote. Terman ought to be stopped, Lippmann urged, adding, "If the impression takes root that these tests really measure intelligence, that they constitute a sort of last judgment on the child's capacity, that they reveal 'scientifically' his predestined ability, then it would be a thousand times better if all the intelligence testers and all their questionnaires were sunk without warning into the Sargasso Sea."[26] That impression did take root, but the drowning of the testers and the tests didn't quite come to pass.

The year Terman published *The Measurement of Intelligence,* Popenoe's close friend Madison Grant published *The Passing of the Great Race; Or, The Racial Basis of European History.* Grant, "never before a historian," practiced what he called "heredity history." He attempted to demonstrate that the "Nordic race" (the "blue-eyed, fair-haired peoples of the north of Europe") was being overrun by stupider people who were "dark-haired, dark-eyed." This, he believed, posed a particular threat to the United States, since "democracy is fatal to progress when two races of unequal value live side by side."[27]

Evolution is an explanation for change over time, which is why arguments about evolution are always arguments about history. J.B.S. Haldane, in *Daedalus,* reflected on "the influence of biology on history." For Grant, the only meaningful force in history was inheritance: really, there was no history; there was only biology.

In 1918, Paul Popenoe and Roswell Hill Johnson wrote *Applied Eugenics* to explain "the practical means by which society may encourage the reproduction of superior persons and discourage that of inferior." It became the most widely assigned college textbook on the topic; it was also translated into German. Popenoe and Johnson deemed miscegenation "biologically wrong" because "the Negro lacks in his germ-plasm excellence of some qualities which the white races possess." For poverty, Popenoe and Johnson blamed the poor, citing a study reporting that 55 percent of retarded children belonged to the laboring class. The solution to want was to sterilize the needy. Following Terman, Popenoe and Johnson opposed old-age pensions, minimum-wage legislation, and child-labor laws: by helping the biologically and mentally unfit, these programs perpetuated a poor gene pool, just as slavery had protected blacks from extinction.[28] Civilization, sympathy, and charity, Popenoe wrote later, "have intervened in Nature's plan."[29]

For much of the world's ills, Grant blamed "swarms of Polish Jews" and "half-breeds," but Popenoe and Johnson blamed other people, too, especially college girls. Women's education, they warned, "is tending toward race suicide": "Many a college girl of the finest innate qualities, who sincerely desires to enter matrimony, is unable to find a husband of her own class, simply because she has been rendered so cold and unattractive, so overstuffed intellectually and starved emotionally, that a typical man does not desire to spend the rest of his life in her company."[30] Popenoe was, at the time, unmarried. Two years later, at the age of thirty-two, he married a nineteen-year-old dancer.

Meanwhile, he lobbied for immigration restriction. In 1924, Congress passed the most restrictive anti-immigration act in U.S. history. But, as a member of the Immigration Restriction League put it, "The country is somewhat fed up on high brow Nordic superiority stuff."[31]

The next year, a Grant-like figure made an appearance in *The Great Gatsby:*

"Civilization's going to pieces," broke out Tom violently. "I've gotten to be a terrible pessimist about things. Have you read 'The Rise of the Colored Empires' by this man Goddard?"

"Why, no," I answered, rather surprised by his tone.

"Well, it's a fine book, and everybody ought to read it. The idea is if we don't look out the white race will be—will be utterly submerged. It's all scientific stuff; it's been proved."

"Tom's getting very profound," says Daisy, to which Jordan replies, "You ought to live in California."[32]

Popenoe turned his attention to marriage. "That something is wrong with marriage today is universally admitted and deplored," he wrote in *Modern Marriage: A Handbook* in 1925. "The number of celibates, of mismated couples, of divorces, of childless homes, of wife deserters, of mental and nervous wrecks; the frequency of marital discord, of prostitution and adultery, or perversions, of juvenile delinquency, tells the story."[33] The following year, he offered policy recommendations in *The Conservation of the Family*, in which he defined the "normal family" as "one in which two adults live together happily and give birth to an appropriate number of healthy and intelligent children." What number was appropriate depended on whether the parents were superior, inferior, or defective, because "among the 1,000 leading American men of science, there is not one son of a day laborer." Defectives should have no children at all: "the interests of society are best fostered if it is made up of families of more than four children among the superior part of the population, and of less than four in the inferior part, ranging down to no children at all among the defectives and genuine undesirables."

Popenoe preferred sterilization to birth control, which he considered dangerous. "If charity begins at home, Birth Control should begin abroad. Continued limitation of offspring in the white race simply invites the black, brown, and yellow races to finish the work already begun by Birth Control, and reduce the whites to a subject race preserved merely for the sake of its technical skill, as the Greeks were by the Romans."[34] The best way to ensure that the superior would have more children was to convince women to lower their expectations: "Most of the dissatisfaction with existing marriage is expressed either by women, or by men who have accepted the woman's point of view of the case." He did not consider marriage tied to procreation because "where both parents are defective, there should be no children at all, and yet the family may be called normal." Most of all, he wanted to keep birth control out of the hands of feminists like Margaret Sanger. "If it is desirable for us to make a campaign in favor of contraception," he wrote to Grant, "we are abundantly able to do so on our own account, without enrolling a lot of sob sisters."[35]

The constitutionality of compulsory sterilization laws was brought before the Supreme Court in 1927 in *Buck v. Bell*. As measured by Terman's Stanford-Binet test, Carrie Buck and her mother, Emma, were feebleminded, a trait that was associated with "moral degeneracy" and, for Terman, criminality. After Buck bore a child out of wedlock at the age of seventeen, she was placed in an asylum in Virginia, run by J. H. Bell, who scheduled a tubal ligation. Buck had been raped by the nephew of her adoptive parents. Her daughter was classed as an imbecile at the age of seven months after a social worker testified that there was something about her "not quite normal, but just what it is, I can't tell." Oliver Wendell Holmes, writing for the eight-to-one majority, concluded that "three generations of imbeciles are enough." Buck was sterilized. (Reporters who met Carrie Buck later in life—she died in 1983—described her as a woman of normal intelligence who liked to do crossword puzzles.)[36]

Gosney founded the Human Betterment Foundation in 1928, with Popenoe, Jordan, and Terman as board members. Popenoe and Gosney published *Sterilization for Human Betterment* the next year; like *Applied Eugenics*, it was translated into German.[37] In 1930, Popenoe opened his marriage clinic. Its services included a premarital conference to eliminate those among the betrothed who "are not qualified to marry." He instructed his staff "that marriage counseling involved essential questions of hereditary fitness."[38] He used a personality test called the Johnson Attitude Inventory, devised by his coauthor from *Applied Eugenics*. It consisted of 182 questions, a Stanford-Binet of nuptial fitness.[39] Popenoe and Terman collaborated, too; Popenoe collected questionnaires taken from more than a thousand married couples to aid Terman in a new project, an effort to derive an "index of marital happiness," which could be used to advise a prospective couple whether or not to proceed with the banns. Terman conducted a detailed analysis of the "correlates of orgasm adequacy in women," concluding that, although the cause of the problem remained a mystery, "almost exactly a third of the wives in our group are inadequate in this respect."[40]

In counseling, Popenoe stressed the importance of sex, believing that nearly "every instance of marital disharmony" arises from "sexual maladjustment," which came down to female orgasmic inadequacy; that lack appeared to be fixed and hereditary, just like intelligence.[41] He recommended that a prospective husband determine whether his bride is "frigid, normal, or ardent," as "some frigid women require surgical treatment."[42] The institute also published a pamphlet titled *Are Homosexuals Necessary?*[43] Dr. Popenoe thought not.

Eugenics relied on a colossal misunderstanding of science and a savage misreading of history. Harvard's William McDougall argued that illiteracy could be eradicated by forbidding people who could read from marrying people who couldn't, as if this followed, naturally, from Mendel, with his peas, wrinkly and smooth.[44] In 1938, Terman took pride in what he considered to be the great success of his IQ tests, noting that "admission to college is denied to thousands of high school graduates every year in part on the basis of their intelligence scores. Other thousands are influenced against applying for admission as a result of the intelligence ratings they have received."[45] Madison Grant cobbled together Spencer, Darwin, and Frederick Jackson Turner to write the history of Western civilization as the Nordic race's epic battle for demographic supremacy.

In the Progressive era, eugenics was faddish. Progressivism ran through both political parties for nearly two decades. Early on, and especially before the First World War, eugenics was championed by all sorts of people—Margaret Sanger and Woodrow Wilson prominent among them—but the movement was, at heart, profoundly conservative: atavism disguised as reform.[46] After a while, the disguise got pretty flimsy.[47] The week Holmes handed down his decision in *Buck v. Bell,* Harvard declined a $60,000 bequest to fund eugenics courses, refusing "to teach that the treatment of defective and criminal classes by surgical procedures was a sound doctrine."[48] In "The Eugenics Cult," an essay Clarence Darrow wrote not long after defending John Scopes, charged with the crime of teaching evolution in Tennessee, Darrow judged that he'd rather live in a nation of ill-matched misfits and half-wits than submit to the logic of a bunch of cocksure "uplifters." "Amongst the schemes for remolding society," Darrow wrote, "this is the most senseless and impudent that has ever been put forward by irresponsible fanatics to plague a long-suffering race."[49]

Lashed by such stinging criticism, only passionately committed eugenicists remained undaunted. At the International Congress on Genetics in Ithaca in 1932, C. C. Little complained, "We are now spending more money on defectives than we are on school children" and promised that "compulsory sterilization is just around the corner." ("Sees a Super-Race Evolved by Science" was the New York Times headline about Little's lecture.)[50] In 1933, Germany passed its first forced sterilization law; Franz Boas's books were burned by Nazis; and Paul Popenoe wrote to J. H. Bell, asking for photographs of Carrie Buck and her mother and daughter for his archive, telling him, "A hundred years from now you will still have a place in this history of which your descendants may well be proud." That year, too, Madison Grant published The Conquest of a Continent: Or, The Expansion of Races in America, a "racial history" based on "scientific interpretation." The book recommended "the absolute suspension of all immigration from all countries," to be followed by the deportation of aliens.[51]

The Conquest of a Continent married eugenics as science and heredity as history: it was pseudoscientific pseudohistory. Popenoe, too, had become something of a historian. Over four years, he'd conducted Grant's research. He'd also compiled the book's bibliography.[52] Unlike The Passing of a Great Race, though, The Conquest of a Continent met with a furious reception. Ruth Benedict, who had been a student of Boas's, said the only difference between it and Nazi racial theory was that "in Germany they say Aryan in place of Nordic." Boas attacked Grant in the New Republic; Melville Herskovits, another Boas student, attacked Grant in the Nation. The Anti-Defamation League said Conquest of a Continent was "even more destructive than Hitler's Mein Kampf."[53]

Popenoe pressed on, insisting in 1934 that Germany's sterilization program had nothing to do with race: its aim was more the elimination of all "undesireable elements among the Aryans, whatever these are, than to hit any of the non-Aryan groups."[54] He also wrote about Mein Kampf admiringly, and at length: "Hitler himself—though a bachelor, has long been a convinced advocate of race betterment through eugenic measures." He concluded, "The present German government has given the first example in modern times of an administration based frankly and determinedly on the principles of eugenics."[55]

Prominent scientists took a different position. In 1936, Abraham Myerson, chair of the American Neurological Association's Committee for the Investigation of Eugenical Sterilization, issued a report which found that "it is not true that the feeble-minded have large families or are more prolific than the general population, nor is this true of the insane"; in a letter to the New York Times, Myerson declared compulsory sterilization "futile," not least because so very little was understood about the heritability of mental diseases. In 1937, Columbia University's L. C. Dunn delivered a radio address condemning American immigration restriction and Germany's sterilization campaign, both of which he attributed to the quackery of eugenics. "What can science do for democracy?" Dunn asked. "It can tell the people the truth about such misuses of the prestige of science."[56]

There was room, too, for a quieter critique, not only about the quackery of eugenics but about human betterment and, more broadly, about science as the hobbyhorse of the age. In 1939, E. B. White visited the World's Fair in New York while suffering from a cold. The fair's theme was "The World of Tomorrow." Its exhibits featured all sorts of futuristic contraptions. White was unimpressed. "When you can't breathe through your nose," he wrote, "Tomorrow seems strangely like the day before yesterday."[57]

By the end of the 1930s, eugenics had faded from public view. David Starr Jordan, Madison Grant, and William McDougall had died. The American Eugenics Society and the Eugenic Research Association had closed shop. The Eugenics Record Office became the Genetics Record Office. The Journal of Heredity proclaimed its distate for eugenics and invited articles repudiating it.[58]

Popenoe pressed on. Not until the end of the Second World War did he stop publishing on racial purity, and then only begrudgingly, complaining in 1945, "When it comes to eugenics, the subject of 'race' sets off such tantrums in a lot of persons that one has to be very long-suffering!"[59] The next year, at the Nuremberg trials, lawyers defending the Nazi doctors cited Madison Grant's work. "My interest in eugenics is as keen as ever," Popenoe wrote, privately, in 1949, "although most of the work I am doing is in a slightly different field."[60] Four years later, *Ladies' Home Journal* began publishing "Can This Marriage Be Saved?"

The history of quackery is a book of many chapters. "Their romancing would not be worth noticing," Darrow once wrote, "were it not for the fact that the public apparently takes it at face value."[61] In eighteenth-century London, troubled husbands and wives could pay fifty pounds a night to sleep in a "magnetico-electric" Celestial Bed.[62] Some people will always think they know how to make other people's marriages better, and, after a while, they'll get to cudgeling you or selling you something; the really entrepreneurial types will sell you the cudgel. They'll use whatever's handy; Darwin's an add-on. But he's not just any add-on. The intellectual history of the last few centuries can be told as the story of the articulation, repudiation, and reassertion of scientific and especially of biological and hereditary explanations for just about everything, right down to who does the vacuuming. Scientific fantasies of marriage betterment did not end with the Second World War.

Paul Popenoe's business launched an industry; marriage clinics popped up all over the country. The American Association of Marriage and Family Therapy, founded in 1942, had, as of 2010, twenty-four thousand members, although the actual number of therapists seeing couples was much higher.[63] But while 80 percent of therapists practiced couples therapy, only 12 percent were licensed to do so.[64] In 2010, 40 percent of would-be husbands and wives received premarital counseling, often pastoral, and millions of married couples sought therapy. Doubtless, many received a great deal of help, expert and caring. Nevertheless, a 1995 *Consumer Reports* survey ranked marriage counselors last, among all other providers of mental health services, in achieving results. And the rise of couples counseling both coincided with and contributed to a larger shift in American life: heightened expectations for marriage as a means of self-expression and personal fulfillment.[65]

"I have a pretty good marriage," Elizabeth Weil wrote in a 2009 cover story for the *New York Times Magazine*, but "it could be better." This is America. Why settle for pretty good? Weil and her husband sought the services of half a dozen therapists.[66] Laurie Abraham's 2010 book, *The Husbands and Wives Club: A Year in the Life of a Couples Therapy Group*, began as a cover story in the *Times Magazine,* too. (The book's tagline—"Can These Marriages Be Saved?"—seemed to allude to Popenoe, but Abraham never mentioned him.) Abraham spent a year observing five couples undergoing group therapy with the Philadelphia clinician Judith Coché, whose work she admired. The group met for six-hour sessions, one weekend a month, including an annual Sex Weekend. Leigh and Aaron had been in Coché's care for a decade; by the end of the year they had broken new ground: "they may still be using the vibrator more than she'd prefer but Aaron is 'really there.'" Michael and Rachael had been discussing Michael's desire to buy a motorcycle. Rachael was against it. Michael was angry. Coché explained, "Rachael is chastising herself for being too emotional and 'overreacting,' echoing her parents' criticism of her; Michael is abruptly dropping his motorcycle dreams, capitulating rather than facing his wife's disapproval and distress." Later, Michael stated the problem differently: "'Um, the trouble is,' he says, 'Rachael's not a man.'" Between his first and second marriages, Michael slept with men. By the book's epilogue, Rachael has had a baby. When Michael professed his love for his wife, "the therapist chuckles deeply. 'That is so *wonderful.*'" Michael and Rachael have "wondered whether they'd still be married without the group." This reader wondered, too.[67]

That same year, Lori Gottlieb recounted her experience with computer dating in *Marry Him: The Case for Settling for Mr. Good Enough.* (Popenoe launched computer dating—an "Electronic Cupid"—in 1956, on a UNIVAC.)[68] Gottlieb was forty-one and a single mother. Determined to find a husband, she tried every possible matchmaking method, from speed dating to something called Cupid's Coach to signing up with Evan Marc Katz, a "personal trainer for love," who set about improving her marital fitness.[69] "Understanding the science of marriage gives us a crystal ball of sorts," wrote Tara Parker-Pope in *For Better: The Science of a Good Marriage,* also from 2010. Did you know that the first three minutes of an argument are the most important? That "strong marriages have at least a five-to-one daily ratio of positive to negative interactions," so that "for every mistake you make, you need to offer five more good moments, kind words, and loving gestures to keep your marriage in balance"? Parker-Pope, the author of the *Well* blog for the *New York Times,* explained that she had investigated the work of "top scientists" because "the best insights about love and relationships are coming from the scientific community." She cited a study titled "Ovulatory Cycle Effects on Tip Earnings by Lap Dancers" to argue that a woman shopping for a husband shouldn't take the Pill, because it suppresses ovulation, and lap dancers command more tips when they're ovulating. In a chapter titled "The Chore Wars," Parker-Pope attributed the "Housework Gap" (men don't clean) to heredity, since cutting-edge research has proven that "natural selection pressures resulted in neurobiological differences related to domestic skill."[70]

The Progressive era's conservative campaign to defend, protect, and improve marriage never really ended, either. Marriage is a stage of life in which the state plays a greater role than in any other. In 2009, the name Popenoe came up in *Perry v. Schwarzenegger*, a California case testing the constitutionality of Proposition 8, the state's 2008 anti-same-sex marriage act, which was modeled on the federal government's 1996 Defense of Marriage Act. Under cross-examination by David Boies, the plaintiff's attorney, a flustered David Blankenhorn, the founder of the Institute for American Values, exposed as having no scholarly expertise whatsoever, cast about for academic authorities to support his opposition to same-sex marriage. "Popenoe says that same sex marriage will reduce hetero marriage rates," Blankenhorn told the court. "I cannot prove in exact word formulation what he said. If he were sitting here, I believe that's what he would say." "I am asking you to tell us what these people have written," said Boies, "not what you think they'd say if they were here." Popenoe wasn't there, but he wasn't a ghost, either. Blankenhorn meant not Paul Popenoe but David Popenoe, Paul Popenoe's son, who once wrote that the institution of marriage "would surely be compromised by incorporating the marriage of same-sex couples."[71]

David Popenoe, a sociologist from Rutgers, was best known for his work on single mothers. In his most influential book, *Life Without Father*, he described what he called "the human carnage of fatherlessness." The nation, he worried, was at risk "of committing social suicide." In the "family values" 1990s, his controversial findings about the damage divorce does to children informed everything from Dan Quayle's attack on Murphy Brown to the 1996 Defense of Marriage Act itself.[72] Blankenhorn and David Popenoe had edited a book together, and each year, Blankenhorn's Institute for American Values and the National Marriage Project, founded by David Popenoe, published "The State of Our Unions," a report on marriage in America. In 2010, "The State of Our Unions" warned of a "mancession":

during an economic downturn, more men than usual were working fewer hours than their wives, making for unhappier husbands and angrier rows. A spike in the divorce rate was anticipated.[73]

Paul Popenoe stepped down as the director of the American Institute of Family Relations in 1976 and died three years later. David Popenoe wrestled, earnestly and openly, with his father's legacy. "What has puzzled me," he once wrote, "is how fast my father's name passed into oblivion." But, well into the twenty-first century, Paul Popenoe was all over the place, in Sex Weekend, in Cupid's Coach, in the hereditability of housework, in Proposition 8. David Popenoe, who had served on the board of directors of his father's American Institute of Family Relations, declined an invitation to take over the institute. In the 1980s, the institute floundered, then disappeared. In 1992, he went out to Los Angeles and drove down Sunset Boulevard, to see the place, near Hollywood and Vine, where his father had worked. Nothing looked familiar, except, on the side of the building, embossed on stucco, the faint shadow of a sign, long gone. He could just make out the letters.[74]

CHAPTER 6

Happiness Minutes

Ordering people around, which used to be just a way to get things done, was elevated to a science in October 1910 when Louis Brandeis, a fifty-three-year-old lawyer from Boston, held a meeting in an apartment in New York with a bunch of experts, including Frank and Lillian Gilbreth, who, at Brandeis's urging, decided to call what they were experts at "Scientific Management."[1] Everyone there, including Brandeis, had contracted "Tayloritis": they were enthralled by an industrial engineer from Philadelphia named Frederick Winslow Taylor, who had been ordering people around, scientifically, for years.[2] He made work fast, and even faster. "Speedy Taylor," as he was called, had invented a whole new way to make money. He would get himself hired by some business; spend a while watching everyone work, stopwatch and slide rule in hand; write a report telling them how to do their work faster; and then submit an astronomical bill for his invaluable services. He is the "Father of Scientific Management" (at least, that's what it says on his tombstone) and, by any rational calculation, the grandfather of management consulting.[3]

Whether he was also a shameless fraud is a matter of some debate, but not, it must be said, much: it's difficult to stage a debate when the preponderance of evidence falls to one side. Taylor fudged his data, lied to his clients, and inflated the record of his success. Why did it appeal to Louis Brandeis, who wasn't easily duped? Brandeis, born in Kentucky in 1856, was so young when he finished Harvard Law School, in 1876, with the highest grades anyone there had ever received, that Charles Eliot, the university's president, had to waive a minimum-age requirement to allow him to graduate. Brandeis swiftly earned a reputation as a hardheaded and public-minded reformer, the "people's attorney." The man who wrote *The Curse of Bigness* earnestly believed—and plainly, to some degree, he was right—that scientific management would improve the lot of the little guy by raising wages, reducing the cost of goods, and elevating the standard of living. "Of all the social and economic movements with which I have been connected," Brandeis wrote, "none seems to me to be equal to this in its importance and hopefulness."[4] Scientific management would bring justice to an unjust world. "Efficiency is the hope of democracy,"[5] he believed, and that's where it's possible to see what Dean Acheson, who clerked for Brandeis, meant when he said his boss was an "incurable optimist."[6]

In October 1910, Brandeis gathered Taylor's disciples—Taylor, busy man, sent his regrets—because he was preparing to argue in hearings before the Interstate Commerce Committee that railroad companies ought not to be allowed to raise their freight rates.[7] Brandeis had met Taylor and had read at least one of his books, *Shop Management* (1903), and he thought the railroads, rather than raising rates, should cut costs by Taylorizing: hire a man like Taylor, have him review their operations, and teach them to do everything more efficiently.[8] Taylor often called what he did "Task Management." The Gilbreths dubbed their system the "One Best Way." For the sake of the case, Brandeis wanted, for the whole shebang, one best name. At that October meeting, someone suggested calling it, simply, "Efficiency," the watchword of the day, but in the end the vote was unanimous in favor of "scientific management," which does have a nice ring to it, just like "home economics."

Scientific management promised to replace arbitrary standards—rules of thumb—with accurate measurements. Before the ICC, in a case for which he accepted no fee, Brandeis began by establishing that the railroads had no real idea why they charged what they did. When he questioned Charles Daly, the vice president of a New York railroad, Daly said that setting prices came down to judgment, and when Brandeis asked him to explain the basis for that judgment, Daly fell right into his trap. "The basis of my judgment," he began, "is exactly the same as the basis of a man who knows how to play a good game of golf. It comes from practice, contact and experience."

MR. BRANDEIS: I want to know, Mr. Daly, just as clearly as you can
  state it, whether you can give a single reason based on anything more
  than your arbitrary judgment, as you have expressed it.
MR. DALY: None whatsoever.
MR. BRANDEIS: None whatsoever?
MR. DALY: None whatsoever.[9]

Brandeis next set about demonstrating that freight rates could be determined—scientifically—by introducing, as evidence, Taylor's work at Bethlehem Steel Works. Before Taylor went to Bethlehem, a gang of seventy-five men loaded 92-pound pigs of iron onto railcars, at a rate of 12.5 tons per man per day. By timing the workers with a stopwatch, Taylor established that a "first-class man" could load pig iron at a rate of 47.5 tons per man per day, if only he would stop loafing. A boss could speed up a man, Taylor believed, the same way he could speed up a machine: with oil. Ironworkers, Taylor thought, were as dumb as dray horses, and ought to be dealt with accordingly. Most of them were also, to Taylor, the wealthy son of Philadelphia aristocrats, altogether foreign, something he made sure to underscore. He told the story of managing a man he called Schmidt.

"Schmidt, are you a high-priced man?"
"Vell, I don't know vat you mean. . . ."
"You see that car?"
"Yes."
"Well, if you are a high-priced man, you will load that pig iron on that car to-morrow for $1.85. Now do wake up and answer my question. Tell me whether you are a high-priced man or not."
"Vell, did I got $1.85 for loading dot pig iron on dot car to-morrow?"
"Yes, of course you do. . . ."
"Vell, dot's all right."[10]

("Who is this Schmidt," journalists asked, "and what ever happened to him?" Taylor wouldn't, couldn't say. He had more or less made him up.)

Brandeis's star witness turned out to be Frank Gilbreth, who, with his wife, Lillian, specialized in motion study. Where Taylor dissected a job into timed tasks, the Gilbreths divided human action into eighteen motions, which they called "therbligs"—it's an eponymous anagram—in order to determine the One Best Way to do a piece of work. Where Taylor used a stopwatch, the Gilbreths used a motion picture camera. On the stand, Gilbreth, a burly former bricklayer and consummate showman whose enthusiasm was contagious, grabbed a stack of law books, pretended they were bricks, and built a wall, explaining how to eliminate wasted motion. The commissioners, mesmerized, craned their necks and leaned over their desks to get a better view.[11] "This has become sort of a substitute for religion for you," said one of them, awed. (The gospel of efficiency, Taylor called it; some people called it the gospel of hope.)[12] With this, Gilbreth could only agree. (In his diary, Gilbreth once jotted down plans to write a book called *The Religion of Scientific Management*.)[13] Then Brandeis hushed the room by making an astonishing claim. The *New York Times* reported it this way:

ROADS COULD SAVE
$1,000,000 A DAY
Brandeis Says Scientific Management
Would Do It—Calls
Rate Increases Unnecessary.[14]

One million dollars a day! Suddenly, those theretofore obscure ICC hearings made national news. Brandeis won the case, and Taylor became a household word. In 1911, Taylor explained his methods—Schmidt and the pig iron, Gilbreth and the bricks—in *The Principles of Scientific Management*, a book the business überguru Peter Drucker once called "the most powerful as well as the most lasting contribution America has made to Western thought since the Federalist Papers."[15] That's either very silly or chillingly cynical, but *The Principles of Scientific Management* was the best-selling business book of the first half of the twentieth century.[16] Taylor had always said that scientific management would usher in a "mental revolution," and it did.[17] Modern life, and not just work life, is Taylorized life.[18] Above your desk, the clock ticks; on the shop floor, the camera rolls. Manage your time, waste no motion, multitask: your phone comes with a calendar, your breast pump comes with a stopwatch. "Who is Schmidt?" journalists wanted to know. Vell, ve are.

In 1908, Edwin Gay, a Harvard economics professor, visited Taylor in Philadelphia. Gay had been frustrated in his efforts to start a business school
at Harvard. "I am constantly being told by businessmen that we cannot
teach business," he complained. After meeting Taylor, Gay felt vindicated,
declaring, "I am convinced that there is a scientific method involved in
and underlying the art of business." If laws, scientific laws, deducible from
observation, govern the management of business, then business, as an academic discipline, was a much easier sell. Harvard Business School opened
the next year, with Gay as its dean. Taylor came to Cambridge and delivered
a series of lectures, which he repeated every year until his death.[19]

Taylor is the mortar, and the Gilbreths the bricks, of every American
business school. But it was Brandeis who brought Taylor national and
international acclaim.[20] He could not, however, have saved the railroads
one million dollars a day—that number was, as one canny reporter noted,
the "merest moonshine"—because, despite the parade of experts and algo-
rithms, one million dollars a day was based on little more than a ballpark
estimate that the railroads were about 5 percent inefficient.[21] That's how
Taylorism usually worked.

How did Taylor arrive at 47.5 tons for Bethlehem Steel? He chose twelve
men at random, observed them for an hour, and calculated that, at the rate
they were working, they were loading 23.8 tons of pig iron per man per day.
Then he handpicked ten "large powerful Hungarians" and dared them to
load 16.5 tons as fast as they could. A few managed to do it in under fourteen minutes; that comes out to a rate of 71 tons per hour. This number
Taylor inexplicably rounded up to 75. To get to 47.5, he decreased 75 by
about 40 percent, claiming that this represented a work-to-rest ratio of the
"law of heavy laboring." Workers who protested the new standards were
fired. Only one—the closest approximation of an actual Schmidt was a
man named Henry Noll—loaded anything close to 47.5 tons in a single day,
a rate that was, in any case, not sustainable. After providing two years of
consulting services, which could have saved Bethlehem Steel a maximum
of $40,000, Taylor billed $100,000 for his services (which works out to be
something like $2.5 million today), and then he was fired.[22]

Brandeis, like very many Progressives, believed Taylor, and believed *in*
him. What shocked him was that the unions didn't. Brandeis had long been
a labor hero. Convinced that lawyers, by taking the side of capital, had

"allowed themselves to become adjuncts of great corporations," he had worked to establish the standard of an eight-hour day and had deftly arbitrated labor disputes, including the New York Garment Workers strike of 1910.[23] But, early in 1911, delivering a speech called "Organized Labor and Efficiency" before the Boston Central Labor Union, he was heckled. "You can call it scientific management if you want to," one woman shouted, "but I call it scientific driving."[24]

Brandeis, ever hopeful, pressed on. The next year, he wrote the preface for Frank Gilbreth's *Primer on Scientific Management*, attempting to explain, once again, why unions should embrace it. "Under Scientific Management men are led, not driven," he insisted.[25] By then, Taylor had come under the scrutiny of the House Committee to Investigate Taylor and Other Systems of Shop Management. In the last months of 1911, the committee took testimony from sixty witnesses—workers and experts alike—and in January 1912, it called Taylor himself. Facing the committee chairman, William Bauchop Wilson, a Democrat from Pennsylvania who had gone down into the coal pits at the age of nine and joined the union at eleven, Taylor didn't offer up Schmidt and the pig iron—he had trotted out that story too many times, and people were getting suspicious—but he did tell another of his favorite yarns, the one about the science of shoveling coal. "The ordinary pig-iron handler," who is as dumb as a dray horse, is not suited to shoveling coal, Taylor said. "He is too stupid." ("Anything above 85 IQ in the case of a barber probably represents so much dead waste," Lewis Terman had written, explaining the great benefit of administering IQ tests to people before assigning them to any particular kind of work. This would speed things up, given that, as Terman believed, it had been well established that 15 percent of the "industrially inefficient" were of "the moron grade.")[26] A first-class man, though, Taylor continued, could lift a shovelful of coal weighing 21.5 pounds, and could move a pile of coal lickety-split.

"You have told us of the effect on the pile," an exasperated committee member said, "but what about the effect on the man?" Wilson wanted to know what happened to workers who weren't "first-class men."

THE CHAIRMAN: Scientific management has no place for such men?
MR. TAYLOR: Scientific management has no place for a bird that can sing and won't sing. . . .
THE CHAIRMAN: We are not . . . dealing with horses nor singing birds.

> We are dealing with men who are part of society and for whose
> benefit society is organized.[27]

Taylor knew he had performed badly. Asked to proof the transcript of his testimony, he ordered a lackey to steal Wilson's copy of *The Principles of Scientific Management*. Taylor had the idea that he could lift passages from his book and dump them into his testimony—replacing what he had actually said, under oath—but the switch would be too risky if Wilson had the chance to compare the transcript with the book.[28] He didn't get away with it. Speedy Taylor had met his match. The next year, the president appointed William Bauchop Wilson secretary of labor. But, by then, Taylorism had permeated the culture. So had therbligs. In 1913, an American magazine published a cartoon illustrating the fifteen unnecessary motions of a kiss.[29]

Speeding up production meant that workers came home knackered. Some of the ironworkers Taylor had timed in Bethlehem were so wrecked after a Taylor-sized day's work that they couldn't get out of bed the next morning. In 1914, Henry Ford announced a five-dollar, eight-hour workday—generous terms, at the start—but after that, salaries froze while the speed of production increased; meanwhile, Ford kept reducing his workforce.[30] As one of Ford's workers later put it, "Ye're worked like a slave all day and when ye get out ye're too tired to do anything."[31] Brandeis hoped that an auto worker might spend his evening at a lecture or a political rally, but more likely, he went home and collapsed on the couch while his wife (who, quite possibly, had put in eight hours at Ford's, too) made dinner and got the children ready for bed—efficiently. For lots of people, probably for most people, speeding up at work—which you might think would mean slowing down at home, enjoying that promised land of leisure—meant just the opposite: home got sped up, too.[32] No one knew that better than Frank Gilbreth's wife, who had rather a lot to say on the subject of exhaustion, and who understood, better than Taylor and Brandeis did, that scientific management isn't the kind of thing you can leave at the office, or on the factory floor.

Lillian Gilbreth, who first met Taylor in 1907, was pregnant with her fifth child when she attended that meeting with Brandeis in New York in October 1910. Taylor taught efficiency; Brandeis championed it; Gilbreth lived it.

Born in Oakland in 1878, she graduated from the University of California in 1900 and married Frank Gilbreth four years later. They agreed to have twelve children, six boys and six girls, and to raise them by the most scientific methods. In 1800, the fertility rate among white women in the United States was over seven; by 1900, it was half that.[33] The Gilbreths' plan was, at some level, a eugenics project: the fit should have more children, and *could* have more children, if only they would follow scientific methods. In an era of rapidly shrinking family size, the Gilbreths' household, a laboratory of efficiency, would show the world what economies of scale were all about.

Between 1905 and 1922, Lillian gave birth thirteen times, at about fifteen-month intervals; one child died, at the age of five, of diphtheria. She breast-fed every baby. The zaniness of the Gilbreths' family life was recalled by two of their children in *Cheaper by the Dozen*, published in 1948 and made into a film, two years later, starring Myrna Loy as "Boss," which is what Frank called his wife.[34] Lillian disliked the book and was embarrassed by the film, not least because both completely ignored the fact that, during those years, she ran a consulting business, became the first pioneer of scientific management to earn a doctorate, and wrote very many books.

Admittedly, it's hard to see past all those pregnancies. In 1906, after the San Francisco earthquake, William Randolph Hearst offered a hundred dollars to anyone who had a baby in one of the city's emergency hospitals. Frank, who was in the city courting building contracts, wrote to his wife, ribbing her, "I think there is a chance for it if you hurry."[35] He named their summer place the Shoe, after the woman with too many children who lived in one and didn't know what to do. Once, when he told a colleague, "Lillie always feels better when she is pregnant," the other guy shot back, "How the hell can she tell?"[36]

It always bugged Lillian that lying-in hospitals took all her pencils and notebooks away.[37] But once she was home, she got back at it. Frank considered postpartum bed rest wasted time ("Dear Boss," he wrote, "*MOTION IS MONEY*"),[38] so Lillian used the weeks after childbirth to edit her husband's books, most of which she also coauthored—or, as some scholars believe, authored entirely, even when her name didn't appear on the title page. (Lillian's prose is distinctively "gabby," as Frank put it.) In 1911, she edited *Motion Study* after giving birth to Frank junior, and it was likely Lillian, not her husband, who really wrote *The Primer of Scientific Management*.[39] The next year, the Gilbreths moved to Rhode Island so that Lillian could enroll in a PhD program at Brown; there she studied psychology, which is what she thought was missing from Taylorism. (She wouldn't have been able to go to Harvard, which refused to grant a PhD to a woman.) In Providence, the Gilbreths lived so close to campus, Frank joked, that Lillian "could go to class and if a child fell out of the window, catch him before he landed on the ground."[40]

Lillian kept what she called "Mother's Daily Schedule." It read, in part:

5.	Begin the day of work	10.00
6.	Work on book	10.00–12.00
7.	With children	12.00–12.15
8.	Lunch	12.15–1.00
9.	With children	1.00–2.00
10.	Nap	2.00–2.30
11.	With baby	2.30–3.00
12.	Work on book	3.00–4.00[41]

Meanwhile, Taylorized workers kept complaining about being bone-tired. In 1912, molders at an arsenal in Watertown, Massachusetts, refused to work under the eye of a timekeeper. During an investigation into the ensuing strike, it came out that Taylor had told his timekeeper not to bother too much with the stopwatch; better to simply make "a rough guess." Pouring a mold and making a gun carriage usually took fifty-three minutes; Taylor's timekeeper told the molders to do it in twenty-four. In a petition to their boss, the molders wrote, "This we believe to be the limit of our endurance. It is humiliating to us, who have always tried to give the Government the best of what was in us. This method is un-American in principle."[42]

Taylor, plagued by controversy, grew ill. He sent Frank Gilbreth to deliver lectures in his stead. The Gilbreths, though, had misgivings about Taylorism. In 1913, when Frank was substituting for Taylor in Chicago, Lillian went along, with a nursing three-month-old. Onstage, Frank was challenged by Emma Goldman. He was pointing to a chart illustrating the hierarchical relationship between the foreman and the worker. "There is nothing in scientific management for the workman," Goldman shouted. "The only scheme is to have the workman support the loafers on top of him." Lillian leaned over and whispered something to Frank, who cheerfully turned the chart upside down.[43] That was a cheap stunt, but Lillian had an argument to make, too, which she put forward in *The Psychology of Management,* published in 1914: "The emphasis in successful management lies on the *man,* not on the *work.*"[44] And maybe even on the women and children, too.

Gilbreth defended her dissertation in June 1915. Three months later, she fell down a flight of stairs, went into labor, and gave birth to a stillborn baby.[45] Taylor had died that spring. After reading in a fawning biography of Taylor how much workers loved him, an appalled Frank Gilbreth scrawled in the margin, "But none came to his funeral, nor to his memorial service."[46] Brandeis was there, though, and delivered a speech, later printed in *Harper's* under the title "Efficiency by Consent." Brandeis's ideas about management were actually far closer to the Gilbreths' than to Taylor's.[47] Taylor thought men were mules. Brandeis advocated industrial democracy: workers must have a voice in how a business is run.[48] One of the Gilbreths' lasting, if futile, workplace innovations is the suggestion box.[49] Taylor took nothing from the Watertown Arsenal strike except that it might be better "not to try to hurry task work too fast."[50] Brandeis insisted that for workers to enjoy sufficient leisure to participate in a democratic society, productivity had to be increased, but he also worried that, without unions, workers would be pushed past the limits of human endurance. That's why unions, he believed, ought to consent to efficiency.[51] The Gilbreths' firm, Gilbreth, Inc., made a policy of requiring contracts to be signed by both shop bosses and representatives from organized labor.[52]

The year after Taylor died, Brandeis was nominated to serve on the Supreme Court. His support of unions made the nomination one of the most controversial in the court's history.[53] The controversy, Brandeis observed, was because he "is considered a radical and is a Jew." Harvard president Lawrence Lowell circulated a petition decrying Brandeis's nomination, but when Lowell's predecessor, Charles Eliot, sent a letter of support, a friend of Brandeis's boasted, "Next to a letter from God, we have got the best."[54] Brandeis took a seat on the court in June 1916; he soon became famous for fastidiously revising his opinions, whose sole purpose, he believed, was to educate. "Now I think the opinion is persuasive," he told one weary clerk, after the umpteenth draft, "but what can we do to make it more instructive?"[55]

The year Brandeis was seated on the court, Lillian Gilbreth wrote a book called *Fatigue Study* while recovering from the birth of her ninth child.

Taylor had written about fatigue, too, but exhaustion was Lillian Gilbreth's specialty. The Gilbreths pioneered what has since come to be called "ergonomics." They built, for instance, special chairs for different types of work and urged a consumer campaign called "Buy of the seated worker." They even opened, in Providence, the Museum of Devices for Eliminating Unnecessary Fatigue.[56] Taylor had studied fatigue, too (he had, after all, offered up that work-to-rest ratio), but Gilbreth had a different kind of firsthand knowledge of what it meant to be at the limits of physical endurance. She also shared Brandeis's view that profit wasn't everything. ("The greater productivity of labor must not be only attainable," Brandeis said, at Taylor's memorial service, "but attainable under conditions consistent with the conservation of health, the enjoyment of work, and the development of the individual.")[57] The whole point of efficiency, Lillian Gilbreth said, was to maximize "Happiness Minutes."[58] Happiness minutes? For Gilbreth, scientific management was a way of life, a habit of mind, and a religion, all at once. It was her science of human life. Happiness wasn't a mansion anymore; it was a minute.

In 1918, Gilbreth was invited to lecture about fatigue at MIT. She must have been practicing the talk at home. One night, the children invited her to play a game of charades. "What do you think the first one was?" she wrote to Frank. "Well, it was 'Fatigue Survey.' How is that for breathing it in?"[59] The day of the lecture, she got five children ready for school, nursed her four-month-old, handed the two toddlers over to her housekeeper, and caught a ten o'clock train. In Cambridge, she talked for twenty minutes about the effects of fatigue and showed thirty-six slides (reporting to Frank that she tried very hard to speak like a scientist and "not like a Lady"), but when asked to stay late, she told her host that she had eight children to get home to. ("That seemed to interest him a lot," she remarked.) She made it back to Providence for the six-thirty p.m. nursing.[60]

In 1919, in childbed after delivering baby number ten, Lillian proofread the galleys of *Motion Study for the Handicapped* (the Gilbreths had worked with soldiers who had lost limbs; aiding the disabled was a long-standing Gilbreth motion-study specialty).[61] And then, in 1924, Frank Gilbreth died at the age of fifty-five, leaving his wife with eleven children under the age of nineteen.[62] Although she didn't have much money, she was determined to send all of them to college. She tried, desperately, to drum up business. She had sometimes published as "L. M. Gilbreth." After discovering that the president of Gilbreth, Inc., was a woman, the Johnson & Johnson company hired her to study menstruation, whereupon Gilbreth dutifully made a thorough study of the sanitary napkin. Many more clients, however, simply dropped their accounts.[63] She scrambled. Finally, she decided to reinvent herself as an expert in a subject about which she knew next to nothing: housekeeping.

Housework used to be everyone's work; industrialization made it merely women's work. Coal-burning stoves meant that men didn't have to cut, haul, and split wood; women still had to tend the stove. That stove saved a man work; it saved a woman nothing. In 1841, in *A Treatise on Domestic Economy,* Catherine Beecher called housework endless; a century and a half later, it was still endless. Women complaining about exhaustion sound almost the same from the seventeenth century to the twenty-first: "I am daily dropped in little pieces and passed around and devoured and expected to be whole again next day." That was written in 1888, but it could have been written a century before or a century later.[64]

Progressives had the idea of making housekeeping a science and, therefore, efficient. The American Home Economics Association was founded in 1909, after some debate over whether to call the field "domestic science." For a while, housekeeping, like business, aspired to be an academic discipline, and on no better grounds.[65] In that effort, Gilbreth seems an unlikely figure. Her husband had always endorsed a three-man plan of promotion. There's the guy at the bottom, studying to be the guy in the middle, and the guy in the middle, studying to be the guy at the top. "Don't waste your time on housework, Boss," he told his wife. "You're studying for *my* job."[66] "She couldn't cook, never had done any laundry, didn't know much about sewing or knitting, and never had run a house of her own," her children said.[67] About kitchens, one of her sons wrote, "Stoves burned her, ice picks stabbed her, graters skinned her, and paring knives cut her." Her housekeeper, an Irishman named Tom Grieves, did all the cooking. Gilbreth knew how to make exactly one meal, which she made on Grieves's day off: creamed chipped beef. Her children called it DVOT: Dog's Vomit on Toast.[68]

Gilbreth might have gotten the idea for turning to the science of housework from Christine Frederick, a Long Island housewife who, in 1912, wrote a series of essays for the *Ladies' Home Journal* that was published the next year as *The New Housekeeping: Efficiency Studies in Home Management* and expanded, in 1915, as *Household Engineering: Scientific Management in the Home.* Frederick, who was married to a business executive, had overheard him talking about scientific management one evening after work and decided she could use the ideas of Taylor and the Gilbreths to manage her home. She eventually turned her Long Island home into the Applecroft Kitchen Home Experiment Station.[69]

In the 1920s, Lillian Gilbreth engineered model kitchens—one was called the Kitchen Efficient—and purported to eliminate, for instance, five out of every six steps in the making of coffee cake. To make a lemon meringue pie, a housewife working in an ordinary kitchen walked 224 feet; in the Kitchen Efficient, Gilbreth claimed, it could be done in 92.[70] The increasingly strange study of fatigue went on without her. In 1926, by which year Gilbreth had become the chief consultant for several American universities' new departments of home economics,[71] the Harvard Business School opened its Fatigue Laboratory: professors put students on treadmills, and kept them on till they dropped.[72] A few years later, a team from the Fatigue Laboratory went to Mississippi to measure the sweat of sharecroppers ("colorfully-dressed, happy, and well-behaved negroes") as against the exertion of mules.[73]

In 1927, Gilbreth published *The Home-maker and Her Job.* The goal of homemaking, she explained, was to maximize Happiness Minutes for everyone in the family.[74] A housewife should make a study of the science of dishwashing, so as to find the One Best Way. "In washing dishes, Mary may have the best posture, Mother may move her eyes and head least, Johnny may move his feet least, Sarah may make the best use of her hands." The trick was to combine the best of everyone's methods, and then Mary, Mother, Johnny, and Sarah could spend more time doing something other than washing the dishes.[75]

In 1935, Lillian Gilbreth, who did not wash dishes, accepted a professorship at Purdue. Her appointment was divided between the university's School of Home Economics and its sibling, the School of Management. Home economics and business management have Lillian Gilbreth in common, and a lot more, too. Scientific housekeeping, with its standards of spotlessness and shininess, was founded on no less a fudge than that 47.5 tons of pig iron.[76] Tom Grieves was Gilbreth's Schmidt. "Nobody but me never washed a Goddam tub around here in their whole lives," Grieves once told Frank junior. "You know what a Motion Study is, Frankie-boy? You study how to get someone else to make all your motions for you, for Christ sake." Grieves refused to work in the Kitchen Efficient. He didn't want a rolling cart: "Hell, I ain't going to be cooped up like a beejeezeley, sweet-smelling, bobbed-haired housewife, pushing a Goddam worktable around." He complained about the old refrigerator—"the same Goddam kind of icebox that the Goddam Pilgrim Fathers had to use, for Christ sake"—but rejected a new one; he was unwilling to give up the sociable daily visits of the iceman, who was a good friend of his.[77] Reporters who wanted to profile Gilbreth couldn't go into her actual kitchen;[78] they had to visit the fake one. About her domestic life, Gilbreth does not appear to have been sentimental. After Gilbreth's youngest child left home, she had her house demolished.[79]

Gilbreth tried to teach people to save time for joy, but not everyone wants to hurry a pie. Sometimes the best part is rolling the dough too thin so you've got some extra for jam tarts, and to play with. In the Taylorized world, something was lost. Neither unions nor businesses lived up to Brandeis's optimism. "If the fruits of Scientific Management are directed into the proper channels," he believed, "the workingman will get not only a fair share, but a very large share, of the industrial profits arising from improved industry."[80] That share went, instead, to shareholders and, later, to CEOs. Meanwhile, home and work, separated since the first stirrings of the Industrial Revolution, began growing back together again. Efficiency was meant to make for a shorter workday, but in the final two decades of the twentieth century, the average American added 164 hours of work over the course of a year; that's a whole extra month's time, but not, typically, a month's worth of either Happiness Minutes or civic participation.[81] Eating dinner standing up while making a phone call to the office, supervising a third grader's homework, and nursing a baby—or pumping your breast milk—is not the hope of democracy.

Lillian Gilbreth died of a stroke in Scottsdale, Arizona, in 1972, at the age of ninety-three. She was cremated. The *New York Times* ran an obituary headed "Dr. Gilbreth, Engineer, Mother of Dozen."[82] She had always believed that what the world needed was "a new philosophy of work."[83] She never did manage to write it.

CHAPTER 7

Confessions of an Amateur Mother

ailing back from a trip to Europe not long after the First World War, George Hecht fell to chatting with a fellow passenger, a charming but fretful lady. "I have failed," she confided to him, "where every woman wants to succeed: as a mother." Hecht, who didn't have any children of his own but who was keeping an eye out for business opportunities, found himself fascinated. When he got back to the States, he started reading child-rearing manuals. "They were all great big thick books," he noticed. During the war, Hecht had served in the government's Office of Public Information, where he'd helped found the Bureau of Cartoons. In 1918, he had published a collection, *The War in Cartoons*, a history of the war in one hundred cartoons. The year after that, he started publishing *Better Times*, "the Smallest Newspaper in the World." Hecht wrote the whole paper, which was a weekly, and pretty good. He liked pictures; he liked little books. He got to thinking that what that lady needed, to learn how to be a better mother, wasn't another great big thick book; it was a well-illustrated magazine.[1]

The first American magazine for mothers, *Mother's Magazine*, was published out of Utica, New York, in the 1830s and '40s, a product of the Second Great Awakening. It was meant to help mothers by filling a "chasm in their library." Its essays included "Family Worship" and "Habits of Prayer, Early Formed." *Mother's Magazine* was pious and evangelical; it was the periodical equivalent of the Mansion of Happiness, teaching mothers "the nurture of the soul" of the child "from its earliest watch over the cradle-dream to the full development of that mysterious being, whose destiny is immortality."[2]

But by the 1920s, *Mother's Magazine* was long gone, and so was that era, and, surely, Hecht thought, motherhood had changed, just as childhood and adolescence and marriage and work had changed. Everything was getting speedier and more scientific. Then, too, if there ever was a moment in American history to launch a magazine, this was it. Americans were buying magazines like never before. DeWitt Wallace started *Reader's Digest* in 1922; Henry Luce and his former Yale classmate Briton Hadden started *Time* in 1923.[3]

Time, in fact, had a great deal in common with Hecht's little newspaper, *Better Times*. It, too, was an abridgment of the week's news. In the Taylorized age of efficiency, speedy Americans, Hecht and Luce and Hadden believed, were too busy to read the daily paper. For people who measured time in Happiness Minutes, the *New York Times*, just like those big, heavy parenting manuals, was too long. It was also "unreadable," too dense, too demanding; *Time* would be everything, abridged: a week's worth of news in twenty-four pages that could be read in an hour. An early bid for subscribers read, "Take TIME: It's Brief."

Hecht's *Better Times* was small, the smallest newspaper in the world, not much bigger than an index card; it measured less than four inches by five. Luce and Hadden came up with a different gimmick, and theirs was slicker and smarter. Their pages would be big, but their stories would be short. Each issue was to contain one hundred articles, none over four hundred words long. They put together dummy issues by cutting sentences out of seven days' worth of newspapers and pasting them onto pages. At first, *Time* was a kind of clipping service, assembly-line news, manufactured in a Taylorized shop. If not for *Reader's Digest* and another rival, the *Literary Digest*, they might have called it a "digest." They sorted the news into categories—national affairs, the arts, sports—which, amazingly, hadn't been done before. "The one great thing was simplification," Luce wrote. "Simplification by organization, simplification by condensation, and also simplification by just being damn well simple." Theodore Roosevelt's Simplified Spelling Board had lobbed the extra "e" from abridgment. Turning the *Times* into *Time* was a savings of a letter, right there. No wasted letters, no wasted thought. As Luce and Hadden explained in the magazine's prospectus, "TIME is interested—not in how much it includes between its covers—but in HOW MUCH IT GETS OFF ITS PAGES INTO THE MINDS OF ITS READERS." They also clipped their prose. "You're writing for straphangers," an old professor of theirs advised. "You've got to write staccato." Hadden marked up a translation of Homer's *Iliad*, underscoring compound phrases, like "wine-dark sea." ("A sea as dark as wine" dragged.) No longer did events take place "in the nick of time"; they happened, instead, "in time's nick."[4]

Time was meant for businessmen; the magazine's advertising department puffed that its subscribers were "America's most important and interesting class—the Younger Business Executive." A poll conducted five years after *Time* began reported that 80 percent of its subscribers were "plainly of the *executive and professional* class"; 62 percent owned stocks and bonds; more than 50 percent had servants; more than 40 percent belonged to country clubs; and 11 percent owned horses. These were the nation's small and big businessmen, striving; one *Time* brochure asked, "Can you afford to be *labeled* as a man from Main Street?"[5]

George Hecht must have paid close attention to the launch of *Time*. He had been beaten at his own game. And so, in 1924, he began raising money for a magazine about parenting—*Time* for parents. Harold Ross was trying to find backers that year, too, writing a prospectus for the *New Yorker*, a magazine meant to be everything *Time* wasn't. Where Luce and Hadden had announced that *Time* would be edited "so that a mind trained or untrained can grasp it with minimum effort," Ross explained that his magazine "will assume a reasonable degree of enlightenment on the part of its readers." It would not save anyone any time; it would not spare anyone any effort. There would be goings-on, but it wasn't going to be newsy. "As compared to the newspapers, *The New Yorker* will be interpretive rather than stenographic," he wrote. Ross wanted his magazine to be distinguished for its wit, art, integrity, and discrimination. He noted, "It will hate bunk." The *New Yorker*, he said, "is not of that group of publications engaged in tapping the Great Buying Power of the North American steppe region by trading mirrors and colored beads in the form of our best brands of hokum."[6]

George Hecht, though, was keen to sell timely bunk, not to mention the nation's best brands of hokum. Modern, speedy mothers were as busy as businessmen, he figured, and just as concerned with success and efficiency and the opinions of Main Street. The sort of women who read zippy books like Christine Frederick's time-saving guides *New Housekeeping* and *Household Engineering* didn't have time to read big, heavy child-rearing manuals. They could read his little monthly magazine. And, to protect their babies and children, they would buy anything, so long as they could be kept good and worried.

For an editor, Hecht wanted a woman. He required "that she be a college graduate, that she should have had an editorial position preferably with a woman's magazine, that she should be able to write if dire necessity ever required it of her, that she be married and that she should be a mother."[7] It might not be a bad idea if she were a worrier, too. He looked around. And then he called into his office Clara Savage Littledale, ex–woman's page reporter, former war correspondent, mother of one, future editor of *Parents* magazine.

If stages of life are artifacts, parenthood seems, at first, different. There have always been parents, and parents have always been besotted by their children, awestruck by their impossible beauty, dopey high jinks, and strange little minds. But the word "parenthood" dates only to the middle of the nineteenth century, and the notion that parenthood is a distinct stage of life, shared by men and women, is, historically, in its infancy. An ordinary life used to look something like this: born into a growing family, you help raise your siblings, have the first of your own half dozen or even dozen children soon after you're grown, and die before your youngest has left home. In the early 1800s, when American women could expect to bear between seven and eight children, life expectancy hadn't reached forty.[8] To be an adult was to be a parent, except that people didn't usually think of themselves as "parents"; they were mothers or fathers, and everyone knew that there was a world of difference between the two.

In George Hecht's day, all that was changing, which is what worried eugenicists like Paul Popenoe. The Gilbreths aside, many people, especially wealthier people, were having fewer children, living longer, and starting families later in life. Why? Economists, sociologists, and anthropologists have offered all sorts of theories to explain this change, including the price of land, the cost of labor, industrialization, the market revolution, and rising literacy rates. But the fertility rate began to fall, in the American colonies, around 1750, a century before it began to fall in most of the rest of the Western world, and long before any real advances in contraception. Methods practiced since antiquity included abstinence, abortion, infanticide, prolonged breast-feeding, herbal abortifacients, barriers like pessaries, and, most commonly, withdrawal. Not until the widespread vulcanization of rubber in the 1850s was there any significant technological advance in contraception. What seems to have happened is that American women, caught up in the late eighteenth century's revolution against authority, accomplished a domestic revolution: they extracted from their husbands help in limiting family size by the most easily available method, withdrawal. They joined the revolution by controlling their childbearing. "At length over wedlock fair liberty dawns," one almanac put it, in 1771. "And the Lords of Creation must pull in their horns."[9] Ahem.

The demographic transition altered both the ages of man and the voyage of life. In the eighteenth century, almost everyone lived in households with children in them. Living longer while having fewer children meant that the slice of the population consisting of adults who did not have children at home—people who would never have children, hadn't had them yet, or had already had them and now had an empty nest—grew. In 1880, 70 percent of American adults lived in households with children under the age of fifteen; by 1920, by which time the average American woman was bearing only about three children, that percentage had fallen to 55.[10] For the first time ever, adulthood no longer implied parenthood. Your chances, as an adult, of living with children at any given moment were not much more than one in two. In the wealthier classes, childbearing and child rearing no longer circumscribed every woman's life; motherhood and fatherhood, while not the same, had more in common than ever before. All these changes, aggregated, transformed parenthood, which began to look mystifying, especially to the increasing numbers of people who had *not* grown up raising their siblings, neighbors, cousins, or nieces and nephews and who, it turned out, had no idea how to bathe or dress or soothe a baby. Looking after babies and little kids is hard work, but as the number of children dwindled, so did the number of middle- and upper-class adults with any real skill at doing it. In stepped experts, who generally wanted to encourage wealthier families to have more children, and poorer families to have fewer. Parental-advice literature, like *Mother's Magazine,* had proliferated beginning in the first half of the nineteenth century, but the science of parenting dates to the Progressive era, when turning middle-class parents into amateur scientists was the work, mainly, of journalists.[11]

Clara Savage, born in Belfast, Maine, in 1891, was the youngest of six children. Her father was a Unitarian minister. She grew up in Medfield, Massachusetts. Starting when she was fifteen, she kept a diary.[12] She wanted to be a reporter, and while still a student at Smith, she wrote features for the *New York Times.* She was just the kind of college girl Paul Popenoe was concerned about. After graduating in 1913, she became the first woman reporter hired by the *New York Evening Post,* where she was assigned to cover the suffrage movement. She had grander ambitions, but at the *Post,* as elsewhere, women weren't allowed into the newsroom; she was named editor of the paper's women's page. (Joseph Pulitzer had started the first women's page in 1886, in the *New York World.* Women's pages lasted for about a century. In 1969, the *Washington Post* renamed its "For and About Women" page the Style section; other newspapers soon followed suit. Motherhood blogs, which turned up in online newspapers in the early twenty-first century, were something of a throwback.)[13] For the *Post,* Savage interviewed Ida Tarbell and Charlotte Perkins Gilman. She wrote about shopgirls and suffrage. She reported, too, on eugenics. "Much telephoning to find out where and when the Executive Committee on Race Betterment would meet," she once wrote in her diary. "It took three of them to tell me. If they're as executive about bettering the race—!"[14]

Savage also fretted, constantly, about what it meant for her to work. "Read 'The Diary of a Working Woman' by Adelheid Popp," she wrote in her own diary one day. (In her autobiography, Popp, an Austrian socialist and labor organizer, chronicles the horrors of toiling in factories and workhouses, from childhood, a life she declared not fit for a human being.)[15] But Savage had scant interest in socialism or social problems like economic inequality. She was young and nervous and ambitious; she was chiefly interested in her plight as a career girl. Her diary is a litany of self-rebuke, one apology nipping at the heels of another. "I ought to be more appealing when I'm out for news and not just think I'm a business woman in same basis as a man reporter," Savage wrote. "Very stupid of me!" She was keenly aware of her professional vulnerability: women reporters were the first fired. "Saw Peiser at lunch," she recorded. "And she told me the Mail had given up its women's page and she and Miss Cole are just suddenly dropped! I'd rather have $20 a wk. on the Post than $40 on the Mail!" She worried, especially, about whether she should be working at all: "I lay on the couch, was tired and *lonesome* for—oh! well, merely for a house, husband and baby!" But when she interviewed working mothers, she found herself judging them. "Put a teacher-mother story together, feeling very archaic because I believe that a mother's place is in the home. Why they want to teach when they have tiny babies is beyond me!"

She wondered, again and again, whether she would ever have a family of her own. "Lunch with Agnes," she wrote, "who propounded the theory that it was economically wrong for every woman to insist on having her own children. 'Adopt orphans!' cried Agnes so loudly that a man sitting opposite dropped his fork to listen." On the subject of raising a family, Savage was both dreamy and frustrated: "Marriage and children are the biggest and most beautiful thing that can come to a woman. I don't see any prospect of either." At the *Post,* she met a Pulitzer Prize–winning reporter named Harold Littledale. Early on, he broached the subject of motherhood, which Savage found more shocking than talking about sex, noting in her diary, "Come to think of it, that's the one thing I've never discussed with a man."

While Clara Savage was dating Harold Littledale, another ambitious New Yorker, Margaret Sanger, was arguing that a lot of things that couldn't be discussed ought to be. Sanger, born in New York in 1879, was the sixth of eleven children, one of whom she helped deliver when she was eight years old. Her mother, a poor and devout Irish Roman Catholic, died at the age of fifty; her father, a stonecutter and a socialist, lived to be eighty-four. Sanger always attributed her mother's ruined health and early death, from tuberculosis, to the exhaustion of bearing and raising children. Sanger suffered from tuberculosis as well. Nevertheless, she trained as a nurse and began caring for poor immigrant women living in tenements on New York's Lower East Side. They begged her for information about how to avoid pregnancy. They could see that wealthy women were having fewer babies: How did they manage it? Sanger wrote, "The doomed women implored me to reveal the 'secret' rich people had, offering to pay me extra to tell them; many really believed I was holding back information for money." Sanger had her own idea of what needed to be on a "women's page." In 1913, she wrote a twelve-part series on sex education for the *Call,* the Socialist Party's daily, titled "What Every Girl Should Know." Since its discussion of venereal disease violated federal obscenity laws, Sanger's final essay, "Some Consequences of Ignorance and Silence," was suppressed, leading the *Call* to publish an announcement in its place: " 'What Every Girl Should Know'—NOTHING."

Sanger and Savage lived in the same city during these years, but they saw that city through very different lenses. Savage met the same desperately poor and overburdened immigrant women Sanger met, and found herself not only not moved to action but mystified and irritated. She wrote in her diary in February 1914, "Off to Ellis Island where I talked to a Russian family—12 children and a Father—the mother in the hospital for another baby. They were fine but I don't see why some people have so many and others none." Both Savage and Sanger went to hear Charlotte Perkins Gilman speak in New York that winter. "All this talk, for and against and about babies, is by men," Gilman said in a speech she gave around that time. "One would think the men bore the babies, nursed the babies, reared the babies."[16] Sanger was impressed.[17] Savage was annoyed, writing in her diary, "She has a lovely face but a harsh voice and I didn't like her especially." Savage went to see Gilman again that April and liked her even less: "she made me *furious.* I dislike her manner and voice so much."

In March 1914, Margaret Sanger, now thirty-four years old and a mother of three, began publishing the *Woman Rebel,* an eight-page feminist monthly, urging her readers to "look the whole world in the face with a go-to-hell look in the eye." In its first issue, Sanger stated her case: "Is there any reason why women should not receive clean, harmless, scientific knowledge on how to prevent conception?"[18] In the *Woman Rebel,* Sanger advocated "birth control," a term she coined. Six of the monthly's seven issues were declared unmailable and seized. Indicted for violating obscenity laws, Sanger fled the country, leaving her husband and children behind.[19]

In New York, Savage, now twenty-three and still single, kept writing stories for the women's page. Assigned to interview "a little woman whose husband goes to war tomorrow leaving her with a tiny baby, no money and no English!" she reported, "I didn't realize *how* bad this was till I saw that woman." But Clara Savage was no more gripped by the plight of the poor or the mission of Margaret Sanger than she had been by Adelheid Popp or Charlotte Perkins Gilman. Although she took a job as press secretary of the National Woman Suffrage Association, her political commitment was lukewarm: "Lunched with Ethel at the Club and of course we talked suffrage which is the dearest thing in life to her—but not to me!"

In 1915, Clara Savage became *Good Housekeeping*'s Washington correspondent.[20] Margaret Sanger returned to the United States in October of that year. After Sanger's five-year-old daughter died of pneumonia, the charges against her were dropped; the prosecution decided that bringing a grieving mother to trial for distributing information about birth control would only aid her cause. She embarked on a national speaking tour. She debated Paul Popenoe in Washington, Popenoe opposing birth control as fervently as Sanger endorsed it.

On October 16, 1916, Sanger opened the United States' first birth control clinic, in Brooklyn. In a poor tenement neighborhood, she rented a storefront from a landlord named Rabinowitz, who lowered the rent when she told him what she was going to use the space for. She wrote a letter to the Brooklyn district attorney, informing him of her plan. Then she posted handbills in English, Italian, and Yiddish:

MOTHERS!
Can you afford to have a large family?
Do you want any more children?
If not, why do you have them?
DO NOT KILL, DO NOT TAKE LIFE, BUT PREVENT
Safe, Harmless Information can be obtained at
46 AMBOY STREET.

On the day the clinic opened, Jewish and Italian women pushing prams and with toddlers in tow lined up around the corner, Sanger recalled, "some shawled, some hatless, their red hands clasping the cold, chapped, smaller ones of their children." They paid ten cents to register. Then Sanger or Byrne met with seven or eight at once to show them how to use pessaries.

Nine days later, an undercover policewoman came, posing as a mother of two who couldn't afford any more children. Mindell sold her a copy of "What Every Girl Should Know." Byrne discussed contraception with her. The next day, the police arrived, confiscated the examination table, shut down the clinic, and arrested Sanger.

Mindell was convicted on obscenity charges; her conviction was eventually overturned. Byrne and Sanger were charged with violating a section of the New York State Penal Code, under which it was illegal to distribute "any recipe, drug, or medicine for the prevention of conception." (The fear was that contraception promotes promiscuity.) Byrne's lawyer argued that the penal code was unconstitutional because it infringed on a woman's right to the "pursuit of happiness." She was found guilty. Sentenced to thirty days, she went on a hunger strike and nearly died. An editorial in the *New York Tribune* begged the governor to issue a pardon, threatening him with the judgment of history: "It will be hard to make the youth of 1967 believe that in 1917 a woman was imprisoned for doing what Mrs. Byrne did."

At Sanger's trial, during which the judge waved a cervical cap from the bench, Sanger hoped to argue that the law preventing the distribution of contraception was unconstitutional: exposing women, against their will, to the danger of dying in childbirth violated a woman's right to life. The judge allowed that doctors could prescribe contraception—which is what made it possible, subsequently, for Sanger to open more clinics—but ruled that no woman has "the right to copulate with a feeling of security that there will be no resulting conception": if a woman isn't willing to die in childbirth, she shouldn't have sex. Sanger went to Queens County Penitentiary. She was sentenced to thirty days.[21]

The month after Sanger was released from prison, she published, in the *Birth Control Review,* an essay by Popenoe, whose point was that "birth control as at present practiced in the United States is the reverse of eugenic."[22] Hard-line eugenicists like Popenoe almost always objected to birth control; but the more eugenicists objected to her agenda, the more vigorously Sanger courted their support.

Meanwhile, eugenicists kept worrying about race suicide, exactly because college-educated women like Clara Savage were working instead of marrying and having babies or, almost as bad, were marrying and having babies but not having enough of them, or not raising them well enough. Eugenicists therefore insisted that Anglo-Saxon parents needed not birth control but parental education, urgently: the unfit races, with their teeming hordes of dark-eyed children, seemed to know how to take care of babies, instinctively, like animals, but fit parents, with their small families, were woefully ignorant. Social services that helped poor mothers were interfering with the workings of natural selection. What were fit women to do?

In the *Journal of Heredity*, in 1916, Popenoe published an influential monograph by Mary L. Read, the educational director of the National Association for Mothercraft Education. Read confessed herself baffled: "It is one of the riddles of history why, when the life and welfare of children are of such vital concern to the family and the race, society has never taken the trouble to see to it that the woman in whose charge these precious baby lives rested were highly trained and fittingly prepared for their responsibility." A well-bred and genetically fit woman who hadn't been taught how to take care of babies, "however pretty and even charming," Read warned, would raise "sickly, peevish, stupid children." If providing social services to the poor couldn't be stopped, then, at a bare minimum, fit parents needed their own social services; they needed parental education.[23]

In 1918, Savage went to Europe as *Good Housekeeping*'s foreign editor; she wanted to cover politics, but she was stymied. When peace came, she quit. In 1920, at the age of twenty-nine, she married Harold Littledale, who went on to become an editor at the *New York Times*. The next year, Sanger founded the American Birth Control League. Sanger fielded letters from women all over the country, begging her for information about contraception. One wrote from Kentucky, "I have Ben married 4 years the 5 december and I have all Redy given Birth to 3 children and all 3 of my children ar Boys and I am all most Broken down and am only 24 yers old. . . . mrs sanger I do want you to write me an Return mail what to do to keep from Bring these Little one to this awfel world."[24]

The Progressive-era debate about parenthood contained within it debates about who had too many children, who had too few, who had a right to write about it, and how. In 1922, at the age of thirty-one, Clara Savage Littledale gave birth to a daughter. Motherhood does not appear to have been all she had hoped for. In 1924, she wrote a short, bitter piece for the *New Republic* about her experience sharing a room in a maternity ward with a woman whose baby had been stillborn. We never learn the woman's name; Littledale calls her "41A." Weirdly, the story, called "Sublimation," which takes the form of a conversation overheard during a visit from 41A's husband, has a lot in common with "Hills Like White Elephants," a short story Hemingway published three years later, in *Men Without Women.* The couple never mentions the dead baby, but everything they say is about the dead baby.

> "Is my aunt cookin' your meals?" she asked.
>
> "Yep, and, say, we had a pie."
>
> "What kind of a pie?" the girl demanded fiercely.
>
> "Apple pie."
>
> "Did she use up those apples I was savin'?" The face of 41A was white and set.[25]

Parenthood came late to Clara Savage Littledale, but for the rest of her life, she wrote about almost nothing else.

Straight after George Hecht met Littledale, he hired her, and then, together, they planned their venture: *Children: A Magazine for Parents.* Paul Popenoe and Lillian Gilbreth served on its advisory board. The first issue came out in 1926. Margaret Sanger wanted to help poor women have smaller families; Hecht and Littledale wanted to help wealthy women raise better babies. The magazine's argument amounted to this: parents' job was to prolong their children's infancy, to baby their babies, because "prolonged infancy makes, through a better preparation for life, a better use of the extended life span which we enjoy today, thanks to modern science." Actually, it went further: childhood was more than a stage of life. It was a right. "If the constitution of the United States were being redrawn to reflect the spirit of the twentieth century," one contributor put it, "along with the 'right to life, liberty, and the pursuit of happiness' might be included a future 'right to childhood,' emphasizing the need of every human being to a protected span of years."[26]

Littledale had a decided editorial vision. She weeded out submissions she hated—gossipy, Victorian-sounding drivel, mainly: "My particular detestation are manuscripts that begin, 'As Mrs. Jones was having tea in the garden with Mrs. Smith the question of Johnny's nail-biting came up.' "[27] She reached out to fathers. In 1927, the year Littledale worked through her second pregnancy, she ran Taylorite articles like "Can a Tired Businessman

Be a Good Father?," which argued for what later came to be called "quality time" ("An hour can be made more significant than a day").[28] Most of all, she solicited contributions from people without either journalistic experience or academic expertise—"Mammas and papas are encouraged to contribute articles and they do"—chiefly to point out what rank amateurs they were.[29]

In 1927, Littledale published "Confessions of an Amateur Mother," the lament of Stella Crossley, a wealthy, well-educated woman who has not the least idea how to take care of her newborn. The article sounds a lot like Littledale's diary. "Why is it that for the women of my type—professional women—motherhood, as a rule, comes so hard?" Crossley asked. Why is it that "we, for whom it should have been comparatively easy, seem to have greater difficulties with our infants than do the uneducated women, the foreign women, the wives of the great mass of toilers?" There are "motherhood clinics aplenty in the districts of the 'poor' women," Crossley complained. "Why not for me?"[30]

Littledale loved this sort of piece, and she printed dozens like it. Meanwhile, Sanger was collecting stories, too. In 1928, she brought out *Motherhood in Bondage,* an anthology of letters she had received from poor women all over the country. "I am the mother of nineteen children, the baby only twenty months old," one woman wrote. "I am forty-three years old and I had rather die than give birth to another child." The expert advice these women wanted was where to get contraception, which, despite Sanger's lobbying efforts, remained illegal. A doctor didn't even have the right to discuss it with patients.

In 1926, Sanger, with colleagues at the American Birth Control League, met with sixty senators and twenty congressmen, and seventeen members of the Judiciary Committee, urging the decriminalization of contraception. They didn't make much headway. (Mary Ware Dennett, of the Voluntary Parenthood League, had pointed out, when she lobbied the New York State Legislature in 1924, that the very men who refused to change the law had wives who broke it: congressional families had an average of 2.7 children.) Notes from the interviews, summarizing the remarks of legistators, read like this: "Knew nothing of the subject," "Has no literature on the subject." Senator James Reed from Missouri told the lobbyists, "He believes that Birth Control is chipping away the very foundation of our civilization. He believes in large families, that women should have many children and that poverty is no handicap but rather an asset." Arizona senator Henry Ashurst told Sanger, "He did not wish to discuss the question with us. Stated that he had not been raised to discuss this matter with women." Spurned by legislators, Sanger turned more of her attention to gaining the support of doctors. By 1930, the American Birth Control League was overseeing fifty-five birth control clinics in twelve states and twenty-three cities. Contraception had become more of a medical issue than a legislative one. And, by now, so had parenthood.[31]

Sanger continued abrasive and impatient, and often reckless and heedless. She also continued to court eugenicists; at one point, the American Birth Control League even proposed a merger with the American Eugenics Society (the society was not interested).[32] But Sanger was unpopular with eugenicists because she was also a socialist, and eugenicists were more commonly laissez-faire conservatives, which is among the many reasons Sanger was at odds with her own organization. A survey conducted of nearly a thousand members of the American Birth Control League in 1927 found its membership to be more Republican than the rest of the country. In a successful bid for respectability as a reform akin to prohibition, the league had attracted to its membership the same wealthy women and men who joined organizations like the Red Cross, the Rotary Club, and the Anti-Saloon League.[33] The next year, Sanger was forged to resign as the league's president; its members objected to her feminism.

Clara Savage Littledale courted much the same Rotarian audience, filling the pages of her parenting magazine with expert advice, offered by the day's leading psychologists and doctors and educators and scholars. But this she did with a twist: she turned her authorities into amateurs. "The staff sits up nights throwing scientific words out of the articles submitted by college professors," she explained. She also domesticated her experts. If the magazine "publishes an article by a Ph.D.," she said, "it hastens to explain that said Ph.D. has a baby or if the Ph.D. is a man that he is the uncle of a dear little tot."[34]

Littledale was making this up as she went because, at the time, science reporting was new. Before the First World War, journalists generally didn't report on science. After the war, scientists tried writing for newspapers and magazines, attempting to explain the value of their work, but most of them weren't any good at it. The number of scientists writing for a popular audience fell, while the number of journalists specializing in science writing rose. And so did the prominence and prevalence of stories about science.

Science didn't become the explanation for everything by happenstance. In 1920, a chemist named Edwin E. Slosson founded a wire service, the Science Service. Initially financed by the newspaper publisher E. W. Scripps, the Science Service was later sponsored by the American Association for the Advancement of Science and the National Research Council. Its purpose was to promote scientific research by feeding stories to newspapers and magazines, which, at a moment when *Time* was becoming a news aggregator, was a good plan, with eager takers. The Science Service, Slosson said, would not "indulge in propaganda unless it be propagandas to urge the value of research and the usefulness of science." By 1930, it reached a fifth of the American reading public.[35]

As science writing grew, it established certain conventions of reporting and prose; certain sorts of stories took shape. An emerging specialty of science journalism was the hair-raising account of a disease that threatens to destroy the human race. Littledale brought that genre into writing about parenting. In her hands, the conquest-of-disease story came to define writing about parenting.[36] Disease stories made good copy. They also sold advertising, especially for hygiene products, like Listerine (first sold over the counter in 1914), Lysol (marketed, in 1918, as an anti-flu measure), Cellophane (1923), and Kleenex (1924, sold as a towel for removing makeup until a consumer survey revealed that people were using it to blow their noses).[37] As George Hecht and Clara Savage Littledale knew very well, these were excellent products to sell to parents.

The germ theory of disease dates, more or less, to the 1870s. Pasteur developed a rabies vaccine in 1885, launching a global battle against infectious illness, a battle whose tremendous success would do so much to lengthen the average life.[38] In the 1910s, "germ" became a household word, and ordinary people learned to blame germs, not God, for catastrophes like the influenza epidemic of 1918—which killed more people than had died in the war. By the 1920s, scientists had developed a vaccine for diphtheria; other vaccines, like the one for polio, would take decades, but hopes ran high. In *The Conquest of Disease,* professor of sanitary science Thurman B. Rice predicted that the eradication of sickness itself was merely a matter of time.[39]

The master of the conquest-of-disease story was a bacteriologist turned journalist named Paul de Kruif. De Kruif had taught at the University of Michigan and worked for the U.S. Sanitary Corps, attempting to isolate the gangrene bacillus. After the war, he turned to writing. In 1925, his collaboration with Sinclair Lewis led to the publication of *Arrowsmith*, a novel about a young doctor fighting an outbreak of bubonic plague—the first medical thriller. The scientist, the *New Republic* noted in its review of the novel, now "sits in the seat of the mighty." De Kruif coauthored the novel and received 25 percent of the royalties. In 1926, while Hecht and Littledale were at work developing their parenting magazine, de Kruif turned to nonfiction, publishing *Microbe Hunters*, a book of profiles of scientists, starting with Leeuwenhoek, who can see tiny things the rest of us can't, things that are trying to kill us.[40] The book, de Kruif wrote, is "the tale of the bold and persistent and curious explorers and fighters of death. . . . It is the plain history of their tireless peerings into this new fantastic world."[41]

The coming plague was Paul de Kruif's bread and butter. Very many of his stories were written for mothers. In 1929, he issued a warning in the lead article in *Ladies' Home Journal*: "In American milk today there lurks a terrible, wasting fever, that may keep you in bed for a couple of weeks, that may fasten itself on you for one, or for two, or even for seven years—that might culminate by killing you." What was this dread malady? Undulant fever. "At least 50,000 people are sick with it at this very moment," their ailment virtually unknown to "their baffled doctors," de Kruif wrote.[42] The article, titled "Before You Drink a Glass of Milk," scared a lot of mothers and sold a lot of magazines. Boasting of its success, the editor of *Ladies' Home Journal* explained, "Nobody had ever heard of undulant fever before."[43]

To sell a magazine about raising children, you have to convince parents that they need that magazine. They need it because, at parenting, they are amateurs. And they need it because their children are in danger. To sell that magazine every four weeks, those children need to be in danger every single month.

For a lesson in the anatomy of a panic, Hecht and Littledale didn't have far to look. The year Paul de Kruif sounded the alarm about undulant fever, Americans fell into a frenzy over yet another disease no one had ever heard of before. " 'Parrot Disease' Baffles Experts," reported the *Washing-*

ton Post, on page 3 of a paper that went to press the night of January 8, 1930, thrilling readers with a medical mystery that would capture the nation's attention with the prospect of a parrot fever pandemic. Reports, cabled and wired and radioed across land and sea, were printed in the daily paper or broadcast, within minutes, on the radio: tallies, theories, postmortems, more to fear.[44] Before it was over, an admiral in the U.S. Navy would order sailors at sea to cast their pet parrots into the ocean.[45] There was talk of the mass extermination of all the birds in the Bronx Zoo. People abandoned their pet parrots on the streets. Every sneeze seemed a symptom. The story grew and grew. Almost as soon as it started, the panic was reclassified as a false alarm. But that sold papers, too. "U.S. Alarm over Parrot Disease Not Warranted," reported the *Chicago Daily Tribune* on January 15, 1930.[46] E. B. White filed a piece for the *New Yorker,* calling parrot fever merely "the latest and most amusing example of the national hypochondria."[47] He figured that the country was suffering from nothing so much as a bad case of the heebie-jeebies.[48] The first American doctor to believe he had seen psittacosis had read about the disease in a Baltimore paper, probably the *Baltimore American,* which included a glossy Sunday supplement called the *American Weekly,* edited by Morrill Goddard. "Nobody heard the word 'psittacosis' until the *American Weekly* printed a page," Goddard boasted.[49]

You could make a parenting panic work the same way. The *New York Times,* where Harold Littledale was an editor, cheerfully greeted Clara Savage Littledale's magazine as "First Aid for Parents."[50] It was first aid for ills it invented. The magazine raced from one panic to the next while, in its pages, selling products that might save children's lives (not the lives of poor children, which were in some peril, but the lives of the children of the anxious affluent). Littledale couldn't possibly report on panics like parrot fever; those came and went too fast for her production schedule. But she did her best to create a new panic every month. In June 1930, just after the parrot fever panic, she ran, alongside ads for Lysol, plenty of disease stories, like "How to Guard Against Colds and Flu," by the New York Public Health Service's Shirley Wynne, who had been much in the news during the parrot fever panic.[51] More pointedly, Littledale ran pieces that turned children's everyday experiences into clinical symptons: "Thumbsucking: Its Dangers and Treatment" and "Have Your Children the Daily Bath Habit?" and "How Well Do We Protect Our Children?"[52] There was more to worry about than colds and flu. What would become of children who sucked their thumbs or who didn't get soaped up every day? They might succumb; they might fail; they might die. So much to worry about, so little time; the magazine, and microbe hunters, had answers. And then, a few months later, you could run a piece about how thumb sucking wasn't so bad after all.

Within a year of *Children*'s first issue, Hecht and Littledale had changed the magazine's name, to the *Parents' Magazine,* which made much sense, since all this business about parenthood had very little to do with kids. As Littledale would explain in 1930,

> Once it was believed that the very physical fact of parenthood brought with it an instinctive wisdom that enabled one to rear children wisely and well. Parents knew best. Today fathers and mothers are unwilling to struggle under such a load of self-imposed omniscience. Even if they were, the facts would be against them. For in this country various studies made in the last ten years present incontrovertible data to prove that devoted but unenlightened parenthood is a dangerous factor in the lives of children.[53]

This almost passes for a definition: Parenthood is being so inept that you're a danger to your own children. "Our want of knowledge is nothing short of criminal," Stella Crossley wrote in "Confessions of an Amateur Mother."[54] That, at least, was the premise of Littledale's magazine, and its price.

By 1931, the *Parents' Magazine* boasted two hundred thousand subscribers.[55] Littledale, however, was frustrated. She wrote a prodigious amount of fiction, odd and rather terrifying stories, many about love gone wrong. She sent them to dozens of magazines, but her efforts to publish them met with little success.[56] Her own magazine, though, kept growing. Its vast readership carried Littledale into broadcasting; she was heard on NBC radio from 1932 to 1943, her show filling Emily Post's noontime slot on Wednesdays, Miss Manners's day off. "I Am a Failure as a Mother" she titled one of her talks.[57] She administered advice by the anecdote. "Fathers Are Parents, Too!" was her answer to a letter from a listener who wished he knew his children better. Littledale's advice was often perfectly sensible. Grown-ups should enjoy living with children, she liked to say, but they shouldn't live *for* them. She didn't much like spanking; she thought kids needed to learn to do things for themselves; she wisely told the listener who said she was a failure as a mother, "One way to be a failure as a mother is to overplay the role." She had six rules for dealing with kids: be fair; be polite; be there; don't wobble; don't pretend to be perfect; and don't be too serious. On more particular matters, such as how to handle a crying baby, Littledale's advice, like her magazine, followed parenting fashion, which changes as often as the length of hemlines.[58] Urgent social issues that affected how very many Americans raised their children—segregation and hunger, for instance—had no place on Littledale's list of parenting problems.

Nor did contraception. But Sanger finally achieved a legal victory, in 1937, with *U.S. v. One Package of Japanese Pessaries*, which ruled that doctors could prescribe birth control. Not long after that, Sanger's Birth Control Clinical Research Bureau merged with the American Birth Control League to become the Birth Control Federation of America. Its leaders, now mostly no longer feminist activists but male doctors, deemed the phrase "birth control" too radical; in 1942, the organization became the Planned Parenthood Federation of America. Sanger was furious, warning, "We will get no further because of the title; I assure you of that."[59]

By the start of the baby boom, confessions of amateur parents had become a stupendously popular genre, and not just in *Parents' Magazine*. In *The Egg and I*, a memoir published in 1945, the same week as *Stuart Little*, Betty MacDonald offered up a parody. MacDonald wrote about motherhood by writing about raising chickens. She told the story of her husband's decision to buy a chicken farm in the Pacific Northwest, dragging his reluctant bride from a comfortable life in the city to a miserable, hardscrabble existence in the country. She discovered that she was bad at raising chickens. At first she just hated the hens and cocks. Then things got worse. "I Learn to Hate Even Baby Chickens" she titled one of her chapters. In the end, she wrote, "I hated everything about the chicken but the egg." *The Egg and I* sold over a million copies and became the best-selling nonfiction title of 1946, even before it was made into a film. "Was there something in my background which kept me from becoming properly adjusted to the chicken," MacDonald wondered, "or was there just too wide a gulf separating a woman and a chicken?"

Although nowhere revealed in the memoir, MacDonald's life as a farm wife had ended badly; long before writing the book, she had divorced her husband and moved to New York. The book ends with an emphatic last line: "The hen is the boss."[60]

By now, Littledale had divorced, too. In 1941, she and her husband were badly hurt when the airplane they were flying in crashed in Georgia. Littledale woke up tangled in a pine tree. Both of her husband's legs were broken. They waited six hours, in the dark, in pouring rain, for a rescue party.[61] "Someway, that accident shook me out of my way of living and I have never been able to go back to it," Littledale wrote to her sister. Harold Littledale spent the rest of his life in a wheelchair. The couple divorced in 1944.[62]

"What Can We Do About Marriage?" Littledale asked in an essay she published in 1947, noting that the divorce rate had risen to nearly three in five. Predictably, she attributed the rising rate to the lack of parental education. If only more people would read her magazine, more marriages would be happier. *Parents' Magazine* had, by then, four hundred thousand subscribers.[63]

During the Second World War, Planned Parenthood touted controlling family size as part of the war effort.[64] Birth control continued to gain religious support. In 1947, more than thirty-five hundred Jewish and Protestant clergy signed a resolution in support of Planned Parenthood.[65] In the 1950s, Planned Parenthood was run by men interested in population control. Barry Goldwater and his wife were active supporters.[66] By 1956, Sanger, who had retired to Tucson, wrote to the national director, "If I told you or wrote you that the name Planned Parenthood would be the end of the movement, it was and has proven true. The movement was then a fighting, forward, no fooling movement, battling for the freedom of the poorest parents and for women's biological freedom and development. The P.P.F. has left all this behind."[67] Sanger was bitter, but she was right. Birth control in the first half of the twentieth century, as the historian David Kennedy once argued, was a liberal reform turned to conservative ends.[68]

In 1955, at the urging of Mary Steichen Calderone, a public health physician who served as Planned Parenthood's medical director, the organization began to wrestle with the subject of abortion. (Abortion had been legal until 1821, when Connecticut became the first state to make abortion after quickening—at about four months—a crime. By the middle of the twentieth century, abortion was illegal throughout the United States, with limited exceptions. It was, nevertheless, widely practiced.) "If there was even a communicable disease that affected that many people in this country," Calderone said, "we would do something about it."[69] Calderone organized a conference and conducted a study. In an article published in 1960, she remarked on the difference between a legal abortion and an illegal one: three hundred dollars and knowing the right person.

Calderone left Planned Parenthood in 1964 to found the Sex Information and Education Council of the United States, Inc. (She wanted to teach people how to talk about sex because, as she once said, "People don't have much of a vocabulary. Or a concept of anything, except fucking.")[70] Alan F. Guttmacher, chief of obstetrics at Mount Sinai Hospital and clinical professor of obstetrics and gynecology at Columbia, became president of Planned Parenthood in 1962.[71] Guttmacher had three priorities: improving Planned Parenthood's relationship with the black community, securing federal support for family planning programs for the poor, and liberalizing abortion law.

In 1940, Planned Parenthood had organized a National Negro Advisory Committee—black doctors, nurses, and public health officials who wanted to reduce maternal death and infant mortality rates among black women and infants through child spacing.[72] Guttmacher hoped to strengthen these alliances, and to build new ones. In 1962, he sent the director of a clinic in Harlem (over whose opening, three decades before, W.E.B. DuBois had presided) to meet with Malcolm X. Malcolm X suggested that Planned Parenthood ought to call its service "family planning instead of birth control." (The meeting notes read, "His reason for this was that people, particularly Negroes, would be more willing to plan than to be controlled.")[73] In 1966, Martin Luther King Jr., who had joined a Planned Parenthood committee as a young minister, was given the Margaret Sanger Human Rights Award. In his acceptance speech, he drew parallels between the birth control and civil rights movements—"There is a striking kinship between our movement and Margaret Sanger's early efforts"—and celebrated Sanger for having "launched a movement which is obeying a higher law to preserve human life under humane conditions."[74] In 1967, after a leader of the Pittsburgh branch of the NAACP called Planned Parenthood a racist project, the chairman of the national organization clarified that the NAACP supported family planning.[75] The next year, a Planned Parenthood clinic in Cleveland was set on fire.[76]

Up to that point, birth control had been mainly privately funded; clinics affiliated with Planned Parenthood ran on donations, grants, and fees-for-service. "I cannot imagine anything more emphatically a subject that is not a proper political or governmental activity or function or responsibility," Dwight Eisenhower said in 1959. "That's not our business." But by 1965, Eisenhower had reversed his position on family planning, serving with Harry Truman as a co-chairman of a Planned Parenthood committee.[77] Meanwhile, the last legal obstacles to contraception were overcome. After Estelle Griswold, executive director of Planned Parenthood of Connecticut, opened a birth control clinic in New Haven, she was arrested and fined under the provisions of a Connecticut statute banning the use of contraceptives; in 1965, the Supreme Court declared that ban unconstitutional. The next year, Guttmacher testified before Congress, "We really have the opportunity now to extend free choice in family planning to all Americans, regardless of social status and to demonstrate to the rest of the world how it can be done. It's time we get on with the job."

In 1968, Paul Ehrlich's *Population Bomb* sold two million copies, Pope Paul VI issued *Humanae Vitae,* reiterating the Catholic Church's prohibition on both abortion and contraception, and Lyndon Johnson appointed a Committee on Population and Family Planning. The next year, Richard Nixon asked Congress to increase federal funding for family planning. In the House, Texas congressman George H. W. Bush said, "We need to make family planning a household word. We need to take the sensationalism out of the topic so it can no longer be used by militants who have no knowledge of the voluntary nature of the program, but rather are using it as a political stepping stone."[78] Nixon signed Title X into law in 1970.[79] "No American woman should be denied access to family planning assistance because of her economic condition," Nixon said then.[80]

By now, George Hecht had joined this fight, too. In July of 1970, Hecht wrote an article in *Parents* titled "Smaller Families: A National Imperative." He sent a copy to Guttmacher, writing to him on the letterhead of a new organization that he'd just founded, "I have recently incorporated the Association for Two-Child Families, Inc. under an association of this kind, rather than as Publisher of Parents' Magazine. I have to be more cautious when writing letters on Parents' Magazine stationery." Hecht invited Guttmacher to join him in writing to major publishers, including S. I. Newhouse, of Condé Nast, to complain about magazine stories urging people to have more babies. But Hecht was cautious—and unwilling to formally ally *Parents* magazine with Planned Parenthood, or even to write to Guttmacher on the magazine's stationery—because Guttmacher had begun campaigning for the legalization of abortion. Planned Parenthood, so closely aligned with the sensibility and agenda of *Parents* in the 1940s and '50s, had become controversial, and Hecht, however much he supported Guttmacher—he personally sent Planned Parenthood pamphlets to *Parents* readers—was unwilling to jeopardize his magazine.[81]

By the beginning of the twenty-first century, *Parents Magazine* was still reaching fifteen million readers, nearly all of them women. The magazine lost its apostrophe somewhere along the way, as well as its purchase on American life, but it still reliably produced confessions of amateur mothers—"*Parents* is for every woman who lives and parents in her own authentic way"—and parental education, along with a column called "Fatherhood 101," that could be read at the magazine's website.[82]

"Remember when everyone was talking about momism, silver-cord mothers, smothering mothers?" Clara Savage Littledale once asked. "Now it's father's turn."[83] If it's not one thing, it's another. She had wearied of it. She died in 1956, having worked, until the day she died, for a magazine that sold the heebie-jeebies.

Margaret Sanger died in 1966, just when questions about parenthood were beginning to dominate American politics. In 1967, Guttmacher edited a book called *The Case for Legalized Abortion Now*. As a young intern in the 1920s, Guttmacher had watched a woman die of a botched abortion, and had never forgotten it. At Mount Sinai, he performed abortions until the hospital told him to stop. Laws liberalizing abortion in the 1960s and early 1970s were urged by doctors and lawyers and supported by clergy. Between 1967 and 1970, some restrictions on abortions were lifted by legislators in Alaska, Arkansas, California, Delaware, Georgia, Hawaii, Kansas, Maryland, New Mexico, New York, North Carolina, Oregon, South Carolina, Virginia, and Washington. Governor Ronald Reagan signed the California law. By 1970, the National Clergy Consultation Service, established to help women find doctors who could conduct abortions safely, offered services in twenty-six states.

Not much involved in any of this agitation were women. Betty Friedan endorsed the liberalization of abortion laws at a meeting of the National Organization of Women in 1966, but women's rights activists only really began to join this effort in 1969, the year NARAL was founded.[84] The conventional narrative—that American politics were poisoned by the Supreme Court's ruling in *Roe v. Wade*—is not borne out by the evidence: a partisan realignment over matters of life and death began before *Roe*. In 1969, in *The Emerging Republican Majority*, Nixon strategist Kevin Phillips offered a blueprint for crushing the Democrats' New Deal coalition by recruiting southerners and Catholics to the GOP. At the time, prominent Democrats, including Edward Kennedy, were vocally opposed to abortion. Nixon's advisers urged him to reconsider his position on abortion and family planning. In 1970, the year he signed Title X, Nixon had ruled that doctors on military bases could perform abortions. In 1971, Patrick Buchanan wrote a memo recommending that the president reverse that ruling as part of a strategy to ensure that George McGovern (the candidate Nixon wanted to run against) would defeat Edward Muskie for the Democratic nomination. Observing that abortion was "a rising issue and a gut issue with Catholics," Buchanan advised Nixon to publicly reverse the Department of Defense. Buchanan wrote, "If the President should publicly take his stand against abortion, as offensive to his own moral principles, ... then we can force Muskie to make the choice between his tens of millions of Catholic supporters and his liberal friends at the New York Times and the Washington Post." A week later, Nixon issued a statement to the DOD reversing his position and borrowing the language of the Catholic Church to speak of his "personal belief in the sanctity of human life—including the life of the yet unborn."

"Favoritism toward things Catholic is good politics," a Nixon strategist wrote in "Dividing the Democrats," a memo to H. R. Haldeman in 1971. "There is a trade-off, but it leaves us with the larger share of the pie." When Nixon supporters balked, Buchanan held firm. Asked whether Nixon might perhaps go back to his original position, Buchanan said that would be stupid: "He will cost himself Catholic support and gain what, Betty Friedan?"

Abortion wasn't a partisan issue until Republicans made it one. In August 1972, a Gallup poll reported that 68 percent of Republicans and 58 percent of Democrats agreed that "the decision to have an abortion should be made solely by a woman and her physician." Supreme Court Justice Harry Blackmun clipped the *Washington Post* story reporting this survey and put it in his *Roe* case file.[85]

Nixon was re-elected in November 1972. Soon after *Roe*, Alan Guttmacher showed up at Brigham and Women's Hospital in Boston to give a lecture, only to be confronted by protesters wearing hospitals scrubs spattered with red paint, crying, "Murderer!" Guttmacher wrote in *Reader's Digest* that "those who oppose and those who favor legalization of abortion share a common goal—the elimination of *all* abortion," through better, safer, cheaper contraception, because, as he saw it, "each abortion bespeaks medical or social failure." This earned him nothing but hate mail. He died not long afterward.[86]

Eight days after the Supreme Court issued its ruling in *Roe*, the newly formed National Right to Life Committee began campaigning for a human life amendment. "This poses real strategy problems," a former president of Planned Parenthood said in an interview in 1974, "because to the degree that any of us fight to keep that out of the Constitution, it brands Planned Parenthood as pro-abortion."[87]

In the late 1970s, GOP strategists Richard Viguerie and Paul Weyrich, both of whom were Catholic, recruited Jerry Falwell into a coalition designed to bring economic and social conservatives together around a "pro-family" agenda, one that targeted gay rights, sexual freedom, women's liberation, the ERA, child care, and sex education. Weyrich wrote that abortion ought to be the centerpiece of the GOP strategy, "since this was the issue that could divide the Democratic Party." Falwell founded the Moral Majority in 1979; Paul Brown, founder of the American Life League, scoffed in 1982, "Falwell couldn't spell abortion five years ago."[88]

Nothing even remotely resembling party discipline on the issue of abortion can be identified on Capitol Hill before 1979. And a partisan divide over this issue only split the country a decade after it showed up in Congress. Meanwhile, opposition to abortion grew violent. In 1985, pro-life protesters picketed at 80 percent of clinics providing abortions.[89] As a consequence, fewer and fewer places were willing to provide abortions, which made Planned Parenthood, in many parts of the country, the last abortion provider left standing.

By 1990, the proportion of Americans living in households with children under the age of fifteen had dropped to 35 percent.[90] Forty percent of American babies born in 2002 were their mother's first; that year, the average age of a woman at the birth of her first child reached twenty-five, an all-time high, and the fastest-growing cohort of first-time mothers was women over thirty-five.[91]

A study conducted by the Guttmacher Institute (formerly the Margaret Sanger Research Bureau) in 2010 found that "virtually all women (more than 99%) aged 15–44 who have ever had sexual intercourse have used at least one contraceptive method" and that one in four of the twenty million American women who used contraception in 2010 received it at a publicly funded clinic.[92] Sanger made birth control legal, and Planned Parenthood made it available to poor women. It remained, nevertheless, not only controversial but the defining issue of American domestic politics.

By 2011, Planned Parenthood had eighty affiliates nationwide. Most received about a third of their funding from the government, a third from grants, and a third from private donations. In April of that year, Republicans in Congress threatened to shut down the federal government unless all funding for Planned Parenthood was eliminated. Nearly everyone running for the GOP presidential nomination in 2011 opposed Planned Parenthood.[93] Planned Parenthood reported that abortions constituted less than 3 percent of its services.[94] But attacking Planned Parenthood neatly tied together opposition to abortion with opposition to government programs for the poor. A century after Clara Savage began reporting on eugenics for the women's pages and Margaret Sanger opened the first birth control clinic in America, there continued to be, in the United States, one set of ideas about parenthood for the poor and another for the wealthy.

Happy Old Age

One Thursday afternoon in 1909, William James took a train from Cambridge to Worcester and caught a ride from the station to the hilltop home of G. Stanley Hall, to which remote destination he had traveled in order to spend the evening with Hall's houseguests, Sigmund Freud and Carl Jung, carrying in his breast pocket, at Hall's request, a report he had written for the American Society of Psychical Research about a medium named Leonora Piper.[1] James was sixty-seven; Hall, sixty-five. Their friendship was fraught. Hall, the father of adolescence, had been James's student at Harvard; he was second only to James as the United States' most important psychologist. But, as will happen, being second irked him something fierce. Hall had once assessed James's *Principles of Psychology* as, mainly, an indulgence: magnificent, impressionistic, and unscientific.[2] Then there was the matter of Mrs. Piper. James found her wonderfully compelling. Hall considered her "without question the most eminent American medium," but this was, in his opinion, so far from a mark of distinction, a badge of infamy, since Hall believed spiritualism the "very sewage," "the ruck and muck of modern culture."[3]

Hall, hosting Freud and Jung in his capacity as president of Clark University, wanted his guests to meet James. He also wanted them to hear all about Mrs. Piper. "I gathered from some remarks of President Hall that William James was not taken quite seriously on account of his interest in Mrs. Piper," Jung later remembered. Neither Freud nor Jung had ever been to the United States before. They crossed the Atlantic on the same boat. (During the voyage, Jung recalled, "we chiefly analysed our dreams.")[4] Hall was their champion; he imported their work to America, and burnished it. "In Europe I felt as though I were despised," Freud wrote, but, in the United States, "I found myself received by the foremost men as an equal"—if not, apparently, by James. Hall, who was the sort of man who told fourteen lies before lunchtime, liked to tell the story of how James, on meeting Freud, said he was a "dirty fellow," which may or may not be true but is a good proxy for the opinion held, at the time, by Freud's European colleagues.[5]

Jung, rather misreading his host, found Hall refined; Freud, more cannily, discerned that he was capable of great mischief.[6] Hall was intellectually ravenous. ("In the beginning was hunger," he liked to say when lecturing on the psychology of food.) On a good day, this gave Hall's work extraordinary vitality; on a bad day, it reduced him to something between a wretch and a fiend.[7] He thought of himself as "the Darwin of the mind," a reference to his commitment to "genetic psychology," the idea that, over the course of our lives, we—not so much our bodies but our minds and, especially, our souls—recapitulate the evolution of the species.[8] He not only invented adolescence but also inspired Franz Boas's student Margaret Mead to debunk him in her writing about Samoa. (Adolescence in Samoa, Mead observed, is "not necessarily a specially difficult period.")[9] Overlooked because overshadowed by his study of adolesence, though, is Hall's study of growing old, or what he preferred to call "senescence."[10]

Hall founded gerontology, but he came at it by way of thanatology.[11] He believed that thinking about aging required thinking about dying. No social science is more extravagantly autobiographical than psychology. Senescence was, for Hall, the flip side of adolescence. You're either growing up or you're growing down. For him, there was—there had been—very little in between. Old age takes everyone by surprise, and no one really ever comes to terms with it. Hall thought that this was because old age is the only stage of life we never grow out of, and can never look back on—not on this earth, anyway. He also thought that because one problem with growing old is that you don't know where you're going anymore, what you should do, when you feel yourself getting stodgy, is think about where you came from: you should think about your history.[12]

Granville Stanley Hall, who lied about, among other things, his age, appears to have been born in 1844 in the small town of Ashfield, Massachusetts, that town not very far from Northampton, where Sylvester Graham was living the last years of his life. Hall's father, a farmer, was descended from Plymouth Colony's William Brewster, a pilgrim who named one of his sons Wrestling, short for "wrestling with God." His mother, who also traced her ancestry to the *Mayflower*, was the granddaughter of an ecstatic preacher. Stanley and his brother and sister, like many New England children—including the March girls, in *Little Women*—wrote their own family newspaper: the *Cottage Weekly News*. Everyone expected him to become a minister. His mother read to him from *Pilgrim's Progress*.[13] He descended the Slough of Despond; he climbed the Hill of Difficulty.

One Sunday when he was fourteen years old, he scrambled up the highest tree he could find and decided he would, one day, leave the farm and "do and be something in the world."[14] Striving to do and be something in this world isn't very John Bunyan; it's more Milton Bradley. Hall left home but, as these things go, he never really escaped. He went first to Williams College, where he was elected class poet and wrote a poem called "A Life Without a Soul."[15] He fell for John Stuart Mill. "I do not think I have got the requirements for a pastor," he wrote home. "What do you think?"[16] He graduated in 1867, having avoided fighting in the Civil War because his father bought him a substitute. He went next to New York, where he enrolled in the Union Theological Seminary. He sneaked out to the stage; he trawled the Bowery.[17] The city thrilled him. To his parents, he sent blandishments: "New York . . . wakes me to depravity all over the world."[18]

He wanted to see that world. He paid a visit to Henry Ward Beecher, known for giving advice to promising young men. "Tell me frankly, are you not more interested in philosophy than in your theological studies?" Beecher asked. Philosophy, said Hall. Beecher wrote him a letter of recommendation and told him, "You ought to go to Germany."[19] Hall set sail.

"Nobody, with few exceptions, goes to church on Sunday," he wrote home from Bonn, wide-eyed.[20] He went to Berlin; he fell for Hegel. He went to see a fortune-teller, who predicted, he said, that "I have some sharp dis-appointments to bear, but all will end well."[21] His parents were not amused. "Just *what* are you doing?" his father wanted to know.[22] He learned to dance; he conducted dissections; he went to the circus; he moved to a tiny village; he swore off speaking English. (All his life he had this immersive, touristic habit. He tramped to prizefights and cockfights, brothels and cre-matoriums, prisons and poorhouses. He had, he said, "a love for glimpsing at first hand the raw side of human life."[23] He attended meetings of radicals and revolutionaries; he never missed a revival meeting.)[24] He soaked up everything and everyone. "If I was a Dickens I should have seen characters enough for a dozen novels," he wrote to his sister. He informed his par-ents that he was thinking about getting a PhD in philosophy. "Now Stanley wherein is the great benefit of being a Ph.D.?" his mother demanded. "I think a *preacher* should be a D.D. Just *what is* a Doctor of Philosophy?"[25]

Hall, boy and man, was subject to enthusiasms. "I sometimes think my life has been a series of fads or crazes," he once wrote.[26] This zest for nov-elty set him against authority, no more so than when he was young. "Never allow yourself to lean to your own understanding when it conflicts with the experience of your elders," his father warned.[27] The general thinking had been for a long time that old people were wiser than young people. To be ancient, as Cotton Mather put it, was to be honorable. Mather dedi-cated *The Old Man's Honour* to a friend: "Were there nothing else to com-mend my Regards for you, besides the Old Age, which your out-living of Three-score Winters has brought you to the Border of, That were enough to give you a room in my Esteem, and Reverence, and Veneration."[28] Ben-jamin Rush thought "none but men of very active minds attain to a high degree of longevity." The French émigré J. P. Brissot, touring the United States, argued that longevity was a measure of the strength of a nation: "Tables of longevity may be everywhere considered the touchstones of government, the scale on which may be measured their excellencies and their defects, the perfection or degradation of the human species."[29]

Americans appeared to be living longer; perhaps they could live even longer.[30] Sylvester Graham had argued that practicing abstemiousness would lengthen life; his followers had founded the *Graham Journal of Health and Longevity*.[31] "A few slothful men have attained to extreme old age, and so have a few gluttons and drunkards, or at least, hard drinkers," one observer remarked in 1859, "but for the most part, and in an incomparably greater proportion, long livers have been distinguished for their sober and industrious habits."[32] When Stanley Hall was growing up, in Young America, there were very many young people but there were also more old people than there used to be, and suddenly they didn't seem quite so venerable after all. "Years do not make sages," a New England almanac put it; "they make only old men."[33]

The history of aging appears to follow this rule: the fewer old people there are, the more esteemed they will be. Scholars have quibbled with this axiom and its grim inverse, pointing out that, even in Cotton Mather's New England, old men, and especially old women, were often ridiculed and held in contempt. Still and all, it holds.[34] As David Hackett Fischer argued, in a landmark study, "The people of early America exalted old age; their descendants have made a cult of youth." In the first U.S. census, in 1790, 2 percent of the population was over age sixty-five; by 1970, 10 percent. By 2030, it will be 20 percent.[35] At the close of the eighteenth century, John Wallis's New Game of Human Life ended at eighty-four. Two centuries later, the fastest-growing segment of the population, in the United States, was people over the age of eighty-five. On Wallis's board, when you get to eighty-five, you're dead.

G. Stanley Hall was born in a circular world and died in a linear one. As a boy, he drove cows to pasture, work that followed the sun and the seasons. He was supposed to be a preacher, retracing the path tread by his forebears or, failing that, a farmer, like his father. Instead, he started out on another trajectory entirely. He placed his faith in scientific solutions, more learned versions of Graham's "science of human life." Caught up in one of the many health crazes of his day ("I eat nothing but brown bread, milk, eggs, and very rare beef"), he wrote home that his father should abandon the farm: "I do hope father will sell the cows and everything and give himself up to the art of prolonging life. Everyone at fifty-five ought to give up everything and call themselves invalids and begin a course of dieting and hygiene."[36]

In Germany, Hall ran out of money; he sailed home without a degree.[37] He took a job at Antioch College, in Ohio, teaching not philosophy but just about everything else, including French, rhetoric, German, and Anglo-Saxon, a language he did not happen to know. He was also the college librarian. He didn't have a chair at Antioch, he liked to say; he had "a whole settee."[38] He fell for Spencer. He fell for Huxley. He fell, hard, for Darwin. In 1876, he left Antioch for Harvard, where he taught English while studying with William James in the philosophy department. In 1878, he finally earned that PhD—the first awarded by Harvard's philosophy department and the first in psychology awarded anywhere in the country.[39] He was thirty-four; he married the next year. In 1884, he was appointed a full professor at Johns Hopkins, where he held a chair in psychology, the first in the United States. Four years later, he left Hopkins to become the founding president of Clark University.

Hall had traversed, in a few years' time, an entire history of ideas: from divinity to philosophy to psychology. He had also come to believe that genetic psychology explains everything: birth, death, faith, eternity. He once wrote a seven-hundred-page book analyzing Jesus, and every line of the Apostles' Creed, by way of Freud. "I am still going in the same direction and in the same path in which my infant feet were first taught to walk," he insisted; he was just going farther.[40] Still, he struggled with the animality of man. Darwinism, the philosopher John Gray has argued, forced Victorians "to ask why their lives should not end like those of other animals, in nothingness. If this was so, how could human existence have meaning? How could human values be maintained if human personality was destroyed at death?"[41] When that happened, Gray argues, we forgot how to die, replacing the hope of life after death with "the faith that death can be defeated."[42] This is as depressing as it is true. In 1883, in *The Possibility of Not Dying,* Hyland Kirk cited Darwin in support of his argument that "the only logical limit to progress is perfection." For Kirk, that perfection was not salvation; it was the defeat, by science, of death.[43]

But maybe there was another way, short of faith in a mansion of happiness, to cheat death. If life isn't a circle but a line, it ends. Or maybe it doesn't? Hence: séances, which aimed to prove an afterlife, of some kind or another. The English Society for Psychical Research was founded in 1882, and the American counterpart followed three years later. Psychology was new; so was psychical research. In the public mind, the two appeared to be one. This Hall could not abide. One, he said, was science; the other, superstition.[44] Nothing's ever that easy. James thought it went the other way around.

"To take sides as positively as you do now, and on general philosophic grounds," James wrote Hall, "seems to me a very dangerous and unscientific attitude." After all, if anyone was being empirical, James pointed out, it was he who was investigating, not Hall, who was holding firm to an untested belief. "I should express the difference between our two positions in the matter, by calling mine a baldly empirical one, and yours, one due to a general theoretic creed," James wrote. "I don't think it exactly fair to make the issue what you make it—one between science and superstition."[45] He was right. It wasn't fair at all.

William James first visited Leonora Piper in 1885, just after the death of his infant son and not long after the death of his father, in whose aftermath he had produced a book called *The Literary Remains of the Late Henry James.* In a trance, Mrs. Piper had offered James the very comfort he must have ached for: mention of his son and "a hearty message of thanks" from his father, for publishing his papers.[46] In grief, solace; in death, life. "For years she has been the more or less private oracle of one of our leading and very influential psychologists," Hall wrote of Mrs. Piper's hold on James. Hall consulted Mrs. Piper himself—he once visited every psychic in New York—probably first sometime in 1890 or 1891, shortly after the deaths of his parents, and just after a family tragedy of his own.[47]

Hall moved to Worcester, to take charge of Clark, early in 1889. He had his work cut out for him, because the university's patron, Jonas Clark, was demanding, unsteady, and changeable, unsure of whether he wanted to found a college for local boys or a first-rate research university. The editors of the local newspaper, the *Worcester Telegram,* wanted only the former. Hall wanted only the latter, but he tried to keep that to himself. The *Telegram* sent a reporter to interview Hall, and described him as looking like "a well-to-do German professor." His best-honed skill was said to be evasion: "Secretiveness is evidently one of President Hall's accomplishments." In March and April 1889, reporters at the *Telegram* produced one exposé after another about the mad science being conducted at the new university by German-born, or German-trained, or German-looking professors. Hall kept laboratory animals locked in a barn behind his house. The *Telegram* ran a story with a half column of headlines:

DOGS VIVISECTED
Scientific Torture at Clark University

HELPLESS ANIMALS ARE KILLED BY INCHES
Cruelty That Is Reduced to a Fine Art.
DUMB VICTIMS WRITHE UNDER THE CRUEL KNIFE.

As the story had it, "Dogs, cats, frogs, rats, mice, and occasionally other animals are scientifically cut up alive in order to satisfy the curiosity of the docents in their research." One of those docents was Franz Boas. "He is a German," the *Telegram* reported, "and has evidently studied vivisection with a rapier, or had it practiced upon himself, as numerous scars on his brow show." Even beloved Worcester family pets were being captured and tortured—sold to Clark, for twenty-five cents each, by boys on the street. The paper also featured the work of the German-trained anatomist Franklin P. Mall. "Dr. Mall was sometime since so very fortunate as to secure a perfect human embryo of about 26 days," the *Telegram* reported, following up with an inquiry: "What good can it ever do the human race?"[48]

Hall fell sick, with diphtheria, and left town; he went to Ashfield to convalesce. The *Telegram* wondered whether he had been made ill by infected animals, in that barn, and whether the whole city was at risk. On May 10, while Hall was still away, his wife and daughter were snuggling together in bed—the girl had blown soap bubbles on the sheets of her own bed, soaking them, and so climbed in with her mother—when someone turned on the gas heat but failed to light a match. They suffocated. Hall, miles away, heard the news after boarding a stagecoach, when a man on the street shouted to the driver, "Is that man in there named Hall? Tell him his wife and daughter are dead."[49]

He sent his nine-year-old son away to boarding school, and barely ever saw him again. And then, suffering "the greatest bereavement of my life—such a one, indeed, as rarely falls to the lot of man," Hall went to see a medium, who, purporting to be channeling his dead wife, told him "that the suffocation and so-called death was absolutely painless."[50] This proved no comfort, and Hall found James's oracle pathetic.[51] Not only an accomplished liar but also an accomplished magician, Hall had taught himself a passel of conjuror's tricks and was sure he knew a fraud when he saw one. Nor did he envy the dead who spoke through the likes of Leonora Piper. "I would deliberately prefer annihilation to the kind of idiotic, twaddling life it appears that these inane ghosts of the dark séance live," he commented. But he did envy James (whose faith in Mrs. Piper he never failed to overstate). "I often wish I could believe in it a little myself," he confided. And he conceded that James's will to believe was nothing if not useful: "Very likely he got more out of his faith than I out of my doubt. And so, if pragmatism is true, he was right and I wrong."[52]

Hall fell into a state he called "the Great Fatigue." He found it hard to write; he could scarcely think straight. Clark began to fall apart. Hall, who was infamously stingy, had nevertheless assembled arguably the best professoriate in the country. The first doctorate in anthropology awarded in the United States was at Clark, under Boas. Some of Boas's most important work began in Worcester. Influenced by Hall's empirical study of childhood, Boas measured the physical growth of twelve thousand Worcester schoolchildren. He concluded that environment, not heredity, accounted for different rates of growth (exactly the opposite of what Lewis Terman would conclude from his measurement of the intelligence of Worcester schoolboys). The *Telegram*, in another series of exposés in 1891, reported that Boas was measuring children in the nude, and intimated more. One article described the scarred German professor visiting a school near campus: "When the children saw him, they became very frightened, fearing that he was going to practice on them." The paper quoted a prominent Worcester native as saying "If I had a sister or children in the school and this Boas came in to measure them, I'd shoot him."[53]

As the *Telegram* told it, the city's children were being exploited and abused and beloved family pets were being captured and tortured, by foreign-born scientists, Germans and Jews. Hall, floundering in depression, proved unable to contend with these problems. Jonas Clark, alarmed and embarrassed by what was reported in the *Telegram*, withdrew his financial support, whereupon Hall lied to his faculty about what he could afford to pay them. In 1892, 70 percent of the students and two-thirds of the instructors, led in their rebellion by Mall, left.[54] Many of the faculty decamped for the new University of Chicago, turning it, overnight, into what Hall had meant Clark to be: the "church of the future."[55]

Meanwhile, rumors spread that Hall's unhappy wife had committed suicide, taking her daughter with her.[56] ("Hall was a perfectly ruthless chap you know," one of his former students later said about Hall as a husband, in an interview the intellectual historian Dorothy Ross conducted for a remarkably astute biography.)[57] Hall aged more than a decade in the space of a few years.[58] He felt, in his heart, that he had become an old man. Much of contemporary developmental psychology, and many popular ideas about childhood and adolescence, can be traced, in one way or another, to Hall's attempt to escape depression. He was rescued from his bereavement not by a séance but by a fascination with the relationship between growing up and growing old, which was a way, in psychology, to think about history. Hall's wife and daughter died—were discovered one morning, dead in that bed—when he was forty-four years old. Old age, he came to believe, begins at forty-five, the age at which we begin to die.[59]

When Hall realized he was old, he wanted to write about it but wasn't sure he ought to, because growing old was a subject, in his view, about which "other old men have written fatuously."[60] What he wanted to do was far more grandiose: he wanted to found a "biological philosophy," with "a view of life far higher, broader and more unified than Plato, Aristotle, Kant, Hegel, or even Darwin, Huxley and Spencer ever dreamed of."[61]

Each of us, he argued, recapitulates, in the course of our lives, the stages of human evolution. Hall's ideas about recapitulation were racial; primitive people were children. "Most savages in most respects are children, or, because of sexual maturity, more properly, adolescents of adult size."[62] Women, too, were doomed to a more primitive state of development. This, Hall posited, in a revealing aside, accounted for both the higher suicide rate among women and the methods women used to kill themselves: "Women prefer passive methods; to give themselves up to the power of elemental forces, as gravity, when they throw themselves from heights or take poison, in which methods of suicide they surpass man."[63]

Adolescence, effervescent and plastic, is when we are most capable of making a leap, and bringing civilization along with us, to the next stage.[64] Adolescents were, to Hall, the future of the race, by which he meant the Anglo-Saxon race. "There is color in their souls, brilliant, livid, loud."[65] The storm and stress of adolescence is, at heart, a crisis of faith. (James, an anti-imperialist, once remarked that perhaps the imperialist Theodore Roosevelt was "still mentally in the Sturm und Drang period of early adolescence.")[66] The work of growing up, Hall argued, is the work of finding something to believe in. But as Ross observed, "what he really described was the crisis of belief of the nineteenth-century intellectual whose religious commitment had been undercut by modern science."[67]

When Hall's two-volume study of adolescence was published, in 1904, one reviewer complained that it was "chock full of errors, masturbation and Jesus. He is a mad man."[68] But its argument that the ages of man are the stages of evolution was also greeted as good parenting advice. The *New York Times* observed, "Many a puzzled and despairing parent will be glad to learn from this volume that the reason why 'that boy is so bad' is not necessarily because he has started on a downward road to wickedness and sin. Probably it is only because he has reached the age when it is necessary for him to live through the cave-man epoch of the race."[69] Most often, Hall's study of adolescence was hailed as visionary, and for reasons that prefigure his theory of senescence. What are we to believe in, when men are animals and death is the end? Sex, science, and youth.[70]

In 1909, Hall brought Freud and Jung to Clark, along with twenty-seven other scholars, to celebrate the university's twenty-year anniversary. (Jonas Clark, in his will, had forbidden Hall contact with undergraduates, but Hall remained at the university as head of the graduate program.) Only Freud and Jung stayed at his house. Hall had been reading their work for years; at least as early as 1903, as Terman remembered it, Hall had mentioned Freud in his lectures.[71] He asked James to come, and to bring his latest paper on Mrs. Piper. When James arrived, he reached into his breast pocket and pulled out not an offprint but a wad of dollar bills. Freud and Jung, who had heard about Hall's reputation for moneygrubbing, found this prank terribly funny—not to mention, given Hall's having told them that James was not taken seriously as a psychologist (which was simply untrue; the reverse was emphatically more the case), well deserved. "It looked to us a particularly happy rejoinder," Jung wrote.[72] James, feigning an apology, then pulled out from another pocket the actual paper, in which he had discussed the case of Richard Hodgson. A former secretary of the American Society for Psychical Research, Hodgson, before he'd died, in 1905, had said he would try to communicate through Mrs. Piper; to prove that it was really him, he promised, he'd speak in "nigger talk." Mrs. Piper obliged. But James concluded that the case presented "no knock-down proof"; Mrs. Piper knew Hodgson too well.[73]

Hall wanted some knockdown proof, too—proof that the whole thing was a sham. He had arranged to host a séance, scheduled for Saturday evening. His plan: to pit psychical research against psychoanalysis. Do the dead speak? Or is it just we, inside our own heads, muttering? This was a dastardly kind of empiricism, closer to vengeance than science. It didn't work. James was called away, to attend a funeral. And the séance, on Saturday, was a disappointment. The medium, a twenty-year-old girl, failed to impress Freud and Jung, who concluded, after a short interview, that her trancelike state derived from thwarted sexual desire. Hall wrote, "The German savants saw little further to interest them in the case."[74]

James died later within the year. Hall began teaching a course called The Psychology of Sex. "After the Freud visit, everything in the university centered around Freudianism," one of his students recalled. "It got to be the sexiest place you can imagine."[75] Meanwhile, Hall had remarried. His wife, a former kindergarten teacher, grew fat; she also grew eccentric. She claimed that he beat her.[76] She fell ill; he committed her to a sanatorium. And then Hall and his graduate students, many of whom were very young women, turned their attention to the study of senescence.[77]

The transformation of old age from a stage of life into a disease was a long time coming. Sylvester Graham had imagined a world without suffering, a world in which one day we are well, and the next we die, without illness, without pain. But the modern medical treatment of aging as a disease, and death as something to be conquered, began in earnest in the first decades of the twentieth century. The word "geriatrics" was coined, in 1909, by I. N. Nascher, a New York doctor originally from Austria. As the story goes, Nascher was making his rounds one day when the attending physician, discussing an elderly woman who was very ill, diagnosed her as suffering from "old age."

"What can be done about it?" Nascher asked.

"Nothing."

Not long after, Nascher wrote an article called "Why Old Age Ends in Death." He thought it might not have to.[78]

Hall followed this research.[79] He had, by now, given up on writing about sex. In 1916, when asked to join the Massachusetts Birth Control League, he declined: "I regret to say that I cannot give the use of my name in connection with your work. If you want to know why, I will tell you frankly that I have borne my share of *odium sexicum* for almost a generation of men. Some fifteen years ago I wrote a book on adolescence advocating what I believed was true and right, and for that have been pilloried severely and ostracized by some of my friends. The same was true because I went into the sex instruction movement. . . . I have done my bit in this movement and am now retiring and am going to have a rest from this trouble for the remainder of my life."[80]

He began his study of old age by making a study of himself, reporting, in 1917, "that early senescence is not so bad as it is painted, but that its study is likely to prove even more interesting than that of adolescence ever was."[81] He didn't publish much on the subject until 1921, when he wrote an essay for the *Atlantic Monthly* called "Old Age." He had just retired; he was seventy-seven. "Now I am divorced from my world," he wrote, "and there is nothing more to be said of me, save the exact date of my death."[82] This was balderdash. Hall dedicated his retirement—to which he objected—to writing an autobiography and to pulling together everything he had been able to discover about life after forty-five. *Senescence: The Last Half of Life* was published in 1922; it was followed, the next year, by *The Life and Confessions of a Psychologist.*[83] The autobiography was very shrewdly reviewed in the *Nation:* "The reading of this book leaves one a trifle depressed. It is a pathetic life-epic in a minor key. It might even be called an apology for failure. Hall, essentially a poet-dreamer, decidedly subjective in temperament, is touched by hard, materialistic science and everywhere its dehumanized hand has either made his work abortive or else left him with a feeling of incompleteness. To overcome this insufficiency he resorted to a new form of religious tenancy."[84]

Hall began *Senescence* by explaining his object. "The one thing I have always planned for this stage of life," he wrote, was to "know more about what it really is, find out its status, estimate its powers, its limitations, its physical and mental regimen; and especially, if I can, look death, which certainly cannot be very far off, calmly in the face." He took stock of his eyesight, his limbs, his acuity. He chronicled every debility of old age, along with its treatment. He visited doctors, only to conclude, "I must henceforth, for the most part, be my own doctor." He read all his old papers, as well as his parents'. James had published his father's "literary remains"; Hall threw his mother's diaries into his fireplace. He noted, "as I watched them burn in the grate one solitary spring at evening twilight, I felt that I had completed a filial function."[85] He wrote his will. It would be discovered after his death that he had hidden away a miser's fortune, in accounts he had taken out in every savings bank in Massachusetts.[86]

Having taken stock of himself, Hall took a look at the lives of other old men. "Napoleon lost Waterloo at 45, Dickens had written all his best at 40, and Pepys finished his diary at 37," he wrote (giving extraordinarily short shrift to *Great Expectations*).[87] Studies, something like actuarial tables, correlating age with productivity were commonplace in those years; it was those studies that led to the invention of retirement.[88] As early as the 1870s, a New York physician had conducted a study of "nearly all the greatest names in history" and examined the course of their lives: "seventy percent of the work of the world is done before forty-five," he'd concluded, "and eighty percent before fifty."[89] From 1874 to 1900, only four American companies had retirement policies; between 1911 and 1915 alone, ninety-nine companies established such policies. In the Taylorized age of efficiency, stopping work at sixty-five became routine and, soon, mandatory.[90]

Hall was dubious. He looked to art, and took heart from Longfellow: "Ah, nothing is too late / Till the tired heart shall cease to palpitate / . . . Chaucer at Wadstock, with the nightingales, / At sixty wrote The Canterbury Tales."[91] Then he sent questionnaires to all the "mostly eminent and some very distinguished old people" he could think of. He asked good questions:

> When did you realize you were getting old?
> To what do you ascribe your long life?
> How do you keep well?
> Are you troubled by regrets?
> What temptations do you feel?
> What duties do you feel?[92]

From all of this, Hall concluded that humanity itself was senescing.[93] "The human stock is not maturing as it should," he wrote, because people were living longer, but they weren't living better.[94] "At no stage of life do we want more to be of service than when we are deprived of our most wonted opportunities to be so," he said. The time had come "to add a new story to the life of man, for as yet we do not know what full maturity really is and the last culminating chapter of humanity's history is yet to be written." A lot of this is Hall's patented mumbo jumbo. But much of it is a howl of pain. "We do not take," he remarked, "with entire kindness to being set off as a class apart."[95]

To the very end, the Darwin of the mind thought he was wiser than everyone, wiser than his parents, wiser than William James. "I am far older than my years," he wrote, on the final page of his autobiography, "for I have laid aside more of the illusions and transcended more of the limitations with which I started than most."[96] As he was dying, he asked to be carried into his study. He had the idea that looking at his books would save his life. Aquinas, Hegel, Freud. A student of his described what happened next: "They brought a wheel chair and bore the indomitable old man into the shabby room which held so many memories of the best part of his life. Here he had thought some of his best thoughts." Hall stared at his desk, the shelves of books. Divinity, philosophy, psychology. Nothing. He collapsed in his chair. "He had placed such hopes upon the study, and the study had failed him."[97] Doctors dissected his brain. It wasn't as distinctive as they had hoped.[98]

CHAPTER 9

The Gate of Heaven

Just before eight o'clock in the morning on October 20, 1975, Thomas Trapasso left the rectory at Our Lady of the Lake, a stone church perched high on a bluff outside the small town of Mount Arlington, New Jersey. He climbed into his car. Through a driving rain, he drove downhill toward Lake Hopatcong, wended his way along the water for a mile or so, and then turned onto Ryerson Road, where he slowed down in front of a two-story bungalow. He could scarcely have missed it. Forty reporters stood in the yard, huddled beneath trees. Mail reached this house even when it bore no more address than "To Karen Quinlan's Family, U.S.A."[1]

Karen Ann Quinlan, twenty-one years old, was not at home. She was a dozen miles away, at Saint Clare's, a Catholic hospital in Denville. She was in a bed, contorted, shriveled, and emaciated. Six months earlier, she had collapsed, mysteriously, after a night out with some friends and had stopped breathing. Before she was successfully resuscitated, her brain had been without oxygen for two periods of about fifteen minutes each.[2] She had never regained consciousness. Since falling into a coma, she had lost half her weight; she weighed less than seventy pounds. Her eyes opened and shut. She flailed, she grimaced: muscle spasms, and nothing more.[3] She had no chance, no conceivable hope, of any sort of recovery at all.[4] A feeding tube and a respirator kept her alive. Her parents, Julia and Joseph Quinlan, talked with Trapasso, their parish priest, who was also Julia Quinlan's boss (she worked in the rectory, as his secretary), and then, in July, they asked their daughter's doctors to remove the respirator. Her doctors refused.[5]

In front of the Quinlans' bungalow on Ryerson Road stood a statue of the Virgin Mary, eyes downcast, arms outspread, palms to the sky. As Trapasso pulled into the driveway, the reporters advanced. When the Quinlans opened a side door, the flashbulbs, Julia Quinlan later remembered, popped like fireworks. "God, see me through this," she prayed, just before she and her husband, a one-armed World War II veteran, made a dash for the priest's car.[6] Trapasso backed out of the drive. The Quinlans had thirty miles of road to go.

This matter of life and death would not be decided in a stone church, perched on a bluff. It would not be decided in the Quinlans' bungalow, down by the lake. It wouldn't even be decided in a hospital room, where a respirator whirred as the rain pattered on the windowpane, sounds Karen Ann Quinlan, who had once taught herself to play the piano by ear, could no longer hear.[7] Through that autumn storm, Trapasso drove, east, and then south, to the county seat. The Quinlans were going to court. When they reached Morristown, where George Washington once quartered his troops, Julia Quinlan thought the Morris County Courthouse looked like Tara, the mansion in *Gone with the Wind,* and the army of reporters camped out front like so many Civil War soldiers, wet, weary, and bedraggled. Inside, a judge was preparing to hear arguments for *In the Matter of Karen Quinlan.*[8] Wrote one reporter for the *Washington Post,* "Whatever the decision, it is one that will haunt us for years to come."[9]

In the Matter of Karen Quinlan marked a fundamental shift in American political history. In the decades following *Quinlan,* all manner of domestic policy issues were recast as matters of life and death: urgent, uncompromising, and absolute.[10] This shift began in 1965, when *Life* published "Drama of Life Before Birth" and the Supreme Court issued its ruling in *Griswold v.*

Connecticut. In 1968, Pope Paul VI issued "On Human Life," asserting the sanctity of life from the very first moment captured by Lennart Nilsson's photographs. Richard Nixon employed this language in 1971, when he reversed his position on abortion as part of a strategy to define the Republican Party around this issue. In 1972, the phrase "sanctity of life" appeared, for the first time, in an opinion of the U.S. Supreme Court, with a death penalty case, *Furman v. Georgia.* The next year, the court's ruling in *Roe v. Wade* galvanized opposition to abortion. In 1975, the Quinlan case brought the right to life and the right to die together, locked in a kind of mortal combat. Reasonable people on all sides agree that profoundly serious and difficult questions lie at the heart of these matters, which is why extremists within the pro-life movement have never managed to tar their opponents as "anti-life" or "pro-death." Nevertheless, in the wake of *Roe* and *Quinlan,* a very small but by no means inconsequential number of people came to believe that Congress, the president, the courts, and assorted unnamed bureaucrats were plotting to deny medical care to the very sick and the very old, to babies born with deformities, to the elderly and infirm, to the ailing and the poor, to the disabled and the insane; that doctors, acting on orders from Washington, would one day soon disconnect respirators, turn off incubators, yank out feeding tubes, unhook IVs, and refuse to renew lifesaving prescriptions; that the machinery of the world's most powerful nation was being turned to the remorseless and unceasing project of euthanizing the weakest members of society.[11] Or something like that. The story changed fairly often. Sometimes it involved organ harvesting. Rarely did Hitler go unmentioned.

For decades, protesters waved poster-sized pictures of Lennart Nilsson's photographs of fetuses. Riders banning abortion, contraception, and sex education tied up bills in committee, bills that, usually, had nothing to do with abortion or contraception or sex education. Judicial nominees faced "litmus tests," explicitly or implicitly, over embryo storage, genetic testing, abortion, stem cell research, and palliative care. In the summer of 2009, after the Obama administration proposed a reform of the health care system, former Republican vice presidential nominee Sarah Palin posted her thoughts on her Facebook page: "The America I know and love is not one in which my parents or my baby with Down Syndrome will have to stand in front of Obama's 'death panel' so his bureaucrats can decide, based on a subjective judgment of their 'level of productivity in society,' whether they

are worthy of health care. Such a system is downright evil."[12] Iowa senator Chuck Grassley agreed that citizens had "every right to fear" that the
government would issue orders about "pulling the plug on grandma"; and
street theater Death Panelists paraded on the Mall wearing masks inspired
by Edvard Munch's *The Scream* and T-shirts picturing the president as the
Grim Reaper.[13]

The fear that the American government was conspiring to hold the
power of life and death over its people kept lingering, and taking on new
forms, because however wildly and dangerously preposterous, it was just
one feature of a newly configured political landscape. Since the 1960s, what
Americans were talking about, even when they seemed to be talking about
something else, was a disputed right to life.

Minooka Comm. H.S. South
Channahon, IL 60410

In November 1963, just days before John F. Kennedy was shot in Dallas,
Richard Hofstadter, a forty-seven-year-old historian from Columbia University, delivered the Herbert Spencer Lecture at Oxford. American politics, Hofstadter argued, is characterized by a "paranoid style." As he took
pains to explain, he didn't mean that clinically; Americans weren't, literally, crazy. Instead, by "style," he meant something like what, in speaking,
is usually termed an accent. Americans talk paranoid and think paranoid;
they use the language of "heated exaggeration, suspiciousness, and con-
spiratorial fantasy"; they have a habit of worrying about dark goings-on
by unnamed, mysterious plotters who lurk, disguised as honorable public
servants, within the very halls of government.[14]

Hofstadter's lecture would have resonated back home even if Kennedy
hadn't been assassinated, but, somehow, that tragedy gained for Hofstadter's account of "angry minds" a special hold on the national psyche.
"The Paranoid Style in American Politics" was published in *Harper's* in
1964. For quite a long time, it was used to explain a great deal, from Joseph
McCarthy, on the floor of Congress in 1951, stirring up fears of Communist
infiltrators in postwar Washington ("How can we account for our present
situation unless we believe that men high in this government are concert-
ing to deliver us to disaster?") to theories about the Warren Commission
and the grassy knoll to Glenn Beck on national television in 2009, ranting
about eugenicists in Barack Obama's White House ("Do you trust these
people enough to give them control over who lives and who dies?").[15]

The essay endured as a consequence of its audacity, which made it capacious. Hofstadter didn't so much nail down an argument as float one. Historians, Hofstadter believed, had a "habit of overvaluing facts for facts' sake." He had a different idea about what was important. "I believe that a conjecture, an insight, even if it proves wrong, is worth a thousand facts," he once wrote; if it proved right, that supposition would be "worth ten thousand facts."[16] With characteristic ambition, sensitivity, and aloofness, Hofstadter claimed, in "The Paranoid Style," to be charting an essentially changeless tradition, worth at least a thousand facts. The essay doesn't contain much historical detail; that wasn't its point. Chiefly concerned with the hard American right from McCarthy to Goldwater, Hofstadter deployed a handful of examples from earlier eras, with stops at the eighteenth-century Bavarian Illuminati and the nineteenth-century Know-Nothings, merely to document the depth of the style he was describing. Partisans of all stripes talk and think paranoid, Hofstadter argued, although "the paranoid style has a greater affinity for bad causes than good." As he saw it, paranoid conservatives of his own day were different from their ideological forebears only in painting their enemies more vividly and attacking them more personally. The Illuminati raved about "little-known papal delegates" undermining democracy, while the people who worried Hofstadter charged FDR himself with heading an international conspiracy to destroy capitalism. What all these people had in common, though, was the belief in "a vast and sinister conspiracy, a gigantic and yet subtle machinery of influence set in motion to undermine and destroy a way of life."[17]

Hofstadter was right about very many things. But this particular argument, forever bound to the moment in which he made it, falls something short of ten thousand facts: the paranoid style is not changeless. It was changing, even as, behind a lectern in front of an audience of Oxford dons, he adjusted his inevitable bow tie, tinkered with his eyeglasses, and took out his stack of notes. When Hofstadter delivered that lecture in 1963, he could not possibly have seen that the ground was shifting beneath his feet, a chasm forming, a whole new sort of paranoia growing in America—not over a way of life, but over life itself.

Before Thomas Jefferson stumbled upon the felicitous phrase "the pursuit of happiness," life, liberty, and property constituted the Enlightenment's list of natural rights. "The inhabitants of the English colonies in North-America," the Continental Congress declared in 1774, "are entitled to life, liberty and property." Jefferson said it better, but his wording didn't assume anything like the status later accorded it until 1826, when the Declaration of Independence was resurrected for the fiftieth Fourth of July. In 1780, when John Adams drafted the Massachusetts Constitution, he rambled on about the people's "right of enjoying and defending their lives and liberties; that of acquiring, possessing, and protecting property; in fine, that of seeking and obtaining their safety and happiness."[18] Whether in three words or a hundred and three, life, liberty, and property have been the rights Americans talk about and fight over. Taking a long view of American history, it's possible to argue that each of these rights has led to a fracture in the body politic, a dispute in which there seemed to be no room for compromise. Urgency, suffering, paranoia, partisanship, violence, political theater, insurrection, and a swirl of disputed ideas have gathered around each of these contested rights. Yet from one era to the next, the ideas have been different. Paranoid may be our enduring political style, but our substance has changed.

In the eighteenth century, colonists on both sides of the struggle for independence worried that their rulers were plotting against their liberties. Americans danced under liberty poles; they sang liberty songs; they wore liberty caps. A conspiracy appeared to be afoot. "A series of occurrences," the people of Boston resolved, "afford great reason to believe that a deep-laid and desperate plan of imperial despotism has been laid, and partly executed, for the extinction of all civil liberty." In 1774, Jefferson concluded that "single acts of tyranny may be ascribed to the accidental opinion of a day; but a series of oppressions . . . too plainly prove a deliberate and systematical plan." The Declaration of Independence is Jefferson's list of those acts of tyranny. Liberty, like all natural rights, was so capacious an idea that it could stretch across both sides of the conflict. When the war began, one in three colonists remained loyal to the Crown, insisting that they, not the so-called patriots, were the "*true* lovers of liberty."[19]

In the nineteenth century, Americans worried about a conspiracy against property—a property in people. In 1820, the Missouri Compromise, which prohibited "this species of property" north of the 36th parallel, divided the country in half. Jefferson called it a national "act of suicide."[20] Four years after the Compromise of 1850 redrew the line between slave and free states, Abraham Lincoln blamed the framers, "who forbore to so much as mention the word 'slave' or 'slavery' " for the disease festering in the body politic. "Thus," he continued, "the thing is hid away, in the constitution, just as an afflicted man hides away a wen or cancer, which he dares not cut out at once, lest he bleed to death."[21] In 1857, in *Dred Scott v. Sandford*, the Supreme Court ruled that the framers had intended to define "the Negro" not as a person but as an item of property, to be "bought and sold and treated as an ordinary article of merchandise."[22] Slave owners feared an abolitionist conspiracy, "a party in the North organized for the express purpose of robbing the citizens of the Southern States of their property."[23] In 1859, John Brown's raid at Harpers Ferry realized those fears.[24] On the floor of the Senate, Jefferson Davis made a threat: "If we are not to be protected in our property and sovereignty, we . . . will dissever the ties that bind us together, even if it rushes us into a sea of blood." The next year, South Carolina became the first state to secede, citing, as its cause, the federal government's failure to honor its "right of property in slaves."[25] The contested right to property led to the Civil War, and six hundred thousand dead.

In the decades since Richard Hofstadter's day—since right around the time the facts of life went extraterrestrial, with Lennart Nilsson's photographs, and abortion entered the partisan arena—Americans have been fighting over the right to life. There are only so many cards in this political deck, and life, it would seem, trumps all.

"The curtain rises on one of the most compelling dramas since the Scopes trial sought to establish the roots of human life," wrote one newsman, filing a report for the New York *Daily News* the day Karen Ann Quinlan's trial began.[26] Only a handful of spectators managed to get through the courthouse door. Prophet Dan, a man with a long white beard who believed "he could cure the stricken girl," had waited four hours to get a seat.[27] (Faith healers had also been turning up at Saint Clare's, asking to lay hands on Quinlan, much to the consternation of the nuns who ran the hospital, the Sisters of the Sorrowful Mother.)[28] Just before nine o'clock, Julia and Joseph Quinlan and Thomas Trapasso made their way inside and climbed the stairs to the courtroom on the second floor, where they settled onto a cushioned mahogany bench, as straight as any pew. It seemed, at first, as if they had entered a chapel, as if the tall, arched windows were made of stained glass. That, though, was only a trick of the eye: wet autumn leaves, yellow and red, glinting through clear panes as the sun broke through the clouds.[29]

Of the 137 seats in the courtroom, 100 were taken by reporters. (The week of the trial, the Quinlans received more than a thousand pieces of mail, not just letters but packages: jars of holy water and little boxes crammed with crucifixes.)[30] No cameras were allowed, and although a reporter offered the Quinlans $100,000 for a photograph of their daughter in her hospital bed ("That was only a starting figure"), they refused, which is why the iconic image of the trial was Karen Ann Quinlan's high school yearbook picture, a head shot, striking in its ordinariness, of a pale and unsmiling eighteen-year-old with long, dark hair.[31]

This story had everything: a pretty girl—"Sleeping Beauty," the press called her—and a handsome young lawyer—the Quinlans' thirty-year-old attorney, Paul Armstrong, looked like he'd come straight out of the 1973 film *The Paper Chase*—and just the sort of edge-of-your-seat high-stakes medical drama television viewers tuned in for in prime time, especially *Emergency!*, NBC's popular series about Los Angeles paramedics, which ran from 1972 to 1977. Reporters had started covering the story in September, when Armstrong filed papers asking the court to appoint Joseph Quinlan as his daughter's guardian. "These poor people really need help," Armstrong told a colleague. "The whole world needs help. It's man against technology."[32]

Intensive care units date only to the 1950s. Dying, which used to happen earlier in life, usually took place at home, and rarely involved an electrical cord. Only beginning in 1958 did the majority of American deaths take place in a hospital. When death moved away from the home, doctors, hospitals, and insurance companies took charge of the end of life.[33] This change, when it came, came fast. By the 1960s, 75 percent of the dying spent at least eighty days in a hospital or nursing home during the last year of life.[34] The longer we live, the longer we die.

As early as 1966, a journalist covering the topic could ask, "Should a new right—the right to die—be added to the triad of 'inalienable rights' to life, liberty and the pursuit of happiness?"[35] Whether machines made to save and extend lives might end up inflicting a sort of torture had revealed itself as a difficult and painful question. More and more patients and their families struggled with doctors and hospitals and health insurance companies. In 1972, the U.S. Senate Committee on Aging held hearings on "death with dignity," and two years later, ABC Television aired a documentary called *The Right to Die*.[36] The Quinlans and their priest had been guided by "The Prolongation of Life," a statement issued by Pope Pius XII in 1957; it obligated Catholics to use only ordinary efforts, rather than "extraordinary means," to extend life.[37] In 1975, the respirator that kept Karen Ann Quinlan alive seemed, to her parents, altogether extraordinary. Their daughter's doctors did not agree. Nor would the court grant this argument. "I thought I'd just go to the clerk and talk to the judge and it would be settled," Joseph Quinlan said.[38] But on September 15, 1975, Judge Robert Muir, a forty-three-year-old Presbyterian, refused to name Quinlan as his daughter's guardian, and instead appointed to that position a part-time public defender named Daniel Coburn.[39] It was on the basis of Muir's refusal that the case had come to trial.[40]

There had been some question, in pretrial proceedings, of whether Karen Ann Quinlan was still among the living. The press wondered, too. "Is Karen Ann Quinlan alive or dead?" *Time* asked.[41] Armstrong had thought he might be able to establish "brain death," a state first described in a report issued in 1968 by the Ad Hoc Committee of the Harvard Medical School to Examine the Definition of Death, a committee that had consisted of ten doctors, one lawyer, one theologian, and one historian. "Under the existing legal and medical definitions of death recognized by the state of New Jersey," Armstrong had insisted, "Karen Ann Quinlan is dead."[42]

Brain death—the cessation of brain function, as measured, more or less, by two flat electroencephalograms, or EEGs, over a period of twenty-four hours—was a legal term whose definition had been intended to standardize practices for transplant surgeons. The definition allowed surgeons to remove organs for transplant from patients whose hearts could be kept beating artificially, without fear of being charged with homicide or wrongful death. The first heart transplant was conducted in 1967; in 1968, doctors transplanted 108 hearts. Brain death, which is something between a medical fiction and a legal one, was intended to facilitate organ transplant; it had very little to do with the kind of decision the Quinlans faced.

In 1975, only eight states had adopted laws defining brain death. New Jersey was not among them. By the time the trial began, Armstrong had agreed that Quinlan did not meet the criterion for "brain death"; her EEG

was not flat. The chief reason she was still alive, six months after collaps-
ing, was that such a criterion existed. Before that 1968 ad hoc committee set
out formal guidelines, and before the rise of malpractice suits (which date
to the 1960s), patients in what is termed a "persistent vegetative state" had
been allowed to die. What was new wasn't pulling the plug or not pulling
the plug. What was new was the plug.[43]

There were nine lawyers in the courtroom. "Not one of those lawyers
looked much more than thirty," Julia Quinlan thought. "So young, to be
arguing about death."[44] Armstrong opened by making an argument about
the afterlife. The Quinlans, he said, "believe that the earthly phase of Kar-
en's life has drawn to a close, that the time of life striving is over, and that
further treatments merely hold her back from the realization and enjoyment of a better, more perfect life." Calling on the language of the nascent
right-to-die movement, Armstrong used the word "dignity" over and over
again. "The answer to the tragedy of Karen Ann Quinlan," he told the court,
"is to be found in the love, faith and courage of her family who ask only
that she be allowed to return to God with grace and dignity." And, citing
Griswold v. Connecticut and *Roe v. Wade,* he argued that the right to die fell
under the right to privacy.[45]

Coburn spoke next. He considered his job to be protecting Quinlan's
"constitutional right to life," a phrase that echoed the central tenet of the
pro-life movement. A chancery court, he insisted, ought not to be asked to
entertain arguments about an afterlife. "This is not a Court of love," said
Coburn. "This is a Court of law."[46] After Coburn took his seat, New Jersey
attorney general William Hyland approached the bench. "It is not for the
executive or the judicial branches of government," he argued, "to evaluate
the quality and usefulness of life and, based upon that assessment, to determine that a citizen's life is not worth preserving."[47] Hyland didn't want the
plug pulled, and, more than that, he didn't want the court to make much of
any sort of decision at all. He believed that doctors knew best.

Next came Ralph Porzio, an attorney retained by the doctors who had
refused to pull the plug. The "cornerstone of our Western culture," Porzio
began, is the "sanctity of life." (That may be, but the phrase "sanctity of life"
appeared in the *Congressional Record* only eight times before 1974, mostly
during prayers.)[48] He then proceeded to imply that the sanctity of life and

the right to life were one and the same, reminding the court that, of the rights listed in the Declaration of Independence, life, liberty, and the pursuit of happiness, "the first is life." And then he said it again: "The first is life."[49]

Karen Ann Quinlan wasn't dead. But, terrifyingly, she wasn't fully alive, either. Maybe she was no longer human: her brain wasn't dead, but the parts of it that made her human were. Her sister, her mother, and one of her friends testified that she had always said she'd rather be dead than kept alive like this. Nearly all of the rest of the witnesses called to testify were doctors, asked to offer a prognosis. A chart of the human brain, three feet tall by five feet wide, was introduced as evidence and displayed in front of the judge's bench.[50] Much of the trial transcript reads like lecture notes from a neurobiology class. When asked to define "decortication," one doctor said, "What it means is that the lesions, or the etiology, whatever it is that causes the condition, has affected certain parts of the neuraxis above the diencephalon," whereupon his questioner confessed, "I lost you."

Lawyers and reporters alike attempted to describe Quinlan's condition in plain English. Groping for words, many settled on one: "fetal." One neurologist told the court that Quinlan's starved and twisted body was "too grotesque, really, to describe in human terms like fetal," but, with that exception, she was almost invariably described in just that way.[51] She was curled up like a fetus in the womb, the respirator her umbilical cord. She was twenty-one and no longer a child and had fallen into a coma after taking Valium and drinking several gin and tonics, but no one ever talked about Quinlan as if she were an adult, or ever had been. She was a girl. She was Karen Ann. (One of her doctors told the court that his own daughter, a toddler, was also named Karen Ann. He couldn't pull the plug. He just couldn't.) And the legal question to be settled, after all, concerned guardianship: Who would take care of this girl? She wasn't somebody's wife, and she was no one's mother: she was somebody's daughter, and her parents wanted to end her life. In some meaningful way, Karen Ann Quinlan seemed, somehow, akin to a baby. Another neurologist compared her brain waves to those of an infant (to point out that they didn't measure up).[52] An attorney asked another medical expert to estimate Quinlan's mental age: Was she like "a two-week-old infant, five-week-old infant, seven-year-old child, or something like that?" The doctor balked at the question's premise—it was a clumsy and ill-considered analogy—but, when pressed, he reluctantly offered this gruesome reply: "The best way I can describe this would be to take the situation of an anencephalic monster. An anencephalic monster is an infant that's born with no cerebral hemisphere. . . . If you take a child like this, in the dark, and you put a flashlight in back of the head, the light comes out the pupils. They have no brain. Okay?"[53]

Those babies born without brains had lately been in the news. In October 1973, nine months after the Supreme Court handed down its decision in *Roe v. Wade*, pediatricians Raymond Duff and Alexander Campbell reported in the *New England Journal of Medicine* that anencephalic and other severely deformed or premature infants were being allowed to die in one of the country's most prestigious hospitals. Between 1970 and 1972, Duff and Campbell reported, 43 of 299 deaths in the special care nursery at Yale–New Haven Hospital were the result of withholding or withdrawing treatment. Even with heroic measures, these babies were not likely to survive beyond a few hours or days. However agonizing the decision to let them die, Duff and Campbell stood by it.[54]

That report, along with other highly publicized cases, fueled the growing pro-life movement. After *Roe v. Wade*, newly founded pro-life organizations across the country, including the National Right to Life Committee, set about searching for cases with which to challenge the ruling. NBC News reported that 58 percent of Americans, including 46 percent of Catholics, approved of legalizing abortion in the first trimester. Pro-life activists concentrated their efforts on putting a stop to late-term abortions. The month Duff and Campbell's study was published, Kenneth Edelin, an obstetrician at Boston City Hospital, conducted an abortion on a seventeen-year-old girl who may have been as far along as twenty-four weeks. In April 1974, Edelin was indicted for manslaughter, largely through the efforts of a group called the Massachusetts Citizens for Life. The state argued that he had delivered a live male infant and killed him. In February 1975, seven months before Karen Ann Quinlan's case went to court, Edelin was found guilty.[55]

In the wake of *Roe v. Wade*, Duff and Campbell's report, and Edelin's conviction, Quinlan's fate rested as much on ideas about abortion as about euthanasia. Historians have called *In the Matter of Karen Quinlan* the most significant medical case in American history.[56] It looked that way even at the time, and as more time passes, it looks only more pivotal. To the press, it was too important a story not to report; it was a very easy story to exploit. It was high; it was low. It was tabloid; it was Plato. There was only one problem: it lacked a villain.[57]

If Muir were to grant the Quinlans' petition, Ralph Porzio warned the court, it would be "like turning on the gas chamber." Enter the villain. Against the sanctity of life, against the first right listed in the Declaration of Independence, Porzio pitted Hitler. "Fresh in our minds are the Nazi atrocities. . . . Fresh in our minds are the Nuremberg Code."[58]

At the end of the Second World War, thirteen different trials were held in the Palace of Justice in Nuremberg, Germany. The medical trials, known popularly as the Doctors' Trial but formally as *U.S.A. v. Karl Brandt et al.,* began on December 9, 1946, two days before the United Nations moved to declare genocide a war crime. (The word "genocide" had been coined in 1943.) Of twenty-three defendants charged with war crimes for conducting experiments on human subjects, twenty were university-trained German physicians, once distinguished scientists. The charges against them included executing a state-run euthanasia program, under which they killed the elderly and the insane, the "feeble-minded" and the lame, crippled children and deformed babies; and conducting experiments on human subjects, during which they maimed, tortured, and murdered hundreds of thousands of Jews, Poles, and Russians, mostly in concentration camps. "A few of the survivors will appear in this courtroom," said the chief prosecutor in his opening statement. "But most of these miserable victims were slaughtered outright or died in the course of the tortures to which they were subjected." After 140 days of testimony, seven of the defendants were acquitted and sixteen convicted.

The trial verdict included a statement about ethical standards for medical research, the Nuremberg Code. As important as the Nuremberg Code later became in the United States—it lay behind the founding, in the 1960s, of the field known as "bioethics"—the trials were virtually ignored in the 1940s. As the historian of medicine David Rothman has pointed out, the American press failed to report on the Nuremberg trials in 1946 and 1947 and paid almost no attention to the execution of seven of its convicted defendants in 1948. To the extent that Americans drew a lesson from Nuremberg, Rothman argues, it was that the government should not have a hand in either science or medicine. "And here," Rothman writes, "the distinction between the Nazi government and all other governments was lost."[59]

The specter of Nazi medicine began to haunt the United States only in the 1960s. *Doctors of Infamy,* a much-redacted version of the Nuremberg Doctors' Trial transcript, was translated from the German and published in New York in 1949, but it received very little attention until it was republished in London in 1962 as *The Death Doctors.*[60] That republication followed the 1961 trial of Adolf Eichmann, who was hanged in 1962. In 1963, the *New Yorker* published Hannah Arendt's *Eichmann in Jerusalem,* her report on the trial. It cast considerable attention on Nuremberg; Dr. Robert Servatius, Eichmann's attorney, had also defended Karl Brandt in 1946. Servatius's defense of Eichmann was more or less the same as his defense of Brandt: these men, implicated in the torture and slaughter of millions of people, were simply following orders. Eichmann was an ordinary civil servant; Brandt, an ordinary doctor. Arendt told of one exchange between Servatius and the court. Eichmann, Servatius insisted, was innocent of charges regarding "the collection of skeletons, sterilizations, killings by gas, and *similar medical matters.*" The judge interrupted him: "Dr. Servatius, I assume you made a slip of the tongue when you said that killing by gas was a medical matter." Servatius: "It was indeed a medical matter, since it was prepared by physicians; *it was a matter of killing, and killing, too, is a medical matter.*"[61]

In the 1960s, Nazi medical atrocities, long ignored by the American press, captured Americans' attention, not least because Americans were, at just that moment, obsessed with death and doctors. When death moved to the hospital, it got scarier: so far from home; so many machines; so many strangers; instruments that poke and prod; bright lights, sleepless nights. The more successfully medicine has staved off death, the less well anyone, including and maybe especially doctors and scientists, has accepted dying. The year the *New Yorker* ran *Eichmann in Jerusalem,* Jessica Mitford published *The American Way of Death.* Some twelve hundred books about death and bereavement came out between 1935 and 1968; twelve hundred more—including Elisabeth Kübler-Ross's 1969 *On Death and Dying*—were published between 1968 and 1973 alone. In 1974, *Publishers Weekly* announced, "Death is now selling books."[62]

It didn't matter that Nuremberg was about Nazi Germany—evil is banal;

it could happen here. If those German doctors had refused to test out the gas chamber in the 1930s, maybe many of the horrors of the twentieth century could have been averted. At the Quinlan trial, Porzio collapsed the distinction between Hitler's Germany and the American government. "If the medical profession in Nazi Germany had shown more independence—if they had refused to partake in human experimentations," Porzio told the court, "perhaps the Holocaust would not have been so great in terms of human lives and deformities."[63] That, Porzio argued, was why the doctors he was representing were unwilling to pull the plug. It wasn't because the machines had gotten the upper hand. It wasn't because those two doctors were afraid of being sued or charged with murder. No. They had refused to allow a severely brain-damaged and comatose woman with no hope of recovery to die . . . because they were not Eichmann. "We're a strange, wonderful, sad country," a *Los Angeles Times* reporter wrote. "We can't decide how to live and we can't decide how to die."[64]

The Quinlan trial adjourned on October 27, 1975. Muir promised to issue his ruling in two weeks.

At seven o'clock in the morning on November 10, 1975, Father Thomas Trapasso held Mass at Our Lady of the Lake. Joseph and Julia Quinlan had breakfast at their house on Ryerson Road, where a copy of Leonardo da Vinci's *Last Supper* hung on the wall above the dining room table.[65] Then Joseph Quinlan drove, through a pelting rain, to Saint Clare's, to visit his daughter, as he had done every day since she had first collapsed, seven months before. At noon, he drove to the rectory to have lunch with his wife and their priest, surrounded by reporters. "It's like eating in a storefront window," said Trapasso. After lunch, they got into Trapasso's car and drove to the Morris County Courthouse.[66]

Television stations interrupted their programming to announce the decision.[67] Muir denied Joseph Quinlan's request. This is "a medical decision and not a judicial one," Muir wrote. "There is no constitutional right to die."[68]

The Quinlans decided to appeal to the New Jersey Supreme Court, which heard the case in Trenton on January 26, 1976.[69] On March 31, the justices issued a unanimous opinion, reversing the lower court. It held that, despite Quinlan's incompetence, her right to refuse medical treatment was protected under the Fourteenth Amendment's protection of liberty, and that her father could exercise that right on her behalf. Agreeing with Armstrong, the court also grounded its ruling in the right to privacy. Finally, it identified a role for the moral sense of the community.[70] "If there is no reasonable possibility of Karen's ever emerging from her present comatose condition to a cognitive, sapient state, the present life-support system may be withdrawn," the justices ruled. Whether there was or wasn't a reasonable possibility of this sort of recovery was to be decided in consultation with "the hospital 'Ethics Committee' or like body of the institution."[71]

The Quinlans had won but, as Armstrong said at the press conference, you couldn't really call being granted permission to watch your daughter die more quickly a victory. In the wake of the ruling, the California legislature began debating a proposed Natural Death Act, which stated, "Every person has the right to die without prolongation of life by medical means." The National Right to Life Committee lobbied against it; during one committee hearing, a testifier placed on the witness table a copy of *The Rise and Fall of the Third Reich*. The sponsor of the bill told the legislature, "Karen Quinlan haunts our dreams."[72]

Karen Ann Quinlan did not die in 1976. Instead of pulling the plug, her doctors slowly weaned her off the respirator. To everyone's surprise, she was able to breathe on her own. In June 1976, she was moved to the Morris View Nursing Home.[73] No one knew how long she might live. Her parents might have asked to remove her feeding tube; they did not. Every time she got sick—respiratory problems, chiefly—reporters kept a deathwatch. One tried to get into the nursing home disguised as a nun.[74] Every day, her father stopped at the nursing home on his way to work, to kiss his daughter good morning, and again on his way home, to kiss her good night. Her mother visited daily, too. Once a week, she brought her parents. Quinlan's grandmother always whispered, "Hurry up and get better, Karen."[75]

The months stretched into years. Karen Ann Quinlan lived through the Reagan revolution of 1980, when evangelicals joined the pro-life movement and brought the movement's style, tactics, and assumptions, if not always its agenda, into nearly all of American politics. She lived through the "Baby Doe" case two years later, when the parents of a baby born with Down syndrome refused to authorize lifesaving surgery for an easily fixed esophageal impairment. The baby starved to death. On the floor of Congress, Mick Staton, a Republican congressman from West Virginia, said the doctors' decision to let the parents refuse surgery had "terrifying similarities to the Nazi Reich's brand of eugenics."[76] In the *Washington Post*, George Will wrote of his own son:

> Jonathan Will, 10, fourth-grader and Orioles fan (and the best Wiffle-ball hitter in southern Maryland), has Down's syndrome. He does not "suffer from" (as newspapers are wont to say) Down's syndrome. He suffers from nothing except anxiety about the Orioles' lousy start.[77]

Matters of life and death are not, inherently, partisan. They have been turned to partisan purposes, and that shift has fundamentally altered American political culture. Americans have always fought about rights, but life is different from liberty and property. When politics turns on a right shrouded in the sacred, issues demanding debate become matters inviolable and political conversation is no longer civil, pluralist, and yielding. And when this happens, day after day, year after year, there is no more politics; there's only one sort of impasse or another.

Karen Ann Quinlan died of pneumonia on June 11, 1985. Her mother was with her, holding, between her hands, her daughter's hands, as bony as bird claws. Julia Quinlan prayed to the Virgin Mary, "To you I come; before you I stand." Her daughter took her last breath. The Quinlan family waited five days to tell the press, and asked only to be left alone. Thomas Trapasso, now a monsignor, celebrated the Mass of Resurrection at Our Lady of the Lake. And then Karen Ann Quinlan's body was taken in a hearse, over miles of winding road, to a cemetery called the Gate of Heaven.[78]

CHAPTER 10

Resurrection

Robert C. W. Ettinger, who thought death was for chumps, drove a rusty white Chevy Lumina with a bumper sticker on the rear that read, "Choose Life!" When I met him, he was ninety years old, bent and crooked. His face was splotched, his goatee grizzled, his white hair wispy and unkempt. He leaned on a worn wooden cane and wore a thick orthopedic shoe on his left foot; he sometimes covered a short distance without the cane by groping from one object to the next, chair to table, table to doorjamb, like a toddler taking his first steps. His legs were smashed when he was hit by German mortar fire in November 1944, just before the Battle of the Bulge. He spent four years in an army hospital in Battle Creek, Michigan, where he had bone grafts and skin grafts; antibiotics saved his life. More recently, he'd undergone angioplasty, cataract surgery, a hemorrhoidectomy, and prostate surgery, twice. That he'd lasted so long was a miracle of science. Actuarially, chances were good that he'd be dying soon. He didn't mind. He wasn't afraid of anything except a stroke; although, if the going got much tougher, he said, he'd kill himself. He'd planned that down to the last detail. He had one concern. "The problem, of course, with suicide," he told me, "is that if you don't do it right, you face autopsy. And then you're no good for freezing."[1]

Ettinger founded the cryonics movement. Cryonics is what happens when ideas about life and death move from the library to the laboratory, from the humanities to the sciences, from the past to the future, and get stuck there. Ettinger planned that, when he died, the blood would be washed out of his body, antifreeze would be pumped into his arteries, and holes would be drilled in his skull, after which he would be stored in a vat of liquid nitrogen at 320 degrees below zero Fahrenheit.[2] His mansion of happiness is a freezer. He expected to be defrosted, sometime between fifty and two hundred years after his death, by scientists who will make him young and strong and tireless.[3] When I went out to Michigan to meet Ettinger in 2009, he had already frozen his mother and his two wives, along with ninety-two other people, who were awaiting resurrection inside giant freezers in a building just a few blocks from his house in Clinton Township.[4]

Clinton Township, population 95,648 at the last census—95,743 if you count the corpses at the Cryonics Institute ("Our patients are not truly dead in any fundamental sense," said Ettinger)—lies twenty miles northeast of Detroit and just a few miles inland from Lake St. Clair. In 1782, Moravian missionaries pitched camp and named the site New Gnadenhutten, which means "tents of grace," but they might have called it Stechmückenhutten, "tents of small, nasty flying insects"; they were badly attacked by mosquitoes. The Moravians buried their dead on top of Indian dead. The township is named after New York's Erie Canal–building governor, DeWitt Clinton, because easterners began arriving in droves soon after the canal was completed in 1825. Ground was broken for a canal to Kalamazoo in 1838, a year after Michigan entered the union, but the railroad came instead.[5] At the Clinton Township Historic Village, which consists of a log cabin, an old Moravian meetinghouse, and a wishing well, the grass was squishy and soggy, as if someone had left the sprinklers on for too long; but it was just the old, abandoned Clinton-Kalamazoo Canal, oozing up. The past has a way of doing that.

There are only three ways to go when you die. You can be buried, burned, or frozen. If there is no God, said Ettinger, your only chance at an afterlife is option 3. I decided to take a closer look at options 1 and 2. Driving along

Cass Avenue, I passed the First Presbyterian Church, where a sign out front read,

LIFE IS SHORT
SO PRAY HARD.

Down the road, I stopped at Clinton Grove Memorial Park, established in 1855, the oldest burial ground around. A canopy of oaks and elms shelters six thousand nineteenth-century dead. Vacancies remain. A brightly lit neon billboard cycled through three messages: CREMATION SPACE $395 . . . MONUMENTS SOLD HERE . . . THINK SPRING!

Across the street were two tombstone firms: Lincoln Granite, family owned and operated since 1903, and Clinton Grove Granite Works, established in 1929. Both offices were closed, so I browsed through the outdoor displays, gravestones of pink and gray granite, their borders engraved with stock sentiments: FOREVER IN OUR HEARTS, inside two valentines; IN GOD'S CARE, on a banner beneath a cross. In the middle of each stone a polished, empty space awaited only a pair of dates and somebody's name. I tried to think spring.

A sign above the blanks caught my eye: RESURRECTION MARKERS & MONUMENTS. Of the thirteen cemeteries in Clinton Township—fourteen if you count the Cryonics Institute—the biggest is a place called Resurrection.

The Cryonics Institute occupies a seven-thousand-square-foot brick-fronted warehouse in an industrial park behind the township's water and sewerage building and just across the street from a condominium development called Still Meadows. Past a shabby waiting room was the small office of Andy Zawacki. Andy constituted half of CI's staff. (Ettinger used to be the other half, but he retired in 2003.) Andy is also one of CI's nearly eight hundred members, which means that he plans to be frozen when he dies. ("Lifetime members" pay $1,250 to join and $28,000 to $35,000 upon "death"; members are encouraged to pay by making the institute the beneficiary of their life insurance policies.)[6] On CI's website, Andy sported a lab coat, as if he were a scientist or a doctor, but mostly he's a handyman. He'd been working for CI since he graduated from high school. He's also the nephew of Ettinger's daughter-in-law. He's lumpy and balding and soft-spoken but, other than that, not a bit like Peter Lorre.

He answered the door and brought me into the office, where Robert Ettinger was waiting. I started to say hello.

"You want to see it?"

Andy led us down the hall and through a door into a storage area with fluorescent lights and twenty-foot-high ceilings. Almost everything else in the room was white or silver, like the inside of a refrigerator just off the truck from Sears. It sounded like a refrigerator in there, too, a faintly throbbing *hrrrmmm*. There were fourteen cylindrical freezers. They looked like propane tanks, the kind you attach to your gas grill, except they were about fifteen feet tall and eight feet wide. Each held six patients. All but four were filled. There were also three older, rectangular freezers, and then there was one more vat, the smallest, and that's where Ettinger was headed. He stopped at a stainless steel thermos about the size of a rain barrel. He lifted the lid. Liquid nitrogen wafted out.

"Cats," he said. He blew into the container and waved his hand, trying to clear the vapor. "Can't see much, I guess."

I peered in. I blew. We blew together. I couldn't see a thing.

"Cats in there?" I asked, peering, blowing.

"Yup."

"How many?"

"Don't know."

Andy interjected: "We've got forty pets. Mostly dogs and cats."

"A few birds," Ettinger added, halfheartedly. He closed the lid.

I stared at the giant freezers. "Are they upside down?" Better for the brain on thawing, I guessed. I pictured hibernating bats.

"Well, not the first ones," Ettinger explained. "We put them in horizontally. Everyone else—in the cylinders—is upside down."

"And, in . . . canisters or something, within the cylinders?"

"No." He shook his head. "In sleeping bags."

"Just regular sleeping bags? Like, from Kmart?"

"No," said Andy. "Walmart."

Ettinger, leaning on his cane, surveyed the room.

"Your mother, and your two wives," I began, hesitantly. "Are they all in this room?"

"Yes."

"And . . . where?"

"No idea." He shrugged. "My mother and my first wife used to be over there," he said, pointing to one corner of the room. "Andy, do you know where they are?"

"That one." Andy nodded, with his chin, at one of the cylinders. "Or maybe that one. One of those two. I can check."

Ettinger, slightly sheepish: "We have a chart."

Robert Ettinger was born in Atlantic City in December 1918. His mother's family came from Odessa; his father was born in Germany. In about 1922, the Ettingers moved to Detroit. Ettinger's father ran a furniture store, and the family lived in a house on Calvert Street, where, in 1927, when he was eight years old, Ettinger started reading *Amazing Stories,* the first magazine of what its editor, Hugo Gernsback, called "scientifiction": "Extravagant Fiction Today . . . Cold Fact Tomorrow."[7] Paul de Kruif's *Microbe Hunters,* which inspired a generation of young readers to pursue careers in science, appeared just months before the first issue of *Amazing Stories,* and much of Gernsback's scientifiction concerns the work of de Kruifian scientists; Gernsback's July 1929 issue included "The Purple Death," the story of a young scientist who keeps a copy of *Microbe Hunters* in his laboratory.[8] Gernsback promised his young readers that everything that happened in his stories, however fantastic, would very likely become established science one day soon. Much of it has. Rockets, television, computers, cell phones. Gernsback's stories also revisited what has been, for millennia, a literary perennial: immortality.

Stories about immortality are ancient, and they always contain within them an argument with history, an argument against history, because to live forever is to conquer time as much as it is to conquer death. Not all stories about time travel involve immortality (think of *A Connecticut Yankee in King Arthur's Court* or *The Time Machine*), but all stories about immortality involve transcending time. (One of CI's competitors is called Trans Time.) About a century and a half ago, stories about immortality got mixed up with stories about scientists. In 1845, Edgar Allan Poe wrote "The Facts in the Case of M. Valdemar," a story about a mesmerist who hypnotizes a dying man at the instant of his death and keeps him in a trance for seven months. When he tries to lift the trance, the poor man cries, "For

God's sake!—quick!—quick!—put me to sleep—or, quick!—waken me!—quick!—I say to you that I am dead!" and promptly melts into a pool of putrescence.[9]

Conquering death is usually gory; conquering time is usually depressing. In 1899, H. G. Wells published *When the Sleeper Wakes,* about a man who falls asleep for two hundred years and awakens to a London he can't understand. In "A Thousand Deaths," Jack London's first short story, also from 1899, the narrator's mad scientist father kills and revives him again and again, leaving him dead for longer and longer stretches: "Another time, after being suffocated, he kept me in cold storage for three months, not permitting me to freeze or decay."[10]

Rot is always a problem for the living dead, which is why resurrectionists borrow a good deal from methods used for preserving food. In 1766, the Scottish surgeon John Hunter tried to animate frozen fish. Benjamin Franklin thought that if he could be preserved in a vat of Madeira wine, he'd like very much to see what the world was like in a century or two.[11] People used to eat their food fresh, canned, or salted, until someone got the idea to sell pond ice, and then those who could afford it paid to have ice delivered by the iceman. Starting in the 1890s, housewives could rent lockers in cold storage warehouses. All this made for some fantastic scientifiction. In January 1930, Gernsback published "The Corpse That Lived," in which a man who dies in a plane crash in the year 2025 is immersed in a bathtub of ice cubes and brought back to life by an electric pulse. The next month's issue included "The Ice Man": Marcus Publius, frozen in Rome in 59 B.C., is defrosted in 1928 by an ingenious professor who happens to be remarkably handy with an electric blanket.[12]

Ettinger dates his interest in immortality to 1931, when he read "The Jameson Satellite" in *Amazing Stories:* in 1958, a dying professor has himself entombed in a rocket and launched into the cold storage of space. Forty million years pass, whereupon a race of mechanical men transplant Jameson's brain into a body like theirs. The Zoromes used to have soft, fleshy bodies, but they gave them up, preferring instead to encase their squishy brains within impenetrable steel helmets attached to six probing tentacles. (Eternity turns out to be crushingly dull if you're stuck on your own planet with no women, which is why the Zoromes are out exploring the universe.) They take Jameson to earth to show him that everyone there has died. Overcome by loneliness, he briefly considers throwing himself off a cliff, calculating that if he could land on his steel head with enough force, he could squash his brain. But then he decides he'd rather be an everlasting Zorome.[13]

When Ettinger was a boy, life expectancy was rising. G. Stanley Hall published *Senescence* in 1922. "How Long Can We Live?" was the question Paul de Kruif posed in *Ladies' Home Journal* in 1930—during the parrot fever panic—chronicling how every success in the twentieth century's battle against infectious disease was lengthening life and marking progress.[14] In 1932, de Kruif published a book called *Men Against Death.* "I grew up with the expectation that one day we would learn how to reverse aging," Ettinger says.[15] Immortality's no good if you're doomed to decrepitude. In the 1920s, a Viennese scientist named Eugen Steinach perfected a surgical technique whose purpose was rejuvenation: the Steinach operation was, basically, a vasectomy. Steinach, much like Sylvester Graham, thought that if men could keep their spermatic fluid, they would enjoy greater potency and live longer, too. Freud had the Steinach operation. So did Yeats. Steinach rejuvenated women by bombarding their ovaries with X-rays. In 1923, his work reached an American audience through a book called *Rejuvenation: How Steinach Makes People Young.*[16]

When Ettinger was shot, during the Second World War, he thought, naturally, about death. In the hospital, he wrote the kind of fiction he'd read as a boy. In 1950, his story "The Skeptic" was published in a Gernsback knockoff called *Thrilling Wonder Stories.* In it, Robert, a soldier in leg casts, scorns his army doctors—"you so-called physicians, you medical midgets, you dope-dispensing dimwits"—and discovers a way to relieve his unbearable pain through mind control. Ettinger's science fiction was autobiographical. Another of his stories, "The Penultimate Trump," also written while he was in the hospital, was published in *Startling Stories* in 1948. The plot concerns H. D. Haworth, who is ninety-two years old and survives only because his doctors have cobbled him together: "They gave him gland extracts, they gave him vitamins, they gave him blood transfusions. They gave him false teeth, eye-glasses and arch-supports. They cut out his varicose veins, his appendix, one of his kidneys." (Ettinger appears to have been influenced by Poe's 1839 story "The Man That Was Used Up.") Haworth, pursuing immortality with the same ruthlessness with which he had pursued an ill-gotten fortune, pays a brilliant young scientist to put him "to sleep in a nice refrigerator until people really know something about the body." The scientist says, "We'd better put the vault in Michigan—very safe country, geologically."[17]

Michigan is also where freezers came from. The first refrigerator for home use was sold in 1918. It was invented in Detroit; refrigeration was an offshoot of the automobile industry. By 1923, the year after the Ettingers moved to Detroit, a company named Frigidaire, owned by General Motors and based in Detroit, began selling refrigerators in cabinets for home use. A chemist hired by General Motors developed Freon-12. In the 1930s, General Foods launched Birds Eye frozen foods. By 1944, more than 85 percent of American homes had refrigerators, but freezers were scarce. During the war, they couldn't be had for love or money; their sale was banned for the duration. When the war ended, Americans had babies and built suburbs and bought appliances, including two hundred thousand freezers in 1946, and twice that many the next year.[18]

Haworth makes his arrangements in secret, sure that if anyone were to find out what he was doing, "everyone would demand a Frigidaire instead of a coffin." He dies; the scientist puts him in a freezer. Three centuries later, he awakens in a room with a beautiful woman doctor, and observes—he is naked—that he is young, strong, and, to his astonished delight, ready: "A long-forgotten stimulus performed its ancient function." Unfortunately, things don't turn out as well as he had hoped. Word had gotten out, long since, and everybody had started going into the "freezatoria." In the absence of any expectation of heaven, people had begun behaving very badly. Scientists had therefore invented the "Farbenstein Probe" to find out if a Sleeper had ever sinned; after scanning Haworth's brain, the probe sentences him to a penal colony on a planet that used to be called Mars. What do they call it now? he asks. He is told, "Now they call it Hell."[19]

Inside the Cryonics Institute, I stood with Ettinger, finding it hard not to think about "The Cerebral Library," which appeared in *Amazing Stories* two months before "The Jameson Satellite," and in which a mad scientist collects five hundred brains in glass jars. This place reminded me of a library, too, or, more, of an archive, a place where people deposit their papers—the contents of their heads—when they're dead, so that someone, some future historian, can find them and bring them back to life.[20]

"Have you got any neuros?" I asked.

A neuro is a severed head; the theory is, scientists in the future, like the Zoromes, will give you a new body, so why bother saving your old one if your brain is all they'll really need? In 2002, when Red Sox baseball great Ted Williams died, his head was sawed off and frozen. It is now stored at the Alcor Life Extension Foundation in Scottsdale, Arizona. Alcor, with nearly nine hundred members and eighty-four patients at the time, was CI's chief rival, although it charges a great deal more for eternal life. After Williams died, his oldest daughter insisted that her father had not wanted to be frozen, and produced, as evidence, a will in which he stated that he wished to be cremated, whereupon his son found, in the trunk of Williams's car, a piece of scrap paper that said something about "bio-stasis."[21]

During the family feud that followed, Ettinger appeared on *ABC World News Tonight* and was interviewed by the *New York Times,* where he was referred to as "Dr. Ettinger"; elsewhere, reporters called him "a Michigan physics professor." Ettinger has two master's degrees, one in physics and one in mathematics, both from Wayne State, which he attended after the war on the GI Bill. Aside from having spent a freshman semester at the University of Michigan in 1937, he had no affiliation with that institution. Many decades ago, he taught at Highland Park Community College, a school that no longer exists.[22] He didn't call himself "Doctor" or "Professor," but he did consider himself a scientist. "I'm a scientist by my own criteria," he told me. That is, he has "a scientific attitude."[23]

"Neuropreservation" has a scientific attitude, too, but that doesn't make it a science; it's more like extremely optimistic cosmetic surgery.[24] The fountain of youth used to be a place, far away; more recently, people have been looking for it in pharmacies and outpatient clinics.[25] In between "The Cerebral Library" and "The Jameson Satellite," Gernsback ran "The Incredible Formula," about a chemist who, in the year 1982, synthesizes an ephedrine-X, granting him eternal youth.[26] Decades later, baby boomers were putting pressure on the Social Security system and getting plastic in their chests and titanium in their knees; they were buying hair dye, Viagra, Rogaine, and anti-aging cream; they were having face-lifts and neck jobs. Cryonics promises to cure hair loss, wrinkles, senescence, impotence, and death, all at once. Nip, tuck, sever, freeze, thaw, rebuild: head job.

Ah, yes, but will it work? Well, it would be going too far to say that stranger things have happened, because they haven't. Reanimating and rejuvenating the dead would be several orders of magnitude stranger than, say, landing on the moon. But it does boast a handful of somewhat prominent promoters and a much larger group of defenders whose position amounts to, basically, What the hell, it's worth a try. Ralph Merkle, a former professor of computer science at Georgia Tech who went on to teach at a place called Singularity University, served on Alcor's board. (Merkle happens to be the great-grandnephew of Fred Merkle, whose base-running error—he failed to touch second—cost the New York Giants the National League pennant in 1908, an error forever after known as the Merkle Boner.)[27] The MIT professor Marvin Minsky, who will await resurrection at Alcor, e-mailed me, in lieu of an explanation, this helpful chart:

CRYONICS	IT WORKS	IT DOESN'T WORK
Sign up	Live	Die, lose life insurance
Do nothing	Die	Die[28]

Which looks a lot like this chart:

GOD	EXISTS	DOESN'T EXIST
Pray hard	Live	Die
Do nothing	Die	Die

And which, while altogether different from faith, is another way of trying to cover all the bases.

As for its scientific plausibility, credentialed laboratory scientists who conduct peer-reviewed experiments having to do with the storage of organic tissue at very low temperatures (embryos, for instance, or organs for transplant) generally don't think the dead will one day awaken.[29] The consensus appears to be that when you try to defrost a frozen corpse, you get mush. And even if, in the future, scientists could repair the damage done to cells by freezing and thawing, they'd have, at best, a cadaver. Merkle believes that nanotechnology will solve this problem—microscopic robots will repair the cells, one by one—but, as Ettinger himself points out, anyone wanting to resurrect and rejuvenate the dead must complete four tasks: cure the person of what killed her, reverse the decay that set in between death and freezing, repair the damage done by the freezing itself, and make her young again. Even Orpheus would be daunted.

And, of course, success would seem to depend on whether the people doing the freezing are doing it well. On August 18, 2003, *Sports Illustrated* published an investigative report by Tom Verducci. Using tapes, photographs, and documents provided to him by Alcor's chief operating officer, Larry Johnson, Verducci described how Williams's head had been "shaved, drilled with holes, accidentally cracked as many as 10 times and moved among three receptacles," until it was finally put in "a liquid-nitrogen-filled steel can that resembles a lobster pot." (The week Verducci's article was published, Johnson, who had cooperated with the investigation, resigned from Alcor and launched a website called freeted.com.)[30] It was Williams's decapitation that brought the Cryonics Institute to the attention of the state of Michigan and resulted in the filing of a cease-and-desist order, three days after Verducci's article appeared.[31]

"No," Ettinger declared. "We don't do neuros."

"But—" Andy began.

"Oh, right." In 1999, CryoCare, a cryonics firm once run by Ben Best, who later replaced Ettinger as president of CI, went out of business.

"We do have two heads," Ettinger said. "Transfers."

Robert Ettinger announced the dawn of what he called the Freezer Era at the height of the Cold War. In 1949, he met his first wife, Elaine, at a Zionist meeting. In the 1950s, they moved to the suburbs and had two children. In the basement of their house in Oak Park, Michigan, Ettinger built a fallout shelter and waited for a scientist to read "The Penultimate Trump" and turn today's extravagant fiction into tomorrow's cold fact.[32] Finally, he decided he'd have to do it himself. In 1960, he wrote a two-page flyer and sent it out to a few hundred people whose names he'd found in *Who's Who*. The response proved underwhelming.[33] In 1962, he wrote a sixty-page manifesto and sent a copy to Frederik Pohl, the editor of the science fiction magazine *Worlds of Tomorrow*. Pohl, who was a regular guest on an all-night New York AM-radio show, *The Long John Nebel Show*, arranged for Ettinger to be invited. One thing led to another and, eventually, Thomas McCormack, a junior editor at Doubleday, agreed to read Ettinger's sixty pages. One day at the office, McCormack was having an argument with Doubleday's science editor. McCormack thought it was not logically impossible to resurrect the frozen dead; the other guy disagreed. Just then, Isaac Asimov, a Doubleday author, happened past. "Asimov walked into the room," McCormack recalls, "and it didn't take him ten seconds to say, 'No, it's not logically impossible.' "[34]

In 1964, the year Doubleday published *The Prospect of Immortality*, *Dr. Strangelove* hit theaters. Through that lens, mortality begins to look rather a lot like mutual assured destruction and immortality at 320 below like nothing so much as a fabulously air-conditioned fallout shelter. In *Strangelove*, the world faces a nuclear Armageddon. On orders from a U.S. Air Force general convinced of a Communist conspiracy to "sap and impurify all of our precious bodily fluids" (shades of Steinach), American airmen have dropped a bomb on Russia, thereby triggering the Soviets' Doomsday Machine. From the war room in Washington, the U.S. president (played by Peter Sellers) entertains proposals made by his scientific adviser, Dr. Strangelove (also Sellers):

> STRANGELOVE: Mister President, I would not rule out the chance to
> preserve a nucleus of human specimens. It would be quite easy, at
> the bottom of some of our deeper mineshafts. . . .
> PRESIDENT: How long would you have to stay down there?
> STRANGELOVE (*pulls out a circular slide rule*): Well, let's see now. . . .
> Hmm. I would think possibly, uh, one hundred years.[35]

No, we're not all going to "die," Ettinger insisted. We're all going into freezers, to be paid for by Social Security. After the Manhattan Project, after *Sputnik*, after dishwashers and electric mixers, either scientists and engineers were on the verge of solving everything (in which case, go into the freezer, because you can be sure the world will be even better when you wake up) or else someone was about to launch an atomic bomb (in which case, go into the freezer, because maybe you'll survive). "Before long," Ettinger predicted, "the objectors will include only a handful of eccentrics." Freezers might even help in the fight against the Reds: Soviet leaders, who "will want immortality for themselves," will be forced to kowtow to the West. Not to mention that since Siberia offered "natural cold storage," it might prove useful, diplomacy-wise, as some kind of trade.[36]

Ettinger did concede that the logistics of freezing the dead could be difficult at first, especially in the "retarded nations," where "makeshifts may be necessary to stretch the rupees, pesos, etc." No one would be left behind, though. In poor, hot countries, "the bodies will be stored in pits insulated with straw and dry ice." Okay, right, yes, that might not actually work; very likely, the dead of the retarded nations will simply rot. No worries. "It will not at first greatly matter how skillfully the bodies are preserved, so long as *hope* is preserved."[37] Hope, after all, springs eternal. But wait: If no one ever dies, won't there be too many people on the planet?

STRANGELOVE (*laughs, distastefully*): Naturally, they would breed prodigiously, eh? There would be much time and little to do.

"The people could simply agree to share the available space, in shifts," Ettinger suggested, "going into suspended animation from time to time, to make room for others." Anyway, overpopulation won't be a problem. While it goes without saying that there will be a great deal of excellent sex in Ettinger's golden age—the men will look like Charles Atlas, the women like Miss Universe—there will be no childbirth; childbirth is gross. Fetuses will be incubated in jars. No woman will dream of breast-feeding, either— blech. "Essentially, motherhood will be abolished," he predicted. Moreover, Ettinger informed me, "When people no longer die of old age, more people will choose to omit children." Why bother? They only disappoint you.[38]

PRESIDENT: But, look here, Strangelove. Won't this nucleus of survivors be so shocked, grief-stricken, and anguished that they will envy the dead, and indeed not wish to go on living?

STRANGELOVE: Certainly not, sir.

Then, too, eugenics will help keep the birthrate down, and deformed babies could be frozen, against the day that someone might actually want them, or figure out how to fix them. "Cretins," for instance, or babies born with cerebral palsy: "would not early freezing be a true mercy?" For the weak-minded, who might find making such a decision difficult, Ettinger offered a philosophical rule of thumb: Ask yourself, "if the child were *already* frozen, and it were within my power to return him to a deformed life, would I do so? If the answer is negative, then the freezer is where he belongs."[39]

On the floor in front of the freezers at the Cryonics Institute were two slot-ted boxes painted white, with a black number in each slot, like the slots in a company mailroom.

"What's this?"

Ettinger didn't answer; he looked away. Andy explained that the numbers refer to the patients, most of whom choose to remain anonymous, and the box is for their families. Over the years, a half dozen have sent flowers, mostly roses, long dead. Attached to one bouquet was a card in an unopened envelope. It turns out that staring at an unopened envelope inside a freezatorium is substantially more depressing than looking at the blank space on a tombstone. Thoughts of spring eluded me.

"Do patients' families ever visit?"

"Not many," Andy said. Ettinger had wandered off toward the office, passing a half-open door I hadn't noticed before.

"What's in there?"

"A storeroom," Ettinger called over his shoulder. "Used to be a library."

We sat down in the conference room. Along the wall hung twenty-six eight-by-ten photographs of patients, beginning with Ettinger's mother. His father, who died in 1984, at the age of eighty-nine, is not among them. "He's in a mausoleum," Ettinger said, shaking his head. "I tried very hard to get him to be frozen, but his second wife was against it. He was too wimpy to stand up to her." In 1964, Ettinger had anticipated this difficulty: "If your husband or wife is mentally competent but opposes freezing, a difficult moral problem arises. The easy way out is compliance and burial, but you will have to live with your conscience for a long time."[40] Ettinger's brother, who died in 2000, proved as weak as his father. "In his last illness he became depressed and told his children he didn't want to be frozen," Ettinger said. "I told them they should freeze him anyway, but I couldn't get them to, and he was lost." This is how Ettinger always put it when he talked about the unfrozen dead. His uncle Herman drove his car into a river: "That was a shame. He was lost."

When Doubleday agreed to publish *The Prospect of Immortality,* it made Ettinger into something of a star. (Thomas McCormack is not a convert. When he dies, he will be lost. "I'll be buried in a place called Valhalla," he told me. "That's the name of the goddamned cemetery, believe it or not.")[41] Ettinger claimed, and he is probably right, that nearly everyone active in cryonics first heard about it, directly or indirectly, from him. Cryonicists talk about where they were when they first read *The Prospect of Immortality* the way some people talk about where they were when Kennedy was shot.[42] Ben Best, who later succeeded Ettinger as CI's president, picked up a copy in a health food store. Stanley Kubrick read it, Ettinger said, and then "bought dozens of copies, gave them to his friends," and arranged to meet with him to talk about signing up and, presumably, to fish for material for *2001*. ("I'm afraid his obsession with immortality has overcome his artistic instincts," Arthur Clarke wrote in his diary in 1965.) In a 1968 interview with *Playboy*, Kubrick said, "Dr. Ettinger's thesis is quite simple." He proceeded to propound it, quoting Ettinger at length, and expressed his own conviction that, within ten years, "the freezing of the dead will be a major industry in the United States and throughout the world."[43]

But when Kubrick died, in 1999, he was lost. He is buried in Hertfordshire.

During a book tour appearance on *The Long John Nebel Show*, Ettinger said he had been gratified by the book's reception: "Almost everybody is willing to take it seriously."[44] Nebel, who believed in UFOs, ghosts, and CIA mind control, took Ettinger seriously. Nebel died in 1978. I don't know if he was lost.

Ettinger says he was also interviewed by David Frost, Steve Allen, Merv Griffin, and Johnny Carson.

"Did these people take you seriously?" I asked.

"Talk-show hosts don't take anything seriously. They're idiots." He told me he was once on a show with William Buckley Jr.

"What did Buckley make of you?"

"He was aghast at everything I said." This is the first time I'd seen Ettinger smile. "He thought it was immoral, unethical, unsanitary, against the will of God!" He laughed. "Buckley understood nothing."

In May 1965, the month after Lennart Nilsson's photographs of the drama of life before birth were published in *Life* magazine, Wilma Jean McLaughlin lay dying of heart disease in a hospital in Springfield, Ohio. Her husband asked Ettinger to freeze her, but at the last minute, the hospital refused to cooperate.[45] The first human being was frozen in 1966; it went badly, and a few months later, the body had to be buried. Ettinger wasn't there for any of it. The next year, a man named James Bedford was frozen by an organization that later became the Cryonics Society of California; Ettinger held a press conference.[46] (What with one snafu and another, most of the people who were frozen in California rotted.) Alcor and Trans Time were founded in 1972. That same year, St. Martin's Press, where McCormack had moved, published Ettinger's second book, *Man into Superman: The Startling Potential of Human Evolution—and How to Be a Part of It.* It begins, "By working hard and saving my money, I intend to become an immortal superman."[47] The following year, *Sleeper* came out. Woody Allen's film is very loosely based on Wells's 1899 novel. Miles Monroe (Allen), who runs a health food store in Greenwich Village, goes into the hospital for an ulcer, but when the surgery goes awry, he is covered in "Birds Eye wrapper" and stuck in a freezer for two hundred years. He eventually falls in love with Luna (played by Diane Keaton), although when first he wakes, he's peevish, especially after his doctor tells him his resurrection is a miracle of science.

> MILES (*pacing*): A miracle of science is going to the hospital for
> a minor operation, I come out the next day, my rent isn't two
> thousand months overdue. That's a miracle of science. This is what
> I call a cosmic screwing. And then: Where am I anyhow? What
> happened to everybody? Where are all my friends?
> DOCTOR: You must understand that everyone you knew in the past has
> been dead nearly two hundred years.
> MILES: But they all ate organic rice![48]

In *Man into Superman,* Ettinger throws around a lot of Nietzsche and George Bernard Shaw but shows more evidence of having whiled away the hours reading *Penthouse,* which started in 1965. The world of tomorrow will be unimaginably better than the world of today. How? There will be transsex and supersex! Scientists will turn woman into a "sexual superwoman . . . with cleverly designed orifices of various kinds, something like a wriggly Swiss cheese, but shapelier and more fragrant." Animals will be bred as sex slaves; even incest might be allowed. Also, scientists will likely equip men with wings, built-in biological weapons, body armor made of hair, and "telescoping, fully adjustable" sexual organs.[49] (Hold on. That last one. Doesn't the existing model already come with that?)

Ettinger saw Allen's film when it came out. His opinion: "He has a lot of good things to say about death."

> LUNA: Oh, I see. You don't believe in science. And you also don't
> believe that the political systems work. And you don't believe in
> God, huh?
> MILES: Right.

LUNA: So then, what do you believe in?

MILES: Sex and death.

Though that opinion is qualified: "But as far as I know, he's never done anything about it."

"Like what?"

"Like sign up."

For a very long time, no one signed up. Ettinger's first patient was his mother, Rhea. He froze her in 1977.

"Did she want to be frozen?"

"I don't know if she was really enthusiastic about it, but she was willing."

Ettinger's second patient was his first wife, who died in November 1987. What did she think about the prospect of being frozen?

"She never talked much about it. It was just taken for granted."

He remarried the following year. One month after Ettinger froze his first wife, Saul Kent froze the head of his mother, Dora, at the Alcor facility. Kent, the author of *Future Sex* (1974) and *The Life-Extension Revolution* (1980), had become a convert to cryonics after reading *The Prospect of Immortality* on the beach. He had also founded the vitamin-peddling Life Extension Foundation, in Hollywood, Florida, which was raided by the Food and Drug Administration in 1987. There was some question of whether Dora Kent was actually dead when her head was cut off. But Kent was never convicted of anything.[50]

Ettinger's second wife, Mae, suffered a stroke in Scottsdale, Arizona, in 2000. Ettinger was with her. It was horrible. She was helpless; he was helpless. "All she was able to do was to move one arm," he said, his voice quavering. Mae knew she would be frozen; Ettinger had paid a retainer to a local funeral home "to practice once a year." She died the day after her stroke. Ettinger took comfort in what happened next. He acted fast: "I pronounced death—anyone can do that in Arizona—and the funeral people were there in a few minutes. We had already started packing her in ice, and the funeral people started right away." She was flown to Detroit. She is Patient 34. She was not lost.

Ettinger finds nothing so uninteresting as history. "When the future expands, the past shrinks," he once wrote. Take literature. In the golden age, no one will read Shakespeare: "Not only will his work be far too weak in intellect, and written in too vague and puny a language, but the problems which concerned him will be, in the main, no more than historical curiosities."[51] Still, Ettinger told me, when I asked, that his mother and both his wives kept photo albums and that they're at the institute, in that storeroom that was once a library, somewhere. He promised we could look for them on the second day of my visit, even though he was baffled by my interest. He showed me the cat vat. He told me about the heads. The future, so gleamy and white. How could anyone possibly care about the musty, dusty past?

The storeroom was a mess. There was an old StairMaster and some folding tables. The bookshelves housed a set of *Encyclopaedia Britannica*, someone's college textbooks—including a copy of *Organic Chemistry*—and a T-shirt on which was printed the periodic table. Along one wall stood a bank of file drawers.

"What's in there?"

"Any patient who wants to can buy a drawer, to put things in," Andy said.

"Really?"

"But not many of them ask."

Mae Ettinger asked. She kept a diary and asked for it to be kept here, marked, "Not to be read until and unless it is deemed useful for the revival." It won't survive, though. Paper turns to dust.

"Anything else?"

"One of our members suggested it would be a good idea to store your computer here," Ettinger said. "No one's done it yet, though."

Andy riffled through drawer after drawer. At last, he found them: ten bulky albums with flesh-toned covers, pink, brown, and beige. He and I lugged them back to the table in the conference room. And then Ettinger and I sat, for a good hour, maybe more, and turned pages. The albums contained mostly photographs, but there were old documents in there, too: a military ID, a college transcript, newspaper clippings. Ettinger hadn't wanted to drag these albums out, but now that he'd decided to indulge me, he was determined to be thorough. He didn't skip a single photograph, even prying apart pages that had gotten stuck. He was bored before we began; I could have looked at that stuff forever.

The earliest albums belonged to his mother: sepia pictures of his babyhood. He offered names. "That's Leo. . . . That's Pee Wee Russell. He married my mother's sister, Mary." He remembered people from his early years best. He was very sharp on the names of his cousins, growing up, and he never missed the name of a dog. He planned to freeze the one he currently had, Mugsy. Mae would like that. His father appeared in a picture or two, then disappeared. There followed dozens of photographs of Ettinger in uniform—handsome, smiling, promising—and, on the next pages, in casts, in wheelchairs, on crutches: a young man cut down. Here was his wedding, under a chuppah. The next albums were Elaine's, snapshots of postwar suburbia: the wading pool, the tricycle, boys in crew cuts, girls in checkered dresses.

And then there was a long gap, until Mae's albums started. There were a handful pictures of Ettinger but many more of a sweetly happy Mae, surrounded by people: her bowling league, her children from her first marriage, her grandchildren from her first marriage. "That's one of Pat's kids," he'd say. Or, more often than not: "Who the hell is that? I don't know who the hell that is."

"When you wake up, nearly everyone in these albums will be gone. Won't you miss them?"

"I hope to see the people I knew before and that I loved before." Ettinger sighed. "Most of the people I grew up with are already gone. That's been true for a long time. Most of the people that anybody grows up with, they lose track of. We lose them."

Unless we save them, in the freezer, in an archive, in our children, forever in our hearts, in God's care. We had gone through one album, two, five, eight. I asked why cryonics is, by any objective measure, a failure. Ettinger talked about something he calls the "legacy effect," the crippling hold of the past. He isn't crippled by it, but other people are. Or else the Freezer Era would actually have dawned, in 1964, when it was supposed to. Idiots. But you can't worry about other people; you have to take care of yourself.

And then, as abruptly as we began, we were done. He pulled himself up to standing, grabbed his cane, and tapped the last page of the final photo album. "Someone should have put labels on these things," he muttered.

Just after I left Michigan, Ettinger self-published a new book, *Youniverse: Toward a Self-Centered Philosophy of Immortalism and Cryonics* (you are the most important person in the world, it says; no one else matters), and the Cryonics Institute admitted a new patient.[52] Patient 93 was born Billie

Joe Bonsall, but he had had his name legally changed to William Constitution O'Rights. He had no known occupation, although he liked to dress up as a priest. Bill O'Rights was forty-three when he "deanimated" in a hospital in Maine on May 9; the next day, his body was flown to Detroit in an icebox. At Faulmann & Walsh funeral home, Jim Walsh opened the body and pumped in eleven liters of ethylene glycol. Then he brought it to CI, where Andy put it into a Walmart sleeping bag and placed it in a cooling box. A few days later, Patient 93 was hoisted up on a forklift and lowered into a freezer, headfirst, like a hibernating bat, beside invisible cats, inside a seven-thousand-square-foot building in an industrial park in the heart of America, where some of the sorriest ideas of a godforsaken and alienated modernity endure.[53]

Robert C. W. Ettinger died on July 23, 2011. He had held on for a very long time, believing that the longer he lived, the better his chances, because in the golden age, or what used to be called Hell, scientists choosing which patients to thaw will follow a simple rule: Last in, first out.

His head was packed in ice; his corpse was carried to the Cryonics Institute. He was ninety-two. He was saved. He is Patient 106.

Last Words

When I was nine, I swiped my mother's *Joy of Cooking* and biked to a place called Annie's Book Swap, where I traded it for *Is Sex Necessary?*, a book I couldn't get out of the public library, where kids were allowed only in a cramped basement, called, rather grandly, the Juvenile Room. It's hard to write a book about life and death without thinking about your own, even when you're trying very hard not to.

Before my mother married my father, who went to Clark University, she worked at the Milton Bradley Company. I was conceived the year Lennart Nilsson's "Drama of Life Before Birth" appeared on the cover of *Life* magazine. As a kid, I played the Game of Life. In 1975, I went to Mass and prayed for Karen Ann Quinlan, although I can't remember, anymore, whether I wanted her to live or to die. I remember only that I was terrified.

E. B. White is the writer who reached through the brambles of my childhood, grabbed me by the pigtails, and yanked. I always wished I could thank him. I once wrote him a letter on my father's typewriter; I never had the gumption to send it. I owe him more thanks, since. "I finished 'Stuart Little,'" a son of mine wrote when he was six. "I think E. B. White is saying, stick with it until you find it."

I have never attended a Sex Weekend or slept in a Celestial Bed, and I do not run a Kitchen Efficient, but I did once work as a secretary at the Harvard Business School, for a management-consulting guru; I used to own a breast pump; my parents have lived longer than their parents; and the rules to the Mansion of Happiness hang by the front door of my house, where,

I like to think, they give strangers pause: "Whoever possesses AUDACITY, CRUELTY, IMMODESTY, or INGRATITUDE, must return to his former situation till his turn comes to spin again, and not even *think* of Happiness, much less partake of it."

I have never frozen anyone. But I did once put someone I love in storage. That, I suppose, is where this book began. She was on her deathbed; I was on an operating table, trying to give birth, fast. She wanted to meet that baby before she died. Every minute mattered. I failed. He was born; she died; she never saw him. I wrote her eulogy from a bed in a maternity ward. Before she got sick, she had been writing a dissertation about *Cheaper by the Dozen* and *The Egg and I,* books she had loved as a kid. She had not gotten very far. When she really liked someone, she would say, "He's a good egg." She was a good egg. She bequeathed to me her books; I put them on my shelves. We scattered her ashes. Then I printed out the contents of her hard drive and carried that sheaf of papers to a library, where it was sorted and cataloged and put in an archive-quality box lined with acid-free paper and stored in a cool, dark, humidity-controlled room, a room where a life on paper lasts forever. I have always believed that the past contains the truth, that history explains, that archives save. I am forever meeting dead people in libraries, and they always have a lot to say. I thought: This should work.

Nine years passed. A nine-year-old in my house wanted to be Headless Ted Williams for Halloween. He trick-or-treated wearing a Red Sox uniform and carrying a papier-mâché head. When Halloween was over, he put Ted's head on top of his dresser. All winter, he left it there.

"How long are you going to keep that thing?" I asked.

He shrugged. "Forever?"

That spring, the tenth birth-and-death day came, and I figured I had waited long enough. I went back to that library and opened that box and read every scrap. And I found out: she is not there. Folder after folder of her papers, and all that shouted out of that box was my grief. I closed the lid, regretted the box, and remembered Ted. And that's why, days later, I flew to Michigan, to meet a man who freezes the dead, and found myself across the hall from hibernating bats and invisible cats, because I had thought: Maybe he can't let go, either.

Most of the chapters in this book started out as essays in the *New Yorker*. I don't know how to thank my editor, Henry Finder, any better than I knew how to thank E. B. White—for a great deal, but especially for sending me to chase a mouse down the halls of the New York Pubic Library and to drive all over New Jersey, looking for the house where Karen Ann Quinlan used to live, to take a picture of a statue of the Virgin Mary in the front yard, for fact-checking. Dear Mr. Finder, It was good to get out. Gratefully, &c.

"A library is a good place to go when you feel bewildered or undecided," E. B. White once wrote, "for there, in a book, you may have your question answered. Books are good company, in sad times and happy times, for books are people—people who have managed to stay alive by hiding between the covers of a book." I met a lot of people in libraries while writing this book. Thanks to librarians and archivists all over the place but especially at the American Antiquarian Society; the Baker Library at the Harvard Business School; the Bryn Mawr Library; the Columbia Rare Book and Manuscripts Library; the Connecticut Valley Historical Museum; Cornell Library's Division of Rare and Manuscript Collections; the Countway Library at the Harvard School of Medicine; the Gilbreth Library of Management at Purdue University; the Goddard Library at Clark University; the Gutman Library at the Harvard School of Education; the Houghton Library at Harvard College; the Milton Bradley Archives at Hasbro; the New-York Historical Society; the New York Public Library; the Schlesinger Library at Radcliffe; the Special Collections Library at Duke University; Time Inc. Archives; UCLA; the University of Florida, Gainesville; and Vassar's Archives and Special Collections.

Many thanks, too, to Dan Frank, at Knopf, for encouragement and wisdom and deft suggestions at every turn. And thanks to Tina Bennett, as ever. Thanks to everyone who commented on portions of this work during lectures and seminars at Colby, Columbia Law School, DePauw, Harvard, Harvard's Kennedy School of Government, Harvard Law School, MIT, Princeton, the University of Chicago School of Law, the University of Connecticut, the University of Massachusetts, and Yale. Thanks, too, to everyone I interviewed, especially Robert C. W. Ettinger. For stints of research along the way, thanks to Molly Morrissey Barron, Heather Furnas, John Huffman, Sara Martinez, Natalie Panno, and especially Emily Wilkerson. Thanks to Latif Nasser, for sharing with me a play he once wrote about an egg named Otto. Heartfelt thanks to friends and colleagues who read drafts of chapters: Elise Broach, Nancy Cott, Amy Kittelstrom, James Kloppenberg, Leah Price, Charles Rosenberg, Dorothy Ross, Bruce Schulman,

Steven Shapin, Laurel Thatcher Ulrich, Sue Vargo, and Michael Willrich. Adrianna Alty navigated me through rough patches, to say nothing of New Jersey; Denise Webb taught me about redemption; and Jane Kamensky has walked me miles, through woods and around ponds and even over ice. And although everyone in my house hates it when I mention them, for which I adore them, here I must, nevertheless, thank They Who Must Not Be Named by promising that I will never serve Dog's Vomit on Toast, or, at least, not ever again.

This book is dedicated to John Demos, who once wrote a book about the Puritan author of a book called *The Redeemed Captive,* whose dedication reads, "Sir, It was a satyrical answer, and deeply reproachful to mankind, which the philosopher gave to that question, What soonest grows old? Replied, *Thanks."* I think, though, that thanks are unaging.

When I came home from Detroit, we put Ted's head in a blue plastic recycling bin and left it out on the curb. He was pulped and bleached and made, I suppose, into a newspaper, ashes to ashes—or, at least, paper to paper. Since then, I have come around to thinking that archives save only what archives can save, nothing more and nothing less. Most of all, I have come to believe that what people make of the relationship between life and death has got a good deal to do with how they think about the present and the past. Hiding between the covers of this book, then, lies a theory of history itself, and it is this: if history is the art of making an argument by telling a story about the dead, which is how I see it, the dead never die; they are merely forgotten or, especially if they are loved, remembered, quick as ever.

A Chronology

A Select Chronology of Works and Events Mentioned

1516   Thomas More, *Utopia*
1550   Thomas Reynalde, *The Birth of Mankind*

1638   Francis Bacon, *A History of Life and Death*
1651   William Harvey, *On Generation*
        Thomas Hobbes, *Leviathan*
1667   John Milton, *Paradise Lost*
1678   John Bunyan, *Pilgrim's Progress*
1684   *Aristotle's Master-piece; Or, The Secrets of Generation*
1689   John Locke, *Two Treatises of Government*
1690   Cotton Mather, *Addresses to Old Men and Young Men and Little Children*
1693   Locke, *Some Thoughts Concerning Education*

1707   Mather, *The Spirit of Life Entering into the Spiritually Dead*
1726   Mather, *A Good Old Age*
1735   Carolus Linnaeus, *Systema Naturae*
1752   Linnaeus, *Step Nurse*
        First issue of the *Lilliputian Magazine*
1758   Linnaeus, *Systema Naturae,* revised
        Benjamin Franklin, *The Way to Wealth*
1762   Jean-Jacques Rousseau, *Émile; Or, On Education*
1790   John Wallis, The New Game of Human Life
1792   Mary Wollstonecraft, *Vindication of the Rights of Woman*
1793   Erasmus Darwin, *Zoonomia: The Laws of Organic Life*

1800   The Mansion of Happiness (British)
        The Mansion of Bliss

1827   Karl von Baer discovers the mammalian egg.
1829   Jacob Bigelow, *Elements of Technology*
       Thomas Carlyle, "Signs of the Times"
       Joel Hawes, *Lectures to Young Men on the Formation of Character*
1831   Sylvester Graham, *Thy Kingdom Come*
1833   Graham, *Lecture to Young Men, on Chastity*
       First issue of *Mother's Magazine*
1834   Moritz Retzsch, *The Chess Players; Or, The Game of Life*
1836   Dorus Clarke, *Lectures to Young People in Manufacturing Villages*
1837   First issue of the *Graham Journal of Health and Longevity*
1838   Hans Christian Andersen, "The Storks"
1839   Edgar Allan Poe, "The Man Who Was Used Up"
       Graham, *Lectures on the Science of Human Life*
1841   Catherine Beecher, *A Treatise on Domestic Economy*
       First U.S. patent for a baby bottle
1843   The Mansion of Happiness (American)
       First issue of the *Child's Friend*
1845   Poe, "The Facts in the Case of M. Valdemar"
1854   Henry David Thoreau, *Walden*
1859   Charles Darwin, *The Origin of Species*
1860   Milton Bradley, The Checkered Game of Human Life
       The Massachusetts Institute of Technology is founded.
1863   Charles Kingsley, *Water-Babies*
1877   Charles Darwin, *The Descent of Man*
1879   Henry George, *Progress and Poverty*
1882   The English Society for Psychical Research is founded.
1883   Hyland Kirk, *The Possibility of Not Dying*
1884   The American Society for Psychical Research is founded.
1886   Joseph Pulitzer publishes the first women's page, in the *New York World.*
1887   Edward Wiebé, *The Paradise of Childhood* (published by Milton Bradley)
       The American Journal of Psychology is founded by G. Stanley Hall.
1889   Clark University is founded.
1896   *Plessy v. Ferguson*
1899   H. G. Wells, *When the Sleeper Wakes*
       Jack London, "A Thousand Deaths"

1900   Rediscovery of Mendel's laws of inheritance
1903   Frederick Winslow Taylor, *Shop Management*
1904   G. Stanley Hall, *Adolescence*
1906   The Race Betterment Foundation is established.
       Lewis M. Terman, "Genius and Stupidity"
1908   E. B. White, age nine, publishes his first poem, about a mouse.
1909   Freud and Jung visit Clark University.
       The Harvard Business School opens.
       The American Home Economics Association is founded.

1910   The Boston Wet Nurse Directory opens.
        The term "scientific management" is coined.
1911   Children's Room at the New York Public Library opens.
        Frederick Winslow Taylor, *The Principles of Scientific Management*
1912   Winfield Scott Hall, *Life's Beginnings: For Boys of Ten to Fourteen Years*
        Frank Gilbreth, *Primer on Scientific Management*
        Christine Frederick, *The New Housekeeping*
1913   First issue of the *Journal of Heredity*
        Winfred Scott Hall, *Sexual Knowledge: In Plain and Simple Language*
        Margaret Sanger, *What Every Girl Should Know*
        Adelheid Popp, *The Autobiography of a Working Woman*
1914   Lillian Gilbreth, *The Psychology of Management*
        Sanger is indicted for publishing the *Woman Rebel*.
1915   The Baby Bollinger case
        Christine Frederick, *Household Engineering*
1916   Terman, *The Measurement of Intelligence*
        Madison Grant, *The Passing of the Great Race*
        Lillian Gilbreth, *Fatigue Study*
        Sanger opens up the nation's first birth control clinic.
1917   Sanger begins publishing the *Birth Control Review*.
1918   Anne Carroll Moore begins reviewing children's literature in *Bookman*.
        Paul Popenoe and Roswell Johnson, *Applied Eugenics*
        The influenza epidemic
1919   First issue of *Better Times*
        Are You Fit to Marry?
1920   Edwin E. Slosson founds the Science Service.
1921   Sanger founds the American Birth Control League.
1922   G. Stanley Hall, *Senescence: The Last Half of Life*
        First issue of *Reader's Digest*
1923   First issue of *Time*
        J.B.S. Haldane, *Daedalus; Or, Science and the Future*
        G. Stanley Hall, *Life and Confessions of a Psychologist*
        Equal Rights Amendment is introduced to Congress.
1924   Clara Savage Littledale, "Sublimation"
1925   First issue of the *New Yorker*
        Paul Popenoe, *Modern Marriage*
        The Scopes trial
        Sinclair Lewis and Paul de Kruif, *Arrowsmith*
1926   Paul Popenoe, *The Conservation of the Family*
        Clarence Darrow, "The Eugenics Cult"
        De Kruif, *Microbe Hunters*
        First issue of *Children: A Magazine for Parents* (later *Parents Magazine*)
1927   Ernest Hemingway, *Men Without Women*
        The first issue of *Amazing Stories*
        Buck v. Bell

Lillian Gilbreth, *The Home-maker and Her Job*

Thurman B. Rice, *The Conquest of Disease*

1928   Sanger, *Motherhood in Bondage*

1929   C. C. Little founds Jackson Laboratory.

Paul Popenoe and E. S. Gosney, *Sterilization for Human Betterment*

James Thurber and E. B. White, *Is Sex Necessary?*

1930   Paul Popenoe founds the Institute for Family Relations.

The parrot fever panic

1931   Aldous Huxley, *Brave New World*

1933   Madison Grant, *The Conquest of a Continent*

Germany passes its first sterilization law.

1936   First issue of *Life*

1937   *U.S. v. One Package of Japanese Pessaries*

1938   "Birth of a Baby," *Life*

"Birth of an Adult," *New Yorker*

1941   E. B. White and Katharine S. White, *The Subtreasury of American Humor*

1942   The American Birth Control League, having merged with Sanger's Birth Control Research Bureau, becomes the Planned Parenthood Federation of America.

The American Association of Marriage and Family Therapists is founded.

1944   Gregory Pincus founds the Worcester Foundation for Experimental Biology.

1945   E. B. White, *Stuart Little*

Betty MacDonald, *The Egg and I*

1946   *U.S.A. v. Karl Brandt et al.*

1947   Thirty-five hundred Jewish and Protestant clergy sign a resolution in support of Planned Parenthood.

1948   Frank Gilbreth Jr. and Ernestine Gilbreth Carey, *Cheaper by the Dozen*

Robert Ettinger, "The Penultimate Trump"

1950   Ettinger, "The Skeptic"

1953   *Ladies' Home Journal* begins publishing "Can This Marriage Be Saved?"

1955   Planned Parenthood begins discussing abortion.

1957   Pope Pius XII, "The Prolongation of Life"

Roth v. United States

1958   La Leche League, *The Womanly Art of Breastfeeding*

1960   The Game of Life

The Pill first sold

1961   Medela introduces the first non-hospital breast pump.

1963   Hannah Arendt, *Eichmann in Jerusalem*

Jessica Mitford, *The American Way of Death*

1964   Stanley Kubrick, *Dr. Strangelove*

Ettinger, *The Prospect of Immortality*

1965   "Drama of Life Before Birth," *Life*

Griswold v. Connecticut

1966   First attempted cryogenic suspension

1967   Alan F. Guttmacher, ed., *The Case for Legalized Abortion Now*

1968   Stanley Kubrick, *2001: A Space Odyssey*
        Pope Paul VI, "On Human Life"
        Paul Ehrlich, *The Population Bomb*
        Gordon Drake, *Is the School House the Proper Place to Teach Raw Sex?*
1969   Elisabeth Kübler-Ross, *On Death and Dying*
        Geraldine Lux Flanagan, *Window into an Egg: Seeing Life Begin*
        David Reuben, *Everything You Always Wanted to Know About Sex (But Were Afraid to Ask)*
        Kevin Phillips, *The Emerging Republican Majority*
        NARAL is founded.
1970   Nixon signs Title X providing federal funding for family planning.
1971   Nixon reverses his position on abortion.
1972   Ettinger, *Man into Superman*
        Woody Allen, *Everything You Always Wanted to Know About Sex* (*But Were Afraid to Ask)*
        Furman v. Georgia
        The ERA passes and goes to the states for ratification.
1973   *Roe v. Wade*
        The first human life admendment is introduced to Congress.
        Peter Mayle, *Where Did I Come From?*
        Woody Allen, *Sleeper*
1974   Saul Kent, *Future Sex*
1975   *In the Matter of Karen Ann Quinlan*
        Peter Mayle, *What's Happening to Me?*
1977   Lennart Nilsson's photographs are first launched into space on board the *Voyager* probes.
1979   Jerry Falwell founds the Moral Majority.
1980   Kent, *The Life-Extension Revolution*
1985   Founding of the Human Milk Banking Association of North America
1991   Medela introduces the Pump In Style breast pump.
1993   U.S. Family and Medical Leave Act
1996   David Popenoe, *Life Without Father*
        U.S. Defense of Marriage Act
1997   Popenoe founds the National Marriage Project.
        The American Academy of Pediatrics issues "Breastfeeding and the Use of Human Milk."
2000   Pepper Schwartz and Dominic Cappello, *Ten Talks Parents Must Have with Their Children About Sex and Character*
2003   *Second Life,* an online virtual world, is launched.
2005   Popenoe, *War over the Family*
2006   Robie Harris, *It's NOT the Stork!*
2007   The Game of Life: Twists and Turns
        U.S. Breastfeeding Promotion Act is introduced.
2008   Proposition 8 (California)

2009 Ettinger, *Youniverse*
Perry v. Schwarzenegger
Jennifer Ashton, *The Body Scoop for Girls*
2010 Laurie Abraham, *The Husbands and Wives Club*
Tara Parker-Pope, *For Better*
Lori Gottlieb, *Marry Him*
U.S. Patient Protection and Affordable Care Act
2011 Robert C. W. Ettinger dies.
Congress debates ending federal funding of Planned Parenthood.
The Mississippi Personhood Amendment is defeated.

Notes

Introduction. THE MANSION OF HAPPINESS

1. Milton Bradley, The Checkered Game of Life (Springfield, MA: Milton Bradley Company, 1866), Liman Collection of American Board Games and Table Games, Henry Luce III Center for the Study of American Culture, New-York Historical Society.

2. Milton Bradley Company, The Game of Life (East Longmeadow, MA: Milton Bradley Company, 1960), in the possession of the author. "Milton Bradley's New 'Family-Fun' Game," *New York Times*, November 6, 1960. For a comparison of the nature of play between the 1860 and 1960 games, see Thomas A. Burns, "*The Game of Life:* Idealism, Reality and Fantasy in the Nineteenth- and Twentieth-Century Versions of a Milton Bradley Game," *Canadian Review of American Studies* 9 (1978): 50–83.

3. *Game and Toy Catalogue* (Springfield, MA: Milton Bradley Company, 1960), 5, Milton Bradley Archives, Hasbro, East Longmeadow, MA.

4. Milton Bradley, "Social Game," U.S. Patent 53,561, issued April 3, 1866.

5. Deepak Shimkhada, "A Preliminary Study of the Game of Karma in India, Nepal, and Tibet," *Artibus Asiae* 44 (1983): 308–22. Andrew Topsfield, "The Indian Game of Snakes and Ladders," *Artibus Asiae* 46 (1985): 203–26. Bruce Whitehill, *Games: American Boxed Games and Their Makers, 1822–1992* (Radnor, PA: Chilton Books, 1992), 24–25. On the popularity of goods from the East in Victorian parlors, see Kristin L. Hoganson, *Consumers' Imperium: The Global Production of American Domesticity, 1865–1920* (Chapel Hill: University of North Carolina Press, 2007).

6. On the diary, see James J. Shea, as told to Charles Mercer, *It's All in the Game* (New York: Putnam, 1960), 19. As recently as 1960, Milton Bradley's papers were housed in the company's archives. But beginning in the 1970s, researchers looking for the papers were turned away, and when I investigated, no one at Hasbro knew what had happened to them. I couldn't find them when I visited the company's archives in November 2006, and my efforts to trace them through Bradley's descendants didn't turn up anything, either.

7. David Parlett, *The Oxford History of Board Games* (New York: Oxford University Press, 1999), 278–86.

8. Thomas More, *Utopia*, trans. Ralph Robynson (London, 1551). Whitehill, *Games*, 45. George Herbert, "115. Upon John Crop, who dyed by taking a vomit," in *Wits Recreations* (London, 1640).

9. Bradley, Checkered Game of Life.

10. Asa M. Bradley, "The Bradleys," typescript, 1907, Milton Bradley Archives, Hasbro, East Longmeadow, MA. See also Shea, *It's All in the Game*, chapter 1; and *Milton Bradley, a Successful Man: A Brief Sketch of His Career and the Growth of the Institution Which He Founded, Published by Milton Bradley Company in Commemoration of Their Fiftieth Anniversary* (New York: J. F. Tapley, 1910), 4. Samuel Penhallow, *The History of the Wars of New-England with the Eastern Indians* (Boston, 1726), 10–11. Cotton Mather, *A Memorial of the Present Deplorable State of New-England* (London, 1707), 33–36. On captivity and redemption, see John Demos, *The Unredeemed Captive: A Family Story from Early America* (New York: Knopf, 1992), and Jill Lepore, *The Name of War: King Philip's War and the Origins of American Identity* (New York: Knopf, 1998).

11. Mather, *Deplorable State of New-England*, 33. Cotton Mather, *The Spirit of Life Entering into the Spiritually Dead* (Boston, 1707), 6–22.

12. The New Game of Human Life (London: John Wallis, 1790). An early work of Edmond Hoyle's was his *A Short Treatise on the Game of Whist* (London, 1742). Robert Lewis, "The Mansion of Happiness: English and American Versions of a Nineteenth-Century Board Game," typescript, Games Collection, Box 1, OS Box 2, American Antiquarian Society, Worcester, MA. See also Jill Shefrin, " 'Make It a Pleasure and Not a Task': Educational Games for Children in Georgian England," *Princeton University Library Chronicle* 60 (1999): 251–75.

13. Plato, *The Republic*, trans. Benjamin Jowett (London: Clarendon Press, 1881), 3. On life as a journey, see Samuel Chew, *The Pilgrimage of Life* (New Haven, CT: Yale University Press, 1962); Elizabeth Sears, *The Ages of Man: Medieval Interpretations of the Life Cycle* (Princeton, NJ: Princeton University Press, 1986); Thomas R. Cole, *The Journey of Life: A Cultural History of Aging in America* (Cambridge: Cambridge University Press, 1992); John Demos, *Circles and Lines: The Shape of Life in Early America* (Cambridge, MA: Harvard University Press, 2004); Michael Kammen, "Changing Perceptions of the Life Cycle in American Thought and Culture," *Proceedings of the Massachusetts Historical Society* 91 (1979): 34–66; and Michael Kammen, *A Time to Every Purpose: The Four Seasons in American Culture* (Chapel Hill: University of North Carolina Press, 2004).

14. Francis Bacon, *A History of Life and Death* (London, 1638).

15. When Noah Webster published a collection of aphorisms in 1786, he quoted Samuel Johnson's "He that embarks in the voyage of life, will always wish to advance rather by the impulse of the wind, than the strokes of the oar," and, on the same page, offered this proverb: "The great art of life is to play for much, and stake little." The two ideas—that life is a game and that life is a voyage—fit together only awkwardly. Are you at the whim of the wind, or are you calculating your odds? Noah Webster, *A*

Grammatical Institute of the English Language (Hartford, CT, 1786), 38. John Bunyan, *The Pilgrim's Progress: From This World to That Which Is to Come* (London, 1678).

16. Benjamin Franklin, *Poor Richard's Almanack* (Philadelphia, 1740).

17. R. C. Bell, *Board and Table Games from Many Civilizations* (London: Oxford University Press, 1969), 14.

18. Nathaniel Cotton, *Visions for the Entertainment and Instruction of Young Minds* (Exeter, NH, 1794).

19. On the game's early use in the United States, see H.S., *The History of the Davenport Family* (Boston, 1798), 30. On playing it as late as the 1870s, see Rose Terry Cooke, "Thanksgiving Then," *Independent*, November 27, 1873, 1485–86.

20. The first Mansion of Happiness was the New, Moral and Entertaining Game of the Mansion of Happiness, printed by Robert Laurie and James Whittle in October 1800.

21. Frederick H. Quitman, *Evangelical Catechism* (Hudson, NY, 1814), 107.

22. T. Newton, The New Game of the Mansion of Bliss: In Verse (London, 1810), 13.

23. E.g., "On her arms she wore the bracelets of her friend, and suspended from her bosom the picture of Mr. Severs—that bosom the mansion of bliss, the fruition of peace which virtue alone can bestow." Miss Hatfield, *She Lives in Hopes; Or, Caroline* (Wilmington, DE, 1802), 164.

24. *Catalogue of Books for Sale and Circulation by Charles Peirce at His Brick Book-store, in . . . Portsmouth, New Hampshire* (Portsmouth, NH, 1806), 91; "A New Game for Children," *Boston Recorder*, December 7, 1843. For sales, see Lewis, "The Mansion of Happiness." Whether the Mansion of Happiness is America's first board game or its second is a matter of some debate. In any event, it was Ives's Mansion of Happiness that inaugurated what is generally known as the golden age of American board games. See also: Margaret K. Hofer, *The Games We Played: The Golden Age of Board and Table Games* (New York: Princeton Architectural Press, 2003); David Wallace Adams and Victor Edmunds, "Making Your Move: The Educational Significance of the American Board Game, 1832 to 1904," *History of Education Quarterly* 17 (1977): 359–83.

25. John Milton, *Paradise Lost* (London, 1674), books 1 and 3.

26. The Mansion of Happiness (Salem, MA, 1843). In the possession of the author.

27. Shea, *It's All in the Game*, 27.

28. Ruth Schwart Cowan, *A Social History of American Technology* (Oxford: Oxford University Press, 1997), 138, 210. Miller, *The Mind in America;* or see him cited in David E. Nye, *American Technological Sublime* (Cambridge, MA: MIT Press, 1994). James Mill, *History of British India* (1817; London: Baldwin, Cradock and Joy, 1820), 1:353. Thomas J. Misa, *Leonardo to the Internet: Technology and Culture from the Renaissance to the Present* (Baltimore: Johns Hopkins University Press, 2004), 101–18. On "men of progress," see Jill Lepore, *A Is for American: Letters and Other Characters in the Newly United States* (New York: Knopf, 2002), epilogue.

29. Thomas Carlyle, "Signs of the Times," *Edinburgh Review*, 1829.

30. On the shape of life, see Demos, *Circles and Lines*. On modernity and historical consciousness, see Dorothy Ross, "Historical Consciousness in Nineteenth-Century America," *American Historical Review* 89 (October 1984): 909–28.

31. Jacob Bigelow, *Elements of Technology* (Boston, 1829). See also Leo Marx, "The Idea

of 'Technology' and Postmodern Pessimism," in *Does Technology Drive History? The Dilemma of Technological Determinism,* eds. Merritt Roe Smith and Leo Marx (Cambridge, MA: MIT Press, 1994), 237–58; Leo Marx and Bruce Mazlish, eds., *Progress: Fact or Illusion* (Ann Arbor: University of Michigan Press, 1996); and Leo Marx, *The Machine in the Garden: Technology and the Pastoral Idea in America* (New York: Oxford University Press, 1964).

32. Jacob Bigelow, *An Address on the Limits of Education* (Boston, 1865), 4.

33. Henry David Thoreau, *Walden and Resistance to Civil Government,* ed. William Rossi (New York: Norton, 1992), 35–73.

34. Review of *Walden* in the New York *Churchman,* September 2, 1854, in *Emerson and Thoreau: The Contemporary Reviews,* ed. Joel Myerson (Cambridge: Cambridge University Press, 1992), 382. Ralph Waldo Emerson, *The Selected Letters of Ralph Waldo Emerson,* ed. Joel Myerson (New York: Columbia University Press, 1997), 15.

35. Shea, *It's All in the Game,* 35–38. See also "Said Pasha," *Littell's Living Age,* November 10, 1855.

36. "The game Tapley brought to the lamp-lighted table was a very old one, apparently, and made in England," a biographer of Bradley once wrote. "It was played on a board with oval discs, like several English and European games." This is a good description of the Mansion of Bliss. "After a week of working steadily, Bradley believed he had perfected his game. But what would he call it? Studying the checkered pattern of the game on his rolltop desk, he thought that it was like the design of his life and the life of nearly everyone he knew: checkered, hazardous, uncertain in its outcome. Life was like a game, and a game—a good game—must be like life itself. You subscribed to fixed rules, you recognized the element of chance, and you exercised all the skill and judgment you possessed to *win* it. He would call it 'The Checkered Game of Life.'" Shea, *It's All in the Game,* 47–49.

37. Benjamin Franklin, "The Morals of Chess," *Columbian Magazine* 1 (December 1786): 159–61.

38. C. Borr. Von Miltitz, *The Game of Life; or, The Chess-Players* (Boston, 1837). Mrs. Frances Sargent Osgood, "The Coquette; Or, The Game of Life," *Graham's Magazine of Literature and Art,* January 1843, 24. "The Web Spun," *Liberator,* July 28, 1848, 118. Lieutenant Murray, "The Duke's Prize," chapter 4, *Gleason's Pictorial Drawing-Room Companion,* July 15, 1854, 19. W.T., "The Game of Chess," *New Mirror,* September 30, 1843, 408. Near the end of the Civil War, *Harper's* printed a version of Retszch's engraving in which Jefferson Davis, president of the Confederacy, plays against Uncle Sam, watched over by the "Goddess of Liberty" ("Check-Mate," *Harper's Weekly,* June 3, 1865, 337). "What a perfect chequer-board is this same game of life," wrote an essayist in 1854; "the various vicissitudes of life make up the chequered field, ourselves the wooden 'men.'"

39. Benjamin Franklin, *Autobiography,* ed. J. A. Leo Lemay and P. M. Zall (New York: Norton, 1986).

40. Shea, *It's All in the Game,* 50–52.

41. *Christian Union,* January 10, 1872, 62.

42. Milton Bradley, "Social Game," U.S. Patent 53,561.

43. Thoreau, *Walden,* 221.

44. Milton Bradley, The Checkered Game of Life (Springfield, MA: Milton Bradley Company, 1866), Games Collection, Box 1, American Antiquarian Society, Worcester, MA.

45. Mark Twain, "The Revised Catechism," New York Tribune, September 27, 1871.

46. Mel Taft, telephone interview with author, November 3, 2006. Reuben Klamer, who designed the 1960 game, told me he had never played the Mansion of Happiness, although when I visited Hasbro, the Mansion of Happiness was hanging in a frame on a wall. Reuben Klamer, telephone interview with author, June 7, 2006. Reuben Klamer to the author, July 14, 2006. On the development of the 1960 game, see also The Milton Bradley Company 100th Anniversary (East Longmeadow, MA: Milton Bradley Company, 1960), an advertising supplement, which also contains a good history of the company; this supplement was printed separately but was also inserted into the Springfield Sunday Republican, February 21, 1960.

47. The Game of Life (East Longmeadow, MA: Hasbro, 1994). In the possession of the author. Hasbro Games Division, interviews with author, February 5, 2007.

48. The Game of Life: Twists and Turns (Pawtucket, RI: Hasbro, 2007). In the possession of the author.

49. Amy Johannes, "Child Advocates Call New Hasbro/Visa Deal 'Sleazy,'" Promo, March 9, 2007, http://promomagazine.com/news/child_advocates_hasbro_visa_deal_030907/.

50. George Burtch, interview with the author, February 5, 2007.

51. Thoreau, Walden, 36.

52. See www.secondlife.com.

53. Before he left his games business to more ambitious men, Bradley had another big hit, just after the Civil War, with croquet, whose rules he patented and whose equipment manufacture he perfected while a fever for the game swept the nation, on the merits of the claim that croquet was just like life. E.g., "Croquet is the game of life, you see," says a character in a Harriet Beecher Stowe novel in 1871 ("My Wife and I," Christian Union, August 9, 1871; the reference is to chapter 32).

54. On this subject, see Scott Sandage, Born Losers: A History of Failure in America (Cambridge, MA: Harvard University Press, 2005).

55. Henry George, Progress and Poverty: An Inquiry into the Cause of Industrial Depressions, and of Increase of Want with Increase of Wealth (San Francisco: 1879; London, 1884), 5. Edward Wiebé, The Paradise of Childhood (Springfield, MA: Bradley, 1887). See also Jennifer L. Snyder, "A Critical Examination of Milton Bradley's Contributions to Kindergarten and Art Education in the Context of His Time," EdD diss., Florida State University, 2005.

56. Shea, It's All in the Game, especially chapter 9; quote from 180.

Chapter 1.   HATCHED

1. "Drama of Life Before Birth," Life, April 30, 1965. Readings of these photographs include Meredith W. Michaels, "Fetal Galaxies: Some Questions About What We See," in Fetal Subjects, Feminist Positions, ed. Lynn M. Morgan and Meredith W.

Michaels (Philadelphia: University of Pennsylvania Press, 1999), 113–32; Barbara Duden, *Disembodying Women: Perspectives on Pregnancy and the Unborn,* trans. Lee Hoinacki (Cambridge, MA: Harvard University Press, 1993), chapter 2; and Valerie Hartouni, *Cultural Conceptions: On Reproductive Technologies and the Remaking of Life* (Minneapolis: University of Minnesota Press, 1997), chapter 3. For a broader and influential analysis of related images, see Ludmilla Jordanova, *Sexual Visions: Images of Gender in Science and Medicine Between the Eighteenth and Twentieth Centuries* (London: Harvester Wheatsheaf, 1989). Related readings include Susan Merrill Squier, *Babies in Bottles: Twentieth-Century Visions of Reproductive Technologies* (New Brunswick, NJ: Rutgers University Press, 1994). Nilsson's photographs were not actually unprecedented, as the editorial department at *Life* acknowledged, at least in internal memos, when readers wrote in to remark on this fact. See, e.g., Mabel Foust to Editorial Reference, memo, May 18, 1965, Lennart Nilsson file, Time Inc. Archives, New York.

2. The editors at *Life* considered this feature the latest in a series of exposés about human reproduction, beginning with the publication of still shots from *The Birth of a Baby* in 1938, and which I discuss in chapter 3. J. McQuiston to *Life* index, "Human Reproduction," memo, May 10, 1965, "Birth of a Baby" file, Time Inc. Archives. Lennart Nilsson, *A Child Is Born: The Drama of Life Before Birth in Unprecedented Photographs* (New York: Delacorte Press, 1965), with text by Axel Ingelman-Sunderg and Claes Wirsén. Display ad, *New York Times,* May 2, 1966.

3. The fetus on the cover, the editors wrote, "was photographed just after it had to be surgically removed from its mother's womb at the age of 4½ months. Though scientists hope some day to be able to keep such early babies alive, this one did not survive." "Drama of Life Before Birth," *Life,* April 30, 1965.

4. "The Unborn Plaintiff," *Time,* April 30, 1965.

5. Nilsson himself kept his distance from the abortion debate, including in 1990, when another series of his photographs of embryos was published in *Life.* Asked when life begins, he said, "Look at the pictures. I am not the man who shall decide when human life started. I am a reporter. I am a photographer." Ray Kerrison, "Backdrop to Bush's Court Selection," *New York Post,* July 25, 1990.

6. The classic account is Joseph Needham, *A History of Embryology* (Cambridge: Cambridge University Press, 1934; repr., New York: Arno Press, 1975). But see also John Farley, *Gametes & Spores: Ideas About Sexual Reproduction, 1750–1914* (Baltimore: Johns Hopkins University Press, 1982); Matthew Cobb, *Generation: The Seventeenth-Century Scientists Who Unraveled the Secrets of Sex, Life and Growth* (London: Bloomsbury, 2006); Clara Correia, *The Ovary of Eve: Egg and Sperm and Preformation* (Chicago: University of Chicago Press, 1997); F. J. Cole, *Early Theories of Sexual Generation* (Oxford: Clarendon Press, 1930); Elizabeth Gasking, *Investigations into Generation, 1651–1828* (London: Hutchinson, 1967); Angus McLaren, *Reproductive Rituals: The Perception of Fertility in England from the Sixteenth to the Nineteenth Century* (London: Methuen, 1984); and, especially, Thomas Laqueur, "Orgasm, Generation, and the Politics of Reproductive Biology," in *The Making of the Modern Body: Sexuality and Society in the Nineteenth Century,* ed. Catherine Gallagher and Thomas Laqueur (Berkeley: University of California Press, 1987), 1–41.

7. Page Smith and Charles Daniel, *The Chicken Book* (Boston: Little, Brown, 1975), 45, 169–70. For another take on philosophy and poultry, see Steven Shapin, "The Philosopher and the Chicken: On the Dietetics of Disembodied Knowledge," in *Never Pure: Historical Studies of Science as if It Was Produced by People with Bodies, Situated in Time, Space, Culture, and Society, and Struggling for Credibility and Authority* (Baltimore: Johns Hopkins University Press, 2010), 237–58.

8. Needham, *History of Embryology*, 22, 25; and Smith and Daniel, *Chicken Book*, chapter 1.

9. A short history of efforts at measurement, along with the sand illustration, can be found in Carl G. Hartman, "How Large Is the Mammalian Egg?," *Quarterly Review of Biology* 4 (1929): 373–88.

10. See Fabricius of Aquapendente, *The Embryological Treatises of Hieronymus Fabricius of Aquapendente: The Formation of the Egg and of the Chick, The Formed Fetus*, a facsimile edition edited and with an introduction, a translation, and a commentary by Howard B. Adelmann (Ithaca, NY: Cornell University Press, 1942).

11. Philip Barbour, *The Complete Works of Captain John Smith* (Chapel Hill: University of North Carolina Press, 1986), 1:276, 128–29, xlv, 232–33. *Captain John Smith*, ed. James Horn (New York: Library of America, 2006), 1101. See also Jill Lepore, "Our Town," *New Yorker*, April 2, 2007.

12. The best biography of Harvey remains Geoffrey Keynes, *The Life of William Harvey* (Oxford: Clarendon Press, 1966). But see also Emerson Thomas McMullen, *William Harvey and the Use of Purpose in the Scientific Revolution* (Lanham, MD: University Press of America, 1998), and Walter Pagel, *William Harvey's Biological Ideas* (New York: S. Karger, 1967). Especially useful is John Aubrey, *Brief Lives* (1669–96), ed. Andrew Clark (Oxford: Clarendon Press, 1898), 1:297–301. For a gendered reading of the politics of Harvey's theory of generation, see Carolyn Merchant, *The Death of Nature: Women, Ecology, and the Scientific Revolution* (New York: Harper & Row, 1980), 155–63, and Eve Keller, "Making Up for Losses: The Workings of Gender in William Harvey's *De Generatione animalium*," in *Inventing Maternity: Politics, Science, and Literature, 1650–1865*, ed. Susan C. Greenfield and Carol Barash (Lexington: University Press of Kentucky, 1999), 34–56.

13. William Harvey, *The Generation of Living Creatures* (London, 1653), especially "The Epistle Dedicatory"; Martin Lluelyn, "To the Incomparable Dr. Harvey," prefatory poem to *De Generatione animalium*. On the language of wonder, see Stephen Greenblatt, *Marvelous Possessions: The Wonder of the New World* (Chicago: University of Chicago Press, 1991).

14. Aubrey, *Brief Lives*, 1:299. On his wife and the parrot, see Keynes, *Life of Harvey*, vii. Harvey thought the parrot was a cock, but when it died and he dissected it, he found an egg inside. McMullen, *William Harvey and the Use of Purpose*, 42.

15. Thomas Reynalde, *The Birth of Mankind: Otherwise Named, The Woman's Book*, edited by Elaine Hobby (1550; repr., Surrey, UK: Ashgate, 2009), 186, 191. This form of diagnosis remained popular a century on; see Jane Sharp, *The Midwives Book* (1671; repr., New York: Garland, 1985), 164.

16. Harvey, *Generation of Living Creatures*, 2, 21, 25, 383, 390.

17. Keynes, *Life of Harvey*, 387–89.

18. Harvey, *Generation of Living Creatures,* 390, 391, 397, 430–31, 532. But see also Needham, *History of Embryology,* 133–34. On Harvey and James I and Charles I, see Christopher Hill, "William Harvey and the Idea of Monarchy," *Past & Present* 27 (1964): 54–72.

19. Harvey, *Generation of Living Creatures,* 25, 390.

20. For an invaluable account of what later came to be called the "scientific revolution," see Steve Shapin, *The Scientific Revolution* (Chicago: University of Chicago Press, 1997).

21. Aubrey, *Brief Lives,* 1:300.

22. Keller, "Making Up for Losses," 43.

23. Keynes, *Life of Harvey,* 344, 348, 368–70, 462.

24. Lluelyn, "To the Incomparable Dr. Harvey."

25. See Laqueur, "Orgasm," and also Mary E. Fissell, *Vernacular Bodies: The Politics of Reproduction in Early Modern England* (Oxford: Oxford University Press, 2004), and Frederick B. Churchill, "The History of Embryology as Intellectual History," *Journal of the History of Biology* 3 (1970): 155–81.

26. Thomas Hobbes, *Leviathan* (London, 1651), "Introduction."

27. Edward G. Ruestow, "Images and Ideas: Leeuwenhoek's Perception of the Spermatozoa," *Journal of the History of Biology* 16 (1983): 185–224, especially 194. See also Farley, *Gametes & Spores,* 17.

28. Aubrey, *Brief Lives,* 1:301.

29. Although both this motto and a misquotation of it, "*Omne vivum ex ovo*" (Everything living comes out of an egg), are often attributed to Harvey, they are not his. He did, however, apparently approve the text of the engraving (Keynes, *Life of Harvey,* 334).

30. Ruestow, "Images and Ideas," 194–96. De Graaf quoted in Farley, *Gametes & Spores,* 16. *The Collected Letters of Antoni van Leeuwenhoek,* edited, illustrated, and annotated by a Committee of Dutch Scientists (Amsterdam: Swets & Zeitlinger, 1939), 1:29–35.

31. Ruestow, "Images and Ideas," 198–200. Leeuwenhoek to Christopher Wren, January 22, 1683, *Letters of Leeuwenhoek,* 4:11–13.

32. Ruestow, "Images and Ideas," 188.

33. *Letters of Leeuwenhoek,* 1:67, 111, 119, 127.

34. Ruestow, "Images and Ideas," 188–89.

35. For a curious account of the transmission of these ideas to New England, see Ava Chamberlain, "The Immaculate Ovum: Jonathan Edwards and the Construction of the Female Body," *William and Mary Quarterly* 57 (2000): 289–322.

36. Laqueur, "Orgasm," 3, 18–19. See also Carole Pateman, *The Sexual Contract* (Palo Alto: Stanford University Press, 1998).

37. Quoted in Laqueur, "Orgasm," 20.

38. Lluelyn, "To the Incomparable Dr. Harvey."

39. Aldous Huxley, *Brave New World* (1931).

40. Von Baer is quoted in C. R. Austin, *The Mammalian Egg* (Oxford: Blackwell, 1961), 4. But for a fuller account, see K. E. von Baer and George Sarton, "The Discovery of the Mammalian Egg and the Foundation of Modern Embryology," *Isis* 16 (1931): 315–30,

and the accompanying reprint of K. E. von Baer, *De Ovi Mammalium et Hominis Genesi*, 331–77.

41. Squier, *Babies in Bottles*, 29–35.

42. Gregory Pincus, *The Eggs of Mammals* (New York: Macmillan, 1936), 8–9. On Pincus and the Pill, see James Reed, *From Private Vice to Public Virtue: The Birth Control Movement and American Society Since 1830* (New York: Basic Books, 1978), chapters 25–27.

43. On the global travels of *Mus musculus*, see Clyde E. Keeler, *The Laboratory Mouse: Its Origin, Heredity, and Culture* (Cambridge, MA: Harvard University Press, 1931), 4–6; on mice and heredity, 7–18. The best study of mice research in the twentieth century is Karen A. Rader, *Making Mice: Standardizing Animals for American Biomedical Research, 1900–1955* (Princeton, NJ: Princeton University Press, 2004).

44. Austin, *Mammalian Egg*, 4–6.

45. Donald Pickens, *Eugenics and the Progressives* (Nashville: Vanderbilt University Press, 1968), 49.

46. J. A. Long and E. L. Mark, *The Maturation of the Egg of the Mouse* (Washington, DC: Carnegie Institution, 1911), 1–6.

47. Rader, *Making Mice*. On chickens, see P. B. Siegel, J. B. Dodgson, and L. Andersson, "Progress from Chicken Genetics to the Chicken Genome," *Poultry Science* 85 (2006): 2050–60.

48. Mall's circular is reproduced in Lynn M. Morgan, *Icons of Life: A Cultural History of Human Embryos* (Berkeley: University of California Press, 2009), 71–72.

49. Morgan, *Icons of Life*, 74–75, 82, 93, 105, 136–37, 141, 149.

50. J.B.S. Haldane, *Daedalus; Or, Science and the Future* (New York: Dutton, 1924), 63–65. Haldane gave the lecture in Cambridge on February 4, 1923. Discussions of Haldane's vision include Spier, *Babies in Bottles*, chapter 2.

51. Reed, *From Private Vice to Public Virtue*, 321. "Rabbits Born in Glass: Haldane-Huxley Fantasy Made Real by Harvard Biologists," *New York Times*, May 13, 1934.

52. Telegram, March 24, 1965, Lennart Nilsson file, Time Inc. Archives. "Drama of Life Before Birth," *Life*, April 30, 1965. Miles Ruben, "Life Before Birth," *Saturday Evening Post*, May–June 1978, 68–69. Joelle Bentley, "Photographing the Miracle of Life," *Technology Review* 95 (November–December 1992): 58. Adrienne Gyongy, "Lennart Nilsson: Sweden's Scientific Eye," *Scandinavian Review* 80 (Winter 1992): 51–55.

53. A good source on the development of the film, from Clarke's point of view, is Arthur C. Clarke, *The Lost Worlds of 2001* (Boston: Gregg Press, 1979). Interviews with Kubrick have been widely reprinted, most usefully in *Stanley Kubrick: Interviews*, ed. Gene D. Phillips (Jackson: University Press of Mississippi, 2001). On Kubrick's interest in *Childhood's End*, see John Baxter, *Stanley Kubrick: A Biography* (New York: Carroll and Graf, 1997), chapter 12. See also Vincent LoBrutto, *Stanley Kubrick: A Biography* (New York: Donald I. Fine, 1997), 258–67. On the filming, see Piers Bizony, *2001: Filming the Future*, with a foreword by Arthur C. Clarke (London: Aurum Press, 2000), which includes a facsimile of MGM's February 23, 1965, press release announcing Kubrick's collaboration with Clarke on *Journey Beyond the Stars* (10–11). And, for a compendium of material on Kubrick's films, see Alison Castle, ed., *The*

Stanley Kubrick Archives (Cologne: Taschen, 2005); a production calendar, compiled by Carolyn Geduld, is on pp. 373–75.

54. "The Playboy Interview: Stanley Kubrick," *Playboy,* September 1968. The complete interview is reprinted in Castle, ed., *Stanley Kubrick Archives,* 398–407.

55. Reviews, diaries, and interviews are reproduced in *The Making of 2001: A Space Odyssey,* selected by Stephanie Schwam (New York: Modern Library, 2000). See especially pp. 5–8 and 83. Clarke's diary entry for October 3, 1965, appears on p. 40.

56. On the modeling of the baby, see Castle, ed., *Stanley Kubrick Archives,* 370. *2001: A Space Odyssey,* directed by Stanley Kubrick (1968; Burbank, CA: Warner Home Video, 2007).

57. Arthur C. Clarke, *2001: A Space Odyssey* (New York: New American Library, 1968), 220–21.

58. Clarke, *2001,* 221.

59. Jay Cocks, "SK," introduction to *The Making of 2001,* xv–xvi.

60. Schlesinger's *Vogue* review is quoted in LoBrutto, *Stanley Kubrick,* 311. The remaining reviews are reproduced in *The Making of 2001,* and quotations are taken from 171, 144–47, 274. See also Barry Keith Grant, "Of Men and Monoliths," in *Stanley Kubrick's* 2001: A Space Odyssey: *New Essays,* edited by Robert Kolker (Oxford: Oxford University Press, 2006), 69–86.

61. "The Playboy Interview: Stanley Kubrick," *Playboy,* September 1968. The *Life* review is reproduced in *The Making of 2001,* and the quotation is taken from p. 171.

62. A replica of "the ultimate trip" movie poster can be found in Castle, ed., *Stanley Kubrick Archives,* 407.

Chapter 2.   Baby Food

1. "Necessity on One Hand, Security on the Other," *New York Times,* September 1, 2006. Transportation Security Administration, "New Policies for Lighters, Electronics, and Breast Milk," http://www.tsa.gov/travelers/sop/index.shtm#milk. The TSA's new policy went into effect on August 4, 2007 (Jeanne Oliver of the TSA to the author, July 25, 2008). The TSA's shifting policies did not end harassment of nursing mothers, as evidenced by a controversy in November 2010. Roger Ebert, "Update on the TSA Breast Milk Incident," *Roger Ebert's Journal* (blog), *Chicago Sun-Times,* http://blogs .suntimes.com/ebert/politics/nbsp-nbsp.html.

2. Jennifer Block, "Move Over, Milk Banks: Facebook and Milk Sharing," *Time,* November 22, 2010.

3. "Board Won't Relent for Breast-feeding Mother," *Boston Globe,* June 23, 2007.

4. On milk banks, see Lois Arnold, "Donor Human Milk Banking: Creating Public Health Policy in the 21st Century," PhD diss., Union Institute and University, 2005.

5. Milkscreen, http://www.milkscreen-moms.com/.

6. Useful histories include Rima D. Apple, *Mothers and Medicine: A Social History of Infant Feeding, 1890–1950* (Madison: University of Wisconsin Press, 1987); Valerie Fildes, *Breasts, Bottles, and Babies: A History of Infant Feeding* (Edinburgh, UK: Edin-

burgh University Press, 1986); Bernice L. Hausman, *Mother's Milk: Breastfeeding Controversies in American Culture* (New York: Routledge, 2003); Harvey Leverstein, " 'Best for Babies' or 'Preventable Infanticide'? The Controversy over Artificial Feeding of Infants in America, 1880–1920," *Journal of American History* 70 (1983): 75–94. And, more broadly, Marilyn Yalom, *A History of the Breast* (New York: Knopf, 1997).

7. A rare early scholarly study is Maia Boswell-Penc and Kate Boyer, "Expressing Anxiety? Breast Pump Usage in American Wage Workplaces," *Gender, Place, and Culture* 14 (October 2007): 551–67.

8. "John McCain & Sarah Palin on Shattering the Glass Ceiling: Interview with McCain and Palin," by Sandra Sobieraj Westfall, *People,* August 29, 2008, http://www.people.com/people/article/0,,20222685,00.html.

9. Julie Hirschfeld Davis, Associated Press, "Capital Culture: New Moms Love Capitol 'Boob Cube,' " *Boston Globe,* December 16, 2010.

10. Kate Zernike, "A Breast-Feeding Plan Mixes Partisan Reactions," *New York Times,* February 18, 2011.

11. On Avent's iQ technology, see http://www.consumer.philips.com/consumer/en/gb/consumer/cc/_categoryid_ADVANTAGE_OF_IQ_AR_GB_CONSUMER/.

12. Linnaeus's work was brilliantly reconstructed and analyzed by Londa Schiebinger in "Why Mammals Are Called Mammals," *American Historical Review* 98 (April 1993): 382–411. See also Gunnar Broberg, "*Homo sapiens:* Linnaeus's Classification of Man," *Linnaeus: The Man and His Work,* ed. Tore Frangsmyr (Berkeley: University of California Press, 1983), especially 170–75. On the length of time Linnaeus's wife nursed, note that one of his maxims was "The newborn should be nourished with mother's milk for several years" (Heinz Goerke, *Linnaeus,* trans. Denver Lindley [New York: Charles Scribner's Sons, 1973], 119).

13. Franklin quoted in Samuel X. Radbill, "Centuries of Child Welfare in Philadelphia: Part II, Benjamin Franklin and Pediatrics," *Philadelphia Medicine* 71 (1975): 320. Benjamin Franklin, *The Life of Dr. Benjamin Franklin. Written by Himself* (Philadelphia, 1794), 19.

14. William Gouge, *Of Domesticall Duties* (London, 1622), 507–13. Cotton Mather, *The A, B, C of Religion* (Boston, 1713). John Cotton's *Spiritual Milk for Boston Babes* was printed in London in 1646, the same year as Robert Abbot's *Milk for Babes; Or, A Mother's Catechism for Her Children.*

15. Ruth Perry, "Colonizing the Breast: Sexuality and Maternity in Eighteenth-Century England," *Journal of the History of Sexuality* 2 (1991): 204–34. See also Paula A. Treckel, "Breastfeeding and Maternal Sexuality in Colonial America," *Journal of Interdisciplinary History* 20 (1989): 25–51. Mary Wollestonecraft, *A Vindication of the Rights of Woman* (Boston, 1782), 256.

16. Erasmus Darwin, *Zoonomia; or, The Laws of Organic Life* (London, 1794), 1:145. See also George D. Sussman, *Selling Mother's Milk: The Wet-Nursing Business in France, 1715–1915* (Urbana: University of Illinois Press, 1982), especially chapter 2.

17. Daguerreotypes of women breast-feeding are housed in the collections of, among other places, the Schlesinger Library at Radcliffe and the Nelson-Atkins Gallery in Kansas City. On antebellum breast-feeding, see also Sally McMillen, "Mothers'

Sacred Duty: Breast-feeding Patterns Among Middle- and Upper-Class Women in the Antebellum South," *Journal of Southern History* 51 (1985): 333–56; and Sylvia D. Hoffert, *Private Matters: American Attitudes Toward Childbearing and Infant Nurture in the Urban North, 1800–1860* (Urbana: University of Illinois Press, 1989).

18. Adrienne Berney, "Reforming the Maternal Breast: Infant Feeding and American Culture, 1870–1940," PhD diss., University of Delaware, 1998, 42. See also Jacqueline H. Wolf, *Don't Kill Your Baby: Public Health and the Decline of Breastfeeding in the Nineteenth and Twentieth Centuries* (Columbus: Ohio State University Press, 2001), 31–33.

19. Joe B. Frantz, "Gail Borden as a Businessman," *Bulletin of the Business Historical Society* 22 (1948): 123–33.

20. Charles Darwin, *The Descent of Man* (London, 1871), chapter 2.

21. In Stephen Jay Gould, *The Mismeasure of Man* (New York: Norton, 1981), 35.

22. Berney, "Reforming the Maternal Breast," 55, 60–63, 262–72, 140–45.

23. Janet Golden, "From Wet Nurse Directory to Milk Bank," *Bulletin of the History of Medicine* 62 (1988): 589–605. See also Henry Dwight Chapin, "The Operation of a Breast Milk Dairy," *Transactions of the American Pediatric Society* 25 (1923): 150–55.

24. Fritz B. Talbot, "An Organization for Supplying Human Milk," *New England Journal of Medicine* (1928): 610–11; "Directory for Wetnurses," *New England Journal of Medicine* (1927): 653–54; "The Wetnurse Problem," *Boston Medical and Surgical Journal* (1913): 760–62; "Two Methods of Obtaining Human Milk for Hospital Use," *Boston Medical and Surgical Journal* (1911): 304–6. James A. Tobey, "A New Foster-Mother," *Hygeia* 7 (1929): 1110–12. Carrie Hunt McCann, "Manual Breast Expression: The Importance of Teaching It to the Mother," *American Journal of Nursing* 28 (1928): 31–32. More on Talbot can be found in the Fritz B. Talbot Papers, Countway Library, Harvard Medical School.

25. For an early pump model, see Calvina MacDonald, "Abt's Electric Breast Pump," *American Journal of Nursing* 25 (1925): 277–80. Storage depended on the rise of freezers, which is discussed in chapter 10, but see also Paul W. Emerson, "The Preservation of Human Milk: Preliminary Notes on the Freezing Process," *Journal of Pediatrics* 2 (1933): 472–77.

26. Judy Torgus and Gwen Gotsh, ed., *The Womanly Art of Breastfeeding*, 7th ed. (Schaumburg, IL: La Leche League International, 2004), 6.

27. On the Healthy People 2000 objectives, and falling short: "The proportion of all mothers who breastfeed their infants in the early postpartum period increased from 52 percent in 1990 to 62 percent in 1997. For select populations, the rate of early breastfeeding increased over the same period as follows—for Black mothers, from 23 to 41 percent; for Hispanic mothers, from 48 to 64 percent; for American Indian/Alaska Native mothers, from 47 to 56 percent. The early breastfeeding rate for low-income mothers increased from 35 percent in 1990 to 42 percent in 1996. The year 2000 target is 75 percent." Department of Health and Human Services, "Progress Review: Maternal and Infant Health," May 5, 1999, http://odphp.osophs.dhhs.gov/pubs/hp2000/PROGRVW/materinfant/maternalprog.htm. The 2010 report card is available at http://www.cdc.gov/breastfeeding/data/reportcard.htm. See also American Academy of Pediatrics, "Breastfeeding and the Use of Human Milk," *Pediatrics*

115 (2005): 496–506; and Karen A. Bonuck, "Paucity of Evidence-Based Research on How to Achieve the Healthy People 2010 Goal of Exclusive Breastfeeding," *Pediatrics* 120 (2007): 248–49.

28. Patient Protection and Affordable Care Act of 2010, Pub. L. No. 111–48, §4207 (2010). But see also "Breastfeeding Laws," National Conference of State Legislatures, http://www.ncsl.org/default.aspx?tabid=14389, and U.S. Department of Labor Wage and Hour Division, "Fact Sheet #73: Break Time for Nursing Mothers Under the FLSA," http://www.dol.gov/whd/regs/compliance/whdfs73.pdf.

29. "Legislative History of Breastfeeding Promotion Requirements in WIC," USDA Food & Nutrition Service, http://www.fns.usda.gov/wic/Breastfeeding/bflegishistory.htm.

30. On Medela's website in 2008.

31. Jodi Kantor, "On the Job, Working Mothers Are Finding a 2-Class System," *New York Times,* September 1, 2006. Rebecca Adams, "A Place to Pump," *Washington Post,* May 13, 2008.

32. Dave Hogan and Michelle Cole, "Political Notebook: Governor Signs Bill for Breast Pump Breaks," *Oregonian,* May 18, 2007.

33. Adams, "A Place to Pump."

34. Pregnancy Discrimination Act of 2005, H.R. 2122, 109th Cong. (2005).

35. See, e.g., Lois Arnold, "Global Health Policies That Support the Use of Banked Donor Human Milk: A Human Rights Issue," *International Breastfeeding Journal* 1, no. 26 (2006): 1–8.

36. David Kocieniewski, "Acne Cream? Tax-Sheltered. Breast Pump? No," *New York Times,* October 26, 2010.

37. Zernike, "A Breast-Feeding Plan."

38. For more on this question, see Joan B. Wolf, "Is Breast Really Best? Risk and Total Motherhood in the National Breastfeeding Awareness Campaign," *Journal of Health Politics, Policy and Law* 32 (2007): 595–636.

39. "Open Letter to the Department of Health and Human Services Secretary Mike Leavitt," National Organization for Women http://www.now.org/issues/mothers/060718breastfeeding.html.

40. Medela's website in 2008 and "2-Phase Expression," Medela, http://www.medela.com/IW/en/breastfeeding/research-at-medela/2-phase-expression.html.

Chapter 3.   THE CHILDREN'S ROOM

1. Anne Carroll Moore (hereafter ACM), *My Roads to Childhood: Views and Reviews of Children's Books* (Boston: Horn Book, 1961). Frances Clarke Sayers, *Anne Carroll Moore: A Biography* (New York: Atheneum, 1972).

2. Sayers, *Moore,* ix, 105–6, 136. Miriam Braverman, *Youth, Society, and the Public Library* (Chicago: American Library Association, 1979), 14.

3. ACM, *My Roads to Childhood,* 65. Braverman, *Youth,* 15.

4. "History of the New York Public Library," New York Public Library, http://www.nypl.org/help/about-nypl/history. On the number of pre-Carnegie and Carnegie branches, see Amy Spaulding, "Moore, Anne Carroll," in *American National Biogra-*

phy Online (2000). Sayers, *Moore,* 140. See also Helen Adams Masten, "The Central Children's Room," *Bulletin of the New York Public Library* 60 (1956): 554.

5. John Locke, *Some Thoughts Concerning Education* (London, 1693), 63, 178. On the "discovery of childhood" (which is much debated), see Philippe Ariès, *Centuries of Childhood: A Social History of Family Life* (New York: Vintage, 1962). For an excellent American exploration of this theme, see Karen Calvert, *Children in the House: The Material Culture of Early Childhood, 1600–1900* (Boston: Northeastern University Press, 1992). On Newbery, see Brian Alderson and Felix de Marez Oyens, *Be Merry and Wise: Origins of Children's Book Publishing in England, 1650–1850* (New York: Pierpont Morgan Library, Bibliographical Society of America, 2006), chapter 5. On American imports of English children's titles, see E. Jennifer Monaghan, *Learning to Read and Write in Colonial America* (Amherst: University of Massachusetts Press, 2005), chapter 11. On Newbery's career, see John Rowe Townsend, ed., *Trade & Plumb-cake for Ever, Huzza! The Life and Work of John Newbery, 1713–1767* (Cambridge: Colt Books, 1994).

6. Phyllis Dain, *The New York Public Library: A History of Its Founding and Early Years* (New York: New York Public Library, 1972), 300–305.

7. Masten, "The Central Children's Room," 551. George Hutchinson, *In Search of Nella Larsen: A Biography of the Color Line* (Cambridge, MA: Harvard University Press, 2006), 171–77. Mary Strang, "Good Labour of Old Days," *Bulletin of the New York Public Library* 60 (1956): 540. Sayers, *Moore,* 68–69. The first registration book was still around in 1986, as it was part of the seventy-fifth-anniversary exhibit. See "75th Anniversary—Children's Room," Box 18, NYPL Archives, Branch Libraries, Donnell Papers, Manuscripts and Archives Division, New York Public Library.

8. Sandburg's testimonial can be found in Box 5, Unnumbered Folder: Commentary About Anne Carroll Moore, ACM Papers, Manuscripts and Archives Division, New York Public Library.

9. It would have taken anyone else 250 years to do for children what Moore did in twenty-five, Carl Van Doren once told her. Carl Van Doren to ACM, October 14, 1931, Box 4, ACM Papers. Sayers, *Moore,* 30. ACM, *My Roads to Childhood,* 23. Leonard S. Marcus, *Minders of Make-Believe: Idealists, Entrepreneurs, and the Shaping of American Children's Literature* (Boston: Houghton Mifflin, 2008), 133. Strang, "Good Labour of Old Days," 543.

10. Ursula Nordstrom to Katharine S. White, June 26, 1974, in *Dear Genius: The Letters of Ursula Nordstrom,* collected and edited by Leonard S. Marcus (New York: Harper-Collins, 1998), 356–57. "One averted one's eyes if possible. I remember when I was a child and something awful happened on the street, you know, one didn't look. Absolutely didn't look—and ACM and *Stuart,* well, it was like a dreadful accident, a horse fallen down." The Moore-White fiasco is reported, in brief, in "Anne Carroll Moore Urged Withdrawal of Stuart Little," *Library Journal* 91 (April 15, 1966): 2187–88, and *School Library Journal* 13 (April 1966): 71–72. Julie Cummins, " 'Let Her Sound Her Trumpet': NYPL Children's Librarians and Their Impact on the World of Publishing," *Biblion* 4 (1995): 97–98.

11. Clyde E. Keeler, *The Laboratory Mouse: Its Origin, Heredity, and Culture* (Cambridge,

MA: Harvard University Press, 1931), 4–6; on mice and heredity, 7–18. Karen A. Rader, *Making Mice: Standardizing Animals for American Biomedical Research, 1900–1955* (Princeton, NJ: Princeton University Press, 2004). For biographical details on White (hereafter EBW), see Scott Elledge, *E. B. White: A Biography* (New York: Norton, 1984).

12. Katharine Sergeant White (hereafter KSW) to Louise Seaman Bechtel (hereafter LSB), undated day in 1941: "Andy remembers of Mt. Vernon that he was not allowed to draw from any of the children's shelves until he reached a certain age. He didn't like it." Box 43, Folder 658, LSB Papers, Archives and Special Collections, Vassar College.

13. EBW, "A Winter Walk," *St. Nicholas Magazine* 38 (June 1911), 757. ACM also contributed, though this does not seem worth noting. See ACM, "Making Your Own Library," *St. Nicholas Magazine* (November 1919), 44–46.

14. Anne Thaxter Eaton, "Reviewing and Criticism of Children's Books," *Bulletin of the New York Public Library* 60 (1956): 559. But see also Richard L. Darling, *The Rise of Children's Book Reviewing in America, 1865–1881* (New York: Bowker, 1968), and ACM, "Writing for Children," in *My Roads to Childhood*, 23. On the founding and early history of the Newbery, see Ruth Allen, *Children's Book Prizes* (Aldershot, UK: Ashgate, 1998). The Newbery is administered by the Association for Library Service to Children, the descendant of the Club of Children's Librarians, formed as part of the American Library Association in 1900. ACM was the club's first chairman. See "History," American Library Association, http://www.ala.org/ala/aboutala/mission history/history/index.cfm.

15. Angell's father read her *Oliver Twist* when she was seven and sent her to the Brookline, Massachusetts, public library, once a week, to choose two books for him. On KSW's childhood reading, see Linda H. Davis, *Onward and Upward: A Biography of Katharine S. White* (New York: Harper & Row, 1987), 22, 24. Like EBW, she won a silver prize from *St. Nicholas*—in her case, for a story about a spider, which is neat, when you think about *Charlotte's Web*. I couldn't find it, but I didn't look for long. KSW's memory of going to the library to pick out books for her father can be found in KSW to LSB, undated 1941, Box 43, Folder 658, LSB Papers, Vassar ("I had to do this because my mother was dead and my father had no time to choose his own books, but read anyway four nights a week"). She had, from childhood, especially adored Austen. "In my sillier moments," she once wrote, "I think of Jane Austen as the perfect *New Yorker* writer."

16. EBW, "The Librarian Said It Was Bad for Children," *New York Times*, March 6, 1966. EBW to Eugene Saxton, March 1, 1939, in *Letters of E. B. White*, rev. ed., ed. Martha White, original ed. Dorothy Lobrano Guth (New York: HarperCollins, 2006), 183. He doesn't call him "Stuart Little" until the revisions in 1938, as far as I can tell. And, for a while in 1944, he seems to decide to call him "Stuart Ames." See the original manuscript of "Stuart Little," EBW Papers, Division of Rare and Manuscript Collections, Cornell University.

17. Sayers, *Moore*, 171–74, 186. For three letters from ACM signed "Nicholas," see "Nicholas" to LSB, December 4, 1927; undated; c. 1931; Box 33, LSB Papers, Vassar. ACM had stationery made with a woodcut illustration of Nicholas writing a letter, and for his

return address: "Nicholas Knickerbocker, 476 Fifth Avenue, New York." The letters are written, at least in places, as if written by Nicholas himself—"I'm the sorriest little Dutch boy you ever knew over your accident"; this from the letter with no date but that LSB has dated 1931.

18. ACM, *Nicholas: A Manhattan Christmas Story* (New York: G. P. Putnam's Sons, 1924), 4-5.

19. Sayers, *Moore,* 110, 124-25.

20. ACM, *My Roads to Childhood,* 339, 365. Dorothy Parker, "Far from Well," *New Yorker,* October 20, 1928, 98-99, and in *The Portable Dorothy Parker* (New York: Penguin, 1976), 518.

21. KSW, "Books for the Babies," *New Yorker,* December 1, 1934, 109-12; "Books for Boys and Girls," *New Yorker,* December 8, 1934, 142-43.

22. KSW to LSB, June 24, 1974, Box 43, Folder 662, LSB Papers, Vassar.

23. Seth Lerer, *Children's Literature: A Reader's History from Aesop to Harry Potter* (Chicago: University of Chicago Press, 2008).

24. KSW, "Books for Younger Children," *New Yorker,* November 30, 1935, 97; "Spring Books for Children," *New Yorker,* May 13, 1939, 103.

25. Reproduced in John Kobler, *Luce: His Time, Life and Fortune* (Garden City, NY: Doubleday, 1968), n.p.

26. Quoted in Alan Brinkley, *The Publisher: Henry Luce and His American Century* (New York: Knopf, 2010), 125.

27. It included a description of where the magazine got its paper ("It is typical of the great NEW YORKER organization, that it owns and operates today the biggest paper forest in the world, covering 29,000,000 or so acres in Canada, Maine and northern New Jersey, under the close supervision of THE NEW YORKER's field superintendent, Mr. Eustace Tilley"). There's also the visit to the Punctuation Farm ("The periods are set out in shallow pans under glass in early Spring, and carefully watered; and after six weeks of sunshine each sends down a tiny root no bigger than a bean (,) which is called a *comma*"). Corey Ford, "The Construction of Our Sentences," *New Yorker,* October 10, 1925; "Securing Paper for THE NEW YORKER," *New Yorker,* August 15, 1925; "The Magazine's Punctuation Farm," *New Yorker,* October 17, 1925.

28. Quoted in Roy Hoopes, *Ralph Ingersoll: A Biography* (New York: Atheneum, 1985), 116.

29. Wolcott Gibbs, "Time . . . Fortune . . . Life . . . Luce," *New Yorker,* November 28, 1936. "Magazine Proposal: True Crime" dated 1937-38, Box 24, *New Yorker* Records, New York Public Library. On the rivalry, see Jill Lepore, "Untimely," *New Yorker,* April 19, 2010.

30. "Cancer Army," *Time,* March 22, 1937. C. C. Little, "A New Deal for Mice: Why Mice Are Used in Research on Human Diseases," *Scientific American* 152 (1935): 16-18. See Rader, *Making Mice,* 135, 152-53.

31. Luce quoted in Brinkley, *The Publisher,* 214, 219, 222-23.

32. The letter is reprinted in the issue itself. The Editors, "This Announcement," *Life,* April 11, 1938. These remarkable pictures, the editors promised, "will be printed on the four centre pages, easily removable if you wish. The final decision must, of

course, be yours." The issue was vetted by the U.S. Postal Service before it was published. P. T. Prentice to Mr. Hinerfeld, April 6, 1938, "Birth of a Baby" file, Time Inc. Archives.

33. P. T. Prentice to Mr. Larsen, memo, April 16, 1938, "Birth of a Baby" file, Time Inc. Archives. The plan, including the proposed band taped around newsstand copies, is detailed in Roy E. Larsen, "Random Thoughts on Use of 'Birth of a Baby,'" typescript, March 24, 1938. On the letters, see copies in the Time Inc. files and also O. P. Swift to Walter K. Belknap, "Birth of a Baby Letter to Newspapermen," memo, April 2, 1938; Swift to Belknap, "Birth of a Baby Woman's Letter," memo, April 2, 1938, "Birth of a Baby" file, Time Inc. Archives. The magazine kept careful track of readers' response. See Anna Goldsborough to Mary Fraser, "Unfavorable letters received on 'The Birth of a Baby,'" memo, June 7, 1938; Anna Goldsborough to C. D. Jackson, "Unfavorable letters received on 'The Birth of a Baby,'" memo, June 13, 1938, "Birth of a Baby" file, Time Inc. Archives.

34. "She is the star": John Thorndike to Sheldon Luce, memo, April 4, 1938, "Birth of a Baby" file, Time Inc. Archives.

35. "The Birth of a Baby," *Life,* April 11, 1938.

36. G. Sugarman to Mr. Longwell, April 6, 1938, memo, "Birth of a Baby" file, Time Inc. Archives.

37. Dr. George Gallup, "America Speaks," *Atlanta Constitution,* April 22, 1938. Geraldine Sartain, "The Cinema Explodes the Stork Myth," *Journal of Educational Sociology* 12 (November 1938): 142–46; quotation on 144.

38. Reports of bans can be found in a scrapbook of news clippings at the Time Inc. Archives, but for a list of cities, see Paul Young to C. D. Jackson, April 15, 1938, memo, "Birth of a Baby" file, Time Inc. Archives. "The Birth of a Baby," *American News Trade Journal,* May 1938. UP Wire Service, April 8, 1938, "Birth of a Baby" file, Time Inc. Archives. William R. Matthews, editor and publisher, *Arizona Daily Star,* to *Life,* telegram, April 8, 1938, "Birth of a Baby" file, Time Inc. Archives. UP Wire service, April 8, 1938, teletype, "Birth of a Baby" file, Time Inc. Archives. "Wide Ban on 'Life' for Birth Pictures," *New York Times,* April 9, 1938. See also "Childbirth Photos Held Not Obscene," *Atlanta Constitution,* April 9, 1938, and "'Life' Ban Spreads to Pennsylvania," *New York Times,* April 10, 1938.

39. Dr. George Gallup, "Public Opposes Ban on Pictures Showing the Birth of a Baby," press release, American Institute of Public Opinion News Service, April 22, 1938, "Birth of a Baby" file, Time Inc. Archives. "Publisher of Life Pushes Court Test," *New York Times,* April 12, 1938. "Court Clears Life on Baby Pictures," *New York Times,* April 27, 1938. Mr. Prentice to Mr. Larsen, April 13, 1938, memo, "Birth of a Baby" file, Time Inc. Archives.

40. EBW, "The Birth of an Adult," *New Yorker,* April 23, 1938. "America Speaks," *Atlanta Constitution,* April 22, 1938. By the end of April, Larsen could declare, "*Life* has definitely turned the corner." The magazine's circulation quadrupled; soon it passed two million. In the first half of 1939, *Life* recorded its first profit, of nearly $1 million. Brinkley, *The Publisher,* 224–25. Circulation cartoon reproduced in Kobler, *Luce.*

41. EBW to James Thurber, April 16, 1938, *Letters of EBW,* 164. EBW, *The Second Tree from the Corner* (New York: Harpers, 1954), 84.

42. EBW, "Children's Books," written in November 1938, as per *One Man's Meat* (Gardiner, ME: Tilbury House, 1997), 19–24; appeared in *Harper's* in January 1939. ACM, "Three Owls' Notebook," *Horn Book* (March 1939), 95, mentions it and tells every reader to read it—"the best critical review of children's books of 1938 I have seen." She also read it aloud to more than one hundred children's librarians (ACM to EBW, January 16–February 2, 1939, EBW Papers, Box 143, Division of Rare and Manuscript Collections, Cornell [the date span is because ACM hesitated for two weeks before sending the letter]).

43. ACM to EBW, January 16–February 2, 1939, Box 143, EBW Papers. EBW to ACM, February 15, 1939, in *Letters of EBW*, 182.

44. ACM to EBW, May [?], 1939, Box 143, EBW Papers. ACM to EBW, February 28, 1939, Box 143, EBW Papers. ACM to EBW, February 18, 1939, Box 143, EBW Papers. In 1939, ACM also wrote to EBW on January 16–February 2, February 28, March 24, and on an unspecified day in May.

45. EBW to Eugene Saxton, March 1, 1939, in *Letters of EBW*, 182–83. EBW to Eugene Saxton, April 11, 1939, in *Letters of EBW*, 184; and EBW to ACM, April 25, 1939, in *Letters of EBW*, 185.

46. Gertrude Stein, *The World Is Round* (London: B. T. Batsford, 1939). KSW, "The Children's Harvest," *New Yorker*, November 25, 1939.

47. KSW quoted (undated) in Editor's Note in *Letters of EBW*, 217.

48. See the original of EBW to ACM, February 15, 1939, in Box 5, ACM Papers, which includes this paragraph: "Our house is a little more orderly, now; we gave away most of the review copies at Christmas, and can now make our way about the rooms. We gave quite a few to a small library in this village, where they were much appreciated, I think. Thanks again for your letter. I will try to get to work on the book. Meantime, please save shelf space in your library, public though it may be, for a copy of 'Quo Vadimus? Or The Case for the Bicycle.'"

49. "What I wonder is whether there are Carnegie funds available for such a library if it were made a free one and to whom I should write to ask about this." Miss Dollard, White carefully told Moore, was a "dear old lady," but she hadn't cataloged a book since 1912 and "won't let people she doesn't like come in the place." KSW to ACM, November 26, 1939, Box 5, ACM Papers. Moore, apparently, was unhelpful, telling White that Carnegie funds would not be forthcoming and that the library could never succeed without a professionally trained librarian. I have not been able to find ACM's reply to KSW, presumably in late 1939 or early 1940. It is not in any of the archives I've checked. But KSW's letter of February 7, 1942 (Box 5, ACM Papers), refers to Moore's response. I suspect the correspondence ceased entirely then, until ACM resumed it on February 1, 1941: "Mr. White and I are supposedly compiling an anthology of American humor and thought it would be fun to have a section in it on humor and children's literature" (KSW to ACM, November 26, 1939, Box 5, ACM Papers).

50. ACM to EBW, February 1, 1941, Box 143, EBW Papers. EBW to ACM, March 2, 1941, Box 5, ACM Papers. (This letter is not in the *Letters*.) ACM wrote to EBW on February 1 and March 6, 1941. KSW to ACM, February 7, 1942, Box 5, ACM Papers. See also KSW to ACM, January 13, 1943.

51. KSW to ACM, February 7, 1942, Box 5, ACM Papers. See also KSW to ACM, January 13, 1943, Box 5, ACM Papers. On KSW's continuing work with the library, in the next decades (the Whites moved back to Brooklin, year-round, in 1957), see, e.g., KSW to LSB, January 16 and February 11, 1953, and LSB to KSW, February 6, 1953, Box 1, KSW Papers, Special Collections, Bryn Mawr.

52. KSW to LSB, undated day in 1941, Box 43, Folder 658, LSB Papers, Vassar.

53. *Subtreasury:* Editors' introduction to a section called "For (or Against) Children": "Our first idea was to collect a section on humor from books written for children. We gave it up because, except for 'The Peterkin Papers' and 'Uncle Remus,' we did not find much humor in early juvenile literature, and the humor in modern books for children is for the most part picture-book humor. So this turned into a section quite as much *about* children as *for* them. Incidentally, it also has a good deal to say about parents." EBW and KSW, eds., *A Subtreasury of American Humor* (New York: Coward-McCann, 1941), 303. Ross's memo about EBW's *Life* circulation parody: "We have oceans of evidence that our parody of the birth-of-a-baby feature in Life was generally, probably unanimously, appreciated in advertising agencies and that our Luce profile was, too." Box 964, *New Yorker* Records, NYPL. There followed much debate over whether this would annoy the *New Yorker*'s own advertisers. Ross insisted, "I don't see who can get mad except Life (which is already mad)." Luce's wife's underwear: Ross to Eric Hodgins (at *Fortune*), March 27, 1940, Box 25. Covering the war: Ross to EBW [May 1941], in Harold Ross, *Letters from the Editor: The New Yorker's Harold Ross*, ed. Thomas Kunkel (New York: Modern Library, 2000), 154.

54. KSW to ACM, May 31, 1944, Box 5, ACM Papers. Davis, *Onward and Upward,* 141–45. "I have no trap, no skill with traps, / No bait, no hope, no cheese, no bread." Elledge, *E. B. White,* 250–52. On the manuscript evidence for the speed of the writing, see Peter F. Neumeyer, "*Stuart Little:* The Manuscripts," *Horn Book* 64 (1988): 593–600. Marcus, introduction to *Dear Genius,* xvii–xxii.

55. Also: "she mounted such campaigns against people and against books. She was absolutely ruthless," Frances Clarke Sayers (hereafter FCS), "Small Felicities of Life," in FCS Oral History, October 19, 1974, transcript, Center for Oral History Research, UCLA, 135–39. Less candid but still bitter reminiscence can be found in FCS, "You Elegant Fowl," *Horn Book* 65 (1989): 748–49.

56. FCS, *Moore,* 242. ACM also refused to review *Stuart Little* for *Horn Book.* It may have been Louise Bechtel who had solicited this review; at the time, Bechtel was associate editor.

57. Editor's Note, *Letters of EBW,* 252. More useful: Ursula Nordstrom, "Stuart, Wilbur, Charlotte: A Tale of Tales," *New York Times,* May 12, 1974. For KSW's view that Nordstrom's article didn't go far enough in vindicating EBW, a vindication that KSW rather urgently wanted by this time, see KSW to LSB, June 24, 1974, Box 43, Folder 662, LSB Papers, Vassar: "She was asked to write it and had a dreadful time with it as they made her do it over and over and in the end changed wordings and added stuff she did not want in there. But she did at least manage to tell a part of the A. C. Moore story. I guess she did not dare correct all the errors in the biography of Miss Moore by Frances Clarke Sayers. . . . Miss Moore had made altered copies of all the

anti-Stuart letters she wrote me." But KSW applauds Nordstrom: "What amazed *me* in Ursula's piece is that Miss Moore had the nerve to order *Ursula* not to publish the book. Ursula and Harper had a lot of courage to go ahead with it under these head-on attacks by the most famous children's librarian, and supposedly the best critic of juvenile literature. Critic, my eye!"

58. What happened to the letter is complicated. On June 20, 1945, ACM sent EBW a letter urging him not to publish *Stuart Little*. KSW later said that this letter consisted of fourteen pages (I believe it is her recollection that informs the Editor's Note, *Letters of EBW*, 252); EBW later said this letter was sixteen pages (EBW to FCS, March 15, 1972, FCS Papers, UCLA). Much suggests that the Whites threw this letter away. It is not among KSW's papers, at Bryn Mawr. It is not among EBW's papers, at Cornell. KSW later insisted that the Whites received not "a letter" but several, including at least two addressed to her and one addressed to EBW, all of which would have to have been dated between June and October of 1945. Everyone who refers to this letter or letters uses summaries that have crept into the discussion over the years or KSW's recollection of the correspondence.

In 2008, an indefatigable archivist at UCLA did find, in the FCS Papers, a six-page letter in ACM's handwriting, marked as ACM's copy of the letter she sent. (The letter had been misfiled, placed in a folder labeled "Resort.") ACM did not know how to type and so did not make a carbon. The copy, therefore, can't really be trusted too far. Sayers reproduced this letter in her 1972 biography of ACM (243–44). It does not differ from the manuscript in Sayers's papers, except that a page is missing from the manuscript. The manuscript original of the copy appears incomplete; it ends with a summary of what the rest of the letter might have contained, or just ACM's notes on this corner of scrap paper, rather than with a closing or a signature. Both EBW and KSW insisted that what Sayers printed was not the letter (or letters) they received. (See EBW to FCS, March 15, 1972, FCS Papers, UCLA.) KSW, who did not see the handwritten copy in Sayers's possession but did see the galleys of Sayers's book, and the book itself, came to think that ACM had destroyed the more complete copy of the letter: "I suspect that Miss Moore regretted her strong words and saw the tide was turning against her and destroyed her copy" (KSW to LSB, August 10, 1974, Box 43, Folder 661, LSB Papers, Vassar). To ACM's June 20, 1945, letter, EBW did not reply. KSW did reply. Her letter includes some internal evidence about to whom ACM's letter was addressed: "Your letter made me quite sick and down-hearted. My husband came home an hour or two after I'd read it, looked at me, and said, 'Well, what's the matter with *you*?' I then read him your letter and felt much better after I found it did not hurt him." Whether the letter KSW opened was addressed to her or to her husband or to both of them is unclear. She might have just opened his mail. She often did.

No further letters survive, although KSW later said that ACM answered her letter of June 26: "She replied to me again and said that was just the trouble, it was a novel for *adults* and attacked the book again. . . . After her second letter I asked her if she had any more to say to please write my husband direct, and she did write him, and this is the letter he referred to in his *Times* article which he was asked by *The Times* to write when 'Stuart Little' was being made into a television show." KSW, note, October 25, 1972, KSW Papers. This, given the above, sounds very strange and even unlikely. It is possible that KSW is confused here and is remembering, instead, the exchange of letters in 1939, which did work this way, except backward: ACM wrote five pestering letters to EBW, after which KSW wrote, asking her to stop bothering her husband, and taking control of the mettlesome correspondence herself. Passing the buck to her husband does not seem to have been her usual inclination. The *Times* essay KSW refers to is an essay EBW wrote in 1966 (*New York Times,* March 6), wherein he gave a slightly different account of what happened: "A letter arrived for me from Anne Carroll Moore, children's librarian emeritus of the New York Public Library. Her letter was long, friendly, urgent, and thoroughly surprising. She said she had read proofs of my forthcoming book called 'Stuart Little' and she strongly advised me to withdraw it. She said, as I recall the letter, that the book was non-affirmative, inconclusive, unfit for children, and would harm its author if published."

When, in 1971, Sayers was preparing her biography of ACM for publication, she sent EBW the galley pages containing her version of ACM's June 20, 1945, letter to him, allegedly from this longhand copy she had in her hands, there in the NYPL. EBW wrote back and said, in effect, that this was not the letter he had received. KSW wrote: "Neither of us recognized it as a letter from Miss Moore to him." EBW was no more than mildly irritated: "My conscience is clear about Anne Carroll Moore." But KSW was troubled. EBW and KSW also searched their attic, to no avail. They asked the archivists at Cornell to search through EBW's papers—again, to no avail. But their search was hampered by EBW's hay fever. "There are cartons and cartons of these letters in the attic still to go to Cornell," KSW wrote to LSB (August 24, 1972, Box 43, Folder 661, LSB Papers, Vassar). KSW assumed that Elledge would clear the matter up in his biography: "Scott probably eventually would straighten it all out if he ever got this biography finished." (Ibid.) He did not. EBW asked Sayers not to print her version of the letter until he could finish looking for the original, but she refused.

At just about this time, KSW was preparing to give her own papers to Bryn Mawr, and EBW was preparing a selection of his letters for publication. In 1972, KSW wrote, "There is nothing he can do now because apparently he put her final letter to him in the wastebasket as we both do with letters that disgust us. Miss Moore implied that the book would be bad for children although all right enough for adults and that she felt his letter was the letter of a sick man." About Sayers's refusal to delay publication until the Whites had a chance to conduct a more thorough search for the June 20, 1945, letter, KSW wrote, "That's what gripes us both but especially me" (KSW to LSB, Box 43, Folder 661, LSB Papers, Vassar, August 10, 1974). In a letter to LSB, October 23, 1972 (KSW Papers), KSW wrote, of the original ACM letter: "I am sure it was dumped in the wastebasket and burned up because Andy often dumps things that displease him and so do I. I threw my two—or three?—away at once." And of Sayers's printed version of the letter: "I believe the original was longer than this and that in her copying it down for her own records she changed Mrs. to Mr. (of course she intended it to go to Mr., but wrote through me). I wrote back and had a second letter. Because Andy cannot come up with the letter, probably neither he nor I will write any correction unless he is directly libeled in some review."

In a note KSW typed on October 25, 1972 (KSW Papers), she refers to the question of to whom the June 20, 1945, letter was addressed: "Of course Miss Moore intended it for him but she wrote to me because she knew me a little, as during my period of reviewing children's books at *The New Yorker* I was invited to and attended the rather dreadful candlelight meetings in the fall of each year in which the children's books were displayed and discussed by Miss Moore to a rather reluctant collection of librarians, children's book critics, and heads of children's book departments in the publishing houses." In an interview published in 1974 (Justin Wintle and Emma Fisher, *The Pied Pipers: Interviews with the Influential Creators of Children's Literature* [New York: Paddington Press, 1974], 128-29), EBW gave this account: "I can't say what was in Anne Carroll Moore's mind when she tried to get me to withdraw the manuscript of 'Stuart Little.' I think she was dead set against an American family having a mouse-boy. I think, too, she found my story inconclusive (which it is), and it seems to me she said something about its having been written by a sick mind. I may be misquoting her, as I haven't got the letter in my possession."

In May 1974, LSB wrote to KSW about the *Stuart Little* fiasco: "You may remember you wrote me at length the horrid details at a time when I thought I could make public use of them. Thank God that is no longer on my conscience. But, my White file will preserve your version of the story for posterity. If only old A.C.M. were here to read it." This may refer to correspondence from 1946 or to a letter from December 29, 1970—"Yours of Dec 29 gave me great pleasure," LSB wrote to KSW on January 8, 1971 (KSW Papers, Bryn Mawr). Or it might refer to their correspondence in 1972, after Sayers's biography was published.

59. "Very difficult to place": ACM to EBW, June 20, 1945, in Sayers, *Moore*, 243-44.

60. EBW, "The Librarian."

61. EBW to Stanley Hart White, July 11-21, 1945, *Letters of EBW*, 253. KSW to ACM, undated, c. July 1945, in *Letters of EBW*, 252. See also KSW on *Stuart Little* in her "Children's Shelf" column, titled "Children's Books: Fairy Tales and the Postwar World," *New Yorker*, December 8, 1945, 120-40.

62. EBW, "Once More to the Lake," in *One Man's Meat*, 202-3.

63. EBW, *Stuart Little* (New York: Harper & Row, 1945), 1-2.

64. EBW, "The Librarian."

65. Malcolm Cowley, "Stuart Little, Or, New York Through the Eyes of a Mouse," review of *Stuart Little*, *New York Times Book Review*, October 28, 1945, 7.

66. *Stuart Little* is also conspicuously absent from the NYPL's Recommended Children's Books for Christmas lists for 1945, 1946, and 1947 (I didn't check any other years). These lists survive in the FCS Papers, Box 24, Folder 5, Special Collections, UCLA. The NYPL lists were apparently hugely influential, and librarians across the country really did use them to make decisions about buying books. Also, on the book not being adopted by libraries across the country, see KSW note on LSB, undated typescript, but c. 1972, Box 1, KSW Papers.

67. Leonard Lyons, "The Lyons Den," *New York Post*, November 23, 1945. Lyons's column

was apparently syndicated. It also appeared, for instance, in the *Washington Post* for November, 27, 1945; in that newspaper it was called "Gossip from Gotham."

68. EBW to FCS, November 24, 1945, in *Letters of EBW*, 255–56. The original, at Cornell, Box 62, is slightly longer but not much different. Sayers refers to this letter in her own letter to EBW, March 6, 1972, in the EBW Papers, Cornell, Box 157. It's possible that the gossipy Louise Bechtel is the person who planted the *Post* squib, but no hint of this appears in EBW to LSB, November 10, 1945, Box 43, Folder 657, LSB Papers, Vassar.

69. EBW to Ursula Nordstrom, November 14, 1945, *Letters of EBW,* 255.

70. EBW, *Stuart Little,* 2, 9.

71. Davis, *Onward and Upward,* 3–7.

72. KSW, *New Yorker,* December 7, 1946, 127. LSB wrote to KSW, approving of her column. KSW wrote back: "I know that what I said about library meetings will be misinterpreted but the whole thing has boiled up in me so long over the years about the modern attitude toward juveniles that I couldn't keep it in any longer. I guess I won't get invited to the candlelit meetings again . . . I'm alarmed by the fact that I have only had letters liking my review and suspect there will be a concerted blast from the others eventually" (KSW to LSB, December 17, 1946, Box 43, Folder 658, LSB Papers, Vassar).

73. EBW, *Stuart Little.*

74. Susan Alder's ending for *Stuart Little* is included with a group of proposed alternate endings to the book sent to EBW by a class of fifth graders from Illinois. Susan DeBushe, secretary, class M, fifth grade, Central School, Glencoe, Illinois, to EBW, February 18, 1946, Box 215, EBW Papers.

75. "A great book": LSB to KSW, [1946], Box 1, KSW Papers. Bechtel discovering the book: KSW note on LSB, undated typescript, but c. 1972; and also KSW, note, October 25, 1972, Box 1, KSW Papers. The Whites did not know that Bechtel had intervened until she told them in 1972. "We were fascinated to hear that it was you who went to the Head Librarian at the main New York Public Library and made Mrs. [*sic*] Moore and Mrs. Sayers pull 'Stuart Little' out of hiding'" (KSW to LSB, August 25, 1972, Box 43, Folder 661, LSB Papers, Vassar). Hopper's response: Franklin F. Hopper to LSB, December 24, 1945, Papers of LSB, Special and Area Studies Collections, George A. Smathers Libraries, University of Florida, Gainesville, Florida. Stuart gnawing his way in: EBW, "The Librarian."

76. The seventh grade of Clifton School, Cincinnati, Ohio, to EBW, March 11, 1946, Box 215, Folder 6, EBW Papers. KSW remembered, however, that libraries in Cleveland also helped break ACM's stranglehold: "It was the Cleveland librarians who first turned against her and decided they weren't going to follow the ban any more, and since then every public library has had its copies of 'Stuart Little'" (KSW to LSB, August 10, 1974, Box 43, Folder 661, LSB Papers, Vassar).

77. LSB at the speech: "After my Bowker speech (which sold more reprints than any other since given) I recall so well the big lecture room [illeg] & ACM at the front *cutting me dead.* Later she either wrote or said how she disliked it. This was a blow indeed, yet there was a fundamental difference in our approaches to reading & espe-

cially to its necessary relation to public education. In my private school teaching, in my teaching writing two seminars at Boulder, in my early 'selling' journeys across the continent, I had a far different experience of books & people than hers. No one could differ with her good taste & high standards, her fine feeling for nonsense, etc., and I did not! But I did have a different angle on *kinds* of reading for all *kinds* of people, & on necessity for more kinds of books [illeg] than she did" (LSB, notes ACM for FSC, Box 33, Folder 476, LSB Papers). LSB's stories are many: ACM hollering at her beneath a streetlight at Fifth Avenue and Eleventh Street about a book about which they disagreed; ACM in a black velvet dress hating LSB's dog jumping in her lap; and so forth. Hoping for prizes: LSB, *Books in Search of Children,* ed. Virginia Haviland (New York: Macmillan, 1940, 1955), 210. ACM sending LSB a blast: LSB to KSW, October [illeg.], 1946, Box 1, KSW Papers.

78. The list of jurors was sent to me by the American Library Committee: Valerie Hawkins, e-mail to the author, May 5, 2008. On how the jury and book selection works, and that the jury consists of children's librarians, see Ruth Allen, *Children's Book Prizes* (Aldershot, UK: Ashgate, 1998), 21. What are now "Newbery Honor Books" used to be called runners-up, but that change, when it was made, was retroactive. Grinding teeth: LSB to KSW, [Spring?] 1946, Box 1, KSW Papers. The letter is (implicitly) dated the morning after the announcement. The Newbery was announced in the June 20, 1946, *New York Times.* More on LSB's backstage maneuvering with KSW for the Newbery: LSB to KSW, February 18, 1946, Box 93, EBW Papers, reporting on meeting a bookseller who "says 'Stuart Little' is my own choice for the Newberry [*sic*] in spite of much controversy." LSB did genuinely love the book. She wrote a rather sweet fan letter to EBW, October 31, 1945, Box 93, EBW Papers: "Please excuse but—today 'the sky is right,' for I have met someone who is 'headed in the right direction.'" EBW wrote back, EBW to LSB, November 10, 1945, Box 43, Folder 657, LSB Papers, Vassar ("Whether children will like the book is a question which time will answer"). Thank you for grinding teeth: KSW to LSB, no date given but must be June or July 1946, Box 43, Folder 662, LSB Papers.

79. Frederic Babcock, "Among the Authors," *Chicago Daily Tribune,* October 7, 1945. On the price of the book, see the display ad in the *Chicago Daily Tribune,* November 11, 1945. For an ad stating that the book is for children "from seven to seventy," see *Washington Post,* October 28, 1945. Also: "I myself have never known whether this book was a juvenile or a novel," Katharine White confessed; but then, she didn't really believe in juveniles. KSW to ACM, undated, c. July 1945, in *Letters of EBW,* 252. See also KSW on *Stuart Little* in her "Children's Shelf," *New Yorker,* December 8, 1945. On the celery-and-olive lunch: EBW to UN, December 17, 1946, and Editor's Note, *Letters of EBW,* 261–62. Nordstrom, "Stuart, Wilbur, Charlotte."

80. KSW, "How Dear to This Heart," *New Yorker,* December 11, 1948. It had taken something out of Katharine White, who, in late 1946, told Louise Bechtel that she had decided to give up the "Children's Shelf." Bechtel convinced her not to, insisting, "This very year is a sort of crisis in children's books." LSB to KSW, October [illeg.], 1946, KSW Papers.

81. UN to EBW, October 23, 1952, in *Dear Genius,* 55–56. Eudora Welty's review of *Charlotte's Web* appeared in the *New York Times Book Review,* October 19, 1952.

82. At noon that day, a reporter from the Associated Press called the Central Children's Room, wanting to know the author of a limerick Kennedy had quoted in his inaugural address:

> There was a young lady of Niger
> Who smiled as she rode on a tiger;
> They returned from the ride
> With the lady inside,
> And the smile on the face of the tiger.

Staff News, NYPL, January 26, 1961. I found this clipped in Box 33, Folder 479, of the LSB Papers. The limerick was written by Cosmo Monkhouse.

83. The letter is: KSW to LSB, September 12, 1961, Box 43, Folder 662, LSB Papers. "I really detest the woman," KSW also wrote. See also KSW to Caroline Angell, Christmas 1976, KSW Papers, Box 29, Folder 1; the copy of the letter in KSW Papers, Box 1, Folder 11; and LSB to KSW, August 21, 1972, KSW Papers. KSW wanted LSB, not FCS, to write the biography of ACM. LSB supplied FCS with much information for the biography, both in letters and over lunches. There is a sense of a conspiracy of silence about ACM's horribleness. After one lunch with FCS, LSB wrote, "Naturally I feel that our talk left much 'unresolved.' I tried again to write out my divergence of basic opinion from ACM's—& then *rewrote* it, & now sensibly am not sending it" (LSB to FCS, August 24, 1961, Box 33, Folder 475, LSB Papers); LSB, on another occasion, warned FCS that "these hastily scribed pages are NOT for quotation!" (undated document, Box 33, Folder 475, LSB Papers, Vassar). LSB, like everyone else, has almost impossibly complicated feelings about ACM: she admired her, had been deeply hurt and humiliated by her, considered her a friend, and was still a little afraid of her reach, even from the grave. It took FSC more than ten years to write the biography. See also, e.g., FCS to LSB, July 19, 1961, and August 23, 1961, Box 33, Folder 474, LSB Papers, as well as LSB's notes, which she sent to FCS but which FCS returned after the biography was published, in 1972. LSB's notes are in Box 33, Folder 475, LSB Papers. FCS makes clear to LSB that she is hugely daunted by the prospect of the biography ("what an assignment!") because of how controversial a figure ACM was, but that she has decided to write a tribute. FSC collected ACM's letters from people ("You said you had too many, but here, forgive me, are more," LSB wrote to FSC, August 24, 1961, Box 33, Folder 475, LSB Papers). When KSW read Sayers's biography, she wrote LSB a long letter with her thoughts, which were about the same as they were when ACM died in 1961: "I really am surprised at what a silly woman Anne Carroll Moore turns out to be" (KSW to LSB, August 10, 1974, Box 43, Folder 661, LSB Papers). Some of what KSW sent LSB left the latter a little worried: "I have carefully refrained from showing your letter to anybody," Bechtel wrote in September 4, 1972. "If her [Sayers's] mistake is to be corrected it should be done by you or E.B." (Box 33, Folder 436, LSB Papers, Vassar). LSB, the very same day, complimented FCS on the biography (LSB to FCS, September 4, 1972, Box 43, Folder 664, LSB Papers). In her biography of Moore, Sayers reported that, sometime near the end of her life, Moore told friends she had been to visit the Whites in North Brooklin. "They have a beautiful place,"

Moore said, "with such delphiniums and other flowers as I haven't seen all summer" (Sayers, *Moore*, 217). Long ago, Katharine White had once or twice extended this invitation—stop by and see my little library—but she hadn't expected Moore to take it up. "Oh *what* a nerve, to come call on you two in Maine!" the ever-gossipy Bechtel exclaimed, on reading Sayers's book. "How did she dare?" But she didn't, White insisted; it was a lie: "I'll bet she just sat in the car and looked at the delphiniums" (KSW to LSB, October 23, 1972, KSW Papers).

Chapter 4.   ALL ABOUT ERECTIONS

1. Karen Gravelle with Nick and Chava Castro, *What's Going on Down There? Answers to Questions Boys Find Hard to Ask* (New York: Walker, 1998), 5.
2. Jacqui Bailey, *Sex, Puberty, and All That Stuff: A Guide to Growing Up* (New York: Barron's, 2004), 47.
3. Lynda Madaras, *On Your Mark, Get Set, Grow!* (New York: Newmarket, 2008).
4. Robie H. Harris, *It's Perfectly Normal: A Book About Changing Bodies, Growing Up, Sex, and Sexual Health* (Cambridge, MA: Candlewick, 2009), 35.
5. Robie H. Harris, *It's So Amazing! A Book About Eggs, Sperm, Birth, Babies, and Families* (Cambridge, MA: Candlewick, 1999), 30.
6. Gravelle, *What's Going on Down There?*, 36, 39, 91, 60.
7. Peter Mayle, *Where Did I Come From? The Facts of Life Without Any Nonsense and with Illustrations* (Secaucus, NJ: Lyle Stuart, 1973), n.p.
8. One young man "sat 'till midnight reading one of them books"; another told a friend he could see it for ten shillings. An account of the "bad book" episode is contained within Ava Chamberlain, "The Immaculate Ovum: Jonathan Edwards and the Construction of the Female Body," *William and Mary Quarterly* 57 (2000): 289–322; see especially 313–18.
9. Stephen Nissenbaum, *Sex, Diet, and Debility in Jacksonian America: Sylvester Graham and Health Reform* (Westport, CT: Greenwood, 1980), 27. Otho T. Beall Jr., "*Aristotle's Master Piece* in America: A Landmark in the Folklore of Medicine," *William and Mary Quarterly* 20 (1963): 210.
10. *Aristotle's Master-piece; Or, The Secrets of Generation* (London, 1694), 99, 10. On this work in England and America, see Roy Porter and Lesley Hall, *The Facts of Life: The Creation of Sexual Knowledge in Britain, 1650–1950* (New Haven, CT: Yale University Press, 1995); Beall, "*Aristotle's Master Piece* in America," 207–22; Mary E. Fissell, "Hairy Women and Naked Truths: Gender and the Politics of Knowledge in *Aristotle's Masterpiece*," *William and Mary Quarterly* 60 (2003): 43–74; Janet Blackman, "Popular Theories of Generation: The Evolution of Aristotle's Works, the Study of an Anachronism," in *Health Care and Popular Medicine in Nineteenth Century England: Essays in the Social History of Medicine,* ed. John Woodward and David Richards (New York: Holmes and Meier, 1977), 56–88; and Vern L. Bullough, "An Early American Sex Manual; Or, Aristotle Who?," *Early American Literature* 7 (1973): 236–46.
11. Bradstreet, "The Four Ages of Man," in *Poems of Anne Bradstreet*, ed. Robert Hutchinson (New York: Dover, 1969).

12. Chamberlain, "Immaculate Ovum," 320. On the language of youth, see Joseph F. Kett, *Rites of Passage: Adolescence in America, 1790 to the Present* (New York: Basic Books, 1977), 11–14. Kett, in pointing out the vagueness of early modern language, uses, instead, the language of dependency, semidependency, and independence.

13. You can see this in Raleigh's *History of the World* (London, 1614):

> Our Infancie is compared to the *Moone,* in which wee seeme only to live and grow, as Plants; the second age to *Mercurie,* wherein we are taught and instructed; our third age to *Venus,* the dayes of love, desire, and vanitie; the fourth to the *Sunne,* the strong, flourishing, and beautifull age of mans life; the fifth to *Mars,* in which we seeke honour and victorie, and in which our thoughts travaile to ambitious ends; the sixth Age is ascribed to *Jupiter,* in which we begin to take accompt of our times, judge of our selves, and grow to the perfection of our understanding; the last and seventh to *Saturne,* wherein our dayes are sad and over-cast, and in which we find by deare and lamentable experience, and by the losse which can never be repayred, that of all our vaine passions and affections past, the sorrow only abideth" (book 1, chapter 2, section 5).

> See also J. A. Burrow, *The Ages of Man: A Study in Medieval Writing and Thought* (Oxford: Clarendon, 1988); Deborah Youngs, *The Life Cycle in Western Europe, c. 1300–c. 1500* (Manchester, UK: Manchester University Press, 2006); Michael Kammen, *A Time to Every Purpose: The Four Seasons in American Culture* (Chapel Hill: University of North Carolina Press, 2004); Elizabeth Sears, *The Ages of Man: Medieval Interpretations of the Life Cycle* (Princeton, NJ: Princeton University Press, 1986). Behind all these works lies Philippe Ariès, *Centuries of Childhood: A Social History of Family Life* (New York: Vintage, 1962). "Until the eighteenth century," Ariès wrote, "adolescence was confused with childhood" (25). Shakespeare, *As You Like It,* act 2, scene 7. John Wallis, The New Game of Human Life (London, 1790).

14. Another: the purpose of Tristram Shandy's father's Tristra-paedia was "to form an INSTITUTE for the government of my childhood and adolescence." Laurence Sterne, *The Life and Opinions of Tristram Shandy,* volume 3, chapter 16.

15. Jean-Jacques Rousseau, *Émile,* trans. William Payne (New York: D. Appleton, 1909), book 4. "If you are not sure of keeping him in ignorance of the difference between the sexes till he is sixteen, take care you teach him before he is ten."

16. See Kett, *Rites of Passage;* Kent Baxter, *The Modern Age: Turn-of-the-Century American Culture and the Invention of Adolescence* (Tuscaloosa: University of Alabama Press, 2008); and Jon Savage, *Teenage: The Creation of Youth Culture* (New York: Viking, 2007).

17. "The birth of a mammal was once a closed book to me," E. B. White wrote ("A Shepherd's Life," in *One Man's Meat,* 126; the essay originally appeared in *Harper's* in April 1940). Histories of sexual education include Claudia Nelson and Michelle H. Martin, eds., *Sexual Pedagogies: Sex Education in Britain, Australia and America, 1879–2000* (New York: Palgrave Macmillan, 2004); M. E. Melody and Linda M. Peterson, *Teaching America About Sex: Marriage Guides and Sex Manuals from the Late Victorians to Dr. Ruth* (New York: New York University Press, 1999); Susan K. Freeman, *Sex Goes to School: Girls and Sex Education Before the 1960s* (Urbana: University of Illinois

Press, 2008); Kristin Luker, *When Sex Goes to School: Warring Views on Sex—and Sex Education—Since the Sixties* (New York: Norton, 2006); Julian B. Carter, "Birds, Bees, and Venereal Disease: Toward an Intellectual History of Sex Education," *Journal of the History of Sexuality* 10 (April 2001): 213–49; Janice M. Irvine, *Talk About Sex: The Battles over Sex Education in the United States* (Berkeley: University of California Press, 2002); and Jeffrey P. Moran, *Teaching Sex: The Shaping of Adolescence in the Twentieth Century* (Cambridge, MA: Harvard University Press, 2000).

18. Susan E. Klepp, *Revolutionary Conceptions: Women, Fertility, and Family Limitation in America, 1760–1820* (Chapel Hill: University of North Carolina Press, 2009), 212.

19. Hans Christian Andersen, "The Storks" (1838), in *Danish Fairy Legends and Tales* (London: W. Pickering, 1846), 83–91.

20. On Andersen, see Jackie Wullschläger, *Hans Christian Andersen: The Life of a Storyteller* (New York: Knopf, 2001). And on his publishing history, see Helle Porsdam, ed., *Copyright and Other Fairy Tales: Hans Christian Andersen and the Commodification of Creativity* (Northampton, MA: Edward Elgar, 2006).

21. Jayme A. Sokolow, *Eros and Modernization: Sylvester Graham, Health Reform, and the Origins of Victorian Sexuality in America* (Rutherford, NJ: Fairleigh Dickinson University Press, 1983), 57.

22. R. T. Trall, "Biographical Sketch of Sylvester Graham," *Water-Cure Journal* (November 1851): 110.

23. Daniel Walker Howe, *What Hath God Wrought: The Transformation of America, 1815–1848* (New York: Oxford University Press, 2007), 186, 167–68.

24. Sylvester Graham, *Thy Kingdom Come: A Discourse on the Importance of Infant and Sunday Schools* (Philadelphia, 1831), 9, 17, 21–22. The lecture was delivered on December 18, 1829, at the Crown Street Church, Philadelphia. On Graham's life, see Nissenbaum, *Sex, Diet, and Debility,* and Sokolow, *Eros and Modernization.*

25. In 1832, Graham blamed a devastating cholera epidemic on "dietetic intemperance and lewdness." Sylvester Graham, *A Lecture on Epidemic Diseases Generally, and Particularly the Spasmodic Cholera* (New York, 1833), 40. See also Charles Rosenberg, *Cholera Years: The United States in 1832, 1849 and 1866* (Chicago: University of Chicago Press, 1962).

26. Joel Hawes, *Lectures to Young Men on the Formation of Character,* 3rd ed. (Hartford, CT: Cooke, 1829), 34. Henry Ward Beecher, *Lectures to Young Men on Various Important Subjects,* 2nd ed. (Salem, MA: John P. Jewett 1846), 120–21. Beecher in John Demos and Virginia Demos, "Adolescence in Historical Perspective," *Journal of Marriage and the Family* 31 (1969): 634.

27. The best discussion is Kett, *Rites of Passage,* especially chapters 1 and 2. Dorus Clarke, *Lectures to Young People in Manufacturing Villages* (Boston: Perkins and Marvin, 1836), 31, 44. Emphasis in original. Campbell Gibson, *American Demographic History Chartbook: 1790 to 2000* (2010), chapter 5, figure 5–1, http://www.demographic chartbook.com. Lindsey Howden and Julie Meyer, *Age and Sex Composition: 2010* (U.S. Census Bureau, May 2011), http://www.census.gov/prod/cen2010/briefs/c2010br -03.pdf.

28. Sylvester Graham, *A Lecture to Young Men, on Chastity, Intended Also for the Serious

Consideration of Parents and Guardians (Boston, 1839), 10. On its publishing history, see Nissenbaum, *Sex, Diet, and Debility*, 28.

29. Graham, *Lecture to Young Men*, 101–26, 20.

30. Graham, *Thy Kingdom Come*, 23.

31. Marcus Cunliffe, introduction to *The Life of Washington*, by M. L. Weems (Cambridge, MA: Belknap Press of Harvard University Press, 1962), xi, xii. Other eighteenth-century treatises on the subject include *Onania: Or, The Heinous Sin of Self-Pollution* (London, 1723); Samuel Auguste Tissot, *Onanism* (London, 1766); and William Farrer, *A Short Treatise on Onanism* (London, 1767).

32. *The Works of Aristotle the Famous Philosopher, in Four Parts* (New England, 1828), Part I. *His Complete Master-piece*, 239, 35.

33. *Aristotle's Compleat Master Piece* (London, 1749), 26.

34. Graham, *Lecture to Young Men*, 20, 85.

35. Ibid., 85, 35, 39, 49–50.

36. Ibid., 102–26.

37. Ibid., 111. The idea that masturbation leads to "immature old age" was not original with Graham; it appears, for instance, in J. H. Smyth, MD, *A New Treatise on the Venereal Disease*, 5th ed. (London, 1771), 52.

38. Massachusetts General Court, *Reports and Other Documents Relating to the State Lunatic Hospital at Worcester, Massachusetts* (Boston, 1837), 114, 161. See also Sokolow, *Eros and Modernization*, 88–89. On this subject, see also R. P. Neuman, "Masturbation, Madness, and the Modern Concepts of Childhood and Adolescence," *Journal of Social History* 8 (1975): 1–27.

39. Graham, *Lecture to Young Men*, 34–35. John D'Emilio and Estelle B. Freedman, *Intimate Matters: A History of Sexuality in America* (New York: Harper & Row, 1988), 68–69.

40. Graham, *Lecture to Young Men*, 35.

41. Ibid., 89–90.

42. Ibid., 12. Nissenbaum, *Sex, Diet, and Debility*, 14.

43. Graham, *Lecture to Young Men*, 12.

44. Ibid., 40. A preface appearing in this edition is dated 1834. On its publishing history, see Nissenbaum, *Sex, Diet, and Debility*, 28.

45. Graham, *Lecture to Young Men*, 14–15.

46. Nissenbaum, *Sex, Diet, and Debility*, 14–15. And, on Graham eating flesh in his final days, see also Trall, "Biographical Sketch of Sylvester Graham," 110.

47. "Death of Sylvester Graham," *Medical Examiner and Record of Medical Science*, November 1, 1851, 726.

48. "Death of Sylvester Graham," *Water-Cure Journal* (October 1851): 89.

49. "Sylvester Graham: The Father of Grahamites and the Godfather of Graham Bread," *Home Journal*, October 11, 1851, 1.

50. G. Stanley Hall, *Life and Confessions of a Psychologist* (New York: D. Appleton, 1923, 1927), 357–58, 131–32. Dorothy Ross, *G. Stanley Hall: The Psychologist as Prophet* (Chicago: University of Chicago Press, 1972), 3–6. Louis N. Wilson, *G. Stanley Hall: A Sketch* (New York: G. E. Stechert, 1914), 15–18.

51. Anne Carroll Moore, *My Roads to Childhood: Views and Reviews of Children's Books* (Boston: Horn Book, 1961), 305. The best discussion of Hall's work on adolescence is John Demos and Virginia Demos, "Adolescence in Historical Perspective," *Journal of Marriage and the Family* 31 (1969): 632–35, but see also Kent Baxter, *The Modern Age*, especially chapter 2, and Jon Savage, *Teenage*, chapter 5.

52. Ross, *GSH*, 336. See also Kett, *Rites of Passage*, chapter 8.

53. G. Stanley Hall, *Adolescence* (New York: D. Appleton, 1904), 2:97, 122–23. For Hall, as Gail Bederman argued, sex wasn't dirty; it was holy (*Manliness and Civilization: A Cultural History of Gender and Race in the United States, 1880–1917* [Chicago: University of Chicago Press, 1995], 104).

54. Baxter, *Modern Age*, 13. See also Steven Mintz, *Huck's Raft: A History of American Childhood* (Cambridge, MA: Belknap Press of Harvard University Press, 2004), 239.

55. G. Stanley Hall, *Adolescence*, 2:97.

56. Notably, Hall, more a Grahamist than a Freudian, was not remotely forgiving of the solitary vice. In a 1907 article he contributed to the *Ladies' Home Journal* called "How and When to Be Frank with Boys," Hall offered tips about how to keep boys' hands out of their pants—"The first trousers should bifurcate low down, be loose, not warm nor rough, and pocketless"—and suggested that, at about age ten, "the boy should be concisely told that there are always certain dirty boys who abuse their bodies, and of the evil effects of this habit, and exhorted to break all acquaintance with such companions." Hall, "How and When to Be Frank with Boys," *Ladies' Home Journal* 24 (September 1907), 26. G. Stanley Hall, *Life and Confessions*, 407–8. Ross, *GSH*, 384.

57. "Sex O'Clock in America" was announced by *Current Opinion* and is quoted in David M. Kennedy, *Birth Control in America: The Career of Margaret Sanger* (New Haven, CT: Yale University Press, 1970), 139.

58. Allan Brandt, *No Magic Bullet: A Social History of Venereal Disease in the United States Since 1880* (New York: Oxford University Press, 1987), 28–31.

59. Winfield S. Hall, *Life's Beginnings: For Boys of Ten to Fourteen Years* (New York: Young Men's Christian Association Press, 1912), 3.

60. Winfield S. Hall, *From Youth into Manhood*, 10th ed. (New York: Association Press, 1918), 34, 59. In an introduction, George J. Fisher writes of Hall: "His theory on the physiology of noctural seminal emissions . . . is most unique" (7).

61. Winfield S. Hall, *Instead of "Wild Oats": A Little Book for the Youth of Eighteen and Over* (New York: Fleming H. Revell, 1912); Winfield S. Hall and Jeannette Winter Hall, *Girlhood and Its Problems: The Sex Life of Woman* (Philadelphia: John C. Winston, 1919); and Winfield S. Hall and Jeannette Winter Hall, *Sexual Knowledge: In Plain and Simple Language* (Philadelphia: International Bible House, 1913), preface, 9.

62. Winfield S. Hall, *Life's Beginnings*, 3.

63. Ibid., 3–5.

64. Ibid., 18, 22–23.

65. James Thurber and E. B. White, *Is Sex Necessary? Or, Why You Feel the Way You Do* (New York: Harper & Brothers, 1929; New York: Perennial, 2004), 113. According to John Updike, White wrote the even-numbered chapters. This is chapter 6. See Updike's foreword, xv.

66. "Stuart Little," *Washington Post,* October 21, 1945. The review is unsigned. On the book's reception as a satire (for adults), note that, in some book pages, it was reviewed under "Humor," not "Juvenile."

67. Geraldine Lux Flanagan, *Window into an Egg: Seeing Life Begin* (New York: Young Scott Books, 1969), 9. Lynn Marie Morgan, in *Icons of Life: A Cultural History of Human Embryos* (Berkeley: University of California Press, 2009), writes, "Chick hatching conveys another important cultural message, which is that life unfolds in the interval between conception and birth. Birth marks the end of the gestational period and the culturally approved beginning of independent life" (38–41).

68. There is some discussion of this case in Irvine, *Talk About Sex,* 21.

69. Gordon Drake, *Is the School House the Proper Place to Teach Raw Sex?* (Tulsa: Christian Crusade, 1968).

70. This battle is best related in Irvine, *Talk About Sex.* She argues that "opposition to sex education was a bridge issue between the Old Right and the New Right" (9).

71. Elders is quoted in Irvine, *Talk About Sex,* 1. See also Paul Richter and Marlene Cimons, "Clinton Fires Surgeon General After New Flap," *Los Angeles Times,* December 10, 1994.

72. Robie H. Harris, *It's NOT the Stork! A Book About Girls, Boys, Babies, Bodies, Families, and Friends* (Cambridge, MA: Candlewick, 2009), 28.

73. Jennifer Ashton, *The Body Scoop for Girls: A Straight-Talk Guide to a Healthy, Beautiful You* (New York: Avery, 2009), 4, 21.

74. Lynda Madaras, *Ready, Set, Grow!* (New York: Newmarket, 2003), 14.

75. Louise Spilsbury, *Me, Myself and I: All About Sex and Puberty* (New York: Hodder Wayland Children's, 2009), 4.

76. Valorie Lee Schaefer, *The Care & Keeping of You: The Body Book for Girls* (Middletown, WI: Pleasant Company, 1998), 42.

77. Gravelle, *What's Going on Down There?,* 17; Ashton, *Body Scoop for Girls,* chapter 9; Schaefer, *Care & Keeping of You,* 17; Jacqui Bailey, *Hair, There, and Everywhere: A Book About Growing Up* (New York: Barron's, 2008), 20.

78. Pepper Schwartz and Dominic Cappello, *Ten Talks Parents Must Have with Their Children About Sex and Character* (New York: Hyperion, 2000), 31. G. Stanley Hall also said, in "How and When to Be Frank with Boys," that what boys need to know can be explained to them in "a ten-minute talk."

Chapter 5. Mr. Marriage

1. Paul Popenoe and Dorothy Cameron Disney, *Can This Marriage Be Saved?* (New York: Macmillan, 1960), 6–20. Dick and Andrea Weymer, like all the names in Popenoe's published cases, were not the couple's real names.

2. Paul Popenoe's picture appeared with this column for a quarter century. He didn't write it, but all the cases came from his marriage clinic. See David Popenoe, *War over the Family* (2005; repr., New Brunswick, NJ: Transaction Publishers, 2008), xii. The magazine called it "the most popular, most enduring women's magazine feature in the world" (228).

3. Popenoe and Disney, *Can This Marriage Be Saved?*, vii. Popenoe's career is discussed in Rebecca L. Davis, *More Perfect Unions: The American Search for Marital Bliss* (Cambridge, MA: Harvard University Press, 2010), 33–37, 72–75, 96, 100, 121–24; Molly Ladd-Taylor, "Eugenics, Sterilisation and Modern Marriage in the USA: The Strange Career of Paul Popenoe," *Gender and History* 13 (2001): 298–327; and Wendy Kline, *Building a Better Race: Gender, Sexuality, and Eugenics from the Turn of the Century to the Baby Boom* (Berkeley: University of California Press, 2001). A biographical sketch is available at the Paul Bowman Popenoe Papers, 1874–1991, American Heritage Center, University of Wyoming. For Popenoe's prominence in the eugenics movement, see, for instance, Kenneth M. Ludmerer, *Genetics and American Society: A Historical Appraisal* (Baltimore: Johns Hopkins University Press, 1972), 9, where Popenoe is listed as one of the movement's six leaders.

4. Kline, *Building a Better Race*, 143–44.

5. Quoted in Ladd-Taylor, "Eugenics, Sterilisation and Modern Marriage," 300, 310.

6. Paul Popenoe, *A Family Consultation Service* (New York: Institute of Family Relations, n.d.), 10–11. Paul Popenoe, "The Institute of Family Relations," *Eugenics* 3 (1930): 134–37. Paul Popenoe, "Divorce and Remarriage from a Eugenic Point of View," *Social Forces* 12 (1933): 48–50; quote from 48.

7. Carl N. Degler, *In Search of Human Nature: The Decline and Revival of Darwinism in American Social Thought* (New York: Oxford University Press, 1991), 42–43.

8. "England gave Darwin to the world," Richard Hofstadter once wrote, "but the United States gave to Darwinism an unusually quick and sympathetic reception." Spencer enjoyed an unusual American popularity as well. By the end of the nineteenth century, Spencer's books had sold more than 350,000 copies. Richard Hofstadter, *Social Darwinism in American Thought*, rev. ed. (Philadelphia: University of Pennsylvania Press, 1944; Boston: Beacon Press, 1992), xiv, 34, 5.

9. Marshall Hyatt, *Franz Boas, Social Activist: The Dynamics of Ethnicity* (New York: Greenwood, 1990), 84–85. Wrote Carl Degler, "Whether called social Darwinism, or social Spencerism, the defense of the social and economic hierarchy of nineteenth-century America that the doctrine was intended to accomplish held little appeal for the men and women who were shaping the emerging fields of sociology, psychology, economics and anthropology at the end of the century." Degler, *In Search of Human Nature*, 13.

10. Isabel Wilkerson, *The Warmth of Other Suns: The Epic Story of America's Great Migration* (New York: Random House, 2010), 41–45.

11. "One has not the right to doubt what the past has transmitted to us" was the assertion, made by a friend of Boas's, that inspired him to a life of research and writing. Abram Kardiner and Edward Preble, *They Studied Man* (Cleveland: World Publishing, 1961), 135, 139. "The Negro Brain," *American Medicine* 13 (April 1907): 197. On Boas, see especially Degler, *In Search of Human Nature*, chapter 3.

12. When Aleš Hrdlička, the curator of what would become the Smithsonian's National Museum of Natural History, solicited "colored" embryos from Mall, Mall was not cooperative. Lynn Marie Morgan, *Icons of Life: A Cultural History of Human Embryos* (Berkeley: University of California Press, 2009), 171–72, and Louis Menand, *The Metaphysical Club* (New York: Farrar, Straus and Giroux, 2001), 269. On Boas's

response to Bean's "Negro Brain," see Hyatt, *Franz Boas,* 91–92. Bean's data and Mall's response are also discussed in Stephen Jay Gould, *Mismeasure of Man,* rev. ed. (1981; repr., New York: Norton, 1996), 109–14.

13. Boas, quoted in Hyatt, *Franz Boas,* 88; DuBois quoted on 99. See also Boas, "What the Negro Has Done in Africa," *Ethical Record* 5 (1904): 106–9; "The Problem of the American Negro," *Yale Review* 10 (1921): 392–95; and Hyatt, *Franz Boas,* chapter 5.

14. Mark A. Largent, *Breeding Contempt: The History of Coerced Sterilization in the United States* (New Brunswick, NJ: Rutgers University Press, 2008), 66. Mark H. Haller, *Eugenics: Hereditarian Attitudes in American Thought* (1963; repr., New Brunswick, NJ: Rutgers University Press, 1984), 137. On Progressive-era fears of race suicide, see also Elaine Tyler May, *Barren in the Promised Land: Childless Americans and the Pursuit of Happiness* (Cambridge, MA: Harvard University Press, 1997), chapters 2 and 3, and Linda Gordon, *The Moral Property of Women: A History of Birth Control Politics in America* (Urbana: University of Illinois Press, 1974), chapters 5 and 6. For a political history of eugenics from late-nineteenth-century populism through mid-twentieth-century pro-natalism, see Laura L. Lovett, *Conceiving the Future: Pro-natalism, Reproduction and the Family in the United States, 1890–1938* (Chapel Hill: University of North Carolina Press, 2007).

15. C. C. Little, "Coat Color in Pointer Dogs," *Journal of Heredity* 5 (1914): 244–48.

16. Gordon, *Moral Property,* 197; David M. Kennedy, *The Birth Control Movement in America: The Career of Margaret Sanger* (New Haven, CT: Yale University Press, 1970), 118–19.

17. For a richly detailed history and analysis of the film, see Martin S. Pernick, *The Black Stork: Eugenics and the Death of "Defective" Babies in American Medicine and Motion Pictures Since 1915* (New York: Oxford University Press, 1996).

18. H. M. Freck, "The Wrong Address," 1905. Postcard in the possession of the author.

19. Pernick, *Black Stork,* 56–57. And on the history of ideas about miscegenation, and its regulation, see Peggy Pascoe, *What Comes Naturally: Miscegenation Law and the Making of Race in America* (New York: Oxford University Press, 2009).

20. Paul Popenoe and E. S. Gosney, *Twenty-eight Years of Sterilization in California* (Pasadena, CA, 1938), preface. California, with 20,108 sterilizations, ranked first overall but third per capita. See Largent, *Breeding Contempt,* 77–78. See also Philip R. Reilly, *The Surgical Solution: A History of Involuntary Sterilization in the United States* (Baltimore: Johns Hopkins University Press, 1991), especially 79–81.

21. Paul Popenoe, "Eugenic Sterilization in California," quoted in Jonathan Peter Spiro, *Defending the Master Race: Conservation, Eugenics, and the Legacy of Madison Grant* (Burlington: University of Vermont Press, 2009), 235.

22. "While offering little positive data on the subject, the study has strengthened my impression of the relatively greater importance of endowment over training, as a determinant of an individual's intellectual rank among his fellows." Lewis M. Terman, "Genius and Stupidity: A Study of the Intellectual Processes of Seven 'Bright' and Seven 'Stupid' Boys," PhD diss., Clark University, 1906, 10, 68.

23. Nicholas Lemann, *The Big Test: The Secret History of the American Meritocracy,* rev. ed. (1999; repr., New York: Farrar, Straus and Giroux, 2000), 17–18. Gould, *Mismeasure of Man,* 178–84, 206.

24. Examining test results of "Indians, Mexicans, and negroes," he concluded that "their dullness seems to be racial." Lewis M. Terman, *The Measurement of Intelligence* (Boston: Houghton Mifflin, 1916), 6–7, 11, 91–92.

25. Ibid., 18.

26. Lippmann's statement in the *New Republic* is reproduced in Ned Joel Block and Gerald Dworkin, eds., "The Lippman-Terman Debate," *The IQ Controversy: Critical Readings* (New York: Pantheon Books, 1976), 4–44, especially 29, 8, 42, and 19. See also Degler, *In Search of Human Nature,* 168–69.

27. Madison Grant, *The Passing of the Great Race; Or, The Racial Basis of European History,* 4th ed. (New York: Charles Scribner's Sons, 1936), vii–viii, xi–xii, 10.

28. Paul Popenoe and Roswell Hill Johnson, *Applied Genetics* (New York: Macmillan, 1920), v, 297, 285, 384–85, 374–75, 368–69.

29. E. S. Gosney and Paul Popenoe, *Sterilization for Human Betterment* (New York: Macmillan, 1929), v.

30. Grant, *Passing of the Great Race,* 91, 85. Popenoe and Johnson, *Applied Genetics,* chapter 12, "Increasing the Marriage Rate of the Superior." See also Donald K. Pickens, *Eugenics and the Progressives* (Nashville: Vanderbilt University Press, 1968), 95–98.

31. Degler, *In Search of Human Nature,* 51–55.

32. F. Scott Fitzgerald, *The Great Gatsby* (1925; repr., New York: Scribner, 2004), 12–13.

33. Paul Popenoe, *Modern Marriage: A Handbook* (1925; repr., New York: Macmillan, 1927), vi.

34. Paul Popenoe, *The Conservation of the Family* (Baltimore: Williams & Wilkins, 1926), 6, 130, 144.

35. Ibid., 250, 6. Paul Popenoe to Madison Grant, April 14, 1928, as quoted in Spiro, *Defending the Master Race,* 189–90.

36. Paul A. Lombardo, *Three Generations, No Imbeciles: Eugenics, the Supreme Court, and Buck v. Bell* (Baltimore: Johns Hopkins University Press, 2008), is the fullest treatment. See also Stephen Jay Gould, "Carrie Buck's Daughter," in *The Flamingo's Smile: Reflections in Natural History* (New York: Norton, 1985), 306–18, and Largent, *Breeding Contempt,* 100–102.

37. Gosney and Popenoe, *Sterilization for Human Betterment,* ix. The book both aspired to and reached a popular audience. See Kline, *Building a Better Race,* 78–80; and see the whole of her chapter 3 for Gosney and Popenoe's research methods, in preparing this study for publication. On the German edition, see Stefan Kühl, *The Nazi Connection: Eugenics, American Racism, and German National Socialism* (New York: Oxford University Press, 1994), 43. More details of Gosney's correspondence with German scientists and of their reaction to *Sterilization for Human Betterment* can be found in Kline, *Building a Better Race,* 103.

38. Davis, *More Perfect Unions,* 35, 123.

39. "Electronic Cupid," *Time,* November 19, 1956.

40. Lewis Terman, *Psychological Factors in Marital Happiness* (New York: McGraw-Hill, 1938), vii, 6, 379, 407.

41. Popenoe, *A Family Consultation Service,* 5.

42. Popenoe, *Modern Marriage,* 159.

43. Kline, *Building a Better Race,* 146.

44. William McDougall, *Is America Safe for Democracy?* (New York: Charles Scribner's Sons, 1921). These were McDougall's Lowell lectures.

45. Terman, *Psychological Factors in Marital Happiness,* vii, 6, 379, 407.

46. Hofstadter, *Social Darwinism in American Thought,* 161–67. Hofstadter discusses Popenoe and Johnson's textbook on 165. He calls eugenics "the most enduring aspect of social Darwinism" (161); he discusses its atavism and its search for biological solutions to political problems. What he calls "the eugenics craze" was appealing because, while deeply conservative, it "had about it the air of a 'reform' " (167). Pickens, in *Eugenics and the Progressives,* writes about the American eugenic tradition as distinctly averse to democracy.

47. On the control of family life as a central project of the movement, see, e.g., Pickens, *Eugenics and the Progressives,* 73.

48. "Harvard Declines a Legacy to Found Eugenics Course," *New York Times,* May 8, 1927.

49. Clarence Darrow, "The Eugenics Cult," *American Mercury* 8 (June 1926): 129–37.

50. William L. Laurence, "Sees a Super-Race Evolved by Science," *New York Times,* August 25, 1932.

51. Paul Popenoe, "The Progress of Eugenic Sterilization," *Journal of Heredity* 25 (1934): 19–26. On the book burning, see Guido Enderis, "Nazi Fires to Get 160 Writers' Books," *New York Times,* May 6, 1933, and Emily Graff, " 'Books Like These Are Burned!': The 1933 Nazi Book Burnings in American Historical Memory" (BA thesis, Harvard University, 2009). On Popenoe and Bell, see Popenoe to Bell, May 23, 1933, as quoted in Lombardo, *Three Generations, No Imbeciles,* 190. Spiro, *Defending the Master Race,* 343. Madison Grant, *The Conquest of a Continent: The Expansion of Races in America* (New York: Charles Scribner's Sons, 1933), vii, 347–51.

52. Grant thanks "his research associate Doctor Paul Popenoe" in his acknowledgments (*Conquest of a Continent,* xi).

53. Spiro, *Defending the Master Race,* 345. Meanwhile, academic geneticists vigorously repudiated eugenics. Dunn's interesting letters are discussed in Ludmerer, *Genetics and American Society,* 127–29; and see, more broadly, chapter 6.

54. Degler, *In Search of Human Nature,* 202–3.

55. Paul Popenoe, "The German Sterilization Law," *Journal of Heredity* 25 (July 1934): 257–60. See also Ladd-Taylor, "Eugenics, Sterilisation and Modern Marriage," 307. As late as 1938, Popenoe was celebrating sterilization—that is, in *Twenty-eight Years of Sterilization,* 22. On the German sterilization law as based on the California statute, see Kline, *Building a Better Race,* 103.

56. Abraham Myerson, "Research Urged" [letter to the editor], *New York Times,* March 15, 1936; see also Abraham Myerson, *Speaking of Man* (New York: Knopf, 1950). Dunn is quoted in Ludmerer, *Genetics and American Society,* 130. Popenoe had defended eugenics to Dunn in 1934 (Degler, *In Search of Human Nature,* 202–3).

57. E. B. White, "The World of Tomorrow," *One Man's Meat* (Gardiner, ME: Tilbury House, 1997), 58–64; quote from 58. First published in the *New Yorker* on May 13, 1939, as "They Came with Joyous Song."

58. Haller, *Eugenics,* 179. Gordon, *Moral Property,* 202.

59. Paul Popenoe to Mariann Olden, May 5, 1945, as quoted in Kline, *Building a Better Race,* 104.

60. Ladd-Taylor, "Eugenics, Sterilisation and Modern Marriage," 314. In 1962, Popenoe wrote, "The major factor in the decline of eugenics was undoubtedly Hitlerism" (cited in Pickens, *Eugenics and the Progressives,* 99).

61. Darrow, "The Eugenics Cult," 132, 137. See also Michael Willrich, "The Two Percent Solution: Eugenic Jurisprudence and the Socialization of American Law, 1900–1930," *Law and History Review* 16 (1998): 104.

62. On the Celestial Bed, see Lydia Syson, *Doctor of Love: James Graham and His Celestial Bed* (Richmond, Surrey, UK: Alma Books, 2008).

63. Davis, *More Perfect Unions,* 3.

64. Laurie Abraham, *The Husbands and Wives Club: A Year in the Life of a Couples Therapy Group* (New York: Touchstone, 2010), 62.

65. Davis, *More Perfect Unions,* 258, 3.

66. Elizabeth Weil, "Married (Happily) with Issues," *New York Times Magazine,* December 1, 2009.

67. Abraham, *Husbands and Wives Club,* 2–3, 280, 96, 19, 245, 284, 274.

68. "Electronic Cupid," *Time,* November 19, 1956.

69. Lori Gottlieb, *Marry Him: The Case for Settling for Mr. Good Enough* (New York: Dutton, 2010), chapter 4, 101, 106.

70. Tara Parker-Pope, *For Better: The Science of a Good Marriage* (New York: Dutton, 2010), 1–3, chapter 9. Earlier, "Ovulatory Cycle Effects on Tip Earnings by Lap Dancers" was awarded an Ig Nobel Prize, a prize given to the junkiest piece of scientific research. "The 2008 Ig Nobel Prize Winners," *Improbable Research,* http://improbable .com/ig/winners/#ig2008.

71. Brian Leubitz, "0 for 2: Blankenhorn Looks Lost," *Prop 8 Trial Tracker* (blog), January 26, 2010, http://www.prop8trialtracker.com/2010/01/26/0-for-2-the-defendants -are-playing-for-some-other-audience/. See also Gary Shih, "Same-Sex Marriage Case, Day 11: Churches," *The Bay Area* (blog), *New York Times,* January 26, 2010, http://bayarea.blogs.nytimes.com/2010/01/26/same-sex-marriage-case-day-11- churches/. David Popenoe, *War over the Family,* 84. On the history of marriage and the state, see Nancy F. Cott, *Public Vows: A History of Marriage and the Nation* (Cambridge, MA: Harvard University Press, 2000).

72. David Popenoe on "social suicide": David Popenoe, *Life Without Father: Compelling New Evidence That Fatherhood and Marriage Are Indispensable for the Good of Children and Society* (New York: Free Press, 1996), 192. Popenoe and Johnson on "race suicide": Popenoe and Johnson, *Applied Genetics,* chapter 12.

73. On their joint publication, see David Popenoe, Jean Bethke Elshtain, and David Blankenhorn, eds., *Promises to Keep: Decline and Renewal of Marriage in America* (Lanham, MD: Rowan and Littlefield, 1996). Institute for American Values and the National Marriage Project at the University of Virginia, *The State of Our Unions: Marriage in America, 2010; When Marriage Disappears—the New Middle America,* http:// www.virginia.edu/marriageproject/pdfs/Union_11_12_10.pdf.

74. David Popenoe, "Remembering My Father: An Intellectual Portrait of 'The Man Who Saved Marriages,'" in *War over the Family*.

Chapter 6.   HAPPINESS MINUTES

1. The story of the meeting at Henry Gantt's apartment and the decision to use "Scientific Management" is described in just about every account of these heady days, but see, especially, Robert Kanigel, *The One Best Way: Frederick Winslow Taylor and the Enigma of Efficiency* (New York: Viking, 1997), 431–42; Frank Barkley Copley, *Frederick W. Taylor: Father of Scientific Management* (New York: Taylor Society, 1923), 2:372; Jane Lancaster, *Making Time: Lillian Moller Gilbreth, a Life Beyond "Cheaper by the Dozen"* (Boston: Northeastern University Press, 2004), 116; and Lewis J. Paper, *Brandeis* (Englewood Cliffs, NJ: Prentice-Hall, 1983), 152. Brandeis attempted to set the record straight in 1914 in a letter to a Columbia University graduate student writing a history of scientific management: Louis Brandeis to Horace Bookwalter Drury, January 31, 1914, *Letters of Louis D. Brandeis*, edited by Melvin I. Urofsky and David W. Levy (Albany: State University of New York Press, 1973), 3:240–41.

2. Daniel Nelson, *Frederick W. Taylor and the Rise of Scientific Management* (Madison: University of Wisconsin Press, 1980), 132.

3. "Speedy Taylor": Kanigel, *One Best Way*, 7. Taylor is buried in Chestnut Hill, Pennsylvania. His tombstone reads, "Frederick Winslow Taylor. Born 1856—Died 1915. Father of Scientific Management."

4. Brandeis quoted in Kanigel, *One Best Way*, 433. Brandeis's brief is most easily read in Louis D. Brandeis, *Scientific Management and Railroads* (New York: Engineering Magazine, 1911). For more on Brandeis's infatuation with scientific management, see Philippa Strum, *Louis D. Brandeis: Justice for the People* (Cambridge, MA: Harvard University Press, 1984), 161–62.

5. Louis Brandeis, "Efficiency and Social Ideas," 1914, in *Brandeis on Democracy*, ed. Philippa Strum (Lawrence: University Press of Kansas, 1995), 33.

6. Acheson is quoted in Strum, *Brandeis on Democracy*, 12.

7. On Taylor too busy to come, see Nelson, *Frederick W. Taylor*, 174.

8. On Brandeis having read *Shop Management* in 1903, see Strum, *Brandeis*, 160.

9. Portions of the transcript are reproduced in Kanigel, *One Best Way*, 431, but the original can be found in *Evidence Taken by the Interstate Commerce Commission in the Matter of Proposed Advances in Freight Rates by Carriers. August to December, 1910*, 61st Cong., 3:2022–24 (1911) (statement of Louis D. Brandeis, attorney).

10. Frederick Winslow Taylor, *The Principles of Scientific Management* (New York: Harper & Brothers, 1911), 42–45; quote from 44–45.

11. Edna Yost, *Frank and Lillian Gilbreth: Partners for Life* (New Brunswick, NJ: Rutgers University Press, 1949), 185–88.

12. Taylor wrote a series of essays called "The Gospel of Efficiency" for *American Magazine* in 1911; "gospel of hope" comes from the preface to Brandeis, *Scientific Management*, n.p.

13. Kanigel, *One Best Way,* 434. Lancaster, *Making Time,* 146.

14. "Roads Could Save $1,000,000 a Day," *New York Times,* November 22, 1910.

15. Kanigel, *One Best Way,* 11.

16. On the *Principles'* publishing history, see Daniel Nelson, "Taylor, Frederick Winslow," in *American National Biography Online* (2000).

17. Kanigel, *One Best Way,* 472.

18. Ibid., 14.

19. Matthew Stewart, *The Management Myth: Why the Experts Keep Getting It Wrong* (New York: Norton, 2009), 39–41.

20. After Brandeis said scientific management could save the railroads $1 million a day, a group of railroad presidents sent him a tongue-in-cheek telegram offering him a job, at a salary of his own naming. Brandeis cabled back, straight-faced: Sure, but keep your money; I never accept payment when serving the public interest. Both telegrams are reproduced in Strum, *Brandeis,* 163. Brandeis actually paid his firm out of his own pocket to cover the time his pro bono work took from his billable hours. Philippa Strum, "Brandeis, Louis Dembitz," in *American National Biography Online* (2000).

21. Paper, *Brandeis,* 153.

22. Stewart, *The Management Myth,* 48–50.

23. Strum, "Brandeis, Louis Dembitz."

24. Strum, *Brandeis,* 166–67.

25. Louis D. Brandeis, foreword (dated May 1912) to *Primer of Scientific Management,* by Frank B. Gilbreth, 2nd ed. (1912; repr., New York: D. Van Nostrand, 1914), vii–viii. Citations come from the 1914 edition.

26. Terman's results were as dodgy as Taylor's. And he stood by them just as faithfully, thereby launching an industry: "The present methods of trying out new employees, transferring them to simpler and simpler jobs as their inefficiency becomes apparent, is wasteful and to a great extent unnecessary. A cheaper and more satisfactory method would be to employ a psychologist to examine applicants for positions and to weed out the unfit." Lewis M. Terman, *The Measurement of Intelligence* (Boston: Houghton Mifflin, 1916), 17–18; Stephen Jay Gould, *The Mismeasure of Man,* rev. ed. (1981; repr., New York: Norton, 1996), 212. Citations come from the 1996 edition. For Terman's own jury-rigged study of the IQ of "hoboes," see Gould's analysis at 182–83.

27. *The Taylor and Other Systems of Shop Management: Hearings Before Special Committee of the House of Representatives to Investigate the Taylor and Other Systems of Shop Management,* H.R. 90, 3:1398–1400, 1478, 1456 (1912) (statement of Frederick W. Taylor, creator of scientific management).

28. Kanigel, *One Best Way,* 481–82.

29. Ibid., 514.

30. Stephen Meyer III, *The Five Dollar Day: Labor Management and Social Control in the Ford Motor Company, 1908–1921* (Albany: State University of New York Press, 1981).

31. Edmund Wilson, *American Jitters: A Year of the Slump* (New York: Charles Scribner's Sons, 1932), 51.

32. See Ruth Schwartz Cohen, *More Work for Mother: The Ironies of Household Technology from the Open Hearth to the Microwave* (New York: Basic Books, 1983), and Juliet

Schor, *The Overworked American: The Unexpected Decline of Leisure* (New York: Basic Books, 1991).

33. Michael R. Haines, "Table Ab1–10—Fertility and Mortality, by Race: 1800–2000," in *Historical Statistics of the United States: Millennial Edition Online*, ed. Susan B. Carter et al. (1949; 1960; 1975; New York: Cambridge University Press, 2006).

34. On the birthing intervals, see Lancaster, *Making Time*, 97–98; on Mary's death as a result of diphtheria, see 123–24. On *Cheaper by the Dozen*, see also Jane F. Levey, "Imagining the Family in U.S. Postwar Popular Culture: The Case of *The Egg and I* and *Cheaper by the Dozen*," *Journal of Women's History* 13 (2001): 125–50.

35. Lancaster, *Making Time*, 101.

36. Ibid., 162.

37. Ibid., 150.

38. Frank Gilbreth to Lillian Gilbreth, [1922], Box 11, Folder 2, Gilbreth Papers, Purdue University.

39. Lancaster, *Making Time*, 117, 164–65. For more on the question of Lillian doing most of the writing, see Laurel D. Graham, "Domesticating Efficiency: Lillian Gilbreth's Scientific Management of Homemakers, 1924–1930," *Signs* 24 (1999): 639.

40. Lancaster, *Making Time*, 127, 129. They lived at 71 Brown Street. Lillian M. Gilbreth, *As I Remember: An Autobiography* (Norcross, GA: Engineering and Management Press, 1998), 121.

41. Gilbreth's "Mother's Daily Schedule" is reprinted in Lancaster, *Making Time*, 130.

42. Hugh G. J. Aitken, *Taylorism at Watertown Arsenal: Scientific Management in Action, 1908–1915* (Cambridge, MA: Harvard University Press, 1960). "Rough guess" is from 137. Regarding timing, etc., see especially 140–50. The petition is reprinted on 150.

43. Lancaster, *Making Time*, 143.

44. L. M. Gilbreth, *The Psychology of Management: The Function of the Mind in Determining, Teaching and Installing Methods of Least Waste* (New York: Sturgis & Walton, 1914), 3.

45. Lancaster, *Making Time*, 161–62.

46. The biography is Copley's (1923); the reference to Gilbreth's marginalia comes from Kanigel, *One Best Way*, 548. Gilbreth's copy of Copley is at Purdue. More evidence of the falling-out: Frank B. Gilbreth and L. M. Gilbreth, "Time Study and Motion Study as Fundamental Factors in Planning and Control: An Indictment of Stop-Watch Time Study" (paper, Taylor Society, New York, December 16, 1920), Box 27, Folder 4, Gilbreth Papers.

47. Brandeis writes about attending the service in a letter to his brother, Alfred, on October 22, 1915; *Letters of Louis D. Brandeis*, 3:617.

48. Louis D. Brandeis, "Testimony Before the United States Commission on Industrial Relations, January 23, 1915," in Strum, *Brandeis on Democracy*, 96–104.

49. Frank B. Gilbreth Jr., *Time Out for Happiness* (New York: Crowell, 1970), 114.

50. Aitken, *Taylorism at Watertown Arsenal*, 161.

51. Remarks by Louis D. Brandeis in *Frederick Winslow Taylor: A Memorial Volume* (New York: Taylor Society, 1920), 72–76.

52. Gilbreths' labor policy: Graham, "Domesticating Efficiency," 639–40.

53. Said one member of the Senate Judiciary Committee, "The real crime of which this man is guilty is that he has exposed the iniquities of men in high places in our financial system." Strum, *Brandeis on Democracy*, 15.

54. Strum, *Brandeis*, 293–95.

55. Strum, *Brandeis on Democracy*, 17.

56. Lancaster, *Making Time*, 164, 15. Frank B. Gilbreth and Lillian M. Gilbreth, *Fatigue Study: The Elimination of Humanity's Greatest Unnecessary Waste; A First Step in Motion Study* (New York: Sturgis & Walton, 1916), 157, 100–102. The Gilbreths' emphasis on reducing fatigue also led them to develop devices to aid the handicapped. See especially Frank B. Gilbreth and L. M. Gilbreth, "Motion Study for Crippled Soldiers" (paper, meeting of the American Association for the Advancement of Science, Ohio, December 27, 1915, to January 1, 1916), Box 27, Folder 2, Gilbreth Papers.

57. Remarks by Brandeis in *Taylor: A Memorial Volume*, 72–76; quote from 73.

58. Gilbreth and Gilbreth, *Fatigue Study*, 149–50.

59. Lillian M. Gilbreth to Frank B. Gilbreth, January 14, 1918, Box 11, Folder 10, Gilbreth Papers.

60. Lancaster, *Making Time*, 176.

61. Ibid., 191, 182–83. See also Edna Yost, in collaboration with Lillian M. Gilbreth, *Normal Lives for the Disabled* (New York: Macmillan, 1944).

62. "Following her husband's orders, she sent his brain to Harvard Medical School." Frank B. Gilbreth Jr., *Time Out for Happiness*, 179.

63. Lancaster, *Making Time*, 237, 244, 247. Vern L. Bullough, "Merchandizing the Sanitary Napkin: Lillian Gilbreth's 1927 Survey," *Signs* 10 (1985): 615–27.

64. Cohan, *More Work for Mother*, 5, 43–44; quote from 43.

65. Home economics entered the curriculum from grade school through graduate programs between 1914 and 1917. See, e.g., Mary S. Hoffschwelle, "The Science of Domesticity: Home Economics at George Peabody College for Teachers, 1914–1939," *Journal of Southern History* 57 (November 1991): 659–80, especially 661, and Sarah Stage and Virginia B. Vincenti, eds., *Rethinking Home Economics: Women and the History of a Profession* (Ithaca, NY: Cornell University Press, 1997); the introduction explains the history of the term.

66. Frank B. Gilbreth Jr., *Time Out for Happiness*, 127.

67. Ibid., 1.

68. Ibid., 209.

69. Lillian Gilbreth's decision to make this switch is in Graham, "Domesticating Efficiency." On Frederick, see all of Frederick's books, but especially the introduction to *The New Housekeeping*. Gilbreth considered Frederick a rival and seems to have been reluctant to help her out. Lillian M. Gilbreth to Frank B. Gilbreth, January 9, 1918: "I have attempted a 'foreword' for Mrs. Christine Frederick's book. Is it business to do one for her? I can't decide" (Box 93, Folder 1, Gilbreth Library of Management, Purdue University). Frederick made money by endorsing products, which Lillian refused to do.

70. Coffee cake: Frank B. Gilbreth Jr., *Time Out for Happiness*, 213. "Making a Lemon Meringue Pie: Original Layout of Kitchen Distance Walked, 224 Feet" and "Making a

Lemon Meringue Pie: Improved Layout of Kitchen Distance Walked, 92 Feet" (blue-prints), Box 71, Folder 1, Gilbreth Library of Management. On the Kitchen Efficient, see Carroll W. Pursell, *White Heat: People and Technology* (Berkeley: University of California Press, 1994), 104–5.

71. Ruth Schwartz Cowan, "Gilbreth, Lillian Evelyn Moller," in *Notable American Women: The Modern Period, A Biographical Dictionary,* ed. Barbara Sicherman and Carol Hurd Green (Cambridge, MA: Belknap Press of Harvard University Press, 1980), 271–73.

72. Jeffrey Cruikshank, *A Delicate Experiment: The Harvard Business School, 1908–1945* (Boston: Harvard Business School Press, 1987), 165–66. For more on the Kitchen Efficient, see "Fatigue Laboratory: Agency History" (unpublished manuscript), Baker Library, Harvard Business School.

73. David Bruce Dill, "Fatigue Studies Among Mississippi Sharecroppers," *Harvard Alumni Bulletin* (October 20, 1939): 113–19. Offprints of this and several other papers reporting on this series of experiments are filed in Fatigue Laboratory: Collected Publications, 1924–1946, Box 2, Folder 190–201, Baker Library, Historical Collections, Harvard Business School. D. B. Dill et al., "Properties of the Blood of Negroes and Whites in Relation to Climate and Season," *Journal of Biological Chemistry* 136 (November 1940): 449–60 (Folder 210–222). W. H. Forbes et al., "Leukopenia in Negro Workmen," *American Journal of the Medical Sciences* 201 (March 1941): 407–12 (Folder 223–233). S. Robinson et al., "Adaptations of White Men and Negroes to Prolonged Work in Humid Heat," *American Journal of Tropical Medicine* 21 (March 1941): 261–87 (Folder 223–233). S. Robinson et al., "Adaptations to Exercise of Negro and White Sharecroppers in Comparison with Northern Whites," *Human Biology* 13 (May 1941): 139–58 (Folder 234–243). J. W. Thompson, "The Clinical Status of a Group of Negro Sharecroppers," *Journal of the American Medical Association* 117 (1941): 6–8 (Folder 244–250).

74. Lillian M. Gilbreth, *The Home-maker and Her Job* (New York: D. Appleton, 1927), 23.

75. Ibid., 96.

76. Cowan, "Gilbreth, Lillian Evelyn Moller."

77. Frank B. Gilbreth Jr., *Time Out for Happiness,* 148; on Grieves's duties, see 193; the icebox, 210–11; the rolling cart, 213.

78. Ibid., 213.

79. Frank B. Gilbreth Jr. and Ernestine Gilbreth Carey, *Belles on Their Toes* (New York: Crowell, 1950), 225–26. Lillian decided not to sell her house, calculating that "people who could afford to run such a large house didn't have families that size any more."

80. Brandeis, foreword (dated May 1912) to Gilbreth, *Primer of Scientific Management,* viii.

81. Arlie Russell Hochschild, *The Time Bind: When Work Becomes Home and Home Becomes Work* (New York: Metropolitan Books, 1997), 6.

82. Lancaster, *Making Time,* 348–50.

83. Ibid., 227. Lillian Gilbreth's best statement of a philosophy of work is in her "Work and Leisure," in *Toward Civilization,* ed. Charles A. Beard (London: Longmans, Green, 1930): 232–52.

Chapter 7.   CONFESSIONS OF AN AMATEUR MOTHER

1. Steven Schlossman, "Perils of Popularization: The Founding of *Parents' Magazine*," *Monographs of the Society for Research in Child Development* 50 (1985): 65–77, and Diane Looms Weber, "Hecht, George Joseph," in *American National Biography Online* (2000). George Hecht, *The War in Cartoons: A History of the War in 100 Cartoons by 27 of the Most Prominent American Cartoonists* (New York: Dutton, 1919).

2. "Prospectus," *Mother's Magazine* 1 (January 1833): 4.

3. The best history of American magazines remains Frank Luther Mott, *A History of American Magazines*, 5 vols. (Cambridge, MA: Harvard University Press, 1938–1968); but see also John Tebbel and Mary Ellen Zuckerman, *The Magazine in America, 1741–1990* (New York: Oxford University Press, 1991).

4. Isaiah Wilner, *The Man Time Forgot: A Tale of Genius, Betrayal, and the Creation of Time Magazine* (New York: HarperCollins, 2006), 83–87, 132. On the prehistory of the magazine, including naming, etc., see especially Alan Brinkley, *The Publisher: Henry Luce and His American Century* (New York: Knopf, 2010), 99. For more on *Time*'s history, see also Angeletti Norberto and Alberto Oliva, *Time: The Illustrated History of the World's Most Influential Magazine* (New York: Rizzoli, 2010), and John Kobler, *Luce: His Time, Life and Fortune* (New York: Doubleday, 1968).

5. Brinkley, *The Publisher*, 138.

6. *Time*'s prospectus appears in Wilner, *The Man Time Forgot*, 85–86. The *New Yorker*'s prospectus is reprinted in Gigi Mahon, *The Last Days of* The New Yorker (New York: McGraw-Hill, 1988), 14–16. "Of All Things," *New Yorker*, February 21, 1925. That the *New Yorker* would not be written for an old lady in Dubuque was a dig at *Time*, but it was a dig at a lot of other magazines, too. Edmund Wilson once wrote to James Thurber that a certain Iowan was an "old cliché of New York editorial offices." Wilson had been on the staff of *Vanity Fair* between 1920 and 1923, when its editor was Frank Crowninshield: "Crowninshield used to say, when confronted with something that he feared was too esoteric: 'Remember, there's an old lady sitting in Dubuque, and she has to be able to understand everything we print.' " Wilson always figured he was kidding. Wilson is quoted in Ben Yagoda, *About Town: The* New Yorker *and the World It Made* (New York: Scribner, 2000), 48. On the rivalry between Ross and Luce, see also Jill Lepore, "Untimely," *New Yorker*, April 12, 2010.

7. Clara Savage Littledale (hereafter CSL), "And George Did It!" undated typescript, Box 2, CSL Papers, Schlesinger Library, Radcliffe.

8. A useful summary of available data is Michael Caines, "Fertility and Mortality in the United States," EH.Net Encyclopedia, ed. Robert Whaples, March 19, 2008; http://eh.net/encyclopedia/article/haines.demography. See also Michael Caines and Richard H. Steckel, eds., *A Population History of North America* (Cambridge: Cambridge University Press, 2001).

9. The literature on demographic transition is vast, but a valuable account of this transition in the United States, along with a summary of the scholarship, can be found in Susan E. Klepp, *Revolutionary Conceptions: Women, Fertility, and Family Limitation in America, 1760–1820* (Chapel Hill: University of North Carolina Press, 2009); the

Essex Almanac for 1771 is quoted on 103. Histories of contraception include Norman E. Hines, *Medical History of Contraception* (Baltimore: Williams and Wilkins, 1936); Angus McLaren, *A History of Contraception: From Antiquity to the Present Day* (London: Basil Blackwell, 1990); and James Reed, *From Private Vice to Public Virtue: The Birth Control Movement and American Society Since 1830* (New York: Basic Books, 1978). But the most important account is Linda Gordon, *Woman's Body, Woman's Right: A Social History of Birth Control in America* (New York: Viking, 1976), and her revision of that work, Linda Gordon, *The Moral Property of Women: A History of Birth Control Politics in America* (Urbana: University of Illinois Press, 2002). Gordon argues that "birth control has always been primarily an issue of politics, not of technology" (2). On the folklore of birth control from antiquity to the twentieth century, see Gordon, *Moral Property*, 13–21.

10. Frances K. Goldscheider et al., "A Century (Plus) of Parenthood: Changes in Living with Children, 1880–1990," *History of the Family* 6 (2001) 477–94.

11. On the history of parenting advice, see especially Peter N. Stearns, *Anxious Parents: A History of Modern Childrearing in America* (New York: New York University Press, 2003), and Ann Hulbert, *Raising America: Experts, Parents, and a Century of Advice About Children* (New York: Knopf, 2003).

12. Biographical and genealogical information can be found in Box 1 of the CSL Papers, Schlesinger Library, Radcliffe. See also Littledale's obituary: "Mrs. Littledale, Magazine Editor," *New York Times*, January 10, 1956. The diaries, which begin on January 1, 1907, can be found in Box 1 of the CSL Papers.

13. Dustin Harp, *Desperately Seeking Women Readers: U.S. Newspapers and the Construction of a Female Readership* (Lanham, MD: Lexington Books, 2007), 22–31.

14. All diary entries can be found in the diaries contained in Box 1 of the CSL Papers.

15. Adelheid Popp, *The Autobiography of a Working Woman* (Chicago, 1913); on life not fit for a human being, see 108–9.

16. Gilman quoted in Gordon, *Moral Property*, 93.

17. For Sanger comparing another speaker favorably to Gilman, see Sanger's diary entry for December 17, 1914, in Margaret Sanger, *The Selected Papers of Margaret Sanger*, ed. Esther Katz (Urbana: University of Illinois Press, 2003–10), 1:106; and for her seeing Gilman speak in New York earlier that year, see 107.

18. *Selected Papers of Margaret Sanger*, 1:69–74.

19. Gordon, *Moral Property*, 143. *Selected Papers of Margaret Sanger*, 1:41. Reed, *From Private Vice to Public Virtue*, 70, 73. Margaret Sanger, *An Autobiography* (New York: Norton, 1938), 89.

20. Savage's stories for *Good Housekeeping* included "Men—and Women's Clubs," *Good Housekeeping* 61 (May 1916), 610–16, and "The Children's Bureau and You," *Good Housekeeping* 66 (January 1918): 53–54.

21. *Selected Papers of Margaret Sanger*, 1:194–5; Reed, *Private Vice, Public Virtue*, 106–7; Gordon, *Moral Property*, 156–57; Sanger, *Autobiography*, 215–21; David M. Kennedy, *Birth Control in America: The Career of Margaret Sanger* (New Haven, CT: Yale University Press, 1970), 82–88.

22. Paul Popenoe, "Birth Control and Eugenics," *Birth Control Review* 1 (April–May

1917): 6, and Roswell H. Johnson, "Birth Control Not Prevention," *Birth Control Review* 1 (April-May 1917): 6. See also Kennedy, *Birth Control in America,* 118.

23. Mary L. Read, "Mothercraft," *Journal of Heredity* 7 (1916): 339–42.

24. [Name omitted] to Margaret Sanger, November 27, 1922, in *Selected Papers of Margaret Sanger,* 1:355.

25. Barbara Straus Reed, "Littledale, Clara Savage," in *American National Biography Online* (2000) and the Finding Aid to the CSL Papers, Schlesinger Library, http://oasis.lib.harvard.edu/oasis/deliver/~sch00098. CSL, "Sublimation," *New Republic,* July 16, 1924.

26. Samuel J. Lewis, "Thumbsucking: Its Dangers and Treatment," *Parents' Magazine,* June 1930, 23, 50–51; A.E.P. Searing, "Have Your Children the Daily Bath Habit?," *Parents' Magazine,* June 1930, 27, 71; Mary Fisher Torrance, "How Well Do We Protect Our Children?," *Parents' Magazine,* June 1930, 20–21, 68–70; quote from 20.

27. CSL, untitled typescript, n.d., Box 2, CSL Papers.

28. J. George Frederick, "Can a Tired Businessman Be a Good Father?," *Parents' Magazine,* April 1927, 15.

29. CSL, "And George Did It!"

30. Stella Crossley, "Confessions of an Amateur Mother," *Children: A Magazine for Parents,* March 1927, 28–29.

31. Margaret Sanger, *Motherhood in Bondage* (1928; repr., Columbus: Ohio State University Press, 2000), 47. Anne Kennedy, Congressional reports 1925 and 1926, Folders 494, 495, and 496, American Birth Control League Records, Houghton Library, Harvard University. And, on the number of clinics in 1930, see Gordon, *Moral Property,* 187–88.

32. Memorandum on Proposed Merger between the American Birth Control League and the American Eugenics Society, March 2, 1933. Planned Parenthood Federation of America Records (hereafter PPFA Records) are at Smith College, Sophia Smith Collection, PPFA I, Series 1, Box 3, Folder 4.

33. Gordon, *Moral Property,* 206–8.

34. CSL, "And George Did It!"

35. Marcel C. LaFollette, *Making Science Our Own: Public Images of Science, 1910–1955* (Chicago: University of Chicago Press, 1990), especially 10–25. The Science Service was founded in 1920 as

a nonprofit syndicate, to distribute "general news of science." Initially financed by newspaper publisher E. W. Scripps, the service was later sponsored by the American Association for the Advancement of Science and the National Research Council, and it represents a turning point for scientists' open and formalized participation in public communications efforts. Its avowed purpose was to promote a positive image of science. The founding editor, chemist and writer Edwin E. Slosson, declared that the Service would not "indulge in propaganda unless it be propagandas to urge the value of research and the usefulness of science." By the mid-1930s, the Service was meeting a subscription list of over 100 newspapers and reaching about one-fifth of the U.S. reading public.

See also Dorothy Nelkin, *Selling Science: How the Press Covers Science and Technology* (1987; repr., New York: Freeman, 1995). For an interesting and slightly different view, see John C. Burnham, *How Superstition Won and Science Lost: Popularizing Science and Health in the United States* (New Brunswick, NJ: Rutgers University Press, 1987). Burnham's chapter 5 is the most relevant. "Between 1920 and 1925," Burnham writes, "the volume of science news doubled in major papers" (174). Also: by 1927, "the Associated Press had two [science] writers and a special science news service" (175).

36. Nancy Tomes, "Epidemic Entertainments: Disease and Popular Culture in Early-Twentieth-Century America," *American Literary History* 14 (Winter 2002): 625–52.

37. Nancy Tomes, *The Gospel of Germs: Men, Women, and the Microbe in American Life* (Cambridge, MA: Harvard University Press, 1998), 183, 249, 251.

38. Bert Hansen, "America's First Medical Breakthrough: How Popular Excitement About a French Rabies Cure in 1885 Raised New Expectations for Medical Progress," *American Historical Review* 103 (1998): 373–418.

39. Thurman B. Rice, *The Conquest of Disease* (New York: Macmillan, 1927).

40. On de Kruif, see Charles E. Rosenberg, *No Other Gods: On Science and American Social Thought* (Baltimore: Johns Hopkins University Press, 1976, 1997), chapter 7, "Martin Arrowsmith: The Scientist as Hero," and also Steven Shapin, *The Scientific Life: A Moral History of a Late Modern Vocation* (Chicago: University of Chicago Press, 2008), 60–63.

41. Paul de Kruif, *Microbe Hunters* (New York: Blue Ribbon Books, 1926), 3.

42. De Kruif, "Before You Drink a Glass of Milk," *Ladies' Home Journal*, September 1929, 8.

43. Loren A. Schuler, "Talk Given by Mr. Loren A. Schuler, Editor of the Ladies' Home Journal," May 26, 1930, Staff Meeting Minutes, Box 8, J. Walter Thompson Company Archives, Special Collections Library, Duke University.

44. " 'Parrot Disease' Baffles Experts," *Washington Post*, January 9, 1930. James A. Tobey, "This Month in Public Health," *American City Magazine*, March 1930, 175. A sample of early newspaper coverage: "Baltimore Woman Dies," *Chicago Tribune*, January 11, 1930; "Parrot Fever Kills 2 in This Country," *New York Times*, January 11, 1930; "Three Ill with Rare Sickness," *Los Angeles Times*, January 9, 1930; "Hunts for Source of 'Parrot Fever,' " *New York Times*, January 12, 1930; "U.S. Opens War on Parrot Fever as 20 Stricken," *San Francisco Examiner*, January 13, 1930; "Trace Parrots Bearing Fatal Disease to U.S.," *Chicago Tribune*, January 12, 1930. For the public health analysis, see Charles Armstrong, "Psittacosis: Epidemiological Considerations with Reference to the 1929–30 Outbreak in the United States," *Public Health Reports* 45 (August 29, 1930): 2013–23; L. Elliocott et al., "The Psittacosis Outbreak in Maryland, December, 1929, and January, 1930," *Public Health Reports* 46 (April 10, 1931): 843–50; and "Psittacosis," *American Journal of Public Health*, July 1930: 756–77. On the outbreak as a whole, see also Jill Lepore, "It's Spreading," *New Yorker*, June 1, 2009.

45. "Parrot Fever Germ Was Found in 1892," *New York Times*, January 14, 1930.

46. "General Cumming Tells of Psittacosis," *Atlanta Constitution*, January 17, 1930. "Parrot Fever Cases Halted in the City," *New York Times*, January 19, 1930. " 'Life' in Sing Sing Offered to All Unwanted Parrots," *New York Times*, January 20, 1930.

47. [E. B. White], Talk of the Town, *New Yorker,* January 25, 1930.

48. A rare exception: "Improvement Seen in Parrot Victims," *Washington Post,* January 10, 1930.

49. Morrill Goddard, "Talk Given at Monday Evening Meeting," March 17, 1930, Staff Meeting Minutes, Box 8, J. Walter Thompson Company Archives, Special Collections Library, Duke University. About beating everyone to the story, though, Goddard was either lying or misremembering. *American Weekly* did not run its story on parrot fever until January 12: "Killed by a Pet Parrot," *American Weekly,* January 12, 1930.

50. The *New York Times* notice calling the magazine "First Aid for Parents" was reprinted in the first issue: *Children: A Magazine for Parents,* November 1926, 50.

51. Shirley W. Wynne, "How to Guard Against Colds and Flu," *Parents',* January 1930, 26, 43.

52. Samuel J. Lewis, "Thumbsucking: Its Dangers and Treatment," *Parents',* June 1930, 23, 50–51; A.E.P. Searing, "Have Your Children the Daily Bath Habit?" *Parents',* June 1930, 27, 71; Mary Fisher Torrance, "How Well Do We Protect Our Children?," *Parents',* June 1930, 20–21, 68–70.

53. CSL, "Parents in Search of Education," typescript of a talk given at Smith College in 1930, Box 2, CSL Papers. In this regard, and for a contrary note, see also Bertrand Russell, "Are Parents Bad for Children?," *Parents',* May 1930, 18–19, 69.

54. Crossley, "Confessions of an Amateur Mother."

55. Schlossman, "Founding," 66.

56. Typescripts of Littledale's short stories, along with files of rejection letters, can be found in her papers at the Schlesinger. See, e.g., *New Yorker* to CSL, May 27, 1935, rejecting her story "Intimations of Love," Box 3, CSL Papers.

57. The transcript of this talk, dated February 24, 1932, is in Box 2, CSL Papers, in a folder titled "Radio talks, January–March 1932." The radio talks run into Box 3 and appear to have run from 1932 to 1943.

58. CSL, "Living with Our Children," April 1937, Box 2, CSL Papers. Littledale's radio addresses, including "Don't Be a Martyr to Your Children," "Fathers Are Parents, Too," and "I Am a Failure as a Mother," can be found in a series of folders in Boxes 2 and 3. She participated in a debate on spanking in 1935; see the transcript titled "Debate: An Old Fashioned Spanking." For Littledale's rules, see "Six Ways to Succeed as a Parent," October 23, 1936, Box 2. On parenting fashion, see CSL, "New Styles in Babies," May 1937, Box 2.

59. Sanger to Robert L. Dickinson, February 20, 1942, in *Selected Papers of Margaret Sanger,* 3:115.

60. Betty MacDonald, *The Egg and I* (Philadelphia: Lippincott, 1945), 145, 96, 137, 143, 136–37. *The Egg and I* was published on October 3, 1945 ("Books Published Today," *New York Times,* October 3, 1945). By December 1945, both it and *Stuart Little* had made it onto lists of the year's ten best books. "Ten Christmas Lists of 'Ten Best,'" *New York Times,* December 2, 1945. "The phenomenal success of this little book is the publishing surprise" of the season, *Life* wrote of *The Egg and I* on March 18, 1946. See also Jane F. Levey, "Imagining the Family in Postwar Popular Culture," *Journal of Women's History* 13 (2001): 125–50.

61. CSL, "Account of Plane Accident as Dictated by Clara Savage Littledale in Crawford W. Long Memorial Hospital, Atlanta, Georgia, March 4, 1941," Box 1, CSL Papers.

62. CSL, to Marion Sabin, September 23, 1944, Box 3, CSL Papers.

63. "What is your community doing about courses for expectant parents—both mothers and fathers?" CSL, "What Can We Do About Marriage?," January 1947, Box 2, CSL Papers.

64. A pamphlet published in 1943 promised that *"more healthy children will be born* to maintain the kind of peace for which we fight." Quoted in Gordon, *Moral Property,* 247; emphasis in original.

65. Cooperation with Religious Leaders, PPFA Records, Smith, PPFA I, Series 1, Box 17, Folder 3.

66. *Selected Papers of Margaret Sanger,* 3:469.

67. Margaret Sanger to D. Kenneth Rose, August 20, 1956, in *Selected Papers of Margaret Sanger,* 3:402.

68. Kennedy, *Birth Control in America,* 272.

69. James W. Reed, interview with Mary Steichen Calderone, M.D., August 7, 1974, transcript, Schlesinger-Rockefeller Oral History Project, Schlesinger Library, Reel A-1, p. 15.

70. Janice M. Irvine, *Talk About Sex: The Battles over Sex Education in the United States* (Berkeley: University of California Press, 2002), 31.

71. Alan F. Guttmacher, "Memoirs," typescript, November 1972, PPFA Records, Smith, PPFA II, Administration, Guttmacher, A. F., Autobiography, Rough Draft, Box 117, Folder 39. Davis, *Sacred Work,* chapter 4.

72. Division of Negro Service, PPFA Records, Smith, PPFA I, Series 1, Box 9, Folder 4. See also Negro Campaign, PPFA I, Series 1, Box 34, Folder 1.

73. Wylda B. Cowles to Alan F. Guttmacher, Memorandum, May 29, 1962, in PPFA Records, Smith, PPFA II, Box 123, Folder 26, "Negro Problem Correspondence."

74. Martin Luther King Jr., *Family Planning—A Special and Urgent Concern* (New York: Planned Parenthood Federation of America, 1966), in PPFA Records, Smith, PPFA I, Negro Campaign, Box 34, Folder 1.

75. See Konrad Reisner to Roy Wilkins, December 20, 1967, and Roy Wilkins to Konrad Reisner, December 28, 1967, in PPFA Records, Smith, PPFA II, Box 123, Folder 26, "Negro Problem Correspondence."

76. Gordon, *Moral Property,* 290. See also "Planned Parenthood Blasted by NAACP," *Dayton Daily News,* December 13, 1967, in PPFA Records, Smith, PPFA II, Box 123, Folder 26, "Negro Problem Correspondence."

77. Kennedy, *Birth Control in America,* viii.

78. Quoted in Gloria Feldt with Carol Trickett Jennings, *Behind Every Choice Is a Story* (Denton: University of North Texas Press, 2002), 94.

79. Gordon, *Moral Property,* 289. See also Deborah R. McFarlane and Kenneth J. Meier, *The Politics of Fertility Control: Family Planning and Abortion Policies in the American States* (New York: Chatham House, 2001).

80. Gordon, *Moral Property,* 289.

81. George J. Hecht, "Smaller Families: A National Imperative," *Parents Magazine,* July

1970. And George Hecht to Alan Guttmacher, August 18, 1970, Box 1, Folder 1, Alan Guttmacher Papers, Countway Library, Harvard University.

82. "A Quality Audience," *Parents* (New York: Meredith Corporation, 2008); http://www .meredith.com/mediakit/parents/print/audience.html.

83. CSL, "Your Dad's a Great Guy!" August 1951, Box 2, CSL Papers.

84. Linda Greenhouse and Reva Siegel, "Before (and After) Roe v. Wade," *Yale Law Journal* 120 (June 2011): 2047, 2049, 2043.

85. Kevin P. Phillips, *The Emerging Republican Majority* (New Rochelle, NY: Arlington House, 1969). Memorandum from Patrick J. Buchanan to the President, March 24, 1971, in Hearings Before the S. Select Comm. on Presidential Campaign Activities, 93d Cong. 4146, 4146–53 (1973); Memorandum from "Research" to Attorney General H. R. Haldeman, October 5, 1971, in Hearings Before the S. Select Comm. on Presidential Campaign Activities, 93d Cong. 4197, 4201 (1973); and Jack Rosenthal, "Survey Finds Majority, in Shift, Now Favors Liberalized Laws," *New York Times*, August 25, 1972, are quoted and discussed in Greenhouse and Siegel, "Before (and After) Roe v. Wade," 2053, 2056, 2031.

86. Alan F. Guttmacher, "Why I Favor Liberalized Abortion," *Reader's Digest*, November 1973, 143–47.

87. James W. Reed, interviews with Loraine Lesson Campbell, December 1973–March 1974, Schlesinger-Rockefeller Oral History Project, Reel A-1, 90.

88. Greenhouse and Siegel, "Before (and After) Roe v. Wade," 2061, 2066–67. Robert Post and Reva Siegel, "*Roe* Rage: Democratic Constitutionalism and Backlash," *Harvard Civil Rights–Civil Liberties Law Review* 42 (2007): 420–21.

89. Greg D. Adams, "Abortion: Evidence of an Issue Evolution," *American Journal of Political Science* 41 (1997): 718, 723. Gordon, *Moral Property*, 309.

90. Goldscheider et al., "A Century (Plus) of Parenthood."

91. Joyce A. Martin et al., "Births: Final Data for 2002," *National Vital Statistics Reports*, vol. 52, no. 10, December 17, 2003; http://www.cdc.gov/nchs/data/nvsr/nvsr52/nvsr52 _10.pdf. For data on the start of this phenomenon earlier in the century, see Jane Riblett Wilkie, "The Trend Toward Delayed Parenthood," *Journal of Marriage and the Family* 43 (1981): 583–91, especially table 2. Wilkie posits the rise of "couples with an idea of adulthood that does not include parenting."

92. Guttmacher Institute, "Facts on Contraceptive Use in the United States," June 2010; http://www.guttmacher.org/pubs/fb_contr_use.html.

93. Jill Lepore, "Birthright," *New Yorker*, November 14, 2011.

94. E.g., Cecile Richards, "We're Not Going Anywhere," *Huffington Post*, April 8, 2011. And see Americans United for Life, "The Case for Investigating Planned Parenthood," July 7, 2011.

Chapter 8. HAPPY OLD AGE

1. On the visit, see Saul Rosenzweig, *The Historic Expedition to America (1909): Freud, Jung and Hall the King-Maker*, rev. ed. (1992; St. Louis: Rana House, 1994); on James's

arrival, see 80–81. Citations come from the 1994 edition. Rosenzweig calls the visit "a watershed for the spread of psychoanalysis in the continents of North America and Europe" (3).

2. G. Stanley Hall (Hereafter GSH), review of *The Principles of Psychology,* by William James, *American Journal of Psychology* 3 (1891): 578–91. On GSH's review, see also Rosenzweig, *Historic Expedition,* 95–96, and Dominic W. Massaro, "A Century Later: Reflections on 'The Principles of Psychology' by William James and on the Review by G. Stanley Hall," *American Journal of Psychology* 103 (1990): 539–45. Many people have commented on what went wrong between James and Hall, who were once close. There was, among other things, a dispute over which man could best claim having established the first psychology laboratory, a dispute that hinged on each man's definition of the field. Revealing is this recollection, from a contemporary: "I spent some time in 1920 with the eminent lawyer, Emery Buckner of Root's firm. He had worked his way through Harvard as James's private secretary and he remarked on the ill-feeling between James and Hall, and implied that Hall had been rather unfair and ungrateful. I knew nothing of the details but was edified by the remark that it was probably due to the fact that James had done so much (too much) to help Hall." Harry Elmer Barnes to Dorothy Ross, April 3, 1962, Box B1-4-5, "Interviews with Contemporaries of G. Stanley Hall," GSH Papers, Clark University. Lorine Pruette, who was Hall's graduate student, has this to offer about Hall's temperament: "He often said unkind things and could make cutting remarks, but he seemed to reserve his sarcasm and reproof for intellectual slackers. It was the man who did not try or the man who was insincere in his thinking for whom Hall brought out his weapons. For the merely stupid he had a marvelous patience, even gentleness. . . . He made a curious distinction between stupidity and insincerity." Lorine Pruette, *G. Stanley Hall: A Biography of a Mind* (New York: D. Appleton, 1926), 45. Finally, this is not related to Hall's viciousness, but it's a wonderfully shrewd and well-stated assessment of what really crippled the man: "Hall's persistent effort to give intellectual form to the full range of his emotional experience was the chief source of both the insight and confusion he would display in his intellectual career." Dorothy Ross, *G. Stanley Hall: The Psychologist as Prophet* (Chicago: University of Chicago Press, 1972), 29.

3. GSH, introduction to *Studies in Spiritism,* by Amy E. Tanner (New York: D. Appleton, 1910), xviii, xxxii. GSH, "Spooks and Telepathy," *Appleton's Magazine* 12 (December 1908): 679.

4. Jung's recollections: C. G. Jung to Virginia Payne, July 23, 1949, in *Letters,* selected and edited by Gerhard Adler (Princeton, NJ: Princeton University Press, 1973), 1:530–32.

5. Harry Elmer Barnes to Dorothy Ross, April 3, 1962, and April 12, 1962, Box B1-4-5, "Interviews with Contemporaries of G. Stanley Hall," GSH Papers. Ross also cites this as a story Hall commonly told (*GSH,* 393).

6. "Hall was justly esteemed as a psychologist and educationalist, and had introduced psychoanalysis into his courses some years before," Freud wrote. "There was a touch of the 'king-maker' about him, a pleasure in setting up authorities and deposing them." Sigmund Freud, *An Autobiographical Study,* trans. James Strachey (1925; repr., New York: Norton, 1963), 57. Citations come from the 1963 Norton edition.

7. Hall regularly gave lectures on the psychology of food (Pruette, *GSH*, 132). Carl Van Doren once mused that writing about GSH got to the heart of the problem of biography: "We all know well enough that in morals there are few blacks and whites, few angels and devils, few heroes and villains. The great difficulty is to instruct the uninformed without dividing the moral universe in this convenient and dramatic way and yet without troubling them in their search for the rules of worthy conduct. At this point the realistic study of biography comes most valuably to the rescue.... Perhaps we Americans, with our republican partiality for simple characters, are specially in need of the study of more complex types, such as President Hall belonged to. As a nation we are very unfamiliar with them; our history lacks them, our literature lacks them, or has lacked them until lately" (Carl Van Doren, introduction to Pruette, *GSH*, ix–x).

8. Hall also wrote about what he called "the man-soul." (He wrote, as well, about "the folk-soul.") An excerpt: "Man is not a permanent type but an organism in a very active stage of evolution toward a more permanent form. Our consciousness is but a single stage and one type of mind: a late, partial, and perhaps essentially abnormal and remedial outcrop of the great underlying life of man-soul." GSH, *Adolescence* (New York: D. Appleton, 1904), 1:vii. For more on the subject, see *Adolescence*, 2:62–63. Hall's work and its relation to social Darwinism is discussed in Donald Pickens, *Eugenics and the Progressives* (Nashville: Vanderbilt University Press, 1968), 132–38.

9. Margaret Mead, *Coming of Age in Samoa: A Psychological Study of Primitive Youth for Western Civilization* (New York: Blue Ribbon Books, 1928; New York: Perennial Classics, 2001); quote from 137. Citation comes from the Perennial edition. See also John Demos, "The Rise and Fall of Adolescence," in *Past, Present and Personal: The Family and the Life Course in American History* (New York: Oxford University Press, 1986), 92–113.

10. Writing about conversion, Hall remarked, "It is thus no accidental synchronism of unrelated events that the age of religion and that of sexual maturity coincide, any more than that senescence has its own type of religiosity" (*Adolescence*, 2:292).

11. So did the journalist Susan Jacoby, in *Never Say Die: The Myth and Marketing of the New Old Age* (New York: Pantheon, 2011). John Gray, *The Immortalization Commission: Science and the Strange Question to Cheat Death* (New York: Farrar, Straus and Giroux, 2011), 207. The best discussion of Hall's study of old age is Thomas R. Cole, "The Prophecy of Senescence: G. Stanley Hall and the Reconstruction of Old Age in America," *Gerontologist* 24 (August 1984): 360–66; see also Thomas R. Cole, *The Journey of Life: A Cultural History of Aging in America* (New York: Cambridge University Press, 1992), chapter 10.

12. The recommendation to review your life is from *Senescence*, but the warning about stodginess is from GSH, "The Dangerous Age," *Pedagogical Seminary* 28 (September 1921): 293.

13. GSH, *Life and Confessions of a Psychologist* (1923; repr., New York: D. Appleton, 1927), 357–58. Citations come from the 1927 edition. Ross, *GSH*, 3–5. Louis Wilson, *G. Stanley Hall: A Sketch* (New York: Stechert, 1914), 16–18.

14. GSH, "Note on Early Memories," *Pedagogical Seminary* 6 (December 1899): 507; and

see Ross, *GSH,* 12. Hall later wrote, "It was a resolve, vow, prayer, idealization, life plan, all in a jumble, but it was an experience that has always stood out so prominently in my memory that I found this revisitation solemn and almost sacramental. Something certainly took place in my soul then" (Pruette, *GSH,* 25).

15. Ross, *GSH,* 16–21.

16. Ibid., 30.

17. Pruette, *GSH,* 64, 34.

18. GSH to Abigail Beals Hall, February 10, 1869, from New York, Box B1-1-2, GSH Papers.

19. Wilson, *GSH,* 37.

20. GSH to Granville Bascom Hall and Abigail Beals Hall, from Bonn, July 9, 1869, Box B1-1-2, GSH Papers. "I am growing deep only if growing at all, but then as applied to men and especially ministers solid is better than surface measure. I am and have been homesick, lonesome, dumpish."

21. GSH to Granville Bascom Hall and Abigail Beals Hall, from Berlin, December 16, 1869, Box B1-1-2, GSH Papers. "I will enclose what a fortune teller says is the spirit photograph of my future wife. Have you ever seen her and how will she do and how does she compare with Robert's?"

22. Granville Bascom Hall to GSH, January 17, 1870, Box B1-1-2, GSH Papers. Hall's father adds, "P.S. Are you having any practice in preaching or religions teaching, or any part in public exercises? Are you in any way doing good as well as getting good? People often inquire for you."

23. GSH, *Life and Confessions,* 578. Pruette writes, "He wanted to 'get the feel' of everything the universe afforded. He liked prize fights and religious revivals, visited poor houses and prisons and asylums for the insane, spent two weeks in a home for the insane, explored the dens of iniquity in most of the large cities of the Occidental world, visited morgues, attended meetings of revolutionists, studied the social evil and became a president of the Watch and Ward Society, and declared: 'I believe that such zests and their indulgence are a necessary part of the preparation of a psychologist or moralist who seeks to understand human nature as it is' " (*GSH,* 63).

24. For more on GSH's human-nature tourism, see Pruette, *GSH,* 63; Ross, *GSH,* 33; GSH, *Life and Confessions,* 578–80.

25. GSH to his sister, from Berlin, January 29, 1870; Abigail Beals Hall to GSH, January 18, 1870, Box B1-1-2, GSH Papers.

26. Pruette, *GSH,* 3. For this reason, Pruette dubbed him "the Playboy of Western Scholarship."

27. Granville Bascom Hall, quoted in Ross, *GSH,* 5.

28. Proverbs 16:31. Cotton Mather, *Addresses to Old Men and Young Men and Little Children,* in *Three Discourses. I. The Old Man's Honour* (Boston: R. Pierce, 1690), dedication. See also Cotton Mather, *A Good Old Age* (Boston: S. Kneeland and T. Green, 1726), 1. And Demos, "Old Age in Early New England," in *Past, Present and Personal,* 139–85.

29. Quoted in W. Andrew Achenbaum, *Old Age in the New Land: The American Experience Since 1790* (Baltimore: Johns Hopkins University Press, 1978), 14, 12.

30. Louis I. Dublin, Alfred J. Lotka, and Mortimer Spiegelman, *Length of Life: A Study of the Life Table,* rev. ed. (1936; New York: Ronald Press, 1949); see especially chapters 2 and 3.

31. Sylvester Graham, *Lectures on the Science of Human Life* (1839). The *Graham Journal of Health and Longevity* ran from 1837 to 1839.

32. Achenbaum, *Old Age in the New Land,* 12–15.

33. Ibid., 47.

34. Pat Thane, for example, points out that old age is not lonelier today than it used to be, because it used to be that if you were old, you had outlived your children. Pat Thane, ed., *The Long History of Old Age* (London: Thames and Hudson, 2005), 9–10.

35. David Hackett Fischer, *Growing Old in America* (New York: Oxford University Press, 1977), 3–4. Jacoby, *Never Say Die,* 28, 4.

36. GSH to his parents, April 9, 1877, GSH Papers, Box B1-1-2.

37. Ross argues, "Anxious to remove any sharp divisions in existence, Hall henceforth tried to find Divinity within nature itself. The reconciliation of religious aspiration with the mechanical world-view propounded by science that Tennyson achieved in poetry, Hall hoped to achieve through philosophy" (*GSH,* 45).

38. Ross, *GSH,* 50–51.

39. Ibid., 61–79. Before leaving Antioch, Hall wrote a short story, which was published: "A Leap Year Romance," *Appletons' Journal* 5 (September 1878): 211–22.

40. GSH, *Jesus the Christ, in the Light of Psychology* (Garden City, NY: Doubleday, Page, 1917), 1:xix: "Senescent insights and adolescent sentiments meet and reinforce each other." And: "As to miracles . . . genetic psychology can have no quarrel with those who cling to them as literally veridical, for this is a necessary stage. They are the baby talk of religious faith, not a disease but an infantile stadium of true belief" (xiii). On the crisis of the Church of Christ and the next necessary step of "re-evolution," see xvi. He wrote this book for his graduate students—it came out of lectures he had been giving since 1897—and saw it as part of his work on adolescence: "My study of adolescence laid some of the foundations of this work, because Jesus' spirit was in a sense the consummation of that adolescence" (xviii).

41. Gray, *Immortalization Commission,* 19.

42. Ibid., 192.

43. Hyland C. Kirk, *The Possibility of Not Dying: A Speculation* (New York: G. P. Putnam's Sons, 1883), 4.

44. He founded the *American Journal of Psychology* with money from the American Society for Psychical Research; in its first year, he published an attack on spiritualism and lost his funding. Although he initially served as a vice president of the American society, he resigned soon after, in either 1886 or 1887. Ross, *GSH,* 164, 170. On the funding of the journal, see also Rosenzweig, *Historic Expedition,* 92–93.

45. William James to GSH, November 5, 1887, *The Correspondence of William James,* edited by Ignas K. Skrupskelis and Elizabeth M. Berkeley (Charlottesville: University Press of Virginia, 1992–2004), 6:282–84.

46. William James, "A Record of Observations of Certain Phenomena of Trance (1890),"

in *Essays in Psychical Research* (Cambridge, MA: Harvard University Press, 1986), 79–88. "A hearty message of thanks" appears on 85.

47. GSH, "Spooks and Telepathy," 681. GSH, introduction to *Studies in Spiritism,* by Tanner, xviii.

48. For the *Telegram*'s hostility to Clark, even before it opened, see "Our University," *Worcester Sunday Telegram,* January 23, 1887. On Hall's appearance and secretiveness, see "What Is Clark University?," *Worcester Daily Telegram,* April 15, 1889. "Dogs Vivisected," *Worcester Sunday Telegram,* March 9, 1890. "Clark University Matters," *Worcester Daily Telegram,* March 13, 1890. "If He Be a Cur Cut Him Up," *Worcester Sunday Telegram,* March 16, 1890. "Docents' Devilish Devices," *Worcester Sunday Telegram,* March 23, 1890. "Snatched from Docents," *Worcester Sunday Telegram,* March 23, 1890. "Cat Crucified and Carved," *Worcester Sunday Telegram,* April 13, 1890. See also Pruette, *GSH,* 94–95, and Ross, *GSH,* 209–10.

49. Dorothy Ross, interview with Hall's only surviving child, Robert G. Hall. Notes & Interviews: Robert G. Hall, 1961, Box B1-4-5, GSH Papers. This account is somewhat at variance with a detailed report in the newspaper: "Wife and Child Die Together," *Worcester Daily Telegram,* May 16, 1890. In the newspaper account, the girl, Julia, was sleeping with her mother because she had been ill; there was no mention of soap bubbles. Also in this account: the gas was thought to have leaked from a light fixture, a chandelier. A medical examiner ruled the deaths accidental: "The most likely is that Mrs. Hall pulled the chain twice before going to bed, and then left the jet opened." Doctors summoned to the scene attempted artificial respiration for more than an hour.

50. GSH, "Spooks and Telepathy," 681–82, and Pruette, *GSH,* 97–98.

51. GSH, introduction to *Studies in Spiritism,* by Tanner, xviii.

52. GSH, "Spooks and Telepathy," 678.

53. "What Franz Boas Must Do," *Worcester Sunday Telegram,* March 8, 1891. "Condemned by Physicians," *Worcester Daily Telegram,* March 9, 1891. "Strip for Measurement!" *Worcester Daily Telegram,* March 10, 1891. Marshall Hyatt, *Franz Boas, Social Activist: The Dynamics of Ethnicity* (New York: Greenwood, 1990), 26–27; see also Ross, *GSH,* 210. On the rise of the modern research university, see Julie A. Reuben, *The Making of the Modern University: Intellectual Transformation and the Marginalization of Morality* (Chicago: University of Chicago Press, 1996).

54. See Florence Rena Sabin, *Franklin Paine Mall: The Story of a Mind* (Baltimore: Johns Hopkins University Press, 1934), 100–104. See also Hyatt, *Franz Boas,* 28–30.

55. GSH, *Life and Confessions,* 340.

56. On the rumors, see Pruette, *GSH,* 95–96.

57. Dorothy Ross, interview with Frank Hankins, March 8, 1961, Box B1-4-5, GSH Papers.

58. Ross, *GSH,* 252.

59. GSH, *Senescence,* vii.

60. Ibid., xxi.

61. GSH, from 1896, quoted in Ross, *GSH,* 264.

62. GSH, *Adolescence,* 2:649.

63. Ibid., 2:194. Stephen Jay Gould, discussing this passage, writes, "In what must be the

most absurd statement in the annals of biological determinism, G. Stanley Hall—again, I remind you, not a crackpot, but America's premier psychologist—invoked the higher suicide rates of women as a sign of their primitive evolutionary status" (*The Mismeasure of Man*, rev. ed. [1981; repr., New York: Norton, 1996], 147; citation comes from the 1996 edition). For more on Hall and social Darwinism, see Carl N. Degler, *In Search of Human Nature: The Decline and Revival of Darwinism in American Social Thought* (New York: Oxford University Press, 1991), 29–30.

64. GSH, *Adolescence*, 2:71. But see the entirety of chapter 10.

65. Ibid., 2:60.

66. James quoted in Richard Hofstadter, *Social Darwinism in American Thought*, rev. ed. (Philadelphia: University of Pennsylvania Press, 1944; Boston: Beacon Press, 1992), 195. Citation comes from the Beacon edition.

67. Ross, *GSH*, 334. On this transition among scholars at American universities, see also Reuben, *Making of the Modern University*. Reuben argues that "the separation of knowledge and morality was an unintended result of the university reforms of the late nineteenth century" (4).

68. Quoted in Ross, *GSH*, 385.

69. "Stanley Hall on Youth's Problems: President of Clark University Discusses Adolescence—the 'Cave-Man' Period of Life," *New York Times*, September 28, 1907.

70. There is a real headiness to this, for Hall. Of genetic psychology: "It appeals to the really young, and would appreciate and meet adolescent needs rather than deal in sad insights which belong only to senescence, whether normal or precocious. It believes youth the golden age of life, the child the consummate flower of creation, and most of all things worthy of love, reverence, and study. . . . It realizes that even pure science, including those departments that deal with mind, is not for its own sake, but that it becomes pure precisely as it becomes useful in bringing a race to ever more complete maturity" (*Adolescence*, 2:55–56).

71. Ross, *GSH*, 382.

72. Jung to Payne, July 23, 1949, *Letters*, 531.

73. William James, "Report on Mrs. Piper's Hodgson-Control," *Proceedings of the American Society for Psychical Research* 3 (1909): 470–500; quote from 498.

74. Rosenzweig, *Historic Expedition*, 104.

75. Dorothy Ross, interview with Frank Hankins, March 8, 1961, B1-4-5, GSH Papers. A significant number of Hall's graduate students were women, partly because Harvard would not admit them (and James sent them to Hall). One of his graduate students from this period, Lorine Pruette, went on to write his biography, which is passionately affectionate. One wonders about the nature of their relationship: "For two years I visited Hall repeatedly, sat in his shabby old study or in the library that never was comfortably warm through the whole New England winter, and talked with him about a multitude of things. For one year I was his student, attending all his lectures and sitting in the famous Monday-night seminars, while for four years he read and criticized practically everything I wrote. Thus the record of his personality may be at all points somewhat warped by my enthusiasm for him, by my remembrance of the stimulation and joy he brought into my life. When I first met 'G. Stanley' he was

in his middle seventies while I was twenty-two; I was old with the excessive luxurious age of youth and he was young as he had always been, the perennial adolescent" (Pruette, *GSH*, 6–7).

76. Hankins told Ross, "His wife was said to be a very beautiful woman when they married, but she got to be a big, fat person. He treated her pretty badly. Hall was a perfectly ruthless chap you know." When Jung met Hall's second wife, in 1909, he wrote, "He has a plump, jolly, good-natured, and extremely ugly wife who, however, serves wonderful food." Hall's son told Ross that his father's wife told people that he beat her but that he himself did not believe this. Pruette's account of Hall's wife's madness, which must be considered suspect, given that it was related to her by Hall, whom she adored, reads: "One night she appeared at a seminar meeting wearing her bedroom slippers; another night she arose suddenly, left her guests and went upstairs to take a bath. She began to stop members of the faculty, and even students, to ask for loans, while at the same time she was spending Hall's money with great extravagance. Here was another occasion for gossip about the University, and the townspeople naturally made the most of it. Florence began to talk more and more wildly, spreading absurd stories about her husband, becoming to him a constant embarrassment and care. A complete separation was finally agreed upon but never entirely maintained, for it seemed as though the poor demented woman could not keep away from Worcester and the University. A paralytic stroke brought her back permanently as a responsibility, and Hall was troubled to the end of his life by unfounded complaints from her regarding her treatment in the sanitarium he had chosen for her. After the separation his friends urged him to put her out of his life, to refuse to look after her personally, since he had already made a generous financial settlement, but this he would not do, and she continued to be a cause of suffering and anxiety to his death" (Pruette, *GSH*, 102–3).

77. E.g., two dissertations from 1915, under Hall's direction: W. T. Sanger, "A Study of Senescence," and R. S. Ellis, "The Attitude Toward Death and Types of Belief in Immortality." GSH cites both in his article "Thanatophobia and Immortality," *American Journal of Psychology* 26 (October 1915), 551. Amy Tanner, also Hall's graduate student, was studying psychical research with him during these years. Hall left Tanner a sizable sum in his will.

78. Fischer, *Growing Old,* 189. On Nascher, see also Gilles Lambert, *Conquest of Age: The Extraordinary Story of Dr. Paul Niehans' Research* (London: Souvenir Press, 1960), 12–13.

79. GSH to his sister, June 1914: "Get Sanford Bennett's book, Old Age Deferred, and try it on. It is wonderful. My face is getting red and full and my hair is coming back all over my head, my muscular development is something wonderful. He is 72 and says he looks 40 and his photos in the book bear it out. I am too old a bird to be caught much by fads but this interested me and will you." Family Letters, 1914–1924, Box B1-1-2, GSH Papers.

80. GSH to the Mary Lawrence East, December 13, 1916, in James Reed, *From Private Vice to Public Virtue: The Birth Control Movement and American Society Since 1830* (New York: Basic Books, 1978), 105.

81. GSH, "A Reminiscence," *American Journal of Psychology* 28 (1917): 297.

82. [GSH], "Old Age," *Atlantic Monthly* 17 (January 1921): 23. The article was published anonymously. Most of it is reproduced in *Senescence.*

83. "There is a wonderful liberty in being old and not anxious about a career, and being able to say what you want to in any way and on any topic," he wrote to his son. December 24, 1923, Letters to Robert G. Hall, 1912–1924, Box B1-1-2, GSH Papers.

84. Kimball Young, "A Man Out of His Time," *Nation,* February 13, 1924.

85. GSH, *Senescence,* xv–xxi.

86. "He wrote his autobiography and made his will, that curious will" (Pruette, *GSH,* 238). Hall left provision for his wife to be taken care of by her guardian, Dr. E. S. Sanford. His bequests were to his sister, his son, the children of another sister, his cousins, his housekeeper, his best friend, and his graduate student and research assistant, Amy Tanner. The remainder of his estate he left to Clark to fund research in genetic psychology. G. Stanley Hall, Last Will and Testament, June 27, 1922, Worcester Probate Court, Worcester, Massachusetts. (I have deposited a photocopy of the will with Hall's papers at Clark.) "At the time of his death it was found that he had a great number of savings-bank books, one apparently from every bank in Massachusetts, each representing a savings account filled up to the limit" (Pruette, *GSH,* 49–50).

87. GSH, *Senescence,* 23.

88. This argument was most aggressively made by William Osler. See Jacoby, *Never Say Die,* 43–55. Osler's brain was dissected and compared with Hall's. Jacoby mentions Hall's reaction to Osler's argument on 54.

89. Quoted in Cole, *Journey of Life,* 163–65.

90. Tamara K. Hareven, "The Last Stage: Historical Adulthood and Old Age," *Daedalus* 105, no. 4 (Fall 1976): 20. Achenbaum, *Old Age in a New Land,* 49. On this subject, see also Carole Haber and Brian Gratton, *Old Age and the Search for Security: An American Social History* (Bloomington: Indiana University Press, 1994).

91. "I looked over such literature, both poetry and prose, as I found within reach, written by aging people describing their own stage of life." GSH, *Senescence,* 149, 100.

92. Ibid., 322–30.

93. He had also concluded that old age is divided into senescence, from forty-five to sixty-five, which is the "dangerous age" because "we aim lower," and senectitude, which is harder. See also GSH, "The Dangerous Age," 275–94.

94. GSH, *Senescence,* 381–82.

95. Ibid., 247, 410.

96. GSH, *Life and Confessions,* 596.

97. Pruette, *GSH,* 258–59.

98. Henry H. Donaldson, "A Study of the Brains of Three Scholars: Granville Stanley Hall, Sir William Osler and Edward Sylvester Morse," *Journal of Comparative Neurology* 46 (August 1928): 1–95.

Chapter 9. THE GATE OF HEAVEN

1. Details about the Quinlans' family life I have generally found in Joseph and Julia Quinlan with Phyllis Battelle, *Karen Ann: The Quinlans Tell Their Story* (Garden City, NY: Doubleday, 1977). Chapter 15 relates the October trial. Mail addressed "To Karen Quinlan's Family, U.S.A." is on 155. For more on the Quinlans' mail, see Steven Rattner, "Quinlan Family Gets Advice and Sympathy in Mail," *New York Times,* October 26, 1975. See also the photograph of the Quinlans sorting through their mail in Julia Duane Quinlan, *My Joy, My Sorrow: Karen Ann's Mother Remembers* (Cincinnati: St. Anthony Messenger Press, 2005), n.p. Mail sent to the judge and the lawyers in the case was turned over to the Morris County sheriff, John Fox. "The people who wrote seemed to take two basic views," explained Fox. "One was 'Don't let Karen die, or we'll kill you.' The other was, 'Let her die, or we'll kill *her.*' " (Quinlans, *Karen Ann,* 171–72.) The Quinlans spent a great deal of time at the rectory. See Bruce Chadwick, "For Quinlans, Weather Was Portent of Ruling," New York *Daily News,* November 11, 1975.

2. Two fifteen-minute periods: *In the Matter of Karen Quinlan: The Complete Legal Briefs, Court Proceedings and Decision in the Superior Court of New Jersey,* 2nd ed. (1975; repr., Frederick, MD: University Publications of America, 1982), 1:542.

3. Physical descriptions can be found in "The Law: The Right to Live—or Die," *Time,* October 27, 1975; "The Law: A Life in the Balance," *Time,* November 3, 1975; and Matt Clark, Susan Agrest, Marianna Gosnell, Dan Shapiro, and Henry McGee, "A Right to Die?," *Newsweek,* November 3, 1975. On the spasms, see the testimony of Dr. Sidney Diamond, October 23, 1975 (*In the Matter of Karen Quinlan,* 1:492–93).

4. On no hope, see Muir's opinion (*In the Matter of Karen Quinlan,* 1:549, but see also 1:560); the testimony of Dr. Julius Korein, October 21, 1975 (*In the Matter of Karen Quinlan,* especially 1:320, where the court debates what "hope" means); "The Law: Between Life and Death," *Time,* September 29, 1975; and "The Law: A Life in the Balance."

5. At the time, public sympathy lay with Julia and Joseph Quinlan. In a nationwide poll, two-thirds of Americans said they believed that family members should be allowed to end life support for a person who is terminally ill, in a coma and not conscious, with no cure in sight. Peter G. Filene, *In the Arms of Others: A Cultural History of the Right-to-Die in America* (Chicago: Ivan R. Dee, 1998), 25, 119–21. The New York *Daily News* telephoned 532 New Yorkers and asked the rather leading question, "Do you agree with Karen Ann Quinlan's parents that she be taken off the respirator and allowed to die in dignity?" As reported in "Most Here Back Parents in Their Decision on Karen," New York *Daily News,* October 27, 1975, 59 percent said yes; 24 percent, no. That poll's results were also broken down by the religion of the respondent. If a majority of the American people agreed about anything, though, it was something that the Quinlans and their daughter's doctors agreed about, too: a judge ought not to be the one to make this kind of decision. See, e.g., "The Law: The Right to Live—or Die," *Time,* October 27, 1975: "To allow the court to decide the Quinlan case, says Dr. David Posqanzer, a neurologist at Massachusetts General Hospital, 'is taking the

judgment of a doctor and putting it in the hands of those not competent to make a decision—the courts.' "

6. Julia Quinlan quoted in Quinlans, *Karen Ann,* 173. The reporters had been laying siege to the bungalow for weeks. "They must have a hundred pictures of me walking out to get the morning paper, and another two hundred pictures of me climbing into the car," Joseph said (Quinlans, *Karen Ann,* 165).

7. That she could no longer hear is mentioned in several places, but see B. D. Colen, *Karen Ann Quinlan: Dying in the Age of Eternal Life* (New York: Nash, 1976), 25. On the singing, see Quinlan, *My Joy, My Sorrow,* 108.

8. Quinlans, *Karen Ann,* 174.

9. B. D. Colen, "Court Rule Asked on Life, Death," *Los Angeles Times,* October 19, 1975. Colen was nominated for a Pulitzer for his coverage of the Quinlan case. A corroborating view: "The outcome of the case of Karen Quinlan will thus be historic. However he decides, Judge Muir will not merely be interpreting the law. He will be making it" ("The Law: A Life in the Balance").

10. The proceedings have been compiled in the two-volume *In the Matter of Karen Quinlan.* For an argument that the abortion issue has contorted American politics, see Ronald Dworkin, *Life's Dominion: An Argument About Abortion, Euthanasia, and Individual Freedom* (New York: Knopf, 1993); Dworkin notes, "Abortion is tearing America apart. It is also distorting its politics, and confounding its constitutional law" (4). Dworkin's first chapter insists on the particular intransigence of this issue in the United States, as compared to Europe (see, in particular, 6).

11. David Rothman has called Karen Quinlan's the most significant medical case ever, in *Strangers at the Bedside: A History of How Law and Bioethics Transformed Medical Decision Making* (New York: Basic Books, 1991), 3 and, especially, 222–28.

12. "Obama's Health Care Town Hall in Portsmouth," *New York Times,* August 11, 2009. Sarah Palin's Facebook page, "Statement on the Current Health Care Debate," August 7, 2009, http://www.facebook.com/note.php?note_id=113851103434.

13. Charlotte Eby, "Grassley: There's 'Every Right to Fear' End-of-Life Counseling Provision," *Globe Gazette,* August 13, 2009.

14. Richard Hofstadter, *The Paranoid Style in American Politics and Other Essays* (New York: Knopf, 1965), 6.

15. Ibid., 3, 6, 24, 29, 35. *The Glenn Beck Program,* Premiere Radio Networks, August 6, 2009. Americans weren't any more paranoid than anyone else, Hofstadter figured; he just thought they were interestingly paranoid and dangerously paranoid; then, too, the United States was his home and his subject. "I choose American history to illustrate the paranoid style only because I happen to be an Americanist," he explained. "It is for me a choice of convenience."

16. Richard Hofstadter Papers, Box 36, Rare Books and Manuscripts Division, Butler Library, Columbia University.

17. Hofstadter, *Paranoid Style,* 5, 24, 29. When revising the essay for publication, he underplayed how far he had jumped around in history. The typescript of Part IV, marked by Hofstadter, begins, "~~If, after our historically discontinuous examples of the paranoid style,~~ we now take the long jump to the contemporary . . ." (Richard Hofstadter Papers, Box 32).

18. The phrase "pursuit of happiness" is not Jefferson's; nor is the list. George Mason wrote about "the enjoyment of life and liberty, with the means of acquiring and possessing property, and pursuing and obtaining happiness and safety" in the Virginia Declaration of Rights in 1776. See Pauline Maier, *American Scripture: Making the Declaration of Independence* (New York: Knopf, 1997), 126–27, 134, 165; Garry Wills, *Inventing America: Jefferson's Declaration of Independence* (New York: Doubleday, 1978), 216–17; Daniel T. Rodgers, *Contested Truths: Keywords in American Politics Since Independence* (New York: Basic Books, 1987), chapter 2, especially pp. 68–70; and David Armitage, *The Declaration of Independence: A Global History* (Cambridge, MA: Harvard University Press, 2007), 3, 165–67. Declaration and Resolves of the First Continental Congress, October 14, 1774.

19. Bernard Bailyn, *The Ideological Origins of the American Revolution* (Cambridge, MA: Harvard University Press, 1967), 119–21, 152. David Hackett Fischer, *Liberty and Freedom* (Oxford: Oxford University Press, 2005), 104–6.

20. Thomas Jefferson to John Holmes, April 22, 1820, Series 1, General Correspondence, 1651–1827, Thomas Jefferson Papers, Library of Congress.

21. Abraham Lincoln, "Speech on the Kansas-Nebraska Act at Peoria, Illinois, October 16, 1854," in *Speeches and Writings, 1832–1858: Speeches, Letters, and Miscellaneous Writings; the Lincoln-Douglas Debates* (New York: Library of America, 1989), 338.

22. *Dred Scott v. John F. A. Sandford*, 60 U.S. 393 (1857).

23. E. N. Elliott, ed., *Cotton Is King, and Pro-Slavery Arguments* (Augusta, GA: Pritchard, Abbott, & Loomis, 1860), iv and especially chapter 2, section 10, 312–19.

24. In 1859, the governor of Virginia called it an invasion "upon slaveholders and upon their property in Negro slaves." In a message to the Virginia legislature, Wise proclaimed, "The home to be invaded was the home of domestic slavery; the persons to be seized were the persons of slaveholders; the property to be confiscated was the property in slaves and the other property of slaveholders alone." State of Virginia, *Governor's Message and Reports of the Public Officers of the State, of the Boards of Directors, and of the Visitors, Superintendents, and Other Agents of Public Institutions or Interests of Virginia* (Richmond, VA: William F. Ritchie, Public Printer, 1859), 3.

25. *Declaration of the Immediate Causes Which Induce and Justify the Secession of South Carolina from the Federal Union and the Ordinance of Secession* (Charleston, SC: Evans & Cogswell, Printers to the Convention, 1860), 8. See also Rodgers, *Contested Truths*, 68–70, on the malleability of property for slave owners.

26. Peter Coutros, "It Is Only a Matter of Life and Death," New York *Daily News*, October 21, 1975.

27. "The Law: A Life in the Balance."

28. Peter Kihss, "Case of Karen Quinlan Gives Hospital Maintenance and Security Problems," *New York Times*, November 5, 1975.

29. Quinlans, *Karen Ann*, 174–75.

30. For mail sent to the hospital, see Jean Joyce, "Mail: Let Her Live," New York *Daily News*, October 23, 1975. One letter writer suggested putting Quinlan in a state of suspended animation until scientists in the future could repair her damaged brain.

31. In his excellent history of the right-to-die movement, Peter Filene points out that four photographs of Quinlan were available to the press but this one was used nine

times out of ten. Filene, *In the Arms of Others,* 79–81. See also M. L. Tina Stevens, *Bioethics in America: Origins and Cultural Politics* (Baltimore: Johns Hopkins University Press, 2000), 110. For a very different photograph of Quinlan, see "Judge: Keep Karen Alive," New York *Daily News,* November 11, 1975. The offer for $100,000: Quinlan, *My Joy, My Sorrow,* 90–91; and for more on the family's position about the photographs, see 46.

32. Armstrong to his colleague as quoted in Stevens, *Bioethics in America,* 125.

33. The best account of this shift is Rothman, *Strangers at the Bedside.*

34. Filene, *In the Arms of Others,* 53, 55.

35. Selig Greenberg, "The Right to Die," *Progressive* 30 (June 1966), 37.

36. Filene, *In the Arms of Others,* 10, 49–50.

37. Pope Pius XII, "The Prolongation of Life," November 24, 1957, *The Pope Speaks* 4 (Spring 1958): 393–98.

38. Joseph Quinlan quoted in Georgie Anne Geyer, "A Question of Life or Death," *Los Angeles Times,* October 27, 1975.

39. And, on Coburn's own investigation, including borrowing a manuscript from Norman Cantor, see *In the Matter of Karen Quinlan,* 1:22–23.

40. The press flocked to New Jersey, Filene has argued, because the story of Karen Ann Quinlan served as an irresistible counterpoint to that of Patty Hearst, who had just been arrested for robbing a bank two years after being kidnapped by the Symbionese Liberation Army; Hearst was "brainwashed" (*In the Arms of Others,* 76–79).

41. "The Law: Between Life and Death," *Time,* September 29, 1975.

42. On the 1968 ad hoc committee, see Stevens, *Bioethics in America,* especially 81. Armstrong quoted in "The Law: The Right to Live—or Die," *Time,* October 27, 1975.

43. See Stevens, *Bioethics in America,* chapters 3 and 4. *Newsweek* claimed that "the Quinlan case appears to be the first in which anyone has sought advance legal permission to withhold such supports" (Merrill Sheils, Susan Agrest, and Elaine Sciolino, "Cruel Questions," *Newsweek,* September 29, 1975). See also Michael Halberstam, "Other Karen Quinlan Cases Have Never Reached Court," *New York Times,* November 2, 1975. "In any other age," observed one theologian, "she would be dead." "The Law: The Right to Live—or Die," *Time,* October 27, 1975.

44. In Quinlans, *Karen Ann,* 175, this statement is attributed to Julia Quinlan, but it is attributed to "an observer" in Frank J. Prial, "The Common Denominator at Coma Trial Is Youth," *New York Times,* October 21, 1975.

45. *In the Matter of Karen Quinlan,* 1:195–96.

46. Ibid., 1:196. For more on Coburn: Coutros, "It Is Only a Matter of Life and Death," New York *Daily News,* October 21, 1975. He waved away Armstrong's argument about the Quinlans' religious convictions. "We don't talk about what the Catholic Church's position may be. That may be binding on the Quinlans; it's not binding on Your Honor."

47. *In the Matter of Karen Quinlan,* 1:200. "While the only certainty in life is death," Hyland observed, "what constitutes death is far from certain." *In the Matter of Karen Quinlan,* 1:84.

48. Until the twentieth century, the phrase "sanctity of life" meant "sacred life." This

usage is commonplace, although the phrase itself is rare. From 1639 to 1800—by my search of *Early American Imprints*, series 1 (Readex, online)—it appears in all of American printed books and pamphlets only twice, both times in religious tracts. In the nineteenth century it appears to be synonymous with "purity of faith" (*Catholic Layman*, 4 [May, 1855]: 51). Although it is now often referred to as a timeless feature of Christian teaching, it dates only to the nineteenth century. See Geoffrey Drutchas, "Is Life Sacred? The Incoherence of the Sanctity of Life as a Moral Principle Within the Christian Churches" (DDiv diss., Lancaster Theological Seminary, 1996), and also Fabián Andrés Ballesteros Gallego, "Sanctity of Life: Exploring Its Significance in Modern Medicine and Bioethics" (PhD diss., McGill University, 2001). In the first decades of the twentieth century, it was used to argue against capital punishment, with something like its modern and less wholly doctrinal meaning. See Herbert L. Stewart, "Euthanasia," *International Journal of Ethics* 29 (October 1918): 56. Schlesinger Sr. uses it to talk about revolutionary rights: Arthur Meier Schlesinger, "The American Revolution Reconsidered," *Political Science Quarterly* 34 (March 1919): 63. The phrase entered the legal lexicon about 1957, chiefly through Glanville Williams, *The Sanctity of Life and the Criminal Law* (New York: Knopf, 1957).

49. *In the Matter of Karen Quinlan*, 1:203, 258–60. This conflation was new in 1975. It has become common. See, e.g., *Cruzan by Cruzan v. Director, Missouri Department of Health*, 497 U.S. 261 (1990) (Stevens, J., dissenting).

50. *In the Matter of Karen Quinlan*, 1:294, 252, 258–60.

51. Ibid., 1:252, 492.

52. This is from the October 23 testimony of Dr. Sidney Diamond (*In the Matter of Karen Quinlan*, 1:493), but is also cited in Bruce Hallett, "3 Docs: Karen's Lost, but Keep Her Living," New York *Daily News*, October 24, 1975.

53. *In the Matter of Karen Quinlan*, 1:328–29.

54. Raymond Duff and Alexander Campbell, "Moral and Ethical Dilemmas in the Special Care Nursery," *New England Journal of Medicine* 289 (October 25, 1973): 890–94; see also Duff and Campbell, "Moral and Ethical Dilemmas: Seven Years into the Debate About Human Ambiguity," *Annals of the American Academy of Political and Social Science* 447 (January 1980), 19–28; quote from 24. Filene, *In the Arms of Others*, 114. Rothman, *Strangers at the Bedside*, 194–204.

55. *Commonwealth v. Kenneth Edelin*, 371 Mass. 497 (1976); Dr. F. J. Ingelfinger, "The Edelin Trial Fiasco" and "Edelin Supported" in *New England Journal of Medicine* 292 (March 27, 1975): 697; 705; Carol Altekruse Berger and Patrick Berger, "The Edelin Decision," *Commonweal* (April 25, 1975): 76–78; Connie Paige, *The Right to Lifers: Who They Are, How They Operate, Where They Get Their Money* (New York: Summit Books, 1983), chapter 1. On the sentencing, see 24.

56. Rothman, *Strangers at the Bedside*, 221. On the importance of the case as landmark jurisprudence, see, e.g., Norman L. Cantor, "Twenty-five Years After Quinlan: A Review of Jurisprudence of Death and Dying," *Journal of Law, Medicine and Ethics* 29 (Summer 2001): 182–96. The case also commonly appears in casebooks—e.g., Gregory E. Pence, *Classic Cases in Medical Ethics: Accounts of Cases That Have Shaped*

Medical Ethics, with Philosophical, Legal, and Historical Backgrounds, 5th ed. (New York: McGraw-Hill, 1990; repr., Boston: McGraw-Hill Higher Education, Inc., 2008), chapter 2; citation comes from the 2008 edition. On the legacy of the issues Quinlan raised, see, e.g., Henry R. Glick, *The Right to Die: Policy Innovation and Its Consequences* (New York: Columbia University Press, 1992), and Robert M. Veatch, *Death, Dying, and the Biological Revolution,* rev. ed. (1976; repr., New Haven, CT: Yale University Press, 1989), especially chapter 5.

57. For an interesting statement on the nonadversarial nature of the proceedings, see Daniel N. Robinson's introduction to the second volume of *In the Matter of Karen Quinlan:* "Even those, driven by chivalric devotion to protect the weak, search in vain for Karen Quinlan's assailant. Karen Quinlan has no avowed enemy in this case; her parents love her, her Church stands ready to commend her soul, her physicians labor with tireless enthusiasm over her wasting body" (xvii).

58. *In the Matter of Karen Quinlan,* 1:203. Also: "You are doing what Hitler did," a reader wrote, in a letter to Duff and Campbell. Duff and Campbell received a great deal of mail in 1974. More than three-quarters of the letters were supportive. The rest of the letter writers objected, strenuously. More than one mentioned Hitler. Duff and Campbell, "Moral and Ethical Dilemmas in the Special Care Nursery." See also Duff and Campbell, "Moral and Ethical Dilemmas: Seven Years into the Debate About Human Ambiguity"; quote is on 24.

59. "The trial itself did not receive extensive press coverage. Over 1945 and 1946 fewer than a dozen articles appeared in the *New York Times* on the Nazi research; the indictment of forty-two doctors in the fall of 1946 was a page-five story and the opening of the trial, a page-nine story. (The announcement of the guilty verdict in August 1947 was a front-page story, but the execution of seven of the defendants a year later was again relegated to the back pages.) Over the next fifteen years only a handful of articles in either medical or popular journals took up Nuremberg" (Rothman, *Strangers at the Bedside,* 62, 63). On the history of bioethics, see Albert R. Jonsen, *The Birth of Bioethics* (New York: Oxford University Press, 1998).

60. Alexander Mitscherlich and Fred Mielke, *Doctors of Infamy: The Story of the Nazi Medical Crimes,* trans. Heinz Norden (New York: Henry Schuman, 1949). A. Mitscherlich and F. Mielke, *The Death Doctors,* trans. James Cleugh (London: Elek Books, 1962). It wasn't only Nazi medical atrocities that Americans ignored in the 1940s and '50s, and that became the object of dedicated fascination by the 1970s, as Peter Novick has argued in *The Holocaust in American Life* (Boston: Houghton Mifflin, 1999).

61. Hannah Arendt, *Eichmann in Jerusalem: A Report on the Banality of Evil* (New York: Viking, 1963; repr., New York: Penguin Books, 1994), 69; citation comes from the Penguin edition. Those italics are Arendt's. On the reception of Arendt's book, see Novick, *Holocaust,* chapter 7.

62. Filene, *In the Arms of Others,* 49.

63. *In the Matter of Karen Quinlan,* 1:518.

64. Geyer, "A Question of Life or Death," *Los Angeles Times,* October 27, 1975.

65. Da Vinci: Quinlans, *Karen Ann,* 53.

66. Bruce Chadwick, "For Quinlans, Weather Was Portent of Ruling," New York *Daily News,* November 11, 1975.

67. Filene, *In the Arms of Others,* 44.

68. *In re Karen Quinlan,* 348 A.2d 801 (N.J. Super. Ct. Ch. Div) (1975).

69. On March 29, 1976, while awaiting the verdict, the Quinlans celebrated Karen's birthday. Trapasso held a Mass in the Quinlans' house. "Twenty-two years ago," he began, "a child was born who will probably in some way change the world." Filene, *In the Arms of Others,* 88. Said the seven-member court to Armstrong: "You seem to say that this is a medical question and at the same time you say that the family and the doctor should make the decision. Well here the doctor has said 'no.' Now what do you want us to do?" Armstrong restated the argument he had made in Morristown. *In the Matter of Karen Quinlan,* 2:222. See also the exchange on 223–25.

70. Two useful assessments of the court's legal reasoning: Cantor, "Twenty-five Years After Quinlan"; Annette E. Clark, "The Right to Die: The Broken Road from *Quinlan* to *Schiavo,*" *Loyola University Chicago Law Journal* 37 (2006): 385–405.

71. *In the Matter of Karen Quinlan:* "they shall consult with. . . . If that consultative body agrees that there is no reasonable possibility of Karen's ever emerging from her present comatose condition to a cognitive, sapient state, the present life-support system may be withdrawn" (2:315). The Quinlans weren't in court to hear the opinion. They were at the Nassau Inn in Princeton. See Quinlan, *My Joy, My Sorrow,* 50.

72. Filene, *In the Arms of Others,* 98–104.

73. Quinlan, *My Joy, My Sorrow,* 59.

74. Ibid., 87–90.

75. Ibid., 64, 66.

76. *Congressional Record,* May 26, 1982.

77. George F. Will, "The Killing Will Not Stop," *Washington Post,* April 22, 1982.

78. Funeral and burial: Quinlan, *My Joy, My Sorrow,* 103–9. An obituary: Robert D. McFadden, "Karen Ann Quinlan, 31, Dies; Focus of '76 Right to Die Case," *New York Times,* June 12, 1985.

Chapter 10.   RESURRECTION

1. Most of this account comes from Robert Ettinger, interviews with author, May 1–3, 2009, but see also R.C.W. Ettinger, *Youniverse: Toward a Self-Centered Philosophy of Immortalism and Cryonics* (Boca Raton, FL: Universal Publishers, 2009), 392–93. For more on Ettinger's suicide plans, see Ettinger, *Youniverse,* 278, 395. Ettinger's views are the subject of *The Philosophy of Robert Ettinger,* ed. Charles Tandy and Scott R. Stroud (Parkland, FL: Universal Publishers/uPUBLISH.com, 2002). There is very little serious scholarship on cryonics, but see Christine Quigley, *The Corpse: A History* (Jefferson, NC: McFarland, Inc., 1996), 233–36, and Ed Regis, *Great Mambo Chicken and the Transhuman Condition: Science Slightly over the Edge* (New York: Addison-Wesley, 1990), chapter 3.

2. The best summary of the practices of the Cryonics Institute, including perfusion,

is "Outline of CI Cryopreservation Procedures for Human Patients," http://www
.cryonics.org/phases.html.

3. "He may have the physique of Charles Atlas if he wants it, and his weary and faded
wife, if she chooses, may rival Miss Universe." Robert C. W. Ettinger, *The Prospect of
Immortality* (Garden City, NY: Doubleday, 1964), 6; on this same theme, see 59, 101,
and 162.

4. In 2003 the state of Michigan placed a cease-and-desist order on the institute until
Ettinger's son, David, and David's wife, Constance, both attorneys, helped arrange its
reopening. Michigan Department of Consumer and Industry Services, "CIS Orders
Cease and Desist for Cryonics Institute," August 26, 2003, Michigan Department of
Licensing and Regulatory Affiars, http://www.michigan.gov/lara/0,4601,7-154-10573
_11472-74066—,00.html, and "State Orders Cryonics Institute to Close," Associated
Press, August 26, 2003. The "state's Department of Consumer and Industry Services
found that the Cryonics Institute, which has frozen both people and pets, is operating an unlicensed mortuary science establishment and a non-registered cemetery"
("Body Freezing-Halt Ordered," *Grand Rapids Press*, August 27, 2003). Ettinger told
the press that CI is not a cemetery: "It's in a new and different category. Obviously
at some point the bureaucracy will have to catch up" ("State Orders Cryonics Lab
to Freeze," UPI, August 27, 2003). The ruling that CI is a cemetery came on January 7, 2004. For more on David Ettinger's role, see Elizabeth Piet, "Cryonics Lab One
of Three in United States," Associated Press, February 16, 2004.

5. Robert F. Eldredge, *Past and Present of Macomb County, Michigan, Together with
Biographical Sketches of Many of Its Leading and Prominent Citizens and Illustrious
Dead* (Chicago, 1905), 621–25; *History of Macomb County, Michigan* (Chicago, 1882);
Clinton Historical Commission, "History of Clinton Township," http://ctwphc.org/
article.html?id=1. See also David Zeisberger, *The Moravian Mission Diaries of David
Zeisberger, 1772–1781*, edited by Herman Wellenreuther and Carola Wessel, trans. Julie
Tomberlin Weber (University Park: Pennsylvania State University Press, 2005).

6. Cryonics Institute, "Becoming a Member: The FAQ," http://cryonics.org/become
.html.

7. Robert Ettinger, "The Past, Present, and Future, and Everything," *Cryonics* 15 (1994):
27–32. Ettinger, *Youniverse*, 388.

8. Jack Barnette, "The Purple Death," *Amazing Stories*, July 1929.

9. Edgar Allan Poe, "The Facts in the Case of M. Valdemar," in *Collected Works of Edgar
Allan Poe*, ed. Thomas Ollive Mabbott (Cambridge, MA: Harvard University Press,
1978), 3:1233–44; quote from 1242. On immortality in science fiction, see George
Slusser, Garry Westfahl, and Eric S. Rabkin, *Immortal Engines: Life Extension and
Immortality in Science Fiction and Fantasy* (Athens: University of Georgia Press,
1996).

10. H. G. Wells, *When the Sleeper Wakes* (New York: Harper & Brothers, 1899). Jack London, "A Thousand Deaths," *Black Cat* 4 (May 1899): 33–42; quote from 40.

11. Benjamin Franklin, "Observations on the Generally Prevailing Doctrines of Life and
Death," in *Works of the Late Dr. Benjamin Franklin* (New York, 1794), 1:61–63. See also
Gerald J. Gruman, "A History of Ideas About the Prolongation of Life: The Evolu-

tion of Prolongevity Hypotheses to 1800," *Transactions of the American Philosophical Society* 56 (1966): 1–102.

12. E. D. Skinner, "The Corpse That Lived," *Amazing Stories*, January 1930. William Withers Douglas, "The Ice Man," *Amazing Stories*, February 1930.

13. Neil R. Jones, "The Jameson Satellite," *Amazing Stories*, July 1931.

14. Paul de Kruif, "How Long Can We Live?," *Ladies' Home Journal*, February 1930.

15. Ettinger quoted in Faye Flam, "Scientists Say Freezing Is Risky Business," *Philadelphia Inquirer*, July 11, 2002. Paul de Kruif, *Men Against Death* (New York: Harcourt, Brace, 1932).

16. Bryan S. Turner, "Longevity Ancient and Modern," *Society* 46 (2009): 255–61. George F. Corners, *Rejuvenation: How Steinach Makes People Young* (New York, 1923).

17. R.C.W. Ettinger, "The Skeptic," *Thrilling Wonder Stories*, February 1950; R.C.W. Ettinger, "The Penultimate Trump," *Startling Stories*, March 1948.

18. Oscar Edward Anderson Jr., *Refrigeration in America: A History of a New Technology and Its Impact* (Princeton, NJ: Princeton University Press, 1953), 3–7, 128, 195–98, 221, 275, 279, 284, 288, 298–300. See also Elaine Tyler May, *Homeward Bound: American Families in the Cold War Era* (New York: Basic Books, 1988, 2008), especially chapter 7.

19. Ettinger, "The Penultimate Trump." For an interesting survey of the life of the damned, see Alice K. Turner, *The History of Hell* (New York: Harcourt Brace, 1993).

20. David H. Keller, "The Cerebral Library," *Amazing Stories*, May 1931.

21. On the Williams case, see, e.g., Maya Bell, "Scientists Scoffing at a Frozen Williams," *Star-Ledger*, July 9, 2002; Rick Anderson, "The Long, Cold Road to Undeath," *Seattle Weekly*, July 18, 2002; and Richard Sandomir, "Please Don't Call the Customers Dead," *New York Times*, February 13, 2005.

22. Henry Fountain and Anne Eisenberg, "Just Chillin'; Putting Mortality on Ice," *New York Times*, July 14, 2002.

23. Ettinger was, I believe, alluding to C. H. Waddington, *The Scientific Attitude* (Harmondsworth, UK: Penguin Books, 1941).

24. On the history of plastic surgery, see Elizabeth Haiken, *Venus Envy: A History of Cosmetic Surgery* (Baltimore: Johns Hopkins University Press, 1997), especially chapter 5.

25. See, e.g., Bryan Appleyard, *How to Live Forever or Die Trying: On the New Immortality* (London: Simon & Schuster, 2007).

26. Paul Ernst, "The Incredible Formula," *Amazing Stories*, June 1931.

27. Ralph Merkle's relationship to Fred is reported in Allen Abel, "The Death of Death," *Maclean's* 118 (October 10, 2005): 160–68.

28. Marvin Minsky, e-mail to the author, May 24, 2009. See also Minsky's articles, e.g., Marvin L. Minsky, "Will Robots Inherit the Earth?," *Scientific American* (October 1994). And Alex Beam, "Immortality and the Chosen, Frozen Few," *Boston Globe*, June 3, 1998.

29. Robert L. Steinback, "Advocates of Cryonics Undeterred by Naysayers," *Miami Herald*, September 21, 2002.

30. Tom Verducci, "What Really Happened to Ted Williams," *Sports Illustrated*, August 18, 2003.

31. Ettinger had earlier commented about neuropreservation to the press. "We don't have any quarrel with the rational," Ettinger told a reporter in 1997, but "it's a public relations negative" (Michael Moss, "Cryonics Entrepreneurs Say Business Is Ice Cold," *Wall Street Journal,* February 2, 1997). For an example of media coverage bringing Ettinger local attention, see "Macomb County Lab Puts People on Ice," *Grand Rapids Press,* August 7, 2002; this is directly reported in "State Orders Cryonics Institute to Close," Associated Press, August 26, 2003.

32. "In 1948 I saw the light and waited patiently for about twelve years," he once explained, "momentarily expecting some prominent scientist to announce the arrival of the freezer era" (Ettinger, *Prospect of Immortality,* 189).

33. Ettinger, "The Past, Present, and Future, and Everything."

34. Thomas McCormack, telephone interview with author, June 15, 2009.

35. *Dr. Strangelove; Or, How I Learned to Stop Worrying and Love the Bomb,* directed by Stanley Kubrick (1964; Culver City, CA: Columbia Tri-Star, 2001), DVD.

36. Ettinger, *Prospect of Immortality,* 1, 99, 179, 125–27.

37. Ibid., 127, 99, 42, 127.

38. Ibid., 117, 161, 59, 162.

39. Ibid., 116, 96–97.

40. Ibid., 73.

41. Thomas McCormack, telephone interview with author, June 15, 2009.

42. Barbara Metzler, "Cryonics: Is Freezing Bodies Visionary Medicine or the Work of Mad Scientists?," Associated Press, January 25, 1988.

43. Ettinger, "The Past, Present, and Future, and Everything." Clarke's diary entry from March 8, 1965, as reprinted in *The Making of 2001: A Space Odyssey,* selected by Stephanie Schwam (New York: Modern Library, 2000), 38. "The Playboy Interview: Stanley Kubrick," *Playboy,* September 1968, and reprinted in *The Making of 2001;* quote from 286. Kubrick also believed in the conquest of aging: "Too many people view senile decay, like death itself, as inevitable. It's nothing of the sort" (289).

44. Robert Ettinger as a guest on *The Long John Nebel Show,* WNBC Radio, New York, June 14, 1964, as transcribed by the author from an audiotape archived at the Paley Center for Media, New York.

45. Robert C. W. Ettinger, "The Frozen Christian," *Christian Century* 82 (1965): 1313–15. And see also R.C.W. Ettinger, "Cryonics and the Purpose of Life," *Christian Century* 84 (1967): 1250–53.

46. On Bedford's freezing in 1967, see Robert F. Nelson as told to Sandra Stanley, with an introduction by Professor R.C.W. Ettinger, *We Froze the First Man* (New York: Dell, 1968). Ettinger flew to California only after Bedford had been frozen; he gave a press conference. See Christine Quigley, *Modern Mummies: The Preservation of the Human Body in the Twentieth Century* (Jefferson, NC: McFarland, 1998), 140–46.

47. Ettinger, *Man into Superman,* 226. See also Saul Kent, *Future Sex* (New York: Morrow, 1974).

48. *Sleeper,* directed by Woody Allen (1973; Santa Monica, CA: Metro Goldwyn Mayer, 2005), DVD.

49. Ettinger, *Man into Superman,* 88 (cheese), 64 (flying), 62 (body armor), 117 (penile

enhancement). See also Osborn Segerberg Jr., *The Immortality Factor* (New York: Dutton, 1974).

50. Metzler, "Cryonics." When Alcor refused to hand over the head to a coroner, six people were handcuffed and taken in for questioning. In the court case that followed, Connie Ettinger filed an amicus brief, and the case was eventually dropped. Robert L. Steinback, "Advocates of Cryonics Undeterred by Naysayers," *Miami Herald,* September 21, 2002.

51. Ettinger, *Prospect of Immortality,* 156.

52. Ettinger, *Youniverse,* 175.

53. Ben Best, "The Cryonics Institute's 93rd Patient," Case Report, http://www.cryonics .org/reports/CI93.html. On preservation techniques, see also Christine Quigley, *Modern Mummies,* 140–46.

Index

Abbott, Anne Wales, xxii

abortifacients, 65, 115

abortion, xiii, 6, 16, 115, 130–1, 132, 158, 163–4,
204n, 256n
late-term, 163
legalized, 133–4, 163
opposition to, 134–6, 154

Abraham, Laurie, 93–4

Acheson, Dean, 98

Adams, John, 157

Adler, Renata, 21

adolescence, 40, 61–80, 137, 138, 146–7,
148–9, 250n, 252n
duration of, 68–9, 79
Graham's apocalyptic vision of, 67–8
increasing storminess of, 79–80,
146
puberty and, 69, 79–80
as science, 76
as stage of life, 63–4, 74, 146
see also sex education

Adolescence (Hall), 74–5

afterlife, xiii, 142, 161, 170

ages of man, xi–xii, xiii, 64, 74, 115

aging, xiii, 40; see also old age
ejaculation as cause of, 70–3

AIDS, 78–9

Alcor Life Extension Foundation, 177, 178,
179, 183, 185, 265n

Alder, Susan, 57, 221n

Aldrin, Edwin, 20

Allen, Woody, 78, 184–5

Amazing Stories, 173, 174–5, 176

American Academy of Pediatrics (AAP),
23, 33

American Association of Marriage and
Family Therapy, 93

American Birth Control League, 121, 123–4,
129

American Breeders' Association, 82, 83

American Home Economics Association, 108

American Institute of Family Relations,
81–2, 96

American Library Association, 39

American Society for Psychical Research,
137, 142, 147–8, 250n

American Society of Magazine
Photographers, 6

Americans with Disabilities Act (1990), 24

American Weekly, 127

Andersen, Hans Christian, 65–6

anencephalic monsters, 163

Angell, Katharine, see White, Katharine
Angell

Anti-Defamation League, 91

Applecroft Kitchen Home Experiment Station, 109

Applied Eugenics (Popenoe and Johnson), 87, 89

Arendt, Hannah, 165

Are You Fit to Marry?, 84–5

Aristotle, xi, 7, 8, 10, 15, 63–4

Aristotle's Master-piece (Anonymous), 63, 64, 67, 70–1

Arizona Daily Star, 47

Armstrong, Neil, 20

Armstrong, Paul, 159, 160–1, 167, 258n, 261n

Arrowsmith (Lewis and de Kruif), 126

Ashton, Jennifer, 79, 80

Ashurst, Henry, 124

Asimov, Isaac, 179–80

Aubrey, John, 8, 9, 12, 13

Baby Bollinger case, 84–5

"Baby Doe" case, 167–8

Bacon, Francis, xx

Bailey, Jacqui, 62

Bean, Robert Bennett, 83, 86

Bechtel, Louise Seaman, 42–3, 51, 57–60
    NYPL lecture of, 57–8, 221n–2n

Beck, Glenn, 155

Bedford, James, 183, 264n

Beecher, Catherine, 108

Beecher, Henry Ward, 68, 139

Bell, J. H., 89, 91

Benedict, Ruth, 91

Best, Ben, 179, 182–3

Bethlehem Steel Works, 99, 101, 102, 103

Better Times, 111, 112

Bigelow, Jacob, xxv

Binet, Alfred, 85, 86

birth control, *see* contraception

Birth Control Federation of America, 129

Birth Control Review, 120

Birth of a Baby, The, 47

"Birth of an Adult, The" (White), 48

Birth of Mankind, The, 10

Blackmun, Harry, 135

Black Stork, The, 84–5

Blankenhorn, David, 95–6

board games, xiii, xv–xxxiii, 18, 40
    ancient Southeast Asian, xvii–xviii
    by mapmakers, xx–xxi
    spiral race, xxi–xxiii, xxix–xxx, xxxi
    square board race, xvii, xxxi

Boas, Franz, 83–4, 91, 138, 144, 145

body politic, 12–13, 14, 68, 70, 157–8

Body Scoop for Girls, The (Ashton), 79

Boies, David, 95

Bollinger family, 84–5

Bookman, 42–3

Borden, Gail, 29

Boston Central Labor Union, 102

Boston Public Library (BPL), 38

Bradley, Daniel, xviii, xxiii, xxv

Bradley, Hannah, xviii–xx, xxvii

Bradley, Jonathan, xxiii

Bradley, Joseph, xviii–xix

Bradley, Lewis, xxiii, xxiv, xxv, 65

Bradley, Milton, xv–xviii, xx, xxiii–xxxiii, 9, 29, 39, 40, 65, 139, 199n, 202n

Bradley family, xviii–xx, xxiii–xxiv

Bradstreet, Anne, 64

brain death, 160–1

Brandeis, Louis, 97–102
    background of, 98
    labor unions supported by, 101–2, 103, 106, 107, 110
    railroad freight rates and, 98–100, 101, 236n
    on Supreme Court, 106
    Taylor's memorial service speech of, 106, 107

Brandt, Karl, 164, 165

Brave New World (Huxley), 14, 17, 25

breast-feeding, 23–37, 77, 104, 105, 107, 110, 115, 181
    by African women, 30
    benefits conferred by, 33
    bottle feeding vs., 31, 32
    as civic duty, 28
    Congress and, 24–5, 26, 34, 35–6
    as human right, 35
    infants' purported feelings about, 29, 31, 32
    initiation rate of, 33
    insufficient production for, 28, 29, 30–1

processed infant foods and, 29, 31, 32, 33
as public health issue, 33–4
by wet nurses, 27–8, 29, 30, 31, 32, 37
workplace and, 24–5, 33–5, 36–7
Breastfeeding Promotion Act (proposed),
26, 35
breast milk, 23–37
cow's milk vs., 29–31
letdown of, 26
as medicine, 23, 31–3, 37
milk banks for, 24, 31–2
on-demand supply of, 34
scientific research on, 32–3
as "species-specific," 33
synthetic formulas vs., 25, 32
taxonomy and, 26–8, 37
breast milk, expressed, 23–6, 31
legal regulation of, 23–4, 26, 33–5
and workplace accommodations, 33–6
breast pumps, 23, 24–6, 32, 34–7, 100, 110
manufacturers of, 25–6, 32, 37
tax breaks for, 25, 35–6
breast shields, 25–6
Brewster, William, 139
Brissot, J. P., 140
Brooklin Library, 50, 51, 59
Buchanan, Patrick, 134
Buck, Carrie and Emma, 89, 90, 91
Buckley, William, Jr., 183
Buck v. Bell, 89, 90
Bunyan, John, xx, xxiii, xxv, 139
Burtch, George, xxxi
Bush, George H. W., 132

Calderone, Mary Steichen, 130–1
California, 35, 88, 133
cryonics in, 183
forced sterilization law of, 84, 85
proposed Natural Death Act of, 167
2008 Proposition 8 of, 95, 96
Call, 118
Campbell, Alexander, 163, 260n
Cappello, Dominic, 80
Carlyle, Thomas, xxiv
Carnegie, Andrew, 39, 50
Carnegie Human Embryo Collection, 17

Case for Legalized Abortion Now, The
(Guttmacher, ed.), 133
Castle, W. E., 15–16
Catcher in the Rye, The (Salinger), 59
Celestial Bed, 93
Centers for Disease Control (CDC), 24, 33
"Cerebral Library, The" (Keller), 176, 177
Chang, Min Chueh, 18
Charles I, King of England, 9, 10–11, 12
Charlotte's Web (White), 59
Cheaper by the Dozen (Gilbreth and Carey),
104
Checkered Game of Life board game, xv–
xviii, xxvi–xxix, xxx, xxxii, 202n
invention of, xvii–xviii, xxvi–xxvii
rules of, xv, xxvii–xxviii, xxxiii
chess, xviii, xxvi–xxvii, xxix
Chess Players, The; Or, The Game of Life
(Retzsch), xxvi–xxvii
childbirth, 28, 181
in hospitals, 25, 31, 33–4, 104, 121–2
premature, 24, 31, 163
risk of death in, 120
stork myth of, 31, 65–6, 69, 84–5
childhood, xiii, 64, 65, 67, 74, 145
as constitutional right, 122
discovery of, 39–40, 45, 59
Childhood's End (Clarke), 19
children's libraries, 38–43, 44, 45, 51, 53, 55,
58, 63, 74
see also Moore, Anne Carroll
children's literature, 38–60
golden age of, 63, 75
illustrators of, 41, 54, 62
Middle Ages and, 45
reviews of, 41–5, 48–50, 51, 52, 56, 59
about sex, 61–3, 64, 67, 70–1, 73, 75, 76–8,
79–80
suitability issue of, 44–5
see also Stuart Little
Child's Friend, xxii
China, xviii, 7
Chutes and Ladders board game, xvii
Civil Rights Act (1964), 35
Civil War, American, xvii, xxix, 139, 157–8
Clark, Jonas, 143, 145, 147

Clarke, Arthur C., 19–21, 183
Clarke, Dorus, 69
Clark University, 16–17, 83, 85, 138, 142, 143–4, 145, 147–8, 254*n*
Clinton, DeWitt, 170
Coburn, Daniel, 160, 161
Coché, Judith, 94
Cocks, Jay, 21
computer dating, 94
"Confessions of an Amateur Mother" (Crossley), 123, 128
Congress, U.S., 21, 102–3, 154, 155, 160, 161, 167–8
    anti-immigration legislation by, 87
    breast-feeding and, 24–5, 26, 34, 35–6
    contraception and, 123–4, 132, 135–6, 154
Conquest of a Continent, The (Grant), 91
Conquest of Disease, The (Rice), 125
Conservation of the Family, The (Popenoe), 88
contraception (birth control), 78, 88–9, 117–21, 130–6
    Congress and, 123–4, 132, 135–6, 154
    as "family planning," 131, 132, 134
    illegality of, 120, 123–4
    legal cases on, 129, 132, 133
    methods of, 18–19, 80, 95, 115; *see also* abortion
    see also Sanger, Margaret
"Corpse That Lived, The" (Skinner), 174
Cotton, Nathaniel, xxi
Cowley, Malcolm, 54–5
Crossley, Stella, 123, 128
Crowninshield, Frank, 240*n*
CryoCare, 179
cryonics (cryogenic suspension), xi, xii, 19, 169–88
    Cold War and, 179–81
    efficacy of, 177–8
    lost dead vs., 182, 183, 185
    methods of, 178–9
    neuropreservation (severed heads) in, 176–7, 179, 185, 264*n*, 265*n*
    overpopulation as danger of, 181
    pioneering efforts in, 183

    rejuvenation in, 170, 177–8, 181
    scientific plausibility of, 178–9
Cryonics Institute (CI), 170–3, 176–9, 181–8
    cease-and-desist order filed against, 179, 262*n*
    cost of, 171
    facilities of, 171–3, 181–3, 188
    location of, 170–1
    members of, 170, 171, 172–3, 185, 187–8
    practices of, 170, 172, 178–9, 188, 261*n*–2*n*
    rivals of, 173, 177, 178, 179, 183, 185
    storeroom of, 182, 186–7
Cryonics Society of California, 183
Curse of Bigness, The (Brandeis), 98

Daedalus (Haldane), 17–18, 87
Daly, Charles, 98–9
Darrow, Clarence, 90–1, 93
Darwin, Charles, xi, 15, 17, 30, 74, 82–3, 93, 142
Darwin, Erasmus, 28–9, 32
Davis, Bette, 62
Davis, Jefferson, 158
Day of a Godly Man's Death Better Than the Day of His Birth, The (Foxcroft), xii
death:
    books about, 165
    brain, 160–1
    in childbirth, 120
    definitions of, 160
    in infancy, 17, 28, 66, 84–5
    in intensive care units, 159, 165
    masturbation as cause of, 71–2
    prenatal, 5–6, 16–17, 18
    scientific defeat of, 142, 148
    spiritual, xix
    by suicide, xv, xviii, 169–70, 251*n*–2*n*
Death Doctors, The (Mitscherlich and Mielke), 165, 260*n*
de Brunhoff, Jean, 44
Declaration of Independence, 157, 162, 164
Defense Department, U.S., 134
Defense of Marriage Act (1996), 95
de Graaf, Regnier, 13
de Kruif, Paul, 126, 173, 175
Dennett, Mary Ware, 123
Denny, Frances Parkman, 31–2

Descent of Man, The (Darwin), 30
Dollard, Annie, 50, 55
Doubleday, 179–80, 182
Doyle, Sir Arthur Conan, 61
Drake, Francis, 9
Dred Scott v. Sandford, 158
Dr. Strangelove, 19, 180, 181
Drucker, Peter, 100
DuBois, W.E.B., 84, 131
Duff, Raymond, 163, 260n
Dunn, L. C., 92

ectogenesis, 14–15, 17–18, 19–21, 181
Edelin, Kenneth, 163
Edwards, Jonathan, 63, 64, 67
"Efficiency by Consent" (Brandeis), 106, 107
Egg and I, The (MacDonald), 129
eggs, xi, 5, 6–16, 66, 79
    in *Brave New World* Hatchery, 14, 17, 25
    chicken, 6, 7–8, 10, 14, 76, 78
    fertilized, constitutional rights of, 22
    mammalian, 7–8, 11, 15–16
    in sex education, 76–7
Eggs of Mammals, The (Pincus), 15
Egypt, xxvi
    ancient, xxi, 7
Ehrlich, Paul, 132
Eichmann, Adolf, 165, 166
Eichmann in Jerusalem (Arendt), 165
Eisenhower, Dwight, 132
Elders, Joycelyn, 79
Elements of Technology (Bigelow), xxv
Eliot, Charles, 98, 106
Emberly, Michael, 62
Emerging Republican Majority, The
    (Phillips), 134
Emerson, Ralph Waldo, xxvi
Émile (Rousseau), 28, 64
Enlightenment, 28–9, 40, 65, 156–7
Equal Rights Amendment (ERA), 21–2
ergonomics, 107
Ettinger, Robert C. W., xi, 19, 169–88
    background of, 173
    death of, 188
    Freezer Era launched by, 179–81, 187, 264n
    photo albums of, 186–7

publications of, 175–6, 179–80, 182–4, 185,
    187
science fiction as inspiration of, 173, 174–5
sexual fantasies of, 184
suicide plans of, 169–70, 261n
wives of, 172–3, 185, 186–7
in World War II, 169, 175, 177, 187
    see also Cryonics Institute
"Eugenics Cult, The" (Darrow), 90–1
eugenics movement, 82–93, 114, 116, 155, 181
    birth control and, 120–1, 124
    blacks and, 83–5, 87
    critics of, 90–2
    decline of, 92–3
    forced sterilization in, 82, 84, 85, 87, 88–9,
        90–2
    Gilbreth's children in, 104
    immigration restriction in, 87, 91, 92
    intelligence testing in, 85–6, 89, 90
    Nazi, 91–2, 168
    normal family in, 88, 89
    political orientation of, 83, 90, 124
    poverty and, 87
    Progressivism and, 82, 90, 95
    race suicide feared by, 87, 120–1
    racial segregation instituted by, 83
    racial theories in, 83–5, 86–7, 88, 90, 91,
        92, 120–1
    social Darwinism in, 82–3
    social welfare programs opposed by, 83,
        86, 87, 121
    women's education opposed by, 87
evolution, xii, 15, 17, 30–1, 82–3, 86–7, 90
    genetic psychology and, 138, 142, 146, 147,
        250n, 252n
    natural selection in, 83, 95, 121

Fabricius, Hieronymus, 8, 10
"Facts in the Case of M. Valdemar, The"
    (Poe), 173–4
Fairley, George E. A., 47
Falwell, Jerry, 135
Family and Medical Leave Act (1993), 33
Fatigue Study (L. Gilbreth), 106–7
feeble-mindedness, 85, 86, 89, 92, 164
Ferrell, Will, 35

fertility rate, xii, 75, 104, 114–15
Fielding, Henry, xii
Fischer, David Hackett, 141
Foley, Samuel J., 47
food, 138, 248n
    frozen, 174, 176
    processed, 29, 31, 32, 33, 69–70, 72
For Better (Parker-Pope), 94–5
Ford, Henry, 103
Formed Fetus, The (Fabricius), 8
Fortune, 46, 52
Fourteenth Amendment, 83, 167
Foxcroft, Thomas, xii
Franklin, Benjamin, xx, xxvi, xxvii, 28, 174
Frederick, Christine, 108–9, 114
freezing of dead, see cryonics
Freud, Sigmund, 31, 74, 77–8, 137–8, 142,
    147–8, 175, 246n–7n
Friedan, Betty, 21, 134, 135
Froebel, Friedrich, xxxii
Furman v. Georgia, 154
Future Sex (Kent), 185

Galen, 7, 14
Gallup poll, 47–8, 135
Game of Life board game, xvi, xxix–xxxii
    rules of, xxix–xxx
    Twists and Turns version of, xxx–xxxii
Games for Soldiers games collection, xxix
games of life, xiii, xv–xxxiii, 40
    see also board games
Gandy, Kim, 36
Gay, Edwin, 101
Geisel, Theodor (Dr. Seuss), 48, 49
generation, secrets of, 5–22, 29, 42, 64
    body politic and, 12–13, 14
    childlessness and, 10, 12
    dissections in research on, 7, 8, 9, 10–11, 13
    Harvey's theory of, 10–13, 14
    seeds and, 7, 8, 10, 13, 14
    see also eggs
Generation of Living Creatures, The (De
    Generatione animalium), (Harvey),
    12–13, 14, 205n
genetic psychology, 138, 142, 146, 147, 250n,
    252n

genetics, see heredity
"Genius and Stupidity" (Terman), 85
genocide, 164
genomes, 16
George, Henry, xxxii
Germany, 16, 74, 87, 89, 173
    G. S. Hall and, 139–40, 141, 143–4
    Nazi, 91–2, 164–6, 168
    Nuremberg trials in, 92, 164–6, 260n
germ theory of disease, 125–6
Gernsback, Hugo, 173, 174, 175, 177
Gibbs, Wolcott, 46
Gilbreth, Frank, 97, 98, 101, 102, 104–7
    books of, 102, 104
    death of, 107
    at ICC railroad hearing, 100
    lectures of, 105–6
    three-man promotion plan of, 108
Gilbreth, Frank, Jr., 104, 110
Gilbreth, Inc., 106, 107–8
Gilbreth, Lillian, 97, 98, 100, 101, 103–10, 122
    background of, 104
    books of, 104, 106–7, 109
    breast-feeding by, 104, 105, 107
    daily schedule of, 105
    death of, 110
    doctorate of, 104–5, 106
    economies of scale demonstrated by, 104
    fatigue studies of, 106–7, 109
    Happiness Minutes as goal of, 107, 109,
        110, 112
    as housekeeping expert, 108–10
    male housekeeper of, 107, 108, 109–10
    MIT lecture of, 107
    Purdue professorship of, 109
    thirteen pregnancies of, 103, 104, 105,
        106, 107
    widowhood of, 107–10
    see also scientific management
Gilman, Charlotte Perkins, 116, 118, 119
Girlhood and Its Problems (Hall and Hall), 76
Go, game of, xvii
God, xviii, xix–xx, xxi, xxix, 8, 20, 26–7,
    72–3, 74, 170
Goddard, Morrill, 127
Goldman, Emma, 105–6

Goldwater, Barry, 130, 156
Good Housekeeping, 119, 121
Gosney, E. S., 82, 89
Gottlieb, Lori, 94
Graham, Sylvester, 67–73, 74, 78, 84, 139, 141, 148, 175
  apocalyptic vision of, 67–8
  book by, 69, 73, 74
  death of, 73, 74
  health regimen recommended by, 72–3, 140
  ill health of, 67, 73
  lectures of, 69, 71, 73
  marital sex deplored by, 70–1
  masturbation decried by, 70–2, 73, 74
  overstimulation deplored by, 69–71
Graham Journal of Health and Longevity, 140
Grant, Madison, 86–8, 89, 90, 91, 92
Grapes of Wrath (Steinbeck), 49–50
Grassley, Chuck, 155
Gravelle, Karen, 62
Gray, John, 142
Great Awakening, 67
Great Gatsby, The (Fitzgerald), 87–8
Grieves, Tom, 108, 109–10
Griswold, Estelle, 132
Griswold v. Connecticut, 153–4, 161
Guttmacher, Alan F., 131, 132–4, 135

Hadden, Briton, 46, 112–13
Haiselden, Harry J., 84–5
Haldane, J.B.S., 17–18, 19, 25, 87
Haldeman, H. R., 134
Hall, Granville Stanley, 85, 137–51
  adolescence in work of, 74–5, 76, 137, 138, 146–7, 148–9, 250n, 252n
  background of, 139–40, 141–2
  bereavements and depression of, 144–6, 251n
  at Clark University, 138, 142, 143–4, 145, 147–8, 254n
  death of, 141, 151
  Freud and Jung hosted by, 137–8, 147–8, 246n–47n
  genetic psychology doctrine of, 138, 142, 146, 147, 250n, 252n

miser's fortune left by, 149, 254n
  personality of, 138, 139, 140, 143, 144, 247n, 249n
  psychical research rejected by, 137–8, 142–3, 144–5, 147–8
  racial theories of, 146
  remarriage of, 148, 253n
  senescence theory of, 138–9, 145–6, 147, 148–51, 175, 254n
  sex education and, 74–5, 76, 148–9
  will of, 149, 253n, 254n
Hall, Jeannette Winter, 76
Hall, Winfield Scott, 76–7
Happiness Minutes, 107, 109, 110, 112
Harper & Row, 49, 52–3, 59
Harper's, 21, 48–9, 106, 155
Harris, Robie, 62, 79
Harvard Business School, 101
  Fatigue Laboratory of, 109
Harvard University, xxv, 15–16, 18, 19, 42, 90, 98, 105, 106, 137, 142, 160, 252n
Harvey, William, xi, 8–14, 15, 22, 26, 76
  blood circulation theory of, 9, 10, 12
  death of, 13
  dissections performed by, 9, 10–11, 13
  generation theory of, 10–13, 14
  women as viewed by, 9–10
Hasbro, xvi, xxx–xxxi, 199n, 203n
Hawes, Joel, 68
Health and Human Services Department, U.S., 33
Health Care Act (2010), 33–4
Hearst, Patty, 258n
Hearst, William Randolph, 104
Hecht, George, 111–14, 122, 125, 126, 132–3
Herbert, George, xviii
heredity (genetics), 15–16, 17, 42, 82, 84, 93
  environment vs., 145
  history and, 86–7, 91
  of housework, 93, 95, 96
  of intelligence, 85, 90, 145
  see also eugenics movement
Herskovits, Melville, 91
"Hills Like White Elephants" (Hemingway), 121–2

History of British India (Mill), xxiv
History of Life and Death (Bacon), xx
Hitler, Adolf, 91, 164, 166, 260n
Hobbes, Thomas, 10, 12–13
Hodgson, Richard, 147
Hofstadter, Richard, 155–8, 233n, 256n
Holmes, Oliver Wendell, 89, 90
home economics, 98, 108–10
Home-maker and Her Job, The (L. Gilbreth), 109
homosexuality, 62, 78, 90
Hopper, Franklin, 57–8
Hounds and Jackal game, xxi
House at Pooh Corner, The (Milne), 44
Household Engineering: Scientific Management in the Home (Frederick), 108–9, 114
House of Representatives, U.S., 132
    Committee to Investigate Taylor and Other Systems of Shop Management, 102–3
housework, 93, 95, 96, 108–10
Human Betterment Foundation, 82, 89
Human Milk Banking Association of North America, 24
Hunter, John, 27, 174
Husbands and Wives Club, The (Abraham), 93–4
Huxley, Aldous, 14–15, 17, 18, 25
Huxley, Julian, 15
Huxley, T. H., 15
Hyena Game, xxi
Hyland, William, 161, 258n

IBM, 19, 20
"Ice Man, The" (Douglas), 174
immigrants, 87, 91, 92, 117–18, 119–20, 121, 123–4
Immigration Restriction League, 87
immortality, xii, 169–88
    as Christian heavenly mansion, xxii
    rejuvenation and, 175
    in science fiction, 173–6, 177, 179, 184–5, 262n
    time transcended in, 173–4
    see also cryonics
"Incredible Formula, The" (Ernst), 177

India, xvii–xviii, xxiv, xxvii, 7
industrialization, 32, 108, 110, 115
infant care, xiii, 23–37
    see also breast-feeding; breast milk; parenthood, parenting
infants, deformed, 84–5, 154, 163, 167–8
influenza epidemic of 1918, 125
Instead of "Wild Oats" (Hall), 76
Institute for American Values, 95–6
intelligence quotient (IQ), 25, 85–6, 90, 102
intelligence testing, 85–6, 89, 90, 145
Interstate Commerce Committee (ICC), 98, 100
ironworkers, 99, 101, 102, 103, 109
Irvin, Rea, 48
Is Sex Necessary? (Thurber and White), 77
Is the School House the Proper Place to Teach Raw Sex? (Christian Crusade), 78
It's NOT the Stork! A Book About Girls, Boys, Babies, Bodies, Families, and Friends (Harris), 79
It's Perfectly Normal (Harris), 62
Ives, W. and S. B., xxii

Jackson Laboratory, 16
James, William, 137–8, 142–3, 144–5, 146, 147–8, 149, 151, 247n
James I, King of England, 8–9
"Jameson Satellite, The" (Jones), 174–5, 176, 177
Jamestown colony, 8–9, 12
Japan, xvii, 42
Jefferson, Thomas, 156–7, 257n
jigsaw puzzles, xx
Jñāna Chaupár board game, xvii, xx
John, Gospel According to, xxii
John Birch Society, 78
Johnson, Larry, 179
Johnson, Lyndon, 132
Johnson, Roswell Hill, 87, 89
Johnson & Johnson, 108
Johnson Attitude Inventory, 89
Jordan, David Starr, 82, 83, 84, 85, 89, 92
Journal of Heredity, 84, 92, 121
Journey Through Europe (Play of Geography) board game, xx
Jung, Carl, 137–8, 147–8, 246n–47n, 253n

Kael, Pauline, 21
Karolinska Institute, 18
Katz, Evan Marc, 94
Kellogg, John Harvey, 72, 84
Kennedy, David, 130
Kennedy, Edward, 134
Kennedy, John F., 59, 155, 182, 223*n*
Kent, Saul, 185
kindergarten movement, xxxii–xxxiii,
    39, 74
Kindergarten Review, xxxii, xxxiii
King, Eleanor, 47
King, Martin Luther, Jr., 131
King James Bible, 8
Kirk, Hyland, 142
Kitchen Efficient, 109, 110
Kübler-Ross, Elisabeth, 165
Kubrick, Stanley, 19–21, 22, 183

labor unions, 101–3, 105–6, 110, 116
Ladies' Home Journal, 81, 93, 109, 126, 175
Larsen, Nella, 41
Larsen, Roy, 47–8
Lawrence, Ruth, 23
Lectures to Young Men (Beecher), 68
*Lectures to Young Men on the Formation of
    Character* (Hawes), 68
*Lectures to Young People in Manufacturing
    Villages* (Clarke), 69
Lecture to Young Men, A (Graham), 69,
    73, 74
Leeuwenhoek, Antoni van, 13–14, 126
Leighton, Robert, 62
Leonardo da Vinci, 8, 29, 166
Lerer, Seth, 45
Leviathan (Hobbes), 12–13
Lewis, Sinclair, 126
life:
    as circle, xi–xii, xxiv–xxv, 141
    fate in, xxx
    as game, xiii, xv–xxxiii, 200*n*–1*n*
    as game of chess, xxvi–xxvii
    as linear, xii, xxiv–xxv, 141
    stages of, 18, 39–40, 63–4, 72–3, 74, 95,
        114–15, 138, 146, 149, 150
    as voyage, xx–xxiii, xxvii–xxxiii, 40, 68,
        69, 74, 115, 200*n*–1*n*

Life, 5–6, 18, 19–20, 21, 51–2, 153, 183, 204*n*,
    214*n*–15*n*
    "Birth of a Baby" issue of, 46–8, 214*n*–15*n*
Life and Confessions of a Psychologist, The
    (Hall), 149
life expectancy, xii, 114–16, 122, 125, 175
Life-Extension Revolution, The (Kent), 185
Life's Beginnings (Hall), 76–7, 79
Life Without Father (D. Popenoe), 95
Lilliputian Magazine, 40
Lincoln, Abraham, xv, xxvi, 158
Linnaeus, Carolus, 26–8, 30
Lippmann, Walter, 86
*Literary Remains of the Late Henry James,
    The* (James), 143, 149
Little, C. C., 15–16, 42, 46, 48, 84, 91
Littledale, Clara Savage, 114, 116–23, 125–30
    background of, 116–17
    childbirth of, 121–2
    death of, 133
    diary of, 116–17, 118, 123
    divorce of, 129–30
    fiction writing of, 128
    journalism career of, 116–17, 118–19, 120
    radio show of, 128–9
    see also Parents Magazine
Littledale, Harold, 117, 121, 127, 129–30
Little Goody Two-Shoes, 58
Little Prince, The (Saint-Exupéry), 52
Lloyd's of London, 20
Locke, John, 9, 40
London, Jack, 174
Long, J. A., 16
longevity, 115, 140–1, 150
Longfellow, Henry Wadsworth, 150
Loves, Lusts, and Sexual Acts of Animals, The
    (Harvey), 12
Lowell, Lawrence, 106
Loy, Myrna, 104
Luce, Henry, 46–8, 51–2, 112–13
Luke, Gospel According to, xix

MacDonald, Betty, 129
machines, xxiv, xxv–xxvi, 20, 30, 31, 33, 40, 69
    life-support, 153, 159–62, 166
Macmillan, 42–3, 57
Madaras, Lynda, 62, 80

Malcolm X, 131

Mall, Franklin Paine, 16–17, 83–4, 144, 145

Man into Superman (Ettinger), 183–4

Mansion of Bliss board game, xxii, xxvi, 201n, 202n

Mansion of Happiness board game, vii, xiii, xxii–xxiii, xxvii, xxviii, xxix, xxx, xxxi, 3, 112, 201n, 203n

"Man That Was Used Up, The" (Poe), 175

Mariner IV space probe, 20

Mark, E. L., 16

marriage, xiii, 69, 75, 78, 81–96, 117
　divorce and, 82, 95, 129–30
　same-sex, 95
　sex within, 70–1, 89–90
　as stage of life, 95
　women's dissatisfaction with, 88–9
　see also eugenics

marriage counseling, 81–2, 88–90, 92–6
　as couples therapy, 93–4
　premarital, 89–90, 93

Marry Him: The Case for Settling for Mr. Good Enough (Gottlieb), 94

Mason, George, 257n

Massachusetts Birth Control League, 148–9

Massachusetts Citizens for Life, 163

Massachusetts Institute of Technology (MIT), xxv, 19, 20, 107, 178

masturbation, 13, 70–2, 73, 74, 78–9
　purported debilitating consequences of, 71–2

masturbatory insanity, 72

maternity leaves, 33–4, 36

Mather, Cotton, xix, xxvii, 28, 140, 141

Maturation of the Egg of the Mouse, The (Long and Mark), 16

Mayle, Peter, 62

McCarthy, Joseph, 155, 156

McCormack, Thomas, 179–80, 182, 183

McDougall, William, 90, 92

McGovern, George, 134

McLaughlin, Wilma Jean, 183

McLaughlin Brothers, xvii

Me, Myself and I (Spilsbury) 80

Mead, Margaret, 138

Measurement of Intelligence, The (Terman), 86

Medela breast pumps, 25–6, 32, 34, 37

Mein Kampf (Hitler), 91

Men Against Death (de Kruif), 175

Mendel, Gregor, 15–16, 17, 90

menstruation, 7, 16, 108

Merkle, Ralph, 178

mice, 84
　fancy, breeding of, 42
　laboratory, 15–16, 19, 42, 46, 48

Mickey Mouse, 16, 54

Microbe Hunters (de Kruif), 126, 173

Middle Ages, xi, 45, 84

milk, 23–37, 126
　cow's, 29–31
　human, *see* breast milk
　as mammalian characteristic, 26–8

Milkscreen, 24

Mill, James, xxiv

Mill, John Stuart, xxiv, 139

Milne, A. A., 44

Milton, John, xxiii, xxv

Milton Bradley Company, xv–xviii, xxvi–xxxiii
　centennial of, xvi, xxix

Minnesota, University of, 37

Minsky, Marvin, 19, 178

Mitford, Jessica, 165

Modern Marriage (Popenoe), 88

Monopoly, xxii, xxxi

Moore, Anne Carroll, 40–6, 49–60, 63, 74, 75
　background of, 38
　children's book published by, 43
　children's literature reviewed by, 41–4, 45, 49–50, 52
　death of, 59–60
　Nicholas Knickerbocker doll owned by, 43, 44
　NYPL Children's Room supervised by, 39, 40–3, 50–1
　post-retirement authority retained by, 52–3, 58
　retirement of, 50–1

Stuart Little opposed by, 42, 52–3, 55, 57–60

Whites' correspondence with, 49, 50–1, 53, 218*n*–20*n*

More, Thomas, xviii

Motherhood in Bondage (Sanger), 123

Mother's Magazine, 111–12, 116

mother's milk, *see* breast milk

motion study, 100, 107, 110

Motion Study (Gilbreth), 104

Mouse Club of America, 16

Muir, Robert, 160, 164, 166, 256*n*

Myerson, Abraham, 92

NARAL, 21, 134

NASA, 5, 6, 19, 20

Nascher, I. N., 148

National Cancer Institute Act (1937), 46

National Clergy Consultation Service, 133

National Marriage Project, 95–6

National Organization for Women (NOW), 21, 36, 133–4

National Right to Life Committee, 135, 163

National Woman Suffrage Association, 119

Nebel, Long John, 179, 183

Newbery, John, 40

Newbery Medal, 58–9

New Game of Human Life board game, xx–xxii, xxvii, 40, 64, 141

Newhouse, S. I., 132

New Republic, 86, 91, 121–22, 126

New York, N.Y., xvii, xxvii, 6, 18, 97, 103, 116–21, 139

public libraries of, 38–9, 40–3

New Yorker, 43, 44–8, 51–2, 54, 59, 127, 165, 240*n*

"Birth of an Adult" lampoon in, 48

cartoons of, 46, 48

"Children's Shelf" column of, 44–5, 49, 50, 51, 52, 56, 59

launch of, 113–14

New York Garment Workers strike (1910), 102

New York League for Sexual Freedom, 78

New York Public Library, 49

Children's Room of, 39, 40–3, 50–1, 52–3, 55, 57–8; *see also* Moore, Anne Carroll

establishment of, 39

New York Times, 18, 21, 91, 92, 94, 100, 110, 112, 116, 121, 127, 147, 177

New York Times Book Review, 44

New York Times Magazine, 93, 94

New York World's Fair (1939), 92

Nicholas: A Manhattan Christmas Story (Moore), 43

Nilsson, Lennart, 5–6, 18, 19–20, 21, 79, 154, 158, 183, 204*n*

Nixon, Richard, 132, 134–5, 154

Noll, Henry, 101

Nordic race, 86, 87, 90, 91

Nordstrom, Ursula, 42, 52–3, 54, 55, 58–9

Nuremberg trials, 92, 164–6, 260*n*

Obama, Michelle, 25, 36

Obama administration, 154–6

obscenity laws, 35, 47–8, 118

Sanger and, 118, 119, 120

sexual explicitness vs., 78

Of Mice and Men (Steinbeck), 46

old age, 137–51

debilities of, 71–2, 149

as disease, 148

increased longevity in, 140–1, 150

productivity and retirement in, 150

as senescence, 138–9, 145–6, 147, 148–51, 254*n*

as stage of life, 138, 149, 150

wisdom of, 140, 150–1

"Old Age" (Hall), 149

Old Man's Honour, The (Mather), 140

Onania (Weems), 70

"Once More to the Lake" (White), 54

On the Generation of Animals (Aristotle), 7

On Your Mark, Get Set, Grow! (Madaras), 62

organ transplants, 160, 178

orgasms, 7, 71

women's inadequate, 89–90

O'Rights, William Constitution "Bill," 187–8

Origin of Species, The (Darwin), 15
ovaries, 13, 14, 175
ovulation, 16, 94–5

pachisi board game, xvii
Palin, Sarah, 24, 154–5
Paradise Lost (Milton), xxiii
Paradise of Childhood, The (Bradley),
    xxxii, 40
"Paranoid Style in American Politics, The"
    (Hofstadter), 155–8, 256*n*
parenthood, parenting, xiii, 80, 111–36, 147
    by amateurs, 128–30
    demographic change and, 114–16
    by fathers, 95, 115, 122–3, 128, 133
    manuals for, 111, 112, 114
    playing board games in, xxi, xxii, xxiii,
        xxviii
    of poor vs. wealthy parents, 114–15, 116,
        117–18, 119–20, 121, 123–4, 127, 130, 131
    quality time in, 122–3
    as stage of life, 114, 115
    see also contraception
Parents Magazine, 111–14, 124–30, 132–3
    conquest-of-disease stories in, 125–6
    editorial policy of, 122–3, 128–9
    editor of, *see* Littledale, Clara Savage
    fathers addressed by, 122–3, 128, 133
    parental anxieties fed by, 126–8
    products advertised in, 125, 127
    science reporting in, 124–6
    success of, 128, 130, 133
Park and Shop board game, xvi
Parker, Dorothy, 44
Parker-Pope, Tara, 94–5
parrot fever (psittacosis), 126–7, 175
Passing of the Great Race, The (Grant),
    86–7, 91
Pasteur, Louis, 125
Patent Office, U.S., xvii, xxiv, xxvi, xxviii,
    29, 31, 32
Paul, Alice, 21
Paul VI, Pope, 132, 154
Pelosi, Nancy, 25
"Penultimate Trump, The" (Ettinger),
    175–6, 179

Percy, George, 8–9
Perry v. Schwarzenegger, 95
personhood amendments, 22
pessaries, 115, 119–20
Phillips, Kevin, 134
Pilgrim's Progress (Bunyan), xx, xxiii, 20,
    45, 139
Pill (oral contraceptive), 18–19, 80, 95
Pincus, Gregory, 15, 18–19
Piper, Leonora, 137–8, 143, 144–5, 147
piss prophecy, 10
Pius XII, Pope, 160
Planned Parenthood Federation of
    America, 129, 130–6
    funding of, 131–2, 136
    National Negro Advisory Committee
        of, 131
Plato, xx
Plessy v. Ferguson, 83
Poe, Edgar Allan, 173–4, 175
Pohl, Frederik, 179
Poor Richard's Almanac (Franklin), xx
Popenoe, David, 95–6
Popenoe, Paul, 81–96, 114, 116, 122
    background of, 82
    birth control opposed by, 88–9, 119,
        120–1
    books by, 87, 88, 89
    "Can This Marriage Be Saved?" column
        of, 81, 93, 94
    computer dating launched by, 94
    death of, 96
    forced sterilization advocated by, 82, 85,
        87, 88–9, 91
    as marriage counselor, 81–2, 88–90, 92–6
    marriage of, 87
    Nazi Germany defended by, 91–2
    see also eugenics movement
Popp, Adelheid, 116, 119
Population Bomb (Ehrlich), 132
population control, 130
Porzio, Ralph, 161–2, 164, 166
Possibility of Not Dying, The (Kirk), 142
Pratt Institute, 39
prenatal development, xiii, 5–22
    conception in, 6–7, 15

ectogenetic, 14–15, 17–18, 19, 181
embryos in, 5, 6, 11, 13, 16–18, 154, 178
fetuses in, 5, 6, 7, 8, 11, 14, 16, 18
in science fiction, 14, 17–18, 19–21, 22
as stage of life, 39–40
see also generation, secrets of; Nilsson, Lennart
Primer on Scientific Management (Gilbreth), 102, 104
Principles of Psychology (James), 137
Principles of Scientific Management, The (Taylor), 100, 103
progress, xxiv–xxvi, xxix, xxxii, 30–1, 40, 82, 86–7, 142
Progress and Poverty (George), xxxii
Progressivism, 76, 77–8, 82, 90, 95, 101, 108, 116
pro-life movement, 6, 22, 135–6, 154, 161, 163, 167–8
Prospect of Immortality, The (Ettinger), 179–80, 182–3, 185
Pruette, Lorine, 247n, 249n, 252n, 253n
Psalms, xx
psychical research, 137–8, 142–3, 144–5, 147–8
Psychology of Management, The (L. Gilbreth), 106
Pulitzer, Joseph, 116, 117
Puritans, xviii–xx, xxi, xxiii, 9, 28, 64, 139
"Purple Death, The" (Barnette), 173

Quayle, Dan, 95
Quinlan, Julia and Joseph, 153, 158–62, 166–8
Quinlan, Karen Ann, 152–68
    condition of, 152–3, 160–1, 162–4
    court-appointed guardian of, 159, 160
    court decisions on, 166–8
    eventual death of, 167–8
    life-support machines hooked to, 153, 159–62, 166, 167, 261n
    Nuremberg trials and, 164–6, 260n
    press coverage of, 153, 158, 159, 163–4, 166, 167, 168, 255n–6n
    significance of, 163–4
    trial of, 158–66
    see also right to die

Race Betterment Foundation, 84
racial theories, 30, 83–5, 86–7, 88, 90, 91–2, 120–1, 146
railroads, xxv–xxvi
    efficiency of, 98–100, 101, 236n
Ramthun, Roy, 35–6
Read, Mary L., 121
Reader's Digest, 112, 135
Ready, Set, Grow! (Madaras), 80
Reagan, Ronald, 133
Reed, James, 123–4
refrigerators, 176
Republic, The (Plato), xx
resurrection, xix, 168; see also cryonics
Retzsch, Moritz, xxvi–xxvii
"Revised Catechism, The" (Twain), xxix
Rice, Thurman B., 125
right to die, xiii, 152–68
    of deformed newborn infants, 84–5, 163, 167–8
    life-support machines vs., 159–61
    and paranoid political style, 155–8
    in political history, 153–5, 168
    see also Quinlan, Karen Ann
right-to-die movement, 161, 257n–8n
right to life, 153–5, 156–7, 158, 159, 161–2, 168
right to privacy, 161, 167
right to property, 156–8, 168, 257n
right to refuse medical treatment, 163, 166–8
Rock, John, 18
Roe v. Wade, 21, 78, 134, 135, 154, 161, 163
Roosevelt, Eleanor, 47
Roosevelt, Theodore, 113, 146
Ross, Dorothy, 145, 146, 253n
Ross, Harold, 43, 113–14
    Luce's battle with, 46–8, 51–2
    Stuart Little and, 54
Roth, Philip, 41
Rothman, David, 164–5
Roth v. United States, 78
Rousseau, Jean-Jacques, 14, 28, 64–5, 69, 76
Royal College of Physicians, 8
Royal Game of Goose board game, xxi
Royal Society, 13
Rush, Benjamin, 140
Rush University Medical Center, 33

Minooka Comm. H.S. South Library
Channahon, IL 60410

Sa'id Pasha, xxvi

Sagan, Carl, 19

Saint-Exupéry, Antoine de, 52

Salinger, J. D., 59

sanctity of life, 154, 161–2, 164, 258n–9n

Sandburg, Carl, 41

Sanger, Margaret, 89, 90, 117–21, 122, 129, 130
    background of, 117
    birth control clinics opened by, 119–20, 124
    death of, 133
    obscenity laws violated by, 118, 119, 120
    poor women counseled by, 117–18, 119–20, 121, 123–4

Saxton, Eugene, 49, 52

Sayers, Frances Clarke, 52–3, 55, 57–8

Schiebinger, Londa, 27

Schlafly, Phyllis, 21

Schlesinger, Arthur, Jr., 21

Schwartz, Pepper, 80

science fiction, 14, 17–18, 25
    films, 19–21, 22, 184–5
    immortality in, 173–6, 177, 179, 184–5, 262n

science journalism, 124–6
    conquest-of-disease stories in, 125–6

Science Service, 125, 242n

scientific management, 97–110
    of arsenal molders, 105, 106
    of coal shoveling, 102–3
    exhaustion produced by, 101, 103, 105, 107
    at Ford Motor Company, 103
    as gospel of efficiency, 100
    House investigation of, 102–3
    of housekeeping, 108–10
    IQ and, 102
    of ironworkers, 99, 101, 102, 103, 109
    labor unions' resistance to, 101–3, 105–6, 110
    motion study in, 100, 107, 110
    naming of, 97, 98
    of railroads, 98–100, 101, 236n
    task timing in, 98, 99, 100, 101
    therbligs in, 100, 103
    work-to-rest ratio in, 101, 107
    see also Brandeis, Louis; Gilbreth, Frank;
        Gilbreth, Lillian; Taylor, Frederick
        Winslow

Scott, William R., 41–2

Scripps, E. W., 125, 242n

Second Great Awakening, 67, 112

Second Life virtual world, xxxi

segregation, racial, 83

Selchow & Righter, xvii

semen, 13–14
    ejaculation of, 6–7, 61, 63, 68, 70–3
    nocturnal emissions of, 71, 76

Senescence: The Last Half of Life (G. S. Hall),
    149–50, 175

"Sentinel, The" (Clarke), 19

Servatius, Robert, 165

Sex, Puberty, and All That Stuff (Bailey), 62

sex education, 61–80, 118, 131, 135, 154
    battle over, 78–9
    children's literature for, 61–3, 64, 67, 70–1, 73, 75, 76–8, 79–80
    curiosity satisfied by, 64–5, 69, 74, 76, 77
    explicit, obscenity laws and, 78
    homosexuality in, 62, 78
    Progressive-era, 76, 77–8
    in public schools, 76, 78
    stork myth and, 65–6, 69
    see also Graham, Sylvester

sexual abstinence, 72, 115

sexual intercourse, 13, 74–5
    benefits of, 70–1, 75
    marital, 70–1, 89–90

Sexuality Information and Education
    Council of the United States, 78

Sexual Knowledge (Hall), 76

Shakespeare, William, 64, 185–6

Shop Management (Taylor), 98

"Skeptic, The" (Ettinger), 175

Sleeper, 184–5

Slosson, Edwin E., 125, 242n

Smith, John, 8–9

Snakes and Ladders board game, xvii

social Darwinism, 82–3, 248n

Some Thoughts Concerning Education
    (Locke), 40

space age, xi, xii, 20–2

Spencer, Herbert, 82, 90
sperm, 5, 79
    as animalcules, 13–14
Spilsbury, Louise, 80
"Spirit of Life Entering into the Spiritually
    Dead, The" (Mather), xix
Stanford-Binet intelligence test, 85–6, 89
Staton, Mick, 167–8
Stearns, Lutie, 39
Stein, Gertrude, 49–50
Steinach, Eugen, 175, 180
Steinbeck, John, 46
"Step Nurse" (Linnaeus), 28
sterilization, forced, 82, 84, 85, 87, 88–9,
    90–2
Sterilization for Human Betterment
    (Popenoe and Gosney), 89
St. Nicholas, 42
stork myth, 31, 65–6, 69
    "black stork" in, 84–5
"Storks, The" (Andersen), 65–6
Stuart Little (White), 42–3, 45, 48, 49, 50,
    52–60
    alternate ending written for, 57, 221*n*
    content of, 55–7
    dream origin of, 43
    final lines of, 56–7
    illustrations of, 54
    Moore's opposition to, 42, 52–3, 55, 57–60
    Newbery Medal denied to, 58–9
    publication of, 54, 129
    reviews of, 54–5, 56
    sex education and, 77–8
    success of, 59, 60
    title character's advent in, 42, 54, 55, 60
"Sublimation" (Littledale), 121–2
Subtreasury of American Humor, The
    (White and White), 50, 51–2, 217*n*
suggestion box, 106
Supreme Court, U.S., 132, 153–4, 158
    Brandeis on, 106
    forced sterilization laws endorsed by,
    89, 90
    Roe v. Wade ruling of, 21, 78, 134–5, 154,
    161, 163
Systema Naturae (Linnaeus), 26–7

Taft, Mel, xxix
Talbot, Fritz, 31–2
taxonomy, 26–8, 37, 83–4
Taylor, Frederick Winslow, 97–110, 112, 150
    books of, 98, 100, 103
    death of, 106
    fees charged by, 97, 101
    at House Committee investigation,
    102–3
    memorial service of, 106, 107
    methods of, 97–8, 99, 100, 101, 102–3, 105,
    109
    tombstone epitaph of, 97, 235*n*
    see also scientific management
*Ten Talks Parents Must Have with Their
    Children About Sex and Character*
    (Schwartz and Cappello), 80
Terman, Lewis M., 85–6, 87, 89–90, 102, 145,
    147, 236*n*
Thoreau, Henry David, xxv–xxvi, xxviii,
    xxxi
"Thousand Deaths, A" (London), 174
Thurber, James, 48, 77, 240*n*
Tilden, Samuel, 38, 39
Time, 6, 16, 21, 46, 112–13, 125, 160, 240*n*
Transportation Security Administration
    (TSA), U.S., 23
Trans Time, 173, 183
Trapasso, Thomas, 152–3, 158, 166, 168,
    261*n*
Travels of Babar (de Brunhoff), 44
Treatise on Domestic Economy, A (Beecher),
    108
Truman, Harry, 132
Turner, Frederick Jackson, 90
Twain, Mark, xxix
2001: A Space Odyssey, 19–21, 22, 183

undulant fever, 126
United Nations, 35, 164
U.S.A. v. Karl Brandt et al., 164–6
U.S. v. One Package of Japanese Pessaries,
    129
Utopia (More), xviii

vaccines, 125

venereal diseases, 62, 75, 76, 118
Verducci, Tom, 179
Victorian era, xvii, xxii, 40, 142
Viguerie, Richard, 135
Vindication of the Rights of Woman
    (Wollstonecraft), 28
Virgil, xix
Voltaire, 28
von Baer, Karl, 15

Wallace, DeWitt, 112
Wallis, John, xx–xxii, 40, 64, 141
War in Cartoons, The (Hecht), 111
Water-Babies: A Fairy Tale for a Land Baby
    (Kingsley), 15
Watertown Arsenal strike (1912), 105, 106
Weems, Parson, 70
Weil, Elizabeth, 93
Wells, H. G., 174, 184
Welty, Eudora, 59
wet nurses, 27–8, 29, 30, 31, 32, 37
Weyrich, Paul, 135
"What Can We Do About Marriage?"
    (Littledale), 130
"What Every Girl Should Know" (Sanger),
    118, 120
*What's Going on Down There? Answers
    to Questions Boys Find Hard to Ask*
    (Gravelle), 62
What's Happening to Me? (Mayle), 62
When the Sleeper Wakes (Wells), 174, 184
Where Did I Come From? (Mayle), 62
White, E. B., 42–5, 48–60, 77–8, 84, 127
    "Birth of an Adult" lampoon written
        by, 48
    Moore's correspondence with, 49, 50–1,
        53, 218n–20n
    at New York World's Fair, 92
    see also Stuart Little

White, Joel, 44
White, Katharine Angell, 43, 44–6, 50–2, 53,
    57–9, 77
    children's literature reviewed by, 44–5, 48,
        49, 50, 51, 52, 56, 59
Whitney, Eli, xxiv
"Why Old Age Ends in Death" (Nascher),
    148
Will, George, 168
Williams, Garth, 54
Williams, Ted, 177, 179
Wilson, Edmund, 54, 240n
Wilson, William Bauchop, 102–3
Window into an Egg: Seeing Life Begin
    (Flanagan), 78
"Winter Walk, A" (White), 42
Winthrop, John, 9
withdrawal, contraceptive, 115
Wollstonecraft, Mary, 28
Womanly Art of Breastfeeding, The (La
    Leche League), 32
Worcester Foundation for Experimental
    Biology, 18
Worcester Telegram, 143–4, 145
workplace, xiii, 67, 69
    breast-feeding and, 24–5, 33–5, 36–7
    maternity leave from, 33–4, 36
    see also scientific management
World Is Round, The (Stein), 49–50
Worlds of Tomorrow, 179
World War I, 41, 90, 111, 121, 124, 125
World War II, 41, 48, 51, 52, 91–2, 93, 130,
    164–6, 169, 175, 176, 177, 187
Wynne, Shirley, 127

Youniverse (Ettinger), 187

Zawacki, Andy, 171–3, 179, 182, 186, 188
Zoonomia (Darwin), 28–9